GW00670365

The Crossworder's List Book

The Crossworder's List Book

John E. Brown and
Margaret H. Brown

CASSELL
LONDON

CASSELL & COMPANY LIMITED
35 Red Lion Square, London WC1R 4SG
and at Sydney, Auckland, Toronto, Johannesburg
an affiliate of
Macmillan Publishing Co. Inc.,
New York.

First published 1977

ISBN 0 304 29882 4

Typeset by Malvern Typesetting Services
Printed in Great Britain by
Lowe & Brydone Printers Limited,
Thetford, Norfolk

To the
immortal memory of
XIMENES
and to those who follow
so worthily
in his train

AZED, JAC and ZANDER

Introduction

Crosswords grow ever more popular; and the men and women who compile crosswords become more and more subtle, more and more diabolically clever. We who enjoy — and suffer — the results of their machinations must seek to arm ourselves with more powerful, more versatile weapons; simply 'hunting through the dictionary' is too time-consuming, even for the most addicted among us, particularly since the search may end in frustration.

This book of lists arms the crossword addict with the kind of specialized help which he (she) might derive from a library of some four dozen reference books. Words and names are listed (a) according to their subject; (b) according to the number of letters which they contain; (c) in alphabetical order.

The range is wide, from admirals to Welsh princes, from bays to universities, from reptiles to British Prime Ministers: a glance through the List of Contents, which serves also as an index, will show the great diversity of subjects included.

Alternative spellings, in proper names as well as common nouns and more esoteric words, have been generously provided, wherever they are supported by authoritative reference books, particularly *Chambers's Twentieth Century Dictionary*.

The compiler wishes to place on record his keen appreciation of the help given by the publishers at every stage of the production of this book.

Although the greatest possible care has been taken to eliminate errors in the compilation of these lists, it may be that some mistakes have been overlooked. The compiler (and the publishers) would be grateful to have any such errors pointed out so that they may be corrected in any future editions.

J.E.B.
July 1976

Contents

x · Contents

Admirals

3	HORTON	**9**	**2**
LAW	HOWARD	ARBUTHNOT	KY
MAY	JERRAM	BERESFORD	
	JERVIS	CALLAGHAN	**3**
4	KEPPEL	CHATFIELD	LEE
BEGG	LE FANU	DUCKWORTH	
BUSH	MADDEN	EFFINGHAM	**4**
BYNG	NELSON	FREMANTLE	PECK
HOOD	NIMITZ	HENDERSON	
HOPE	OLIVER	ST VINCENT	**5**
HOWE	PARKER	VON HIPPER	BOYLE
JOHN	POPHAM	VON SCHEER	EVANS
KERR	RAMSAY	WARRENDER	
SIMS	RAWSON		**6**
TOGO	RODNEY	**10**	GRANDY
	WILLIS	CODRINGTON	HARRIS
5		CUNNINGHAM	NEWALL
ANSON	**7**	EVAN-THOMAS	PORTAL
BACON	BURNABY	HILL-NORTON	TEDDER
BLAKE	BURNETT	KEMPENFELT	WALKER
BOYLE	DAMPIER	MOUNTEVANS	
BRAND	DE CHAIR	SOMERVILLE	**7**
BROCK	DOENITZ	TROUBRIDGE	BROCARD
BROKE	EXMOUTH	VILLENEUVE	BURNETT
COWAN	HOPKINS	VON TIRPITZ	DICKSON
DEWAR	JACKSON		DOUGLAS
DRAKE	MARKHAM	**11**	GOERING
FIELD	RAINIER	COLLINGWOOD	JOUBERT
HAWKE	RALEIGH	ELPHINSTONE	SALMOND
JAMES	RONARCH	MOUNTBATTEN	SLESSOR
KEITH	SEYMOUR		
KEYES	STURDEE	**12**	**8**
MAHAN	TIRPITZ	CULME-SEYMOUR	BRANCKER
MILNE	VON SPEE	WESTER-WEMYSS	ELWORTHY
MOORE	WATKINS		PRICKETT
NOBLE		**13**	
SCOTT	**8**	CORK AND ORRERY	**9**
STARK	BERKELEY		ELLINGTON
TOVEY	BOSCAWEN	**14**	FAIRCHILD
TRYON	CALDWELL	ROZHDESTVENSKY	SPOTSWOOD
TWISS	COCHRANE		TRENCHARD
	COCKBURN		
6	COLVILLE		
BEATTY	CRADDOCK		
BRIDGE	CUSTANCE		
BRUEYS	DE ROBECK		
CALDER	FANSHAWE		
COLOMB	JELLICOE		
CREASY	KING-HALL		
DARLAN	MUSELIER		
DUNCAN	RICHMOND		
FISHER	SAUMAREZ		
FRASER	TYRWHITT		
FREWEN	VAN TROMP		
HORTHY	VILLARET		

Air-Marshals

Animals (see also Dogs; Horses; Reptiles)

2	CONY	PUMA	DOGIE	SABLE	BEEVES	JUMENT
AI	COON	QUEY	DRILL	SAIGA	BEZOAR	KALONG
KY	CRAB	RANA	ELAND	SAJOU	BHARAL	KITFOX
OX	DAUW	REEM	EQUUS	SASIN	BOBCAT	KITTEN
	DEER	ROAN	FAUNA	SEROW	BURHEL	KOODOO
3	DIEB	RUNT	FELIS	SHEEP	BURREL	KOULAN
APE	DOUC	RUSA	FILLY	SHOAT	CABIAI	KUKANG
ASK	EURO	SAKI	FITCH	SHREW	CHACMA	KUPAIA
ASS	EVET	SEAL	FOSSA	SKUNK	CHETAH	KYLOES
BAT	EYRA	SKUG	GAYAL	SLOTH	CHITAL	LANGUR
BOK	FAWN	SORE	GENET	SOREL	COAITI	LIONEL
CAT	FOAL	STAG	GORAL	SPADE	COSSET	MACACO
COW	FROG	STOT	GRICE	SPADO	COUGAR	MALKIN
CUB	GAUR	TAIT	HARPY	STEER	COYOTE	MALMAG
DAM	GILT	TEGG	HINNY	STIRK	CRABER	MAMMAL
DOE	GOAT	TITI	HORSE	STOAT	DESMAN	MARGAY
DOG	GUIB	TOAD	HUTIA	SWINE	DEXTER	MARMOT
EFT	GYAL	UNAU	HYENA	TABBY	DIK-DIK	MARTEN
ELK	HARE	URUS	HYRAX	TAKIN	DOG-FOX	MAWKIN
EWE	HART	URVA	INDRI	TAPIR	DONKEY	MAZAMA
FOX	HIND	VARI	IZARD	TATOU	DRAGON	MAZAME
GIB	HOGG	VOLE	JOCKO	TIGER	DUGONG	MERINO
GNU	IBEX	WOLF	KAAMA	URIAL	DUIKER	MESSAN
HOG	JOEY	WORM	KALAN	URSON	DUYKER	MONKEY
KID	KINE	ZATI	KIANG	VISON	DZEREN	MORKIN
KIT	KOBA	ZEBU	KOALA	VIXEN	DZERIN	MUSANG
KOB	KUDU	ZOBO	KULAN	WHALE	DZERON	MUSK-OX
MAN	LAMB	ZUNA	KYLOE	WHELP	ERMINE	MUSTAC
MUG	LION		LAPIN	YAPOK	FARROW	NILGAI
PIG	LYNX	**5**	LEECH	ZEBRA	FENNEC	NILGAU
PUP	MAKI	ADDAX	LEMUR	ZERDA	FERRET	OCELOT
RAM	MARA	AGUTI	LLAMA	ZIBET	FISHER	ONAGER
RAT	MARE	AMMON	LORIS	ZIZEL	FOUSSA	OORIAL
RIG	MICO	ARIEL	MAGOT	ZORIL	FOX-BAT	OVIBOS
ROE	MINK	ASKER	MANIS	ZORRA	GALAGO	PALLAH
SAI	MOCO	BEAST	MANUL	ZORRO	GERBIL	PANTER
SOW	MOHR	BIPED	MHORR		GIBBON	PARDAL
TEG	MOKE	BISON	MOOSE	**6**	GIBCAT	PELUDO
TOD	MOLE	BITCH	MORSE	AGOUTA	GOPHER	PORKER
TUP	MONA	BOBAC	NAGOR	AGOUTI	GRISLY	POSSUM
URE	MULE	BOBAK	OKAPI	ALIPED	GRISON	PYGARG
WAT	MUSK	BONGO	ORANG	ALPACA	GRIVET	QUAGGA
YAK	NAPU	BROCK	ORIBI	ANGOLA	GUENON	RABBIT
ZHO	NEAT	BRUIN	OTARY	ANGORA	HACKEE	RACOON
	NEWT	BURRO	OTTER	ANKOLE	HEIFER	REEBOK
4	NOWT	CAMEL	OUNCE	AOUDAD	HOGGET	RENARD
ALCE	OONT	CIVET	PANDA	ARGALI	HOWLER	RHESUS
ANOA	ORYX	COATI	PEKAN	AYE-AYE	HYBRID	RODENT
BEAR	OXEN	CONEY	PHOCA	BABOON	IMPALA	SAMBAR
BOAR	PACA	CONGO	PONGO	BADGER	INDRIS	SAMBUR
BUCK	PACO	COYPU	POTTO	BANDAR	INYALA	SARLAC
BULL	PARD	CRONE	PUPPY	BARROW	JACKAL	SARLUK
CALF	PEBA	CUDDY	RANNY	BAUSON	JAGUAR	SEA-APE
CAVY	PIKA	DAMAN	RATEL	BAWSON	JERBOA	SEA-COW
COLT	PUDU	DIPUS	ROYAL	BEAVER	JUMART	SERVAL

SIMPAI
SORREL
SPONGE
SUSLIK
TAGUAN
TAPETI
TARAND
TELEDU
TENREC
THEAVE
TOMCAT
TUPAIA
TURTLE
TUSKER
VERMIN
VERVET
VICUNA
WALRUS
WAPITI
WEASEL
WEEPER
WETHER
WIVERN
WOMBAT
WOW-WOW
WYVERN
YAPOCK
ZORINO

7
ACOUCHY
ANT-BEAR
AUROCHS
AXOLOTL
BANTENG
BANTING
BAUSOND
BAWSINT
BIG-HORN
BLESBOK
BLUE-CAT
BLUE FOX
BONASUS
BOSHBOP
BRAWNER
BROCKET
BRUSHER
BUBALIS
BUFFALO
BULCHIN
BULLOCK
BUSHCAT
CAPE ELK
CARABAO
CARACAL
CARIBOO
CARIBOU
CATTALO

CENTAUR
CETACEA
CHAMOIS
CHEETAH
CHEVIOT
CHIKARA
CHIMERA
CHITWAH
COLOBUS
COON CAT
DASYPOD
DASYPUS
DASYURE
DOLPHIN
DRAFT-OX
EANLING
ECHIDNA
EPIZOAN
EPIZOON
ERMELIN
FATLING
FINBACK
FITCHET
FITCHEW
FOUMART
GAZELLE
GELDING
GEMSBOK
GENETTE
GERENUK
GIRAFFE
GLUTTON
GNU-GOAT
GORILLA
GRAMPUS
GRAY FOX
GRIFFIN
GRIZZLY
GUANACO
HAMSTER
HANUMAN
HEXAPOD
HOOLOCH
HUANACO
HULLUCK
ICE BEAR
JACCHUS
JACKASS
KARAGAN
KARAKUL
KEITLOA
KIDLING
KLIPDAS
LAGOMYS
LAMBKIN
LEMMING
LEOPARD
LEVERET

LIBBARD
LINSANG
LIONESS
MACACUS
MACAQUE
MADOQUA
MAMMOTH
MANATEE
MANGABY
MANX CAT
MARKHOR
MARMOSE
MINEVER
MINIVER
MOLERAT
MOLLUCK
MOLLUSC
MONGREL
MORLING
MORMOPS
MOUFLON
MUFFLON
MUGLAMB
MUNTJAK
MUSIMAN
MUSKHOG
MUSKRAT
MUSTELA
MYCETES
MYLODON
NANDINE
NASALIS
NOCTULE
NYLGHAU
ONDATRA
OPOSSUM
PACK RAT
PADDOCK
PAINTER
PANTHER
PARDALE
PECCARY
POLECAT
POTOROO
PRICKET
PROCYON
RACCOON
RED DEER
ROCK DOE
ROEBUCK
ROE DEER
ROOF RAT
RORQUAL
SAGOUIN
SAIMIRI
SAMBHUR
SAPAJOU
SASSABY

SCIURUS
SCORPIO
SEA BEAR
SEALION
SIAMANG
SOLIPED
SONDELI
SOUNDER
SPITTER
STEMBOK
SUMPTER
TADPOLE
TAMARIN
TARSIER
TIGRESS
TOXODON
TREE FOX
TWINTER
UNICORN
VAMPIRE
VANSIRE
VIVERRA
WALLABY
WART-HOG
WATER OX
WILD ASS
WILD CAT
WILD DOG
WISTITI
WOOD RAT
ZAMOUSE
ZEBRASS
ZORILLE
ZORILLO

8
AARDVARK
AARDWOLF
ANTEATER
ANTELOPE
AQUATOAD
BABIRUSA
BASILISK
BEHEMOTH
BETTONGA
BLACK CAT
BLACK FOX
BLACK RAT
BRANT FOX
BROWN RAT
BULLCALF
BUSHBABY
BUSHBUCK
CACHALOT
CACHOLOT
CAPIBARA
CAPUCHIN
CAPYBARA

CARCAJOU
CAVICORN
CHIGETAI
CHIMAERA
CHIPMUNK
CIVET CAT
COLOCOLA
COTSWOLD
CRICETUS
DEMIWOLF
DORMOUSE
DUCKBILL
ELEPHANT
ENTELLUS
FILANDER
FINWHALE
GALLOWAY
GRYSBOCK
HEDGEHOG
HEDGEPIG
HOGGEREL
HOG-STEER
HYLOBATE
JAVELINE
KANGAROO
KINGCRAB
KINKAJOU
LAMANTIN
LANDCRAB
LIMOUSIN
MACROPOD
MANDRILL
MANGABEY
MARKHOOR
MARKHORE
MARMOSET
MASTODON
MATAMATA
MERIONES
MILCH COW
MONGOOSE
MUD-PUPPY
MULE-DEER
MUSK-DEER
MUSQUASH
PACKMULE
PANGOLIN
PARDALIS
PHYSETER
PLATYPUS
POLAR FOX
POLLIWIG
POLLYWOG
PORKLING
PORPOISE
REINDEER
RUMINANT
SCORPION

SEA-OTTER
SELADANG
SEWER RAT
SQUIRREL
STAGGARD
STEENBOK
STINKARD
STEINBOK
SURICATE
SWIFT FOX
TABBY CAT
TALAPOIN
TIGERCAT
TUCUTUCO
TUCUTUCO
TUCUTUCU
TWINLING
VISCACHA
WALLAROO
WALL-NEWT
WANDEROO
WARRAGAL
WARRIGAL
WATER-HOG
WATER-RAT
WEANLING
WHARF RAT
WHISTLER
WHITE FOX
WILD BOAR
WILD GOAT
YEANLING
YEARLING
ZEBRINNY

9
ADELOPODE
ANGOLA-CAT
ARCTIC FOX
ARMADILLO
BABIRUSSA
BANDICOOT
BARBASTEL
BLACK BEAR
BLACK BUCK
BROWN BEAR
BRUSH-DEER
BRUSH-WOLF
CATAMOUNT
CHICKAREE
COTTON RAT
DEERMOUSE
DEER TIGER
DELUNDUNG
DESERT-RAT
DINOCERAS
DRAUGHT-OX
DROMEDARY

DZIGGETAI
FLYING-CAT
FLYING-FOX
GALLIWASP
GLYPTODON
GRIMALKIN
GROUND-HOG
GRUNTLING
GUINEA-PIG
HAMADRYAD
HARTBEEST
HONEY-BEAR
ICHNEUMON
JAGUARETE
LEVIATHAN
MARSUPIAL
MONOCEROS
MOUSE DEER
ORANG-UTAN
PACHYDERM
PADEMELON
PADYMELON
PETAURIST
PHALANGER
PINEMOUSE
PIPISTREL
POCKET RAT
POLAR BEAR
PORCUPINE
PRONG-BUCK
PRONG-HORN
REARMOUSE
REERMOUSE
REREMOUSE
ROSMARINE
SHREW-MOLE
SILVER FOX
SKUNK BEAR
SOUTHDOWN
SPRINGBOK
STEERLING
STEINBOCK
STONEBUCK
TATOUPEBA
THYLACINE
WATERBUCK
WATERVOLE
WHITE BEAR
WHITE WOLF
WOLVERENE
WOLVERINE
WOODCHUCK
WOODSHOCK
YOUNGLING

10
ANGWANTIBO
ARCTIC HARE

ASSAPANICK
BABIROUSSA
BARBARY-APE
BATRACHIAN
BELL-WETHER
BEZOAR GOAT
BUCKJUMPER
BUCKRABBIT
CAMELOPARD
CHAROLLAIS
CHEVROTAIN
CHIMPANZEE
CHINCHILLA
COATIMONDI
COATIMUNDI
COCKATRICE
COTTONTAIL
DEINOCERAS
FALLOW-DEER
FIELDMOUSE
FREEMARTIN
GIANT PANDA
GRISLY BEAR
HARTEBEEST
HERMIT-CRAB
HERRING-HOG
HIPPOGRIFF
HIPPOGRYFF
HIPPOGRYPH
HOUSE-MOUSE
JACK-RABBIT
JAGUARONDI
JAGUARUNDI
LEOPARD-CAT
LEOPARDESS
MEXICAN HOG
MUSK-BEAVER
NATTERJACK
PADDYMELON
PERSIAN CAT
PICHICIAGO
PLIOHIPPUS
POUCHED RAT
PRAIRIE-DOG
RHINOCEROS
RIVER-HORSE
ROCK-BADGER
SALAMANDER
SHREWMOUSE
SPECTRE-BAT
SPRINGBUCK
STARVELING
SYRIAN BEAR
TIMBERWOLF
VAMPIRE-BAT
WILDEBEEST

11
BARBESTELLE
BELGIAN HARE
BLACK CATTLE
BLOODSUCKER
CAPE BUFFALO
CARDOPHAGUS
CATERPILLAR
CAT-SQUIRREL
CONGO MONKEY
COTTON-MOUSE
FLICKERTAIL
FOX-SQUIRREL
GRIZZLY BEAR
JUMPING-DEER
KANGAROO-RAT
MEADOW-MOUSE
MEGATHERIUM
ORANG-OUTANG
POCKET-MOUSE
PRAIRIE-WOLF
ROCK-WALLABY
SEA-ELEPHANT
SIVATHERIUM
SPECTRE-CRAB
SPERMOPHILE
SWAMP-RABBIT
WISHTONWISH

12
AMERICAN LION
BARBARY-SHEEP
BENGAL-MONKEY
CASHMERE GOAT
CATAMOUNTAIN
CINNAMON-BEAR
FLICKERMOUSE
FLINDERMOUSE
FLITTERMOUSE
FLYING MARMOT
GOAT-ANTELOPE
GREY SQUIRREL
HARVEST-MOUSE
HIPPOPOTAMUS
JUMPING-MOUSE
KLIPSPRINGER
MOUNTAIN GOAT
MOUNTAIN LION
POCKET-GOPHER
POUCHED MOUSE
RHESUS-MONKEY
ROCK-SQUIRREL
SPECTRE-LEMUR
SPIDER-MONKEY
SPOTTED HYENA
STRIPED HYENA
TREE-KANGAROO
TREE-SQUIRREL

VIRGINIA-DEER
WATER-BUFFALO

13
ABYSSINIAN CAT
ANOPLOTHERIUM
ANOPLOTHEROID
AUSTRALIAN CAT
BACTRIAN CAMEL
BRUSH-KANGAROO
CHAPMAN'S ZEBRA
GALEOPITHECUS
GOLDEN HAMSTER
HIGHLAND STEER
INDIAN BUFFALO
KANGAROO-MOUSE
LAUGHING-HYENA
MOUNTAIN-SHEEP
MOUNTAIN-ZEBRA
PARRY'S WALLABY
RINGTAILED CAT
SABLE ANTELOPE
SHORTHORN BULL
SPINY-ANTEATER
SPOTTED HYAENA
STRIPED HYAENA
TASMANIAN WOLF
TREE-PORCUPINE
WOOLLY MAMMOTH

14
BRIDLED WALLABY
BURCHELL'S ZEBRA
CRAB-EATING SEAL
FLYING SQUIRREL
GROUND-SQUIRREL
HIGHLAND CATTLE
HUNTING LEOPARD
INDIAN ELEPHANT
INDIAN PANGOLIN
JERBOA-KANGAROO
LAUGHING-HYAENA
SNOWSHOE-RABBIT
TASMANIAN-DEVIL
TASMANIAN-TIGER
THIAN SHAN SHEEP

15
AFRICAN ELEPHANT
AMERICAN BUFFALO
EUROPEAN POLECAT
FLYING PHALANGER
IMPERIAL MAMMOTH
LAUGHING JACKASS
MARCO POLO'S SHEEP
MOUNTAIN-PANTHER
SABRE-TOOTHED CAT

Archbishops of Canterbury

(Earlier archbishops had Christian names only. Later archbishops are entered twice in the following list: for example, the 101st Archbishop of Canterbury, His Grace the Most Reverend Dr F. D. Coggan, who signs himself 'Donald Cantuar', appears below as DONALD and as FREDERICK DONALD COGGAN).

3
ODO

4
JOHN

5
COSMO
HENRY
RALPH
ROGER
SIMON

6
ALFRIC
ALSINE
ANSELM
DONALD
EDMUND
EDWARD
ETHELM
GEORGE
HUBERT
JUSTUS
LYFING
ROBERT
THOMAS
WALTER

7
AEFSIGE
AELFRIC
ALPHEGE
BALDWIN
CHARLES
DUNSTAN
EADSIGE
GILBERT
MATTHEW
MICHAEL
NOTHELM
RANDALL
RICHARD
SIGERIC
STEPHEN
STIGAND
WILLIAM

WULFELM
WULFRED

8
BONIFACE
CEOLNOTH
CUTHBERT
ETHELGAR
ETHELRED
FLEOGILD
GEOFFREY
HONORIUS
JOHN KEMP
LANFRANC
MELLITUS
REGINALD
TAETWINE
THEOBALD
THEODORE

9
ARCHIBALD
AUGUSTINE
BERHTHELM
BERHTWALD
BREOGWINE
DEUSDEDIT
ETHELHELM
ETHELNOTH
FREDERICK
JAENBERHT
JOHN MOORE
PLEGEMUND

10
EDMUND RICH
ETHELHEARD
HENRY DEANE
JOHN MORTON
JOHN PECHAM
JOHN POTTER
LAURENTIUS
SIMON ISLIP

11
GEORGE ABBOT
JOHN PECKHAM

ROGER WALDEN
WILLIAM LAUD
WILLIAM WAKE

12
EDWARD BENSON
HUBERT WALTER
JOHN DE UFFORD
JOHN STAFFORD
JOHN WHITGIFT
REGINALD POLE
SIMON LANGHAM
SIMON SUDBURY
THOMAS BECKET
THOMAS SECKER
WILLIAM JUXON

13
EDMUND GRINDAL
HENRY CHICHELE
JOHN STRATFORD
JOHN TILLOTSON
MATTHEW HUTTON
MATTHEW PARKER
RALPH DESCURES
THOMAS ARUNDEL
THOMAS CRANMER
THOMAS HERRING
THOMAS TENISON
WILLIAM HOWLEY
WILLIAM TEMPLE
WILLIAM WARHAM

14
GILBERT SHELDON
HENRY CHICHELEY
JOHN BIRD SUMNER
RALPH DE TURBINE
RICHARD LE GRANT
ROBERT KILWARDY
SIMON DE MEOPHAM
STEPHEN LANGTON
THOMAS FITZALAN
WALTER REYNOLDS

15
COSMO GORDON LANG

FREDERICK TEMPLE
RANDALL DAVIDSON
RICHARD BANCROFT
ROBERT KILWARDBY
THOMAS BOURCHIER
WILLIAM SANCROFT

16
ROBERT WINCHELSEA
THOMAS BRADWARDEN
WILLIAM COURTENAY
WILLIAM WITTLESEY

17
RICHARD WETHERSHED
THOMAS BRADWARDINE
WILLIAM DE CORBEUIL

18
ARTHUR MICHAEL RAMSEY
FREDERICK CORNWALLIS
REGINALD FITZ-JOCELIN

19
CHARLES MANNERS-SUTTON
CHARLES THOMAS LONGLEY

21
ARCHIBALD CAMPBELL TAIT
FREDERICK DONALD COGGAN
GEOFFREY FRANCIS FISHER

Archbishops and Bishops of York

(Early archbishops and bishops had Christian names only. Later archbishops are entered twice in the following list: for example, the Most Reverend Dr A. M. Ramsey, who signed himself 'Michael Ebor', appears below as MICHAEL and as ARTHUR MICHAEL RAMSEY.)

4
BOSA
CEAD
CHAD
JOHN

5
COSMO
CYRIL
EDWIN
HENRY
ROGER
SEWAL

6
ALFRIC
DONALD
EDMUND
EDWARD
EGBERT
GEORGE
GERARD
OSWALD
ROBERT
SAMUEL
THOMAS
TOBIAS
WALTER

7
AELFRIC
CHARLES
EALDRED
EALDULF
EANBALD
EBORIUS
GODFREY
MATTHEW
MICHAEL
NICOLAS
OSKETYL
RICHARD
WIGMUND
WILFRID
WILLIAM

8
ACCEPTED
GEOFFREY

JOHN KEMP
KINESIGE
LANCELOT
LAWRENCE
NICHOLAS
PAULINUS
REDEWALD
THURSTAN
WULFHERE
WULFSIGE
WULFSTAN

9
ALEXANDER
EDWARD LEE
ETHELBALD
ETHELBERT
JOHN PIERS
JOHN SHARP

10
JOHN DOLBEN
WALTER GRAY

11
CHRISTOPHER
EDWIN SANDYS
HENRY BOWETT
HENRY MURDAC
HENRY NEWARK
JOHN GILBERT
JOHN LE ROMAN
THOMAS YOUNG

12
JOHN THORESBY
JOHN WILLIAMS
NICOLAS HEATH
RICHARD NEILE
ROBERT WALDBY
SEWAL DE BOVIL
THOMAS SAVAGE
THOMAS WOLSEY
WILLIAM BOOTH
WILLIAM DAWES

13
EDMUND GRINDAL
GEORGE NEVILLE

LAWRENCE BOOTH
MATTHEW HUTTON
NICHOLAS HEATH
RICHARD SCROPE
RICHARD STERNE
ROBERT HOLGATE
THOMAS ARUNDEL
THOMAS HERRING
TOBIAS MATTHEW
WALTER GIFFARD
WILLIAM MELTON
WILLIAM TEMPLE
WILLIAM ZOUCHE

14
ACCEPTED FREWEN
EDWARD HARCOURT
SAMUEL HARSNETT
THOMAS LAMPLUGH
THOMAS MUSGRAVE
WILLIAM MARKHAM
WILLIAM THOMSON

15
COSMO GORDON LANG
GEORGE MONTEIGNE
THOMAS CORBRIDGE
THOMAS ROTHERHAM
WILLIAM WICKWAIN

16
ALEXANDER NEVILLE

17
ROBERT HAY DRUMMOND
WILLIAM GREENFIELD

18
LANCELOT BLACKBURNE
WILLIAM CONNOR MAGEE

19
ARTHUR MICHAEL RAMSEY
CYRIL FORSTER GARBETT

20
CHARLES THOMAS LONGLEY

21
CHRISTOPHER BAINBRIDGE
FREDERICK DONALD COGGAN

24
WILLIAM DALRYMPLE MACLAGAN

Architects

4
ADAM
KENT
LOOS
MIES
NASH
SHAW
WEBB
WOOD
WREN

5
AALTO
BARRY
GAUDI
GIBBS
JONES
LE VAU
NERVI
PORTA
PUGIN
SCOTT
SOANE
WYATT

6
ASHBEE
BROSSE
CAMPEN
JENNEY
KLENZE
LEDOUX
LESCOT
PARLER
PERRET
PISANO
RENNIE
SMIRKE
UTZORN
VOYSEY
WRIGHT

7
ALBERTI
ARNOLFO
ASPLUND
BEHRENS
CORTONA
DELORME
FISCHER
GARNIER
GEDYMIN
ICTINUS
LETHABY
LUTYENS

MADERNA
MADISON
MANSART
NEUMANN
PERUZZI
VIGNOLA

8
AGOSTINO
ANTELAMI
BRAMANTE
CAMPBELL
CHAMBERS
HOFFMANN
KOLDEWEY
PERRAULT
SANGALLO
SCHINKEL
SOUFFLOT
SULLIVAN
THORNTON

9
BORROMINI
COCKERELL
HAUSSMANN
HAWKSMOOR
LABROUSTE
LEMERCIER
SANSOVINO
VITRUVIUS

10
ARCHIPENKO
BERRUGUETE
HONNECOURT
MACKINTOSH
MENDELSOHN
MICHELOZZO
PRANDTAUER
RICHARDSON
ROSSELLINO
ZIMMERMANN

11
HILDEBRANDT
LE CORBUSIER

12
BRUNELLESCHI
MICHELANGELO
VIOLLET-LE-DUC

15
PIETRO DA CORTONA
VITRUVIUS POLLIO

16
AGOSTINO DI DUCCIO

Art terms

3
BUR
MAT

4
BUST
DADA
DAUB
ETCH
FLAT
GILD
ICON
LIMN
MATT
NUDE
POSE
TONE
WASH

5
BATIK
BRUSH
BURIN
CHASE
CRAFT
DELFT
DORIC
DUTCH
EASEL
GENRE
GRAVE
GREEK
GROUP
HATCH
IMAGE
IONIC
JAPAN
MODEL
MOUNT
MURAL
ORDER
PRIME
PRINT
PUTTI
PUTTO
SCENE
SEPIA
SHADE
STUDY
TORSO
TRACE
UMBER
UMBRA
VIRTU

6
CARVER
CRAYON
CUBISM
CUBIST
DESIGN
ECTYPE
EMBLEM
EMBOSS
ENGILD
FICTOR
FIGURE
FRESCO
FYLFOT
GOTHIC
GROUND
INCISE
KITCAT
LIMNER
MASTIC
MEGILP
MOBILE
MOSAIC
MOSTIC
NIELLO
OXGALL
PALLET
PASTEL
PATINA
PENCIL
PLAQUE
POSING
POUNCE
REFLEX
RELIEF
ROCOCO
SEVRES
SHADOW
SITTER
SKETCH
STATUE
STUDIO
SYMBOL
TUSCAN

7
ART DECO
ASIATIC
ATELIER
BAROQUE
BOSCAGE
CARTOON
CARVING
CERAMIC
CHASING

CLOISON
COLLAGE
COMPOSE
DADAISM
DADAIST
DIAGRAM
DIORAMA
DRAWING
DRESDEN
EBAUCHE
ENGRAVE
ETCHING
FAIENCE
FAUVISM
FAUVIST
FLEMISH
GILDING
GOUACHE
GRAPHIC
GRECIAN
IMAGERY
IMPAINT
IMPASTO
IMPRESS
ITALIAN
LACQUER
LIMNING
LINOCUT
LOST-WAX
LUNETTE
MEISSEN
MONTAGE
MONTURE
OUTLINE
PALETTE
PICTURE
PIGMENT
POINTEL
PRIMING
PROFILE
REALISM
REALIST
RELIEVO
REPLICA
SCUMBLE
STENCIL
STIPPLE
TABLEAU
TEMPERA
TESSERA
TRACING
WOODCUT

8
ABSTRACT
ACADEMIC
ANAGLYPH
AQUATINT

CERAMICS
CHARCOAL
CREATION
DAMASKIN
DEMITINT
DRY POINT
ENGRAVER
EXTERIOR
FIGURINE
FREEHAND
FUTURISM
FUTURIST
GARGOYLE
GOLD-SIZE
GRAFFITI
GRAFFITO
GRAPHICS
GROUPING
HATCHING
IDEALISM
INCISION
INTAGLIO
INTERIOR
MAJOLICA
MANDORLA
MAQUETTE
MEDIEVAL
MOUNTING
NEGATIVE
OILPAINT
PAINTING
PANORAMA
PASTICHE
PASTORAL
PORTRAIT
PRINTING
REPOUSSE
ROMANTIC
SEAPIECE
SEASCAPE
STATUARY
TOREUTIC
TRIPTYCH
VIGNETTE
VIRTUOSO

9
BAS-RELIEF
BRIC-A-BRAC
BYZANTINE
CEROGRAPH
CLASSICAL
CLOISONNE
CRAFTWORK
DAMASCENE
DAMASKEEN
DAMASQUIN
DISTEMPER

EMBLEMATA
ENCAUSTIC
FACSIMILE
GOTHICISM
GOTHICIST
GRADATION
GRISAILLE
INDELIBLE
INDIAN INK
JAPANNING
LANDSCAPE
LAY FIGURE
LITHOTINT

MAHLSTICK
MANNEQUIN
MANUAL ART
MARQUETRY
MAULSTICK
MEDIAEVAL
MEZZOTINT
MODERNISM
MODERNIST
NAUMACHIA
NEOGOTHIC
PASTICCIO
PEN-AND-INK
PORTRAYAL
PRIMITIVE
SCULPTURE
SCUMBLING
STATUETTE
STILL LIFE
STIPPLING
SYMBOLISM
SYMBOLIST
TABLATURE
TENEBRIST
TENEBRITY
VORTICISM
VORTICIST
XYLOGRAPH

10
ANAGLYPHIC
ART NOUVEAU
BACKGROUND
CARICATURE
CIRE PERDUE
CLASSICISM
CLASSICIST
CORINTHIAN
CORNUCOPIA
EMBROIDERY
FOREGROUND
GRECO-ROMAN
HAIR-PENCIL
HALF-LENGTH
INDIA-PAPER

JUGENDSTIL
KEY PATTERN
LITHOGRAPH
MARIONETTE
METALCRAFT
MEZZOTINTO
MONOCHROME
NATURALISM
NATURALIST
NIGHT-PIECE
PAINTBRUSH
PENCILLING
PENTIMENTO
PHOTOGRAPH
PIETRA-DURA
PORT-CRAYON
RAPHAELISM
RAPHAELITE
ROMANESQUE
SILHOUETTE
SURREALISM
SURREALIST
TERRACOTTA
WOODCARVER
XYLOGRAPHY

11
AQUATINTING
BAMBOCCIATA
BATTLEPIECE
CALLIGRAPHY
CHROMOGRAPH
CONNOISSEUR
DELINEATION
DISPOSITION
DRAUGHTSMAN
ELECTROTYPE
GRAECO-ROMAN
GROUND PLANE
HELIOCHROME
HELLENISTIC
ICHNOGRAPHY
LITHOGRAPHY
MASTERPIECE
OIL PAINTING
PASTEL SHADE
PERSPECTIVE
PHOTOGRAPHY
PLASTIC-CLAY
POINTILLISM
POINTILLIST
PORTE CRAYON
PORTRAITURE
PRIMITIVISM
PRIMITIVIST
RENAISSANCE
RESTORATION
ROMANTICISM

ROMANTICIST
ROTOGRAVURE
SILVERPOINT
STENCILLING
TESSELLATED
WOODCARVING
XYLOGRAPHER
ZINCOGRAPHY

12
BACKPAINTING
CLARE OBSCURE
CLARO OBSCURE
CLASSICALISM
ECTYPOGRAPHY
ILLUMINATION
ILLUSTRATION
LITHOGRAPHER
MESOPOTAMIAN
MEZZO-RILIEVO
MONOCHROMIST
NATURALISTIC
ORTHOGRAPHIC
PHOTOGRAPHER
PHOTOGRAVURE
STEREOCHROMY
SURREALISTIC
ZINCOGRAPHIC

13
BLACK-AND-WHITE
FINGER PAINTER
IMPRESSIONISM
IMPRESSIONIST
MURAL PAINTING
NEO-CLASSICISM
NEO-CLASSICIST
NEO-PLASTICISM
PRE-RAPHAELITE
SCENE PAINTING
SOCIAL REALISM

14
ABSTRACTIONIST
ACTION PAINTING
PLASTER-OF-PARIS
POSTER PAINTING
STEEL ENGRAVING
TRADITIONALISM
TRADITIONALIST

15
CHURRIGUERESQUE
IMPRESSIONISTIC
PRE-RAPHAELITISM
TEMPERA PAINTING

16
PRE-IMPRESSIONISM
PRE-IMPRESSIONIST
SOCIALIST REALISM

17
CONVERSATION PIECE
POST-IMPRESSIONISM
POST-IMPRESSIONIST

Astronomical terms

3
ORB
RAY
SUN

4
AXIS
CUSP
HALO
LIMB
MOON
NODE
NOVA
RILL
STAR

5
APSIS
COMET
DIGIT
EPACT
EPOCH
ERROR
FLARE
LABEL
LUNAR
MARIA
NADIR
NODAL
ORBIT
PHASE
RILLE
SOLAR
TRINE
UMBRA

6
ALBEDO
APOGEE
ASPECT
ASTRAL
AURORA
BINARY
CORONA
COSMIC
CRATER
EPOCHA
GALAXY
GNOMON
LUNARY
MASCON
METEOR
NEBULA
ORRERY

				Authors
PARSEC	EPICYCLE	SOLAR WIND	PHOTOSPHERE	
PERIOD	EVECTION	STARGAZER	PLANETARIUM	
PLANET	FIREBALL	STARLIGHT	PLANETOIDAL	
PULSAR	LATITUDE	SUBASTRAL	TERRESTRIAL	**3**
QUASAR	LUNATION	SUBLUNARY		FOX
RADIUS	MERIDIAN	SUPERNOVA	**12**	FRY
SPHERE	METEORIC	SYNODICAL	ASTROGEOLOGY	GAY
SUN-DOG	MILKY WAY	TELESCOPE	ASTRONOMICAL	HAY
SYZYGY	MOONGLOW	URANOLOGY	ASTROPHYSICS	KYD
TROJAN	OCCULTED	VIA LACTEA	CHROMOSPHERE	LAW
VECTOR	PARALLAX		ECCENTRICITY	POE
VERTEX	PENUMBRA	**10**	HELIOCENTRIC	
ZENITH	PERIGEAN	ABERRATION	INTERMUNDANE	**4**
ZODIAC	PERILUNE	ACRONYCHAL	INTERSTELLAR	AMIS
	QUADRANT	ALTAZIMUTH	LUNAR ECLIPSE	AYER
7	QUARTILE	APPARITION	PERTURBATION	BALL
ANNULAR	QUINTILE	ASTEROIDAL	SOLAR ECLIPSE	BEDE
APOGEAN	RED SHIFT	BELT BOLIDE	SPATIOGRAPHY	BELL
APOLUNE	SIDEREAL	COPERNICAN	TOTAL ECLIPSE	BOLL
APPULSE	SOLSTICE	DEPRESSION	VAN ALLEN BELT	CARY
AURORAL	SOUTHING	EARTH-SHINE		CATO
AZIMUTH	SPECTRUM	ELONGATION	**13**	COKE
CEPHEID	SPHEROID	EPHEMERIST	ASTROPHYSICAL	COLE
CLUSTER	STARLESS	EXALTATION	CONSTELLATION	DELL
COMETIC	SUBLUNAR	GEOCENTRIC	DIPLEIDOSCOPE	EDEN
CURTATE	UNIVERSE	HOUR CIRCLE	INTERGALACTIC	FORD
ECLIPSE	VARIABLE	LUNAR MONTH	SPECTROSCOPIC	FYFE
EQUATOR	X-RAY STAR	METEOREOUS		GALT
EQUINOX	ZODIACAL	NUTATIONAL	**14**	GIDE
METONIC		OPPOSITION	ASTROGEOLOGIST	GLYN
MOCK-SUN	**9**	OUTER SPACE	AURORA BOREALIS	GORE
NEBULAE	BLACK HOLE	PERIASTRON	INTERPLANETARY	GREY
NEBULAR	CANICULAR	PERIHELION	LUNAR DISTANCES	HALL
NODICAL	CELESTIAL	PRECESSION	PARTIAL ECLIPSE	HART
NUCLEUS	COSMOLOGY	PROMINENCE	RADIOASTRONOMY	HOGG
PERIGEE	CURTATION	QUADRATURE	RIGHT ASCENSION	HOOK
RADIANT	DEEP SPACE	REFRACTION	SUMMER SOLSTICE	HOPE
SEXTILE	ELEVATION	RETROGRADE	WINTER SOLSTICE	HUGO
SPUTNIK	EPHEMERIS	SELENOLOGY		HUME
STELLAR	EPICYCLIC	SIDEROSTAT		INGE
SUNSPOT	FIRMAMENT	TELESCOPIC		JOAD
SYNODIC	HOUR-ANGLE	TERMINATOR		KANT
TEKTITE	IMMERSION	TRAJECTORY		KING
TRANSIT	LIBRATION	TRANSLUNAR		KNOX
	LIGHT YEAR	URANOMETRY		LAMB
8	LONGITUDE			LANG
AEROLITE	LUNAR YEAR	**11**		LEAR
AEROLITH	LUNISOLAR	CIRCUMPOLAR		LIVY
APHELION	MAGNITUDE	CONJUNCTION		LOON
APOAPSIS	METEORITE	CULMINATION		LOOS
ASTERISM	NORTH STAR	DECLINATION		LYLY
ASTEROID	PARHELION	GEGENSCHEIN		LYND
CISLUNAR	PERIAPSIS	INCLINATION		MAIS
COMETARY	PLANETARY	METEOROLITE		MANN
DRACONIC	PLANETOID	MURAL CIRCLE		MARX
ECLIPTIC	PTOLEMAIC	NEUTRON STAR		MILL
EMERSION	RADIO STAR	NONAGESIMAL		MORE
EMPYREAN	SATELLITE	OCCULTATION		NASH

OMAN	GREEN	VERGA	CURZON	MUNTHE	BERGSON
PARK	GRIMM	VERNE	DARWIN	MURRAY	BLUNDEN
PENN	HARDY	WAUGH	DEKKER	MUSSET	BULLETT
POLO	HARTE	WELLS	DOBSON	NEWMAN	BURGESS
READ	HASEK	WHITE	DOWDEN	O'CASEY	BURNETT
RHYS	HEBER	WILDE	DRYDEN	O'NEILL	CARLYLE
SADE	HEGEL	WOLFE	EUCLID	ORWELL	CARROLL
SAKI	HEINE	WOOLF	EVELYN	OSSIAN	CELLINI
SAND	HENRY	YATES	FARNOL	PASCAL	CHAPMAN
SHAW	HENTY	YEATS	FARRAR	PICARD	CHARDIN
SNOW	IBSEN	YONGE	FISHER	PINERO	CHEKHOV
WARD	JAMES	YOUNG	FOWLER	PORTER	CHEYNEY
WEBB	JEANS	ZWEIG	FRANCE	POTTER	CLEMENS
WEST	JONES		FROUDE	POWELL	COBBETT
ZOLA	JOYCE	**6**	GARVIN	PROUST	COCTEAU
	KAFKA	ALCUIN	GIBBON	RACINE	COLETTE
5	KEBLE	ANDRES	GODWIN	ROHMER	COLLINS
ACTON	LASKI	ANSTEY	GOETHE	RUSKIN	COPPARD
AESOP	LEWIS	ARCHER	GRAVES	SARDOU	CORELLI
AGATE	LOCKE	ARNOLD	GREENE	SAPPER	DA VINCI
ARDEN	LODGE	ASCHAM	HALLAM	SAPPHO	DEEPING
ARLEN	LUCAS	AUBREY	HAMSUN	SARTRE	DE STAEL
AYRES	MASON	AUSTEN	HANNAY	SAYERS	DICKENS
BABEL	MAUDE	BALZAC	HARRIS	SENECA	DIDEROT
BACON	MILNE	BARHAM	HEMANS	SEWELL	DODGSON
BARRY	MOORE	BARING	HENSON	SIDNEY	DOUGHTY
BATES	MURRY	BARKER	HILTON	SMILES	DOUGLAS
BEITH	ORCZY	BARRIE	HOBBES	SQUIRE	DUNSANY
BLAIR	OTWAY	BEETON	HOLMES	STEELE	DURRELL
BLAND	OUIDA	BEGBIE	HOLTBY	STERNE	EMERSON
BLUNT	PAINE	BELLOC	HOWARD	STOKER	ERASMUS
BURKE	PALEY	BELLOW	HUDSON	STRONG	FARADAY
CAINE	PATER	BENSON	HUGHES	TAGORE	FARJEON
CAMUS	PEPYS	BESANT	HUXLEY	TAYLOR	FLECKER
CRANE	PLATO	BIERCE	IRVING	TEMPLE	FLEMING
CROCE	PLINY	BINYON	JACOBS	THRALE	FORSTER
CURIE	POUND	BIRREL	JEROME	VALERY	FRANKAU
DEFOE	PRIOR	BORROW	JEVONS	VIEIRA	FREEMAN
DILKE	PUSEY	BRECHT	JONSON	WALTON	GALILEO
DONNE	READE	BRETON	JOWETT	WATSON	GALLICO
DOYLE	RENAN	BRIDIE	JUNIUS	WESKER	GARNETT
DUMAS	RILKE	BRONTE	KELLER	WEYMAN	GASKELL
DURAS	SAGAN	BROWNE	KEYNES	WILDER	GAUTIER
ELIOT	SCOTT	BUCHAN	LANDOR	WRIGHT	GILBERT
ELLIS	SHUTE	BUNYAN	LE FANU		GISSING
EVANS	SKEAT	BURNEY	LONDON	**7**	GOGARTY
FABRE	SMITH	BUTLER	LOWELL	ABELARD	GOLDING
FREUD	SPARK	CAESAR	LUTHER	ADDISON	GRAHAME
FROST	STAEL	CALVIN	LYTTON	AQUINAS	GUNTHER
GIBBS	STEAD	CAXTON	MACHEN	ARIOSTO	GUTHRIE
GIONI	STEED	CHEKOV	MAILER	ASHFORD	HAGGARD
GOGOL	STEIN	CHURCH	MALORY	BAGEHOT	HAKLUYT
GORKI	STORM	CIBBER	MANNIN	BALFOUR	HALDANE
GORKY	SWIFT	CICERO	MASSON	BECKETT	HAWKINS
GOSSE	SYNGE	CONRAD	MILLER	BENNETT	HAZLITT
GOULD	TAINE	COOPER	MOFFAT	BENTHAM	HERBERT
GOWER	TWAIN	COWARD	MORGAN	BENTLEY	HEWLETT
GRASS	TYNAN	CRONIN	MORLEY	BERGMAN	HEYWOOD

Aviation

3
RADAR
RADIO
RIGID
STALL
STRUT

ACE
FIN
FLY
GAP
GAS
JET
RIB

4
BANK
BUMP
COWL
DIVE
DOPE
DRAG
FIDO
FLAP
HULL
KITE
LIFT
LOOP
SLIP
SOAR
SPAN
SPAR
SPIN
STOL
TAIL
TAXI
TRIM
VTOL
WING
ZOOM

5
BENDS
BLIMP
CABRE
CHORD
CLEAT
CRASH
DRIFT
DRONE
FLAPS
FLOAT
GLIDE
GROUP
G-SUIT
LORAN
PILOT
PITCH
PLANE
PRANG
PYLON

6
BASKET
BOMBER
CAMBER
CANARD
CANOPY
DROGUE
ELEVON
FABRIC
FLIGHT
FLOATS
GASBAG
GLIDER
HANGAR
NOSE-UP
RADOME
RAMJET
RUDDER
RUNWAY
TANDEM
TURRET
VECTOR

7
AILERON
AIRFOIL
AIRPORT
AVIATOR
AVIETTE
AVIONIC
BALLAST
BALLOON
BANKING
BIPLANE
BLISTER
CATWALK
CEILING
CHASSIS
COCKPIT
COWLING
DIEDRAL
ECHELON
FAIRING
FIGHTER
FLYPAST
GLIDING
GONDOLA
HELIBUS
HELIMAN

HOUSING
INFLATE
LIFT-OFF
MACH ONE
MACH TWO
MAE WEST
NACELLE
NOSECAP
RIPCORD
RIPLINE
SOARING
SPINNER
SPONSON
STAGGER
TAIL FIN
TAKE OFF
TRACTOR
TRIMMER
ZOOMING

8
AEROFOIL
AIRCRAFT
AIRFIELD
AIRSCREW
ALTITUDE
AUTOGIRO
AVIONICS
BALLONET
BOMBRACK
BUOYANCY
DIHEDRAL
ELEVATOR
ENVELOPE
FUSELAGE
GYROSTAT
HELIPORT
HYDROGEN
INTER-COM
JET-PLANE
LONGERON
MACH CONE
NON-RIGID
NOSEDIVE
NOSE-OVER
PULSOJET
RADIATOR
SEAPLANE
SQUADRON
STALLING
TAILBOOM
TAIL SKID
TAIL SPIN
TAIL UNIT
TRIPLANE
TURBOJET
WARPLANE
WINGFLAP

9
AERODROME
AEROPLANE
AIRPOCKET
ALTIMETER
AMPHIBIAN
ASTRONAUT
COSMONAUT
DAMBUSTER
DIRIGIBLE
EMPENNAGE
INFLATION
INTER-COMM
LOW-FLYING
MACH METER
MONOCOQUE
MONOPLANE
NOSEWHEEL
PARACHUTE
PROPELLER
RUDDER-BAR
SEMI-RIGID
STABILITY
SWEEP BACK

10
AEROBATICS
AERONAUTIC
AEROPHOBIA
AEROSTATIC
ANEMOMETER
ANEMOSCOPE
BALLOONING
BALLOONIST
CANTILEVER
DIVE-BOMBER
FLIGHTDECK
FLIGHT PATH
FLYING-BOAT
HELICOPTER
HIGH-FLYING
HOVERCRAFT
HOVERPLANE
HYDROPLANE
ROTORCRAFT
ROTORPLANE
SLIPSTREAM
STREAMLINE
SUPERSONIC
TACHOMETER
TURBOPROPS
VOLITATION

11
AEROSTATICS
AIRSCREW-HUB
ASPECT-RATIO
BLIND FLYING
BOMB-CARRIER

CONTRA-PROPS
DIVE-BOMBING
DUAL-CONTROL
EJECTOR-SEAT
FIRE-BALLOON
GROUND STAFF
HEAT-BARRIER
HEAVY BOMBER
INSTABILITY
KITE-BALLOON
LAMINAR FLOW
LEADING EDGE
MONTGOLFIER
MOORING-MAST
ORNITHOPTER
PARACHUTING
PARACHUTIST
RADIO-BEACON
RUDDER ANGLE
STREAMLINED

12
AERODYNAMICS
AEROEMBOLISM
AERONAUTICAL
AIRSCREW-SLIP
ANTI-AIRCRAFT
ARRESTER-GEAR
ARRESTER-HOOK
BALLON D'ESSAI
BELLY-LANDING
CONTROL-CABIN
CONTROL-TOWER
FUEL-INJECTOR
GLIDING ANGLE
HEDGE HOPPING
LANDING WIRES
NIGHT FIGHTER
PILOT-BALLOON
RADAR-SCANNER
SOUND BARRIER

13
AIRWORTHINESS
CONTROL COLUMN
CRUISING SPEED
ESCORT FIGHTER
HYDRO-AIRPLANE
SHOCK-ABSORBER
UNDERCARRIAGE
WHEEL-COWLINGS

14
HEAVIER-THAN-AIR
HYDRO-AEROPLANE
LOOPING-THE-LOOP
PANCAKE-LANDING

15
AIRCRAFT-CARRIER

Battles, Land

3
ACS
ULM

4
ALMA
CAEN
CEVA
DEGO
IVRY
JENA
LAON
LENS
LODI
LOOS
METZ
MONS
NAAS
NIVE
NOVI
SOOR
TARA
WAWZ
ZAMA
ZELA

5
ADOWA
AISNE
ALAMO
ALLIA
ANJOU
ANZIO
BOYNE
BUXAR
CRECY
CRETE
CUZCO
DELHI
DOURO
DREUX
DUNES
EL TEB
EUTAW
EYLAU
GOREY
HANAU
IPSUS
ISSUS
KALKA
KAZAN
KHART
KOLIN
LARGS
LEWES

LIGNY
LIPAU
MAIDA
MORAT
MUDKI
MUNDA
MURET
NARVA
NEDAO
ORMUZ
PARMA
PATAY
PAVIA
PYDNA
RIETI
SEDAN
SELBY
SESIA
SOMME
STOKE
TOURS
UCLES
VALMY
VARNA
VILNA
WAVRE
WORTH
XERES
YPRES
ZENTA

6
ACTIUM
ALFORD
ALIWAL
ANGORA
ARBELA
ARCOLE
ARGAUM
ARKLOW
ARNHEM
ARQUES
ASPERN
ASSAYE
ATBARA
AUNEAU
BARNET
BATAAN
BAYLEN
BERLIN
BOXTEL
BRAILA
BUSACO
CAMDEN
CANNAE

CITATE
CUNAXA
DIEPPE
DUNBAR
ENSLIN
FAMARS
GUJRAT
HARLAW
HEXHAM
HIMERA
INCHON
INGOGO
INGOUR
JARNAC
KADESH
KALISZ
KOHIMA
KONIEH
KURDLA
LANDEN
LIOPPO
LONATO
LUTZEN
MAJUBA
MARGUS
MINCIO
MINDEN
MOHACS
MUKDEN
MULTAN
NACHOD
NAJARA
NARVIK
NASEBY
NESBIT
NOVARA
OBIDOS
ORTHEZ
ORTONA
OULART
PINKIE
PLEVNA
PODOLL
PRAGUE
QUEBEC
RIVOLI
ROCROI
ROLICA
SADOWA
SANGRO
SHILOH
SUAKIN
TARBES
TESTRI
THABOR
TORGAU
TOWTON
TUDELA

VERDUN
VIENNA
WAGRAM
WARSAW
XIMENA
ZURICH

7
ABOUKIR
ABU KLEA
ALAMEIN
ALARCOS
ALBUERA
ALMANSA
ANTIOCH
ASUNDEN
ATLANTA
AUGHRIM
BADAJOZ
BAPAUME
BARROSA
BASSANO
BAUTZEN
BELFORT
BELMONT
BITONTO
BORISOV
BRECHIN
BRESLAU
BRIENNE
BULL RUN
CARRHAE
CASSANO
CASSINO
CHALONS
COLENSO
CORINTH
CORONEA
CORUNNA
COUTRAS
CRAONNE
CZASLAU
DEVIZES
DRESDEN
DUNKIRK
ECKMUHL
ENGHIEN
EVESHAM
FALKIRK
FLEURUS
FORNOVO
GLENCOE
GROCHOW

8
HASBAIN
HERRERA
IDSTADT
KILSYTH
KLISSOW

KOSSOVO
KRASNOI
LEIPZIG
LEUCTRA
LEUTHEN
LIBENAU
LINCOLN
LUCKNOW
MAGENTA
MAGNANO
MARENGO
MILAZZO
MOCKERN
MOHILEV
MONDOVI
NEWBURN
NEWBURY
NEW ROSS
OKINAWA
ORLEANS
OURIQUE
PANIPAT
PLASSEY
PLATAEA
POLOTZK
PULTOWA
PULTUSK
RAUCOUX
RAVENNA
REDINHA
RIO SECA
SAGUNTO
SAINTES
SAKARIA
SALERNO
SEMPACH
SENEFFE
SKALITZ
SOBRAON
TANAGRA
THAPSUS
TOURNAI
TREBBIA
VILAGOS
VIMIERO
VITEBSK
VITORIA
VOUILLE
WAITZEN
WINWAED
ZALLACA

8
AIZNADIN
ALBUFERA
ALMENARA
ANTIETAM
ARDENNES

ASSANDUN
AYACUCHO
BASTOGNE
BELGRADE
BERESINA
BIR HAKIM
BLENHEIM
BLUMENAU
BORODINO
BOUVINES
CASTALLA
CAWNPORE
CHATALJA
CHIPPEWA
CLONTARF
COURTRAI
CULLODEN
CUSTOZZA
DROGHEDA
DRUMCLOG
EDGEHILL
EDINGTON
FAIR OAKS
FLUSHING
FONTENOY
FORMIGNY
GEMBLOUX
GITSCHIN
GRANICUS
HASTINGS
HATFIELD
HOMILDON
INKERMAN
JEMAPPES
KATZBACH
KULIKOVO
KUMANOVO
LAFFELDT
LAKE ERIE
LANDSHUT
LANGPORT
LANGSIDE
LANSDOWN
LAUFFELD
LIAOYANG
LIEGNITZ
MAGNESIA
MALVALLI
MANTINEA
MARATHON
METAURUS
MOLLWITZ
MONASTIR
NANTWICH
NIVELLES
NORMANDY
OMDURMAN
PALESTRO

PALO ALTO
PELUSIUM
PIACENZA
POITIERS
PYRAMIDS
PYRENEES
ROSSBACH
ROVEREDO
ST ALBANS
SARATOGA
SEIDLITZ
SEMINARA
SIMANCAS
SOISSONS
SORAUREN
SPION KOP
SYRACUSE
SZEGEDIN
TALAVERA
TALIKOTA
THE BULGE
THE MARNE
TOULOUSE
TRUELLAS
VALEGGIO
VALTEZZA
VOLTURNO
WATERLOO
WURSCHEN
WURZBURG
YORKTOWN
ZORNDORF

9
AGINCOURT
AGNADELLO
AKHALZIKH
AUERSTADT
AYLESFORD
BALACLAVA
BENEVENTO
BIG BETHEL
BORGHETTO
BRENTFORD
CAPORETTO
CASTILLON
CASTLEBAR
CERIGNOLA
CHAERONEA
CHALGROVE
CHEBREISS
DENNEWITZ
DETTINGEN
DORYLAEUM
DRUMOSSIE
EL ALAMEIN
ELCHINGEN
ESPIERRES

FRIEDLAND
GAUGAMELA
HOCHKIRCH
KISSINGEN
LA BICOCCA
LAINGSNEK
LEXINGTON
LINCELLES
LIPPSTADT
MANZIKERT
MARIGNANO
MILLESIMO
MOESKIRCH
MORGARTEN
NASHVILLE
OLTENITZA
OTTERBURN
OUDENARDE
PELEKANON
PHARSALIA
PIRMASENS
PORTO NOVO
RAMILLIES
RATHMINES
ROOSEBEKE
RUREMONDE
SALAMANCA
SARAGOSSA
SEDGEMOOR
SINGAPORE
SOLFERINO
STEENKIRK
TCHERNAYA
TRAUTENAU
VALTELINE
VAUCHAMPS
VICKSBURG
VIMY RIDGE
WAKEFIELD
WANDIWASH
WORCESTER
ZULLICHAU

10
ADRIANOPLE
ALEXANDRIA
ARGENTARIO
ASPROMONTE
AUSTERLITZ
BENNINGTON
BLORE HEATH
BRANDYWINE
BUENA VISTA
BUNKER HILL
CALATAFIMI
CEDAR CREEK
CHATEAUDUN
COLD HARBOR

DANNEVIRKE
DONNINGTON
DUNGAN HILL
FEHRBELLIN
FIROZSHAHR
GERMANTOWN
GETTYSBURG
GRAVELOTTE
GUINEGATTE
IMJIN RIVER
KONIGGRATZ
KUNERSDORF
LULE-BURGAS
LUNDY'S LANE
LUTZELBERG
MAHARAJPUR
MALPLAQUET
MASERFIELD
MILLI DUZOV
MONCONTOUR
MONTEBELLO
MONTENOTTE
MOUNT BADON
MOUNT TABOR
NEERWINDEN
NEW ORLEANS
NORDLINGEN
OSTROLENKA
PAARDEBERG
PORT ARTHUR
QUATRE BRAS
SAINT-DENIS
SANTA-LUCIA
SHREWSBURY
SOLWAY MOSS
STALINGRAD
STRASBOURG
TANNENBERG
TEL-EL-KEBIR
TEWKESBURY
TINCHEBRAY
WILDERNESS

11
BANNOCKBURN
BELLEAU WOOD
BRIARS CREEK
BRUNANBURGH
CASTELNUOVO
CASTIGLIANO
CHAMPAUBERT
CHATTANOOGA
CHICKAMAUGA
CHILIANWALA
CLIFTON MOOR
DARDANELLES
DIEN-BIEN-PHU
GROSS BEEREN

GUADALAJARA
HALIDON HILL
HENNERSDORF
HOHENLINDEN
ISANDLHWANA
KESSELSDORF
KIRK-KILISSE
LANGENSALZA
MARSTON MOOR
MODDER RIVER
MONTINIRAIL
MOOKERHEEDE
NORTHAMPTON
PFAFFENDORF
PHILIPHAUGH
PRESTONPANS
RHEINFELDEN
RIETFONTEIN
RORKE'S DRIFT
SAARBRUCKEN
SAINT ALBANS
SAINT-DIZIER
SAINT-MIHIEL
SHERIFFMUIR
TAGLIACOZZO
THERMOPYLAE
VILLAFRANCA
VINEGAR HILL
WHITE PLAINS

12
ARCIS-SUR-AUBE
ATHERTON MOOR
CARBERRY HILL
CAUDINE FORKS
CHICKAHOMINY
ELANDSLAAGTE
FLODDEN FIELD
GREAT MEADOWS
MEUSE-ARGONNE
MUNCHENGRATZ
MURFREESBORO
SAINT-ANTOINE
SAINT-QUENTIN
SARANTOPORON
SERINGAPATAM
VILLAVICIOSA
WILLIAMSBURG

13
BOSWORTH FIELD
CYNOSCEPHALAE
KILLIECRANKIE
LAKE TRASIMENE
LITTLE BIG HORN
MAGERSFONTEIN
MILVIAN BRIDGE
MONS BADONICUS

NAVAS DE TOLOSA
NEVILLE'S CROSS
NEWTOWNBUTLER
NICHOLSON'S NEK
NORTHALLERTON
PASSCHENDAELE
SPOTTSYLVANIA
WHITE MOUNTAIN
WHITE OAK SWAMP
YENIDJE VARDAR

14
BOTHWELL BRIDGE
CHATEAU-THIERRY
CONSTANTINOPLE
CROPREDY BRIDGE
FREDERICKSBURG
FUENTES DE ONORO
HOHENFRIEDBERG
LAKE TRASIMENUS
MORTIMER'S CROSS
PUSAN PERIMETER

15
RESACA DE LA PALMA
TEUTOBURGERWALD
TEUTOBURG FOREST

16
CHANCELLORSVILLE
GROSSJAEGERNDORF
LINLITHGOW BRIDGE

17
BURLINGTON HEIGHTS

Battles, Naval

4
ACRE
JAVA
LADE
ORAN
YALU

5
CADIZ
DOVER
HANGO
LAGOS
LISSA
SAMOS
SIRTE
SLUYS
TEXEL

6
ACTIUM
ARMADA
BASQUE
LEMNOS
MALAGA
MALAYA
MANILA
MIDWAY
NARVIK
SINOPE
USHANT

7
ABOUKIR
ALGIERS
CORONEL
DUNKIRK
HARWICH
JUTLAND
LA HOGUE
LEPANTO
MATAPAN
MESSINA
MINORCA
OKINAWA
SALAMIS
TARANTO
THE NILE

8
AIX ROADS
CORAL SEA
DANNOURA
DOMINICA
ITAMARCA
JAPAN SEA

NAVARINO
PORTLAND
QUIBERON
ROSAS BAY
SANTIAGO
TCHESINE
THE DOWNS
TSU SHIMA

9
ALGECIRAS
ARGINUSAE
CARTAGENA
CHAMPLAIN
DUNGENESS
LEYTE GULF
NEGAPATAM
ST VINCENT
SANTA CRUZ
THE SAINTS
TRAFALGAR
YELLOW SEA
ZEEBRUGGE

10
ALEXANDRIA
BEACHY HEAD
CAMPERDOWN
COPENHAGEN
DOGGER BANK
FINISTERRE
GUADELOUPE
HELIGOLAND
NEW ORLEANS
PLATE RIVER
RIVER PLATE
SEVASTOPOL

11
AEGOSPOTAMI
BISMARCK SEA
PASSARO CAPE

12
AEGATES ISLES
GIBRALTAR BAY
HAMPTON ROADS
PEARL HARBOUR
SAINT VINCENT
SOUTHWOLD BAY

13
FALKLAND ISLES
LAKE CHAMPLAIN
NORTH FORELAND
PHILIPPINE SEA

14
MACASSAR STRAIT

Bays of the British Isles

(When the word 'Bay' is included in the title, it is not given in the list. When another word is used, both forms are given: e.g. FORTH as well as FIRTH OF FORTH; LOCH LAXFORD as well as LAXFORD; LOUGH TARBERT as well as TARBERT.)

3
EWE
MAL
TAY

4
BUDE
CLEW
FYNE
GOIL
LONG
LORN
LUCE
LYME
RYAN
SAND
WASH

5
BROAD
BROOM
CLYDE
DULAS
ENARD
FORTH
FOYLE
HERNE
HOURN
LUNAN
MORAY
SHEEP
SLIGO
START
WOODY

6
BANTRY
CEMLYN
COLWYN
CRUDEN
DINGLE
DUNNET
GALWAY
LIGGER
MANNIN
MOUNT'S
NEIGWL
ST IVES
SOLWAY
SWILLY
TORBAY

TRALEE
VERYAN
WEMYSS

7
ARDMORE
BELFAST
BRANDON
BIGBURY
COULAGH
DONEGAL
DORNOCH
DUNDALK
DUNDRUM
GRUNARD
INCHARD
KILLALA
LAXFORD
LOCH EWE
NEWPORT
PADSTOW
PEGWELL
PORLOCK
SNIZORT
SWANSEA
TARBERT
WEXFORD
WHITLEY
WIGTOWN

8
BIDEFORD
BLACKSOD
CARDIGAN
CROMARTY
DROGHEDA
DUNMANUS
DUNVEGAN
FALMOUTH
GAIRLOCH
HOLYHEAD
LOCH FYNE
LOCH GOIL
LOCH LONG
LOCH RYAN
RED WHARF
ST BRIDE'S
ST FINAN'S
TORCROSS
TORRIDON
TREMADOC

9
ABERFFRAW
BEAUMARIS
FISHGUARD
GWEEBARRA
HOLLESLEY
KILKIERAN
LISCANNOR
LOCH BROOM
LOCH HOURN
MORECAMBE
PORT ISAAC
ST AUSTELL
SAINT IVES
SCAPA FLOW
SINCLAIR'S
TRE-ARDDUR
WATERGATE

10
BRIDGWATER
BROADHAVEN
CARMARTHEN
CLONAKILTY
FIRTH OF TAY
LOUGH FOYLE
MALLTRAETH
MORAY FIRTH
ROBIN HOODS
SHEEP HAVEN

11
BALLYCOTTON
BERTRAGHBOY
BRIDLINGTON
FIRTH OF LORN
LOCH INCHARD
LOCH LAXFORD
LOCH SNIZART
LOUGH SWILLY
PORTH NEIGWL
SAINT BRIDE'S
SAINT FINAN'S
SOLWAY FIRTH

12
BELFAST LOUGH
DORNOCH FIRTH
EDDRACHILLIS
FIRTH OF CLYDE
FIRTH OF FORTH

LOCH DUNVEGAN
LOCH TORRIDON
LOUGH TARBERT
SAINT AUSTELL

13
CROMARTY FIRTH

14
BALLINSKELLIGS

In the lists of bays which follow, the various words for *bay* are omitted.

Bays of Europe (excluding the British Isles)

4	TARANTO	13
HANO	TRIESTE	KIPARISSIAKOS
JADE	VECCHIO	MECKLENBURGER
KOGE		
LION	8	15
RADE	CAGLIARI	MONT SAINT MICHEL
	GASCOGNE	
5	MAZARRON	
ARHUS	ORISTANO	
CADIZ	QUIBERON	
FAKSE	ST BRIEUC	
GAETA	SAN JORGE	
GENOA	STA MANZA	
GIENS	VALENCIA	
GIOIA	WHITE SEA	
PALMA		
PATTI	9	
ROSAS	ARGOLIKOS	
SAROS	BOURGNEUF	
SEINE	CAP BRETON	
VIGSO	LAKONIKOS	
	ST EUFEMIA	
6	ST FLORENT	
ALBAEK	SAINT MALO	
ALBORG	SARONIKOS	
ARANCI	SQUILLACE	
BISCAY	TERRACINA	
DANZIG	TORONAIOS	
KIELER		
LUBECK	10	
NAPLES	BELOYE MORE	
NAPOLI	CHESHSKAYA	
OROSEI	DOUARNENEZ	
PALMAS	HELIGOLAND	
ST MALO	POLICASTRO	
SEGONE	POMERANIAN	
SEJERO	SANTA MANZA	
TANNIS	SINGITIKOS	
VENICE	THERMAIKOS	
7	11	
AJACCIO	JAMMERBUGHT	
ALCUDIA	MANFREDONIA	
ALMERIA	MESSINIAKOS	
ASINARA	PAGASITIKOS	
BOTHNIA	SAINT BRIEUC	
CATANIA	SANT' EUFEMIA	
CORINTH	STRIMONIKOS	
FINLAND		
GALERIA	12	
NAPOULE	KARKINITSKIY	
SALERNO	KORINTHIAKOS	
SETUBAL	MONT ST MICHEL	
	SAINT FLORENT	

Bays of Asia

4
ADEN
BONE
MAYA
OMAN
ORAS
SIAM
TOLO

5
AQABA
CUTCH
DAVAO
GAMAY
HAIFA
IZMIR
KERME
KOREA
KUMAI
KUTCH
LAMON
PANAY
PO HAI
RAGAY

6
BENGAL
BRUNEI
CAMBAY
CATEEL
CHIHLI
DARVEL
FINIKE
ILLANA
KRESTA
LIANGA
MANAAR
MANILA
MANNAR
MARUDU
PELENG
PINADA
POLLOC
RED SEA
SAMPIT
SEBUKU
SMYRNA
TOMINI

7
BACULIN
BAGANGA
BANGKOK
BISLING
EDREMIT

FETHIYE
IMURUAN
LAGONOY
OBSKAYA
PAMUKAN
PERSIAN
SUMBANG
TARTARY
UDSKAYA
YANSKIY

8
ALAMINOS
CANDARLI
CORONADO
HANG-CHOU
KALLONIS
KLUMPENG
LIAOTUNG
LINGAYEN
MARTABAN
SABANGAN
SIBUGUEY
SUKADANA
TONGKING

9
BUORKHAYA
MANDALAYA
PANABUTAN
SAN MIGUEL
SARANGANI
SINDONGON
TATARSKIY
ULBANSKIY

10
ANADYRSKIY
BALIKPAPAN
OLENEKSKIY
SHELEKHOVA

11
KHATANGSKIY
OLYUTORSKIY
YENISEYSKIY

12
PENZHINSKAYA
SAKHALINSKIY
SANGKULIRANG

13
BAYDARATSKAYA

14
KOLYUCHINSKAYA

Bays of Africa

4
SUEZ

5
ALGOA
ARABS
BENIN
FALSE
GABES
MEMBA
PEMBA
SALUM
SIRTE

6
BEJAIA
BIAFRA
BUNBAH
CINTRA
GUINEA
WALVIS

7
ALMEIDA
LEVRIER

8
ANTONGIL
HAMMAMET
LAMBERTS
ST HELENA

9
BOMBETOKA
MAHAJAMBA
ST FRANCIS

10
CONCEPTION
ST AUGUSTIN

11
SAINT HELENA

12
SAINT FRANCIS

13
SAINT AUGUSTIN

Bays of North America

4
BACK
COOS
HOME
OWEN

5
FUNDY
HAZEN
PEARD
PELLY

6
ALASKA
ALEXIS
ARTHUR
CAMDEN
ESTERO
HADLEY
HOOPER
HUDSON
MAUMEE
MEXICO
NORTON
ONSLOW
PIGEON
QUINCY
UNGAVA

7
BOOTHIA
BRISTOL
CAPE COD
CHALEUR
FORTUNE
HAMMOND
JAMAICA
RARITAN
SAGINAW
THUNDER

8
BUZZARDS
DEADMANS
DELAWARE
FRANKLIN
GEORGIAN
HALF MOON
HARRISON
KOTZEBUE
MONTEREY
MORICHES
PLYMOUTH
SANDUSKY
SAN PABLO
SAN PEDRO

9
APALACHEE
COMMITTEE
FOXE BASIN
FROBISHER
HECKSCHER
KUSKOKWIM
LIVERPOOL
LONG POINT
MACKENZIE
MATAGARDO
MUSCONGUS
NOTRE DAME
PENOBSCOT
QUEEN MAUD
SANDY HOOK
SMITHTOWN

10
CALIFORNIA
CHESAPEAKE
CORONATION
CUMBERLAND
FRENCHMAN'S
MARBLEHEAD
PELHAM PARK
SOUTH HAVEN
WACCASASSA
WINCHESTER

11
ATCHAFALAYA
NORTON SOUND
NOTTAWASAGA
SANTA MONICA
SOUTH OYSTER

12
LOWER NEW YORK
NARRAGANSETT
SAN FRANCISCO
UPPER NEW YORK

13
GRAND TRAVERSE
MASSACHUSETTS
SANTA CAROLINA

14
LITTLE TRAVERSE

Bays of Central America and the West Indies

4
BUFF
LONG
YUMA

5
COCOS
GUAPO
HENNE
LISAS
PARIA
URABA
VISTA

6
DARIEN
GALION
MAIMON
MATURA
MAYARA
NICOYA
PANAMA
ST ANN'S
SALINE
SAMANA

7
ANNOTTO
FONSECA
MARACAS
MONTEGO

8
AMATIQUE
BATABANO
CHIRIQUE
CORONADO
ESCOCESA
GUADIANA
HONDURAS
PORTLAND

9
MOSQUITOS
SAINT ANN'S
SAN MIGUEL

10
MANZANILLA

11
GUACANAYABO
NORTH FRIARS

SOUTH FRIARS
TEHUANTEPEC

12
FORT-DE-FRANCE

13
ALLIGATOR POND

15
SAN JUAN DEL NORTE

Bays of South America

4
CUMA
FIJO

5
ANCON
CUCAO
OTWAY
PARIA
UNION

6
BLANCA
CUPICA
DARIEN
GRANDE
MARAJO
SALADO

7
ANEGADA
CARNERO
MANZANO
OYAPOCK
SAN JUAN
SAO JOSE
SECHURA
TURIACU

8
CARAQUEZ
CARRIZAL
SAN JORGE
SAN PEDRO
SAO MARCO
SEPETIBA

9
GUARATUBA
GUAYAQUIL
SAN JULIAN
SAN MATIAS

10
CONCEPCION
PICHIDANGU
SANTA ELENA

11
SAMBOROMBON

12
BUENAVENTURA
SAN SEBASTIAN

13
TODOS OS SANTOS

Bays of Australasia

4
KING
YORK

5
ANSON
BREAM
DUSKY
HAWKE
IRION
PAPUA
SHARK
STORM

6
AWARUA
GOLDEN
LIMMEN
OHARIU
OYSTER
PLENTY
TASMAN
THAMES

7
CASWELL
COLLIER
ELLIOTT
EXMOUTH
FOWLER'S
HALIFAX
HAURAKI
ISLANDS
KARAMEA
MILFORD
MORETON
PEGASUS
POVERTY

8
ANDERSON
DOUBTFUL
PALLISER
TARANAKI
TE WAEWAE

9
ADMIRALTY
ENCOUNTER
VAN DIEMEN

10
CANTERBURY
PORT PHILIP

11
CARPENTARIA

15
GREAT AUSTRALIAN
JOSEPH BONAPARTE

Biblical Characters
Men of the Bible

2
ER
OG
ON

3
ASA
DAN
ELI
GAD
GOG
HAM
HEN
HUR
JOB
LOT
NOE
PUL
RAM
ZUR

4
ABEL
ADAM
AGAG
AHAB
AHAZ
AMOS
ANAK
ARBA
BOAZ
CAIN
DOEG
ENOS
ESAU
EZRA
JEHU
JOAB
JOEL
JOHN
KISH
LEVI
LUKE
MARK
MOAB
NAUM
NOAH
OBED
OMRI
ONAN
PAUL
SAUL
SETH
SHEM

UZZA
ZIBA

5
AARON
ABDON
ABIAH
ABIHU
ABNER
ABRAM
AMASA
AMMON
AMNON
AMRAM
ANNAS
ARIEL
ASAPH
ASHER
ASHUR
ASSUR
BALAK
CALEB
CYRUS
DAVID
ELIAB
ELIAS
ELIHU
ENOCH
FELIX
GAIUS
HAMAN
HEROD
HIRAM
HOSEA
ISAAC
JABEZ
JACOB
JAMES
JASON
JESSE
JESUS
JOASH
JONAH
JONAS
JORAM
JOSES
JUBAL
JUDAH
JUDAS
KORAH
LABAN
MICAH
MOSES

NABAL
NADAB
NAHUM
ORNAN
PEKAH
PETER
REHUM
REZIN
RUFUS
SHAUL
SIHON
SILAS
SIMON
TITUS
TUBAL
URIAH
UZZAH
ZADOK
ZARAH
ZEBUL
ZERAH
ZIMRI

6
ABDIEL
ABIJAH
ABIJAM
ABIRAM
AGABUS
AHIKAM
AMALEK
ANDREW
AQUILA
ASAHEL
BALAAM
BARUCH
CAESAR
CEPHAS
DANIEL
DARIUS
ELIJAH
ELISHA
ELYMAS
ESAIAS
FESTUS
GALLIO
GEHAZI
GIDEON
HAGGAI
HUSHAI
ISAIAH
ISRAEL
JAIRUS

JESHUA
JETHRO
JOSEPH
JOSHUA
JOSIAH
JOTHAM
JUSTUS
LAMECH
LEMUEL
LUCIUS
MANOAH
MARCUS
NAAMAN
NABOTH
NAHASH
NATHAN
NIMROD
PASHUR
PAULUS
PHAREZ
PHILIP
PILATE
RECHAB
REUBEN
SAMSON
SAMUEL
SHEBNA
SHELAH
SHIMEI
SIMEON
SISERA
THOMAS
TOBIAH
UZZIAH
UZZIEL
ZOPHAR

7
ABIEZER
ABISHAI
ABRAHAM
ABSALOM
AGRIPPA
AHAZIAH
AHIMAAZ
ALPHEUS
AMAZIAH
ANANIAS
ANTIPAS
APOLLOS
AZARIAH
CLEMENT
CLEOPAS
CRISPUS
DIDYMUS
ELEAZAR
ELIAKIM
ELIEZER

ELIPHAZ
ELISEUS
ELKANAH
EPHRAIM
ERASTUS
EZEKIEL
GABRIEL
GOLIATH
ISHMAEL
JAPHETH
JEHOASH
JEHORAM
JOHANAN
JONADAB
LAZARUS
LEBBEUS
MALACHI
MALCHUS
MATTHEW
MESHACH
MICHAEL
NICANOR
OBADIAH
PHARAOH
PONTIUS
SERAIAH
SERGIUS
SHALLUM
SHAMMAH
SHAPHAN
SHAPHAT
SHIMEAH
SHISHAK
SOLOMON
STEPHEN
TERTIUS
TIMOTHY
ZEBEDEE
ZEBULUN

8
ABEDNEGO
ABIATHAR
ABINADAB
ADONIJAH
ALPHAEUS
AUGUSTUS
BARABBAS
BAR-JESUS
BARNABAS
BENJAMIN
CAIAPHAS
ELNATHAN
EUTYCHUS
GAMALIEL
HABAKKUK
HEZEKIAH
ISSACHAR

JEPHTHAH
JEREMIAH
JEROBOAM
JESHURUN
JOHN MARK
JONATHAN
MAASEIAH
MANASSEH
MATTHIAS
MORDECAI
NAPHTALI
NEHEMIAH
ONESIMUS
PARMENAS
PELATIAH
PHILEMON
POTIPHAR
REHOBOAM
SHADRACH
SHAMMUAH
SHEMAIAH
SILVANUS
TYCHICUS
ZACCHEUS
ZEDEKIAH

9
ABIMELECH
AHASUERUS
AHIMELECH
ALEXANDER
ARCHELAUS
BARTIMEUS
BOANERGES
CORNELIUS
DEMETRIUS
DIONYSIUS
HADADEZER
JEHOIAKIM
JEHONADAB
JERUBBAAL
NATHANAEL
NETHANIAH
NICODEMUS
RAB-SHAKEH
SHELEMIAH
STEPHANAS
TERTULLUS
TIMOTHEUS
TUBAL-CAIN
ZACCHAEUS
ZACHARIAH
ZALMUNNAH
ZECHARIAH
ZEPHANIAH

10
AHITHOPHEL
ARTAXERXES
BARTIMAEUS
BELSHAZZAR
ISHBOSHETH
JEHOIACHIN
METHUSELAH
SHEPHATIAH
SIMON PETER
THEOPHILUS
ZELOPHEHAD
ZERUBBABEL

11
ARISTARCHUS
BARTHOLOMEW
JEHOSHAPHAT
MELCHISEDEK
ONESIPHORUS
SENNACHERIB
SHESHBAZZAR

12
EVIL MERODACH
MEPHIBOSHETH
SIMON ZELOTES

13
JUDAS ISCARIOT
PONTIUS PILATE
SERGIUS PAULUS

14
NEBUCHADNEZZAR

Women of the Bible

3
EVE

4
ANNA
JAEL
LEAH
LOIS
MARA
MARY
RUTH

5
CHLOE
DINAH
HAGAR
LYDIA
NAOMI
ORPAH
PHEBE
RAHAB
RHODA
SARAH
SARAI
TAMAR

6
ACHSAH
BILHAH
DORCAS
ESTHER
EUNICE
HANNAH
HOGLAH
JOANNA
MARTHA
MICHAL
MILCAH
MIRIAM
PHOEBE
RACHEL
RIZPAH
SALOME
TIRZAH
VASHTI
ZILPAH

7
ABIGAIL
ABISHAG
AHINOAM
BERNICE
CANDACE
DAMARIS
DEBORAH

DELILAH
JEZEBEL
KETURAH
REBECCA
REBEKAH
SUSANNA
TABITHA
ZERUIAH

8
ATHALIAH
DRUSILLA
HERODIAS
SAPPHIRA
ZIPPORAH

9
BATHSHEBA
ELISABETH
ELIZABETH
JEHOSHEBA
PRISCILLA

13
MARY MAGDALENE

Biblical place-names

2			4	
AI	RAMA	KEDAR	ABEL	ELATH
AR	ROME	LAISH	ADAM	ENDOR
ED	SEIR	LIBYA	ANAB	ETHAM
NO	TEMA	LYDDA	ARAM	GEBIM
ON	TYRE	LYDIA	ARBA	GERAR
UR	ZEEB	MAGOG	ASIA	GOLAN
UZ	ZION	MAMRE	AVEN	HARAN
	ZOAN	MARAH	BACA	HAZOR
	ZOAR	MEDIA	CAIN	HELAM
3		MEROM	CANA	ITALY
DAN	**5**	MEROZ	DURA	JAHAZ
DOR	ABDON	MIZAR	EBAL	JAZER
GOB	ACCHO	MYSIA	EDEN	JEBUS
GUR	ACHOR	OPHEL	EDOM	JOPPA
HAI	ADMAH	PARAN	ELAH	JUDAH
HAM	AIOTH	PERGA	ELIM	JUDEA
KIR	AMANA	RAHAB	ENON	KANAH
LUZ	AMMAH	RAMAH	ETAM	
NOB	APHEK	SALEM	EZEL	**6**
ONO	ARGOB	SARON	GATH	ABARIM
SIN	AROER	SHEBA	GAZA	ACHAIA
ZIN	ARPAD	SHUAL	GEBA	ACHZIB
	BABEL	SIDON	GIAH	AHAVAH
4	BAMAH	SIHON	IRON	AJALON
ABEL	BEREA	SINAI	MOAB	ARABIA
ADAM	BEZEK	SODOM	MYRA	ARARAT
ANAB	CABUL	SOREK	NAIN	ARPHAD
ARAM	CALEB	SPAIN	NEBO	ASHDOD
ARBA	CALNO	SYRIA	NOPH	ATHENS
ASIA	CAMON	TABOR	OREB	AZEKAH
AVEN	CHIOS	TEKOA	PEOR	BAJITH
BACA	CRETE	TROAS		BASHAN
CAIN	DEBIR	TYRUS		BETHEL
CANA	DIBON	ZIDON		BETHER
DURA	DUMAH	ZOBAH		BEULAH
EBAL	EDREI	ZORAH		ROCHIM
EDEN	EGYPT			
EDOM	EKRON	**6**		

6	5	7	7	8
BOZRAH	SHINAR	ABILENE	MERIBAH	ACHSHAPH
CALDEA	SILOAH	ADULLAM	MILETUM	ANATHOTH
CALNEH	SILOAM	ANTIOCH	MILETUS	ASHKELON
CANAAN	SIRION	ARMENIA	NINEVEH	BENJAMIN
CARMEL	SMYRNA	ASKELON	PATHROS	BETH-AVEN
CYPRUS	TADMOR	ASSYRIA	PHENICE	BETHEMEK
CYRENE	TARSUS	ATAROTH	PHRYGIA	BETHESDA
DOTHAN	TEKOAH	ATTALIA	PISIDIA	BETH-PEOR
EMMAUS	ZEBOIM	BABYLON	PUTEOLI	BETH-SHAN
ENGEDI	ZELZAH	BAHURIM	RABBATH	BITHYNIA
GADARA	ZIKLAG	BETHANY	REPHAIM	CAESAREA
GALEED		BETHUEL	RHEGIUM	CASIPHIA
GALLIM	**7**	BETHZUR	SALMONE	CENCHREA
GESHUR	ABILENE	BETONIM	SAMARIA	CHORAZIM
GIBEAH	ADULLAM	CALVARY	SAREPTA	COLOSSAE
GIBEON	ANTIOCH	CAPHTOR	SHECHEM	DALMATIA
GILBOA	ARMENIA	CESAREA	SHILOAH	DAMASCUS
GILEAD	ASKELON	CHALDEA	SHITTIM	DIBON-GAD
GILGAL	ASSYRIA	CHARRAN	SHUSHAN	EBENEZER
GINAEA	ATAROTH	CHEMOSH	SUCCOTH	EPHRATAH
GOSHEN	ATTALIA	CHITTIM	TABERAH	ETHIOPIA
GRECIA	BABYLON	CILICIA	TIMNATH	GABBATHA
GREECE	BAHURIM	CORINTH	ZEBULUN	GOLGOTHA
HAMATH	BETHANY	EL-ELOHE		GOMORRAH
HAMMON	BETHUEL	ELTEKEH	**8**	HACHILAH
HEBRON	BETHZUR	EN-ROGEL	ACHSHAPH	HAMON-GOG
HERMON	BETONIM	EPHESUS	ANATHOTH	HANATHON
ITUREA	CALVARY	EPHRAIM	ASHKELON	HAZEROTH
JABESH	CAPHTOR	GALATIA	BENJAMIN	LAODICEA
JUDAEA	CESAREA	GALILEE	BETH-AVEN	LYCAONIA
KADESH	CHALDEA	GERIZIM	BETHEMEK	MAHANAIM
KEILAH	CHARRAN	HADRACH	BETHESDA	MARS HILL
LIBNAH	CHEMOSH	HAMMATH	BETH-PEOR	MEGIDDON
LYSTRA	CHITTIM	HESHBON	BETH-SHAN	
MASSAH	CILICIA	ICONIUM	BITHYNIA	
MELITA	CORINTH	ITURAEA	CAESAREA	
MIDIAN	EL-ELOHE	JABNEEL	CASIPHIA	
MIZPAH	ELTEKEH	JERICHO	CENCHREA	
MIZPEH	EN-ROGEL	KARNAIM	CHORAZIM	
MORIAH	EPHESUS	KERIOTH	COLOSSAE	
NAIOTH	EPHRAIM	LACHISH	DALMATIA	
PAPHOS	GALATIA	LEBANON	DAMASCUS	
PARBAR	GALILEE	MAGDALA	DIBON-GAD	
PATARA	GERIZIM	MEGIDDO	EBENEZER	
PATMOS	HADRACH	MEMPHIS	EPHRATAH	
PENIEL	HAMMATH		ETHIOPIA	
PENUEL	HESHBON		GABBATHA	
PERSIA	ICONIUM		GOLGOTHA	
PISGAH	ITURAEA		GOMORRAH	
RABBAH	JABNEEL		HACHILAH	
RHODES	JERICHO		HAMON-GOG	
RIMMON	KARNAIM		HANATHON	
SAPHIR	KERIOTH		HAZEROTH	
SARDIS	LACHISH		LAODICEA	
SHALEM	LEBANON		LYCAONIA	
SHALIM	MAGDALA		MAHANAIM	
SHARON	MEGIDDO		MARS HILL	
SHEBAH	MEMPHIS		MEGIDDON	

MERODACH
NAZARETH
NEAPOLIS
PERGAMOS
PHILIPPI
PHOENICE
REHOBOTH
REPHIDIM
SELEUCIA
SHALISHA
TARSHISH
THYATIRA
TIBERIAS

9
APOLLONIA
AREOPAGUS
ARIMATHEA
ASHTAROTH
BAAL-HAMON
BAAL-TAMAR
BEER-SHEBA
BETHABARA
BETH-GAMUL
BETH-HORON
BETHLEHEM
BETHPHAGE
BETHSAIDA
CAPERNAUM
DECAPOLIS
HAMMON-GOG
HAROSHETH
ILLYRICUM
JERUSALEM
MACEDONIA
MACHPELAH
NICOPOLIS
PADAN-ARAM
PALESTINA
PAMPHYLIA
PHILISTIA
ZAREPHATH

10
ALEXANDRIA
AMPHIPOLIS
APPII-FORUM
BAAL-ZEPHON
CHESULLOCH
DABBASHETH
EZION-GEBER
GATH-HEPHER
GATH-RIMMON
GENNESARET
GETHSEMANE
KIRIATHAIM
SEPHARVAIM

11
BAAL-PERAZIM
BETH-SHEMESH
EPHES-DAMMIN
KIR-HARASETH
KIRIATHARIM
KIRJATH-ARBA
MESOPOTAMIA
TRACHONITIS

12
BAAL-SHALISHA
BETH-HACCEREM
JABESH-GILEAD
JEHOVAH-JIREH
KADESH-BARNEA
PHILADELPHIA
RAMOTH-GILEAD
THESSALONICA

13
CALEB-EPHRATAH
KIRJATH-JEARIM

14
BETHLEHEM-JUDAH
JEHOVAH-SHAMMAH

16
CAESAREA PHILIPPI

Biblical brooks and rivers

4
ENON
NILE

5
ABANA
GIHON
GOZAN
HAROD

6
CEDRON
JABBOK
JORDAN
KERITH
KIDRON
TIGRIS

7
CHERITH
PHARPAR

9
EUPHRATES

Birds

3
AUK
COB
DAW
EMU
FUM
HEN
HUI
JAY
KAE
KEA
MEW
MOA
NUN
OWL
PEN
PIE
POE
POY
REE
ROC
RUC
TIT
TUI

4
BARB
CHAT
CIRL
COCK
COOT
CRAX
CROW
DODO
DOVE
DUCK
ERNE
EYAS
FOWL
GIER
GOWK
GUAN
GULL
HAWK
HERN
HUIA
IBIS
JYNX
KITE
KIWI
KNOT
KORA
LARK
LOON
LORY
MINA

MONK	EIDER	WADER	LINTIE	TURBIT	FINIKIN
MYNA	FINCH	WHAUP	LORIOT	TURKEY	FLICKER
NYAS	GALAH	WONGA	MAGPIE	TURTLE	FLUSHER
PAVO	GLEDE		MARTIN	WEAVER	GADWALL
PERN	GOOSE	**6**	MERLIN	WHYDAH	GOAT-OWL
PICA	GOURA	AUKLET	MISSEL	WIGEON	GOBBLER
POUT	GREBE	AVOCET	MONAUL	WILLET	GOBURRA
PYAT	HARPY	AVOSET	MOPOKE	YAFFLE	GORCOCK
PYET	HERON	BANTAM	MOT-MOT	ZOOZOO	GORCROW
PYOT	HOBBY	BARBET	MUD-HEN		GOSHAWK
RAIL	JAGER	BONXIE	MUSKET	**7**	GOSLING
RHEA	JUNCO	BOOMER	NANDOO	ANT-BIRD	GRACKLE
ROCH	MACAW	BROLGA	NESTOR	ARACARI	GRAYLAG
ROCK	MADGE	BULBUL	ORIOLE	AWL-BIRD	GREY HEN
ROOK	MAVIS	CANARY	OSPREY	BABBLER	GREYLAG
RUFF	MERLE	CHEWET	PARROT	BARN-OWL	GREY OWL
RUKH	MONAL	CHOUGH	PAVONE	BEEBIRD	HAGBOLT
RUNT	MURRE	CONDOR	PEAHEN	BEEHAWK	HAGDOWN
RYPE	MYNAH	CORBIE	PECKER	BITTERN	HAGGARD
SHAG	NANDU	COUCAL	PEEPER	BLEATER	HALCYON
SKUA	NODDY	CUCKOO	PEEWEE	BLUECAP	HARFANG
SMEE	OUSEL	CULVER	PEEWIT	BLUE JAY	HARRIER
SMEW	OUZEL	CURLEW	PETREL	BLUE TIT	HAWK-OWL
SORA	OWLET	CUSHAT	PHOEBE	BULL-BAT	HEN-HARM
SORE	OX-EYE	CYGNET	PIGEON	BUNTING	HOATZIN
SPOT	PEWET	DARTER	PLOVER	BUSTARD	HOOT-OWL
SWAN	PEWIT	DICKEY	POUTER	BUZZARD	HORN OWL
TAHA	PIPIT	DIPPER	PUFFIN	CAPE-HEN	ICEBIRD
TEAL	POAKA	DRONGO	PULLET	CAPONET	IMPEYAN
TERN	POULT	DUCKER	QUEEST	CARVIST	JACAMAR
TODY	QUAIL	DUNLIN	REDCAP	CAT-BIRD	JACINTH
WAVY	RAVEN	EAGLET	REELER	CHEEPER	JACKDAW
WEKA	REEVE	ELANET	ROLLER	CHEWINK	JACOBIN
WREN	RIFLE	EVEJAR	ROTCHE	CHICKEN	KAMACHI
YITE	ROBIN	FALCON	SAWNEB	COAL-TIT	KESTREL
YUNX	ROTCH	FULMAR	SCAMEL	COBSWAN	KILLDEE
	SAKER	GALEEN	SCAURY	COLE-TIT	KINGLET
5	SCAPE	GAMBET	SCOTER	COLIBRI	LAPWING
AGAMI	SCAUP	GANDER	SCRAYE	COTINGA	LAVROCK
ARDEA	SCRAY	GANNET	SEA-COB	COURLAN	LEGHORN
ARIEL	SERIN	GARROT	SEA-MAW	COWBIRD	LICH-OWL
BIDDY	SHAMA	GENTLE	SEA-MEW	CREEPER	MALLARD
BOOBY	SNIPE	GENTOO	SEA-PIE	CROPPER	MANAKIN
BOSUN	SOLAN	GODWIT	SHRIKE	DORHAWK	MANIKIN
BRANT	SPINK	GRAKLE	SISKIN	DORKING	MAN-O'-WAR
BRENT	SPREW	GROUSE	SMEATH	DOTTREL	MARABOU
CAPER	SQUAB	HAGDEN	SMEETH	DOVEKIE	MARTLET
CAPON	STARE	HAGDON	SOLAND	DOVELET	MOORHEN
CHICK	STILT	HARELD	STRICH	DUN-BIRD	OIL-BIRD
COLIN	STINT	HERMIT	TAKAHE	DUNNOCK	ORTOLAN
CRAKE	STORK	HONKER	TARCEL	EGG-BIRD	OSTRICH
CRANE	SWIFT	HOOPOE	TARSEL	EMU-WREN	OVEN-TIT
DANDY	SYLPH	JABIRU	TERCEL	ESTRICH	PANDION
DHYAL	TEREK	JACANA	THRUSH	FANTAIL	PARTLET
DIVER	TWITE	JAEGER	TOMTIT	FEN-DUCK	PEACOCK
DRAKE	UMBRE	KAKAPO	TOUCAN	FERN-OWL	PEAFOWL
EAGLE	URUBU	LANNER	TOWHEE	FIG-BIRD	PELICAN
EGRET	VEERY	LINNET	TROGON	FIN-FOOT	PENGUIN

PERCHER	VULTURN	EAGLE-OWL	PEETWEET	ZOPILOTE
PHOENIX	WAGTAIL	ESTRIDGE	PETCHARY	
PICARIA	WAPACUT	FAUVETTE	PHEASANT	**9**
PINNOCK	WARBLER	FIG-EATER	PHILOMEL	ALBATROSS
PINTADO	WAXBILL	FINNIKIN	POORWILL	ARCHANGEL
PINTAIL	WAXWING	FISH-HAWK	POPINJAY	BALD-EAGLE
POCHARD	WHOOPER	FLAMINGO	PUFF-BIRD	BALTIMORE
POE-BIRD	WIDGEON	FOOL-DUCK	RAINBIRD	BARGANDER
POY-BIRD	WITWALL	GAIRFOWL	REDSHANK	BEAN-CRAKE
PUTTOCK	WOOD-OWL	GAMECOCK	REDSTART	BEAN-GOOSE
QUABIRD	WREN-TIT	GANG-GANG	REEDBIRD	BECCACCIA
QUETZAL	WRYBILL	GAREFOWL	RICEBIRD	BECCAFICO
RADDOCK	WRYNECK	GARGANEY	RINGDOVE	BERGANDER
RAINBOW		GREAT AUK	RINGTAIL	BIRGANDER
REDBIRD	**8**	GREAT TIT	ROCKBIRD	BLACKBIRD
REDHEAD	AIGRETTE	GREY CROW	ROCKDOVE	BLACK-COCK
REDPOLL	ALCATRAS	GREY FOWL	ROCK-HAWK	BLACKGAME
REDWING	ARAPUNGO	GROSBEAK	ROCK-WREN	BLACKHEAD
ROOSTER	AVADAVAT	GUACHARO	ROSY-BILL	BLACK SWAN
ROSELLA	BALDPATE	HANGBIRD	SCREAMER	BLACK TERN
ROTCHIE	BAR-GOOSE	HAWFINCH	SEA-EAGLE	BLUE CRANE
RUDDOCK	BATELEUR	HOBBY-OWL	SHELDUCK	BLUE POKER
SAGE-HEN	BEAM-BIRD	HORNBILL	SNOWBIRD	BOATSWAIN
SAWBILL	BEE-EATER	KILLDEER	SOFTBILL	BOWER-BIRD
SCOOPER	BELL-BIRD	KINGBIRD	SONGBIRD	BRAMBLING
SEABIRD	BLACKCAP	LANDRAIL	SONGSTER	BROWN GULL
SEA-COCK	BLACK-NEB	LANNERET	SPAR-HAWK	BULLFINCH
SEA-CROW	BLUEBACK	LAVEROCK	SQUEAKER	BUZZARDET
SEA-DOVE	BLUEBIRD	LORIKEET	STALLION	CAMPANERO
SEA-DUCK	BLUE HAWK	LOVEBIRD	STARLING	CASSOWARY
SEA-FOWL	BLUE ROCK	LYREBIRD	TAWNY OWL	CEDARBIRD
SEAGULL	BLUE-TAIL	MANNIKIN	TEAL-DUCK	CHAFFINCH
SEA-HAWK	BLUE WING	MARABOUT	THRASHER	CHATTERER
SEA-LARK	BOATBILL	MARSH-HEN	THRESHER	CHICKADEE
SENEGAL	BOBOLINK	MARSH TIT	THROSTLE	CHICKLING
SERIEMA	BOB-WHITE	MEGAPODE	TITMOUSE	CHURCH-OWL
SIRGANG	BOCKEREL	MINA-BIRD	TIT-PIPIT	COCKATIEL
SKIMMER	BOCKERET	MIRE-CROW	TOMNODDY	COLUMBINE
SKYLARK	BRANCHER	MIRE-DRUM	TOUCANET	CORMORANT
SNOW-OWL	BROWN HEN	MOOR-BIRD	TRAGOPAN	CORNCRAKE
SPARROW	CALANDRA	MOORCOCK	UMBRETTE	CROSSBILL
SQUACCO	CARACARA	MOORGAME	WALLBIRD	CURRAWONG
STANIEL	CARDINAL	MOORPOUT	WATERHEN	DANDY-COCK
SUNBIRD	CARGOOSE	MOREPOKE	WHEATEAR	DICKYBIRD
SWALLOW	CLOT-BIRD	MORILLON	WHIMBREL	EAGLE-HAWK
SWIMMER	COCKATOO	MUIRPOOT	WHINCHAT	EIDER DUCK
TADORNA	COCKEREL	MUIRPOUT	WHIPBIRD	FIELD-DUCK
TAKAHEA	CURASSOW	MUSK-DUCK	WHISTLER	FIELDFARE
TANAGER	CUTWATER	MUTE SWAN	WILD DUCK	FIG-PECKER
TARROCK	DABCHICK	MYNA-BIRD	WILDFOWL	FLEDGLING
TIERCEL	DAKER-HEN	NIGHTJAR	WOODCHAT	FRANCOLIN
TINAMOU	DANDY-HEN	NUTHATCH	WOODCOCK	FRIARBIRD
TITLARK	DIAL-BIRD	OVEN-BIRD	WOOD-DUCK	FROGMOUTH
TITLING	DIDAPPER	PAITRICK	WOOD-FOWL	GALLINULE
TOTANUS	DOTTEREL	PARAKEET	WOODLARK	GERFALCON
TOURACO	DUCK-HAWK	PAROQUET	YELDRING	GIER-EAGLE
TUMBLER	DUCKLING	PEACHICK	YELDROCK	GOLDCREST
VULTURE	DUN-DIVER	PEESWEEP	YOLDRING	GOLD-DRAKE

GOLDEN-EYE	SANDPIPER	BRENT GOOSE	MEADOW-LARK
GOLDFINCH	SAPSUCKER	BUDGERIGAR	MISSEL-BIRD
GOLDSPINK	SCAUP-DUCK	BURROW-DUCK	MUTTONBIRD
GOOSANDER	SCRATCHER	BUSH-SHRIKE	NIGHT HERON
GRASSBIRD	SCREECHER	BUTTERBACK	NIGHT-RAVEN
GRASS-LARK	SCRUBFOWL	BUTTER-BIRD	NUTCRACKER
GRASSWREN	SCRUBWREN	BUTTERBUMP	PEEWEE-LARK
GREENWING	SEDGEBIRD	CANARY-BIRD	PETTICHAPS
GREY GOOSE	SEDGE-WREN	CANVASBACK	PIGEON-HAWK
GROSSBEAK	SHEARTAIL	CAPE PIGEON	PRATINCOLE
GUILLEMOT	SHELD-DUCK	CHIFFCHAFF	PURPLE-BIRD
GUINEA HEN	SHELDRAKE	CHITTAGONG	PURPLE-COOT
GYRFALCON	SHOVELLER	CODDY-MODDY	QUAIL-SNIPE
HAWK-EAGLE	SILVER-DUN	COMMON GULL	REGENTBIRD
HORNED OWL	SKUNK-BIRD	CRESTED JAY	ROADRUNNER
JACK-SNIPE	SNAKEBIRD	CRESTED TIT	ROCK-HOPPER
JENNY-WREN	SNOWFLECK	CROW-SHRIKE	ROCK-PIGEON
JERFALCON	SNOWFLICK	DICKCISSEL	ROCK-PLOVER
KITTIWAKE	SNOWGOOSE	DICKEYBIRD	ROCK-THRUSH
LINT-WHITE	SPINEBILL	DISHWASHER	SAGE-GROUSE
LITTLE AUK	SPOONBILL	DOLLAR-BIRD	SANDERLING
LITTLE OWL	STILTBIRD	EMBER-GOOSE	SANDMARTIN
MACARTNEY	STINKBIRD	EYAS-MUSKET	SCREECH-OWL
MALLEE-HEN	STOCKDOVE	FALLOW-CHAT	SEA-SWALLOW
MALLEMUCK	STONECHAT	FLEDGELING	SHEARWATER
MANGO-BIRD	STONEHAWK	FLYCATCHER	SILVERBILL
MARSH-HAWK	STORMCOCK	GOATSUCKER	SOLAN-GOOSE
MERGANSER	TALEGALLA	GOLD-HAMMER	SONGTHRUSH
MEROPIDAN	TETRAONID	GRASS-FINCH	STONE-HATCH
MIRE-SNIPE	THICKHEAD	GREASEBIRD	STONE-SNIPE
MOUSEBIRD	THORNBILL	GREENFINCH	STRUTHIOID
MOUSE-HAWK	TIERCELET	GREENSHANK	TAILOR-BIRD
NIGHTHAWK	TROCHILUS	GREY FALCON	TIT-BABBLER
OSSIFRAGE	TRUMPETER	GREY PARROT	TIT-WARBLER
PARDALOTE	TURNSTONE	GREY PLOVER	TOCO-TOUCAN
PARAQUITO	WATERFOWL	GROUND-DOVE	TREE-PIGEON
PARRAKEET	WIDOW-BIRD	GROUNDLARK	TROPIC-BIRD
PARROQUET	WILD GOOSE	GUINEA COCK	TUFTED DUCK
PARROTLET	WILLOW-TIT	GUINEA FOWL	TURKEYCOCK
PARTRIDGE	WINDHOVER	HARPY-EAGLE	TURTLEDOVE
PEASEWEEP	WOODSHOCK	HEN HARRIER	WATER-OUZEL
PEREGRINE	WOODSPITE	HERMIT BIRD	WATTLE-BIRD
PHALAROPE	WYANDOTTE	HOODED CROW	WEASEL-COOT
PHILOMELA	YELLOW-OWL	HOODIE-CROW	WEAVERBIRD
PICTARNIE	ZOSTEROPS	HOUSEFINCH	WHIDAH-BIRD
PIED FINCH		INDIGO BIRD	WHITE FRONT
PTARMIGAN	10	JUNGLE-COCK	WHYDAH-BIRD
QUAIL DOVE	ABERDEVINE	JUNGLE-FOWL	WILLOW-WREN
QUAIL-HAWK	ANT-CATCHER	KINGFISHER	WONGA-WONGA
RAZORBILL	ARCTIC SKUA	KING-PARROT	WOODPECKER
REDBREAST	ARCTIC TERN	KOOKABURRA	WOODPIGEON
RED GROUSE	BANK-MARTIN	LITTLE GULL	YELLOWBIRD
RIFLEBIRD	BEARDED TIT	LITTLE TERN	YELLOWLEGS
RING-OUSEL	BELL-MAGPIE	LOVE-PARROT	YELLOWPATE
RING-OUZEL	BLUE-BONNET	MALLEE-BIRD	ZEBRA-FINCH
ROCK-OUZEL	BLUE-BREAST	MARSH-DIVER	
ROCK-PIPIT	BLUE-THROAT	MARSH-GOOSE	11
RUDDY DUCK	BRAND-GOOSE	MARSH-QUAIL	BANK-SWALLOW

BLACK-FALCON
BLACKGROUSE
BONEBREAKER
BRISSEL-COCK
BROWN GANNET
BRUSH-TURKEY
BURGOMASTER
BUSH-CREEPER
BUTCHER-BIRD
BUTTON QUAIL
CANADA GOOSE
CARRION-CROW
CHANTICLEER
CHIMNEY-HAWK
CIRL-BUNTING
DRAGOON-BIRD
FAIRY-MARTIN
FALLOW-FINCH
FRIGATE-BIRD
FRUIT-PIGEON
GNATCATCHER
GNAT-SNAPPER
GOLDEN EAGLE
GREY WAGTAIL
HERRING GULL
HOUSE-MARTIN
HUMMINGBIRD
ICELAND GULL
LAMMERGEIER
LAMMERGEYER
LEATHERHEAD
LITTLE GREBE
LITTLE STINT
MAN-O'-WAR BIRD
MEADOW PIPIT
MOCKINGBIRD
MOOR-BUZZARD
NANKEEN-HAWK
NIGHTINGALE
PIED WAGTAIL
QUAIL-PIGEON
QUAIL-THRUSH
REED-BUNTING
REED-SPARROW
REED-WARBLER
ROCK-SPARROW
ROCK-WARBLER
ROSEATE TERN
SCISSORBILL
SCISSORTAIL
SCREECH-HAWK
SCRUB-TURKEY
SINGING-BIRD
SNOW-BUNTING
SONGSPARROW
SPARROWHAWK
STONECURLEW
STONEFALCON

STONE-PLOVER
STORM-PETREL
SWALLOWTAIL
TREE-CREEPER
TREE-SPARROW
TREE-WARBLER
WHITETHROAT
WHOOPER SWAN
YELLOWAMMER

12
ADJUTANT-BIRD
BERWICK'S SWAN
BRAMBLE-FINCH
CAPERCAILLIE
CAPERCAILZIE
CARDINAL-BIRD
CEDAR WAXWING
CHIMNEY-SWIFT
COAL-TITMOUSE
COLLARED DOVE
COW-BLACKBIRD
DRONGO-CUCKOO
DRONGO-SHRIKE
FIELD-TITLING
GLAUCOUS GULL
GOLDEN ORIOLE
GOLDEN PLOVER
GRASS-SPARROW
GRASS-WARBLER
GREAT BUSTARD
GROUND-CUCKOO
GROUND-THRUSH
HARRIER-EAGLE
HEDGE-SPARROW
HERMIT-THRUSH
HONEY-BUZZARD
HONEY-CREEPER
HOUSE-SPARROW
LONG-EARED OWL
MANDARIN DUCK
MARSH-HARRIER
MISSEL-THRUSH
MISTLE-THRUSH
MOURNING-DOVE
NANKEEN-CRANE
NUTMEG-PIGEON
PAINTED FINCH
PAINTED SNIPE
POWERFUL-FOWL
PURPLE MARTIN
RAZOR-GRINDER
RING-DOTTEREL
RINGED PLOVER
ROCK-PARAKEET
RUFFED GROUSE
SAGE-THRASHER
SANDWICH-TERN

SEDGEWARBLER
SHRIKE-THRUSH
STONE-CHATTER
STONE'S-MICKLE
STORMY PETREL
STUBBLE-GOOSE
TIGER-BITTERN
WATER-WAGTAIL
WHIP-POOR-WILL
WHITE GOSHAWK
YELLOWHAMMER
YELLOWTHROAT

13
BALTIMORE-BIRD
BARNACLE-GOOSE
BROWN THRASHER
CARRIER-PIGEON
COACHWHIP-BIRD
COMMON BUZZARD
GREY PHALAROPE
GREY SANDPIPER
HERMIT-WARBLER
LESSER REDPOLL
LITTLE BITTERN
LITTLE BUSTARD
LONG-TAILED TIT
LOVE-PARRAKEET
MOCKING-THRUSH
NORFOLK PLOVER
OYSTER-CATCHER
PIED BLACKBIRD
RHINOCEROS-AUK
ROCK-PARTRIDGE
ROCK-PTARMIGAN
SECRETARY-BIRD
SHORT-EARED OWL
SPIDER-CATCHER
SPOONBILL DUCK
TURKEY-BUZZARD
TURKEY-VULTURE
WILLOW-WARBLER
YELLOW-BUNTING
YELLOW-WAGTAIL

14
ALPINE ACCENTOR
BABBLING-THRUSH
BIRD-OF-PARADISE
BLACK GUILLEMOT
CHIMNEY-SWALLOW
GOLDEN PHEASANT
GREAT BLACKBACK
GREEN SANDPIPER
MARSH-BLACKBIRD
NANKEEN-KESTREL
PIED FLYCATCHER
RAZOR-BILLED AUK

REDNECKED GREBE
RHINOCEROS-BIRD
ROBIN REDBREAST
SCARLET TANAGER
SKUNK-BLACKBIRD
SLAVONIAN GREBE
STILT SANDPIPER
SWAMP-BLACKBIRD

15
AMERICAN BITTERN
BLACKHEADED GULL
BLUE-WINGED GOOSE
GOLDCRESTED WREN
GREEN WOODPECKER
LAUGHING JACKASS
LESSER BLACKBACK
MISTLETOE-THRUSH
PASSENGER-PIGEON
PINK-FOOTED GOOSE

Boats and Ships

3
ARK
BAC
CAT
COG
COT
GIG
HOY
RAM

4
BARK
BRIG
BUSS
CAIC
DHOW
DORY
FLAT
GRAB
HULK
JUNK
KEEL
KOFF
PINK
PRAM
PRAU
PROA
PUNT
RAFT
SAIC
SCOW
SNOW
YAWL

5
BALSA
BARGE
BOYER
CANOE
CAPER
COBLE
CRAFT
E-BOAT
EIGHT
FERRY
FLOAT
FOIST
FUNNY
JOLLY
KAIAK
KAYAK
KETCH
LINER
PILOT
PRAAM

PRAHU
PRORE
Q-BOAT
RACER
RAZEE
SAICK
SCOUT
SCULL
SHELL
SKIFF
SLOOP
SMACK
TRAMP
U-BOAT
UMIAK
WHIFF
XEBEC
YACHT

6
ARGOSY
BANKER
BARQUE
BAWLEY
BIREME
CAIQUE
CARVEL
COALER
COBBLE
COCKLE
COGGLE
CONVOY
CUTTER
DECKER
DINGHY
DOGGER
DROGER
FRIGOT
GALEAS
GALIOT
GALLEY
HOOKER
HOPPER
LAUNCH
LORCHA
LUGGER
PACKET
PIRATE
PUFFER
RANDAN
RIGGER
SAIQUE
SAMPAN
SLAVER
TANKER

TARTAN
TENDER
TORPID
TRADER
TROUGH
UMIACK
WAFTER
WHALER
WHERRY

7
ALMADIA
BUDGERO
BUMBOAT
CARAVEL
CARRACK
CATBOAT
CLINKER
CLIPPER
COASTER
COLLIER
CORACLE
CORSAIR
CRUISER
DREDGER
DRIFTER
DROGGER
DROGHER
FELUCCA
FLYBOAT
FOUR-OAR
FRIGATE
GALLEON
GALLIOT
GONDOLA
GUNBOAT
ICE-BOAT
LIGHTER
MAN-O'-WAR
MISTICO
MONITOR
PAIR-OAR
PATAMAR
PINNACE
PIRAGUA
PIROGUE
POLACCA
POLACRE
PONTOON
ROWBOAT
SCULLER
SHALLOP
STEAMER
SWEEPER
TARTANE

TOWBOAT
TRAWLER
TRIREME
TUGBOAT
WANIGAN
WARSHIP

8
BILANDER
BUDGEROW
COCKBOAT
COROCORE
COROCORO
CORVETTE
EIGHT-OAR
FALTBOAT
FIRE-BOAT
FIRE-SHIP
FLAGSHIP
FLATBOAT
FOLDBOAT
GALLEASS
GALLIASS
GALLIVAT
HOVELLER
ICE-CANOE
ICE-YACHT
INDIAMAN
IRONCLAD
KEELBOAT
LIFEBOAT
LOG-CANOE
LONGBOAT
LONGSHIP
MAILBOAT
MAN-OF-WAR
MOSQUITO
POSTBOAT
SAILBOAT
SCHOONER
SHOWBOAT
TALL SHIP
TILT-BOAT
TRIMARAN
WOODSKIN

9
AUXILIARY
BLOCKSHIP
BOMB-KETCH
BUCENTAUR
CANAL-BOAT
CARGO-BOAT
CATAMARAN
DAHABEEAH
DAHABIYAH
DAHABIYEH
DESTROYER

FERRYBOAT
FREIGHTER
FRIGATOON
GUARD-BOAT
GUARD-SHIP
HORSE-BOAT
HOUSEBOAT
JOLLYBOAT
LIGHTSHIP
MINELAYER
MOTORBOAT
OIL-TANKER
OUTRIGGER
PETERBOAT
PILOT-BOAT
PILOT-BRIG
PILOT-SHIP
POWER-BOAT
PRIVATEER
RIVER-BOAT
ROTOR-SHIP
SHIP-OF-WAR
SPEEDBOAT
STEAMBOAT
STEAMSHIP
STORESHIP
SUBMARINE
TRANSPORT
TROOPSHIP
TWO-DECKER
WAR-GALLEY
WHALEBOAT
WHEELBOAT

10
ADVICE-BOAT
BARKENTINE
BATTLESHIP
BOMB-VESSEL
BRIGANTINE
CANAL-BARGE
CATTLE-BOAT
HOVERCRAFT
HYDROPLANE
ICE-BREAKER
KNOCKABOUT
OCEAN LINER
PACKET-BOAT
PADDLEBOAT
PATROL-BOAT
PICKET-BOAT
PILOT-COBLE
PIRATE SHIP
QUADRIREME
REPAIR-SHIP
ROWING BOAT
TARGET-SHIP
TEA-CLIPPER

TURRET-SHIP
WINDJAMMER

11
ASSAULT-BOAT
BARQUENTINE
CAPITAL SHIP
CHASSE-MAREE
COCKLESHELL
FISHING-BOAT
GALLEY-FOIST
LANDING-SHIP
MERCHANTMAN
MINESWEEPER
MOTOR-LAUNCH
PENTECONTER
PILOT-CUTTER
PRIZE-VESSEL
QUINQUEREME
ROB ROY CANOE
STEAM-LAUNCH
SUPERTANKER
THREE-DECKER
TORPEDO-BOAT
VICTUAL-SHIP

12
CABIN-CRUISER
COASTING-BOAT
COASTING-SHIP
DESPATCH-BOAT
DISPATCH-BOAT
DOUBLE-DECKER
FISHING-FLOAT
HOSPITAL-SHIP
MERCHANT-SHIP
MOSQUITO-BOAT
PLEASURE-BOAT
SCREW-STEAMER
SQUARE-RIGGER
TRAMP-STEAMER

13
AUXILIARY-BOAT
BATTLE-CRUISER
ESCORT-CARRIER
FISHING-VESSEL
HOVELLING-BOAT
MOTOR-LIFEBOAT
PADDLE-STEAMER
PASSENGER-BOAT
PASSENGER-SHIP
REVENUE-CUTTER
SAILING VESSEL

14
AIRCRAFT-TENDER
AMMUNITION-SHIP

COASTING-VESSEL
FLOTILLA-LEADER
TORPEDO-GUNBOAT

15
AIRCRAFT-CARRIER
ARMOURED CRUISER
CABLE-LAYING-SHIP
CABLE-REPAIR-SHIP
FLOATING BATTERY
SEAPLANE-CARRIER
SUBMARINE-CHASER

Books of the Bible . . .

3
JOB

4
ACTS
AMOS
EZRA
JOEL
JOHN
JUDE
LUKE
MARK
RUTH

5
HOSEA
JAMES
JONAH
KINGS
MICAH
NAHUM
PETER
TITUS

6
DANIEL
ESTHER
EXODUS
HAGGAI
ISAIAH
JOSHUA
JUDGES
PSALMS
ROMANS
SAMUEL

7
EZEKIEL
GENESIS
HEBREWS
MALACHI
MATTHEW
NUMBERS
OBADIAH
THE ACTS
TIMOTHY

8
HABAKKUK
JEREMIAH
NEHEMIAH
PHILEMON
PROVERBS

9
EPHESIANS
GALATIANS
LEVITICUS
ZECHARIAH
ZEPHANIAH

10
CHRONICLES
COLOSSIANS
REVELATION

11
CORINTHIANS
DEUTERONOMY
PHILIPPIANS
SONG OF SONGS

12
ECCLESIASTES
LAMENTATIONS

13
SONG OF SOLOMON
THE REVELATION
THESSALONIANS

14
THE SONG OF SONGS

16
THE SONG OF SOLOMON

17
ACTS OF THE APOSTLES

. . . and the Apocrypha

5
TOBIT

6
BARUCH
ESDRAS
JUDITH
WISDOM

8
MACCABEES

12
REST OF ESTHER

14
ECCLESIASTICUS

15
BEL AND THE DRAGON
EPISTLE OF JEREMY
THE REST OF ESTHER
WISDOM OF SOLOMON

16
DANIEL AND SUSANNA
HISTORY OF SUSANNA
LETTER OF JEREMIAH

17
A LETTER OF JEREMIAH
AN EPISTLE OF JEREMY
THE SONG OF THE THREE

18
THE WISDOM OF SOLOMON

19
THE PRAYER OF MANASSEH
THE PRAYER OF MANASSES

20
DANIEL, BEL, AND THE SNAKE

Canals of the British Isles

6
OXFORD

7
CHESTER
REGENT'S

8
ANDERTON
COVENTRY
ROCHDALE

9
ELLESMERE
LANCASTER

10
CALEDONIAN
GRAND UNION
MANCHESTER

11
BRIDGEWATER
GRAND SURREY
SANKEY BROOK
STROUDWATER

13
FORTH AND CLYDE
GRAND JUNCTION
KENNET AND AVON

14
TRENT AND MERSEY

15
THAMES AND SEVERN

17
LEEDS AND LIVERPOOL

21
GLOUCESTER AND BERKELEY
WILTSHIRE AND BERKSHIRE

22
BIRMINGHAM AND LIVERPOOL

30
STAFFORDSHIRE AND WORCESTERSHIRE

Canals, Overseas

4
ERIE
GOTA
KIEL
MIDI
SUEZ

6
ALBERT
DU MIDI
GANGES
PANAMA

7
BOURBON
CORINTH
ORLEANS
TWENTHE
WELLAND

8
BURGUNDY
HOLSTEIN
WHITE SEA

9
AMSTERDAM

10
MITTELLAND

11
MOSCOW-VOLGA

12
AMERICAN ERIE
ELBE AND TRAVE
SEINE ET LOIRE

14
SAULTE STE MARIE

15
PRINCESS JULIANA

17
KATTEGAT AND BALTIC
SAULTE SAINTE MARIE
WHITE SEA AND BALTIC

19
BORDEAUX AND NARBONNE
MICHIGAN-MISSISSIPPI

21
LENINGRAD AND KRONSTADT

Capes of the British Isles

(The various alternatives for 'Cape' are omitted from the following lists: point, head, ness, bill, mull, rubha; but in some well-known capes, both forms are given: thus, BEACHY and BEACHY HEAD, SELSEY and SELSEY BILL.)

2
OA

3
AIR
EYE
RUE
TOE

4
AIRD
AYRE
BOLT
BRAY
CLAY
COD'S
FAIR
FIFE
HAG'S
HOOK
HORN
LOOP
MARE
MINE
MULL
NASH
NAZE
RORA
SLEA

5
BARRA
BERRY
BLACK
BOLUS
CLEAR
COUPE
ERRIS
FANAD
KERRY
LEWIS
MALIN
MIZEN
REIDH
SEVEN
SLYNE
SPURN
START
STOER
SYBIL
WORMS
WRATH

6
ACHILL
BEACHY
BENWEE
BLOODY
BRADDA
BROUGH
BUCHAN
BUDDON
BURROW
CAHORE
DODMAN
DOULUS
DUNANY
DUNNET
DURSEY
FORMBY
GALLEY
GARRON
GIRDLE
HILSEA
HUNISH
LINNEY
LIZARD
ORFORD
PRAWLE
ROCQUE
ROSSAN
RUDH'RE
ST ABBS
ST BEES
SELSEY
SHEEP'S
TARBAT
TOLSTA

7
ARDNAVE
BENBANE
BRANDON
CAIGHER
CLOGHER
DIZZARD
DONEGAL
FORLORN
GLENGAD
GROSNEZ
HELVICK
KINTYRE
MARWICK
MUCKROS
NEEDLES
RATTRAY
ST JOHN'S
STRATHY
THE NAZE
TREVOSE
WICKLOW

8
BAGINBUN
CARNSORE
COD'S HEAD
COIGEACH
DURLSTON
FORELAND
FOULNESS
GALLOWAY
GREENORE
HAG'S HEAD
HARTLAND
LAND'S END
LANGNESS
LA ROCQUE
MAUGHOLD
PENALLAN
PORTLAND
ST ALBANS
ST DAVIDS
ST GOVAN'S
ST MARTIN
STRUMBLE
TINTAGEL

9
CORSEWALL
DUNCANSBY
DUNGENESS
GREAT ORME
KINNAIRDS
MALINMORE
PLEINMONT
SAINT ABBS
SAINT BEES
ST MARTIN'S

Capes of Europe (excluding the British Isles)

10
BEACHY HEAD
BUCHAN NESS
BUDDON NESS
GREAT ORME'S
GREENSTONE
LITTLE ORME
RHU COIGACH
SAINT JOHN'S
SELSEY BILL
THE NEEDLES

11
BUTT OF LEWIS
DOWNPATRICK
JOHN O' GROATS
RUDNA HUNISH
SAINT ALBANS
SAINT DAVIDS
SAINT GOVAN'S
SAINT MARTIN
THE FORELAND

12
ARDNAMURCHAN
BALLYQUINTIN
ST CATHERINE'S
SAINT MARTIN'S

13
NORTH FORELAND
SOUTH FORELAND

14
BLOODY FORELAND

15
SAINT CATHERINE'S

16
OLD HEAD OF KINSALE

3
NAO
RAZ

4
BUSA
CALA
DORO
FYNS
GATA
GRIS
HEVE
HORN
LEVI
MAKA
MELE
NORD
NUSO
PERA
ROCA
ROUX
SKAW
STAD
YORK

5
AIGLE
ALICE
ASPRO
BENAT
CORSE
CREUS
EMINE
GRECO
HAGUE
KANIN
KOLKA
KUNNA
MAKEA
MESCO
NORTH
PALOS
PAPAS
PAYRE
PENAS
PENNA
PLAKA
PLATE
PONTA
PUNTA
SAIRE
SALOU
SINES
VARES
YASUN
YOROS

6
ARKONA
BLANCO
CALAVA
CHERNY
CHEVRE
CORSEN
COUBRE
EUROPA
FERRET
FREHEL
GJOGUR
GRIVEL
GROUIN
HIGUER
KEFALI
KOUTRI
KULLEN
LICOSA
LINARO
MABRES
MOUNDA
PINNES
PRASSO
SALINS
SARYCH
SPATHA
STABER
TINOSO
VORION
WALKER
YERIMO

7
AKRANES
AKRITAS
AMBELOS
ANTIBES
ANTIFER
ARNAUTI
ATHERAS
CAMARAT
CERBERE
CHATEAU
COLONNE
DARTUCH
DE CREUS
DE VARES
DUEODDE
ENTINAS
FORMAES
GARGANO
GRIS NEZ
KAPELLO
KEFALOS

KIKLOPS
KOPANES
LARDIER
LERVILY
LIVADHI
MARMARI
MATAPAN
MELISSA
MONDEGO
MOSTING
NORD CAP
OKTONIA
ORTEGAL
PASSERO
PODONIT
RIFSNES
RIZZUTO
SALINAS
SANDNES
SAN VITO
SKINARI
SOUNION
STAVROS
SVYATOY
TEULADA
THE SKAW
TORTOSA
TRIONTO
TRIPITI
YERAKAS

8
AGERNAES
AIGUILLE
AKROTIRI
BALEINES
BURYNDYK
CALIACRA
CORRENTI
COURONNE
D'ANTIBES
DOUKATON
ESPICHEL
FILIPPOS
GILBJARG
HEGEMANN
HELGENES
KARTSINO
KHONDROS
LANGANES
LITHINON
MARATHIA
MARROQUI
MARTELOS
PLOUEZEC

ST GILDAS
SCARAMIO
SHAKHOVA
SIDHEROS
STADLAND
TORINANA
VATICANO

9
ANDIRRION
ATHERIDHA
CARVOEIRA
DHRAPANON
FORMENTOR
FYNS HOVED
HANTSHOLM
KHERSONES
KOLLUMULI
KORMAKITI
LE CONQUET
LINDESNES
MONS KLINT
NORTH EAST
PONTUSVAL
POSIDHION
REYKJANES
RIFSTANGI
ST ANDREAS
ST MATHIEU
ST VINCENT
SKAGAFLOS
SKILLAION
SKIOLDNES
STABER HUK
STRAUMNES
TRAFALGAR
ZHELANIYA

10
BRUSTER ORT
CABALLERIA
CALA BURRAS
CAMPANELLA
DARSSER ORT
DOONSKLINT
FINISTERRE
GEDSER ODDE
GROSS KLUTZ
KNUDSHOVED
KOLKOS RAGS
KOTLUTANGI
MACHICHACO
MONTE SANTO
NORD VAGSOY
PIETRE NERE

RIGSCLAGEN
TOULINGNET
TRAKLANKUT
WASHINGTON

11
BJARGTANGER
DAHMESHOVED
HERBAUDIERE
KANASTRAION
SAINT GILDAS
SARAKINIKON
SLETTERHAGE
SPARTIVENTO
STAVNSHOVED
STEVNSKLINT
TERIBERSKIY

12
AYIOS IOANNIS
BLAAVUNDS HUK
GLETTINGANES
MORRIS JESSUP
SAINT ANDREAS
SAINT MATHIEU
SAINT VINCENT
VEJSNES NAKKE

13
BARDHSNESHORN
GILBJARG HOVED
MARKELSDORFER
ONDVERDNARNES
S MARIA DI LEUCA

14
RUSSKIY ZAVOROT
SJAELLANDS ODDE

15
GROSS KLUTZ HOVED

16
MARKELSDORFER HUK

17
NORTH EAST FORELAND
SANTA MARIA DI LEUCA

Capes of Asia

2
PO

3
API
IOT
IRO
KUH
LAI
NOS
NUH
OMA
SUE
TOI
TUA
URA

4
AROE
BABA
BAKE
DAKO
EAST
ESAR
HADD
HEDO
INCE
IRIS
KEGA
KURO
LASO
NASO
NOMA
OMAE
PIAI
POLA
SIFA
SUSA

5
AL KUH
ANIVA
ASWAD
BAROS
BESAR
BOTOK
CAMAU
ERIMO
FALSE
GAMOV
INUBO
JAGIN
JIBSH
JIZOU
KANDI

KERPE
KIOGA
LIANT
MALAN
MONZE
MORNE
NORTH
PARIT
PEDRO
RAKAN
ROKKO
SAMIT
SIRIK
SUNGI
TANAH
TAPPI
TAVOY
TOHQR

6
ALEVIN
AL HADD
ANAMUR
BAGASE
BARIDA
BLANCO
CABULI
CHU-MAY
DONDRA
ENGANO
FLESKO
GELANG
HATIBA
ILIGAN
JABUNG
KO SAKI
LUBONG
MANDAR
MEDANG
MUROTO
NOSHAP
NOZIMA
OENDOE
PATANI
SATANO
SIATON
SIPANG
TINACA
UNSANG
VALSCH

7
ABU-MALI
APATANA
ASIZURI

BANGKAI
BASTION
COMORIN
DEZHNEV
ED DAMUR
ESTAGNO
GARANBI
GENTENG
KAROSSA
KEREMBE
KIDEPIL
KRAWANG
KURINSK
KURKUMA
LOPATKA
MAIDANI
MISHA'AB
NAVARIN
NEGRAIS
NOIMINA
NORDVIK
ONG-KONO
OZERNOY
PADARAN
PINGMAR
PISHKAN
POETING
RACHADO
SELATAN
SHAKUAN
SHINOMI
SHIRIYA
SRISROL
SVYATOY
TANAJIB
TANJONG
TANNURA
TOURANE
VARELLA

8
AL JUNAIZ
BATANGAU
BOJEADOR
BYELKINA
CALAVITE
CALIMERE
CAMBODIA
CORONADO
GOOD HOPE
MAYRAIRA
MUI DUONG
MUSANDUM
PESCHANY
SENEBOEI
TARIGTIG
TOYO SAKI
VICTORIA

9
AL KHAIMAH
BILLINGSA
BULILUYAN
BUNG-KWIUA
BYANDOVAN
EL KHANZIR
KINKWA SAN
MANIMBAYA
MUSHEIRIB
NEGRI LAMA
NGOENDJOE
OLYMPIADY
OLYUTORSK
PAMARUKAN
PEMBOEANG
ST JACQUES
SAMBALANG
SOUTH WEST
TOKARISHO

10
CHELYUSKIN
CHUKOTSKIY
KHELIDONIA
MALATAJOER
NEDERBURGH
NISEMENNII
OVSYANKINA
SAN AGUSTIN
SHELAGSKIY
SHIREITOKO
SOYA MISAKI
YELIZAVETY

11
MANGKALIHAT

12
SAINT JACQUES
SAMPANMANGIO
SAN ILDEFONSO
SERDSTE KAMEN

13
JAVA'S ZUIDHOEK
PANGKALASEANG

14
KITASIRETOKOMI

Capes of Africa

3
BON
TIN

4
OLBA
ROSA
ROXO

5
AAMER
AMBER
BENAS
BLANC
BULAU
CANTU
HAFUM
KASAR
LOPEZ
MILHA
MIRIK
RAWAI
VERDE
VERGA

6
BARBAS
BLANCO
CANTIN
FIGALO
GARNET
PALMAS
RECIFE
ST PAUL
SERRAT
UFERNI

7
ABU DARA
AGULHAS
ALEM RUM
BADGLEY
BOJADOR
DELGADO
EL CANTU
ESTANTE
INFANTA
PADRONE
ST ANDRE
ST LUCIA
SPARTEL
TIMIRIS

8
CORVEIRO

DURNFORD
GOOD HOPE
MOHAMMED
MUHAMMED
NAAS NAAS
RAS BENAS
STE MARIE
ST MARTIN
SLANG KOP

9
CAPE POINT
COLUMBINE
GUARDAFUI
ST FRANCIS
SAINT PAUL
SEVEN CAPS

10
ABU SHAGARA
BARRACOUTA
RAS EL CANTU
SAINT ANDRE
SAINT LUCIA
SANTA MARIA

11
SAINTE MARIE
SAINT MARTIN
SIERRA LEONE
THREE POINTS

Capes of North and Central America

3
ANN
CAY
COD
FER
FOX
LOW
MAY
ORE
RAY
SUR

4
BAJA
BEAR
CRUZ
FEAR
GORE
HARO
HURD
KNOX
LYON
MALA
MONO
PINE
RACE
ROXO
SHOE
TERM
TIAN
TORO

5
ADAIR
AMOUR
ARENA
BAKER
BAULD
BEATA
BLAKE
DOBBS
ELENA
FALSO
GORDA
HECLA
HENRY
MAISI
MERCY
MUZON
NORTH
OTTER

PARRY
PELEE
PINAS
REYES
RICHE
SABLE
SCOTT
STONY
TOKER
TOSCA
VELAS
WHALE

6
ATHOLL
AVINOF
BARROW
BATATA
BLANCO
BURICA
CHACON
CROKER
ESKIMO
ESTERO
FATHER
FERMIN
FISHER
FREELS
GRATES
GURNET
GYPSUM
HEWETT
HOOPER
JOSEPH
LEYSON
NORMAN
PATUCA
RABAST
RODNEY
ROMAIN
ROMANO
ROSIER
ST JOHN
ST MARY
SAMBRO
TATNAM
TULLET
WILSON

7
ABROJOS

ADELAER
BALLARD
BEECHEY
CAMARON
CATOCHE
CHIDLEY
COLNETT
COMFORT
DESPAIR
DOUGLAS
FLOWERS
FRANCIS
HERRERO
KELLETT
KENDALL
LAMBERT
LAMBTON
LLERENA
LOOKOUT
MANNING
MARIATA
MARIATO
MOHICAN
MONOMOY
MUGFORD
OMMANEY
PUERCOS
ROMANOF
ST ELIAS
ST JAMES
SAN BLAS
SCULPIN
SPENCER
STEVENS
TEJUPAN

8
ANGUILLE
ARGUELLO
BATHURST
BEAUFORT
BISMARCK
CARLETON
CHIBUKAK
COLUMBIA
FAREWELL
FERROLLE
FLATTERY
HARRIGAN
HATTERAS
HEGEMANN
HENLOPEN
HONDURAS
HUATULCO
ISACHSEN
KEWEENAW
LAND'S END
LES TROIS

LISBURNE
MARSOUIN
MATAPALO
MECATINA
MOKHOVIK
NEWENHAM
PEMBROKE
PORTLAND
ROMANZOF
ST GEORGE
SAKONNET
SAN LUCAS
SARICHEF
SEAHORSE
SUCKLING
VALIENTE
WRANGELL
YALKUBUL

9
CANAVERAL
CARACOLES
CHURCHILL
DALHOUSIE
ELIZABETH
ESCUMINAC
ESPENBERG
FULLERTON
GARGANTUA
MCDONNELL
MADELEINE
MENDOCINO
MURCHISON
NORTH EAST
NORTH WEST
PARTRIDGE
ST CHARLES
ST GREGORY
SAINT JOHN
SAINT MARY
SANDY HOOK
SAN FELIPE
SAN LAZARO
SOUTH EAST
SOUTHWEST
VACAMONTE
VANCOUVER

10
BEAUCHAIRE
BYAM MARTIN
CABALLERIA
CONCEPCION
COPPERMINE
CORRIENTES
DESOLATION
DORCHESTER
ENGLEFIELD

HENRY KATER
MANIKUAGAN
MANZANILLO
MENDENHALL
SAINT ELIAS
SAINT JAMES
ST NICHOLAS
SAN ANTONIO
SAN DOMINGO
SAN JUANICO
STRATHFORD
TRES PUNTAS
WALSINGHAM

11
CONSTANTINE
FAIRWEATHER
JOSEPH HENRY
SAINT GEORGE
SOUTHAMPTON
SOUTH NEGRIL

12
ALFRED ERNEST
CONSTITUTION
FRANCIS VIEJO
GRACIAS A DIOS
HOPES ADVANCE
PRINCE ALFRED
SAINT CHARLES
SAINT GREGORY
SANTA EUGENIA

13
PRINCE OF WALES
SAINT NICHOLAS

14
DISAPPOINTMENT
PIEDRAS BLANCAS

16
ARENA DE LA VENTANA

Capes of South America

3
SUD

4
CHAO
ESTE
HORN
RASO
VELA

5
AGUJA
ARAYA
COLES
GORDA
MARZO
MORRO
NORTE
PATOS
PILAR
PLATA
QUOIN
TETAS
VIGIA

6
ARENAS
BALEIA
BEWARE
BLANCO
CRUCES
ESPADA
GROSSA
GRUESA
HORNOS
MACEIA
NINFAS
PASADO
PEDRAS
QUILAN
SIERRA
TAITAO
TAPAGE

7
ANGAMOS
ATALAIA
BALLENA
BARIMAS
BERMEJO
CORUMBA
DELGADA
MAGUARY
MANGLES

PARINAS
PIEDRAS
REDONDA
SAN JUAN
TIBURON

8
CARRANZA
CASTELHA
DOLPHINI
ESTRELLA
GALLINAS
GUARDIAN
GUASCAMA
LOS LOBOS
MACBRIDE
MEDANOSA
MEREDITH
PEMBROKE
SAN DIEGO
SAN PABLO
SAN PEDRO
SAN ROMAN
SAO ROQUE
SAO THOME
VIRJENES

9
CASSIPORE
DOS BAHIAS
DUNGENESS
MASTARDAS
TOPOCALMA

10
CHARAMBIRA
CORRIENTES
LA PUNTILLA
PUNTA NORTE
SANTA MARIA

11
ARISTIZABAL

12
BUYUSSUCANGA
LENGUA DE VACA

13
ESPIRITU SANTO
FALSE CAPE HORN
MANGUES VERDES

17
FALSO CABO DE HORNOS

Capes of Australasia and the Pacific Islands

3
RAM

4
ABUT
BALD
GRIM
HOWE
KNOB
UNDU
YORK

5
BANKS
BLUFF
BORDA
BOYER
CORNY
EVANS
HAWKE
JAFFA
KAENA
KALAE
KAUNA
NDOUA
NORTH
OTWAY
PERON
RICHE
SALIA
SANDY
TABLE
TOUHO
UPOLU
VATIA
WRECK

6
ARNHEM
CONRAN
COUDIE
DOMBEY
EGMONT
INDIAN
JERVIS
KAHUKU
KASARI
KAUIKI
KNOBBY
KOHALA
LAFOND
NELSON
PASLEY
PILLAR
QUIROS

ROSSEL
SORREL
TASMAN
TORBAY
WOODED

7
BOUVARD
BUSTARD
DUIFKEN
LEEUWIN
LEVEQUE
LIPTRAP
LISBURN
LOOKOUT
MAKOLEA
ROUSSIN
RUNAWAY
SPENCER
TACKING
TAPANGA
UPSTART
UVERITE
WAIPAPA

8
BALD HEAD
BEECROFT
DEFLOTTE
DUMOULIN
FAREWELL
FLATTERY
FOULWIND
GOSSELIN
GOULVAIN
KUMUKAHI
LOW ROCKY
MANIFOLD
MATUTULA
MENTELLE
PALLISER
PILBARRA
PORTLAND
POUATETI
ST HELENS

9
EDDYSTONE
FRANKLAND
FREYCINET
GRENVILLE
NORTH WEST
SOUTH EAST
SOUTH WEST
TURNAGAIN

VANCOUVER

10
CUMBERLAND
GANTHEAUME
KIDNAPPERS
PALMERSTON
PROVIDENCE
WILLOUGHBY

11
LESCHENAULT
LONDONDERRY
NATURALISTE
SAINT HELENS
WOODED BLUFF

12
BOWLING GREEN

13
BUNGAREE NORAH

14
D'ENTRECASTEAUX
NORTHUMBERLAND

Capitals of Europe and the Mediterranean

4
BONN
OSLO
ROME

11
SAINT HELIER
ST PETER PORT
VATICAN CITY

5
BERNE
PARIS
SOFIA
VADUZ

14
ANDORRA LA VELLA
SAINT PETER PORT

6
ATHENS
BERLIN
DUBLIN
LISBON
LONDON
MADRID
MONACO
MOSCOW
PRAGUE
TIRANA
VIENNA
WARSAW

7
BELFAST
CARDIFF
DOUGLAS
NICOSIA

8
BELGRADE
BRUSSELS
BUDAPEST
HELSINKI
ST HELIER
THE HAGUE
VALLETTA

9
AMSTERDAM
BUCHAREST
EDINBURGH
GIBRALTAR
LUXEMBURG
REYKJAVIK
SAN MARINO
STOCKHOLM
THORSHAVN

10
COPENHAGEN
EAST BERLIN
LUXEMBOURG

Capitals of Asia

4
ADEN
†DILI
DOHA
MALE

ULAN BATOR
VIENTIANE

10
QUEZON CITY

5
AMMAN
DACCA
DELHI
HANOI
KABUL
MACAO
MACAU
SANA'A
SEOUL
TOKYO

11
KUALA LUMPUR

12
KOTA KINABALU

17
BANDAR SERI BEGAWAN

6
ANKARA
BEIRUT
KUWAIT
MANAMA
†MANILA
MUSCAT
PEKING
RIYADH
†SAIGON
TAIPEI
TEHRAN

7
BAGHDAD
BANGKOK
COLOMBO
JAKARTA
KUCHING
RANGOON
TEHERAN
THIMPHU

8
ABU DHABI
DAMASCUS
DJAKARTA
KATMANDU
NEW DELHI
VICTORIA

9
ISLAMABAD
JERUSALEM
KATHMANDU
PHNOM PENH
PYONGYANG
SINGAPORE

† former capital

Capitals of Africa

4
LOME

5
ACCRA
CAIRO
DAKAR
LAGOS
PRAIA
RABAT
TUNIS
†ZOMBA

6
BAMAKO
BANGUI
BANJUL
BISSAU
JIBUTI
KIGALI
LUANDA
LUSAKA
MALABO
MAPUTO
MASERU
MORONI
NIAMEY
UMTATA

7
ABIDJAN
ALGIERS
CONAKRY
†EL AAIUN
FUNCHAL
KAMPALA
MBABANE
NAIROBI
ST DENIS
SAO TOME
TRIPOLI
YAOUNDE

8
CAPE TOWN
DJIBOUTI
*FORT LAMY
FREETOWN
GABORONE
KHARTOUM
KINSHASA
LILONGWE
MONROVIA
N'DJAMENA
PRETORIA
VICTORIA
WINDHOEK

9
BUJUMBURA
EDINBURGH
JAMESTOWN
MOGADISHU
PORT LOUIS
PORTO NOVO
SALISBURY

10
ADDIS ABABA
GEORGETOWN
LIBREVILLE
NOUAKCHOTT
SAINT DENIS
TANANARIVE

11
BRAZZAVILLE
DAR-ES-SALAAM
†MADINA DO BOE
OUAGADOUGOU
*SANTA ISABEL

12
PONTA DELGADA

14
*ST PAUL DE LUANDA

15
*LOURENCO MARQUES

16
*SAO PAULO DE LUANDA

17
*SAINT PAUL DE LUANDA

* former name
† former capital

Capitals of North and Central America

6
HAVANA
NASSAU
OTTAWA
ROSEAU

7
MANAGUA
ST JOHN'S
SAN JOSE
SAN JUAN

8
BELMOPAN
CASTRIES
GODTHAAB
HAMILTON
KINGSTON
PLYMOUTH
ROAD TOWN
ST PIERRE

9
GRAND TURK
GUATEMALA
KINGSTOWN
ST GEORGE'S

10
BASSETERRE
BASSE-TERRE
BRIDGETOWN
GEORGE TOWN
MEXICO CITY
PANAMA CITY
SAINT JOHN'S
WASHINGTON
WILLEMSTAD

11
PORT OF SPAIN
SAINT PIERRE
SAN SALVADOR
TEGUCIGALPA

12
FORT DE FRANCE
PORT AU PRINCE
SAINT GEORGE'S
SANTO DOMINGO

13
BALBOA HEIGHTS
GUATEMALA CITY

15
CHARLOTTE AMALIE

Capitals of South America

4
LIMA

5
LA PAZ
QUITO

6
BOGOTA

7
CARACAS
CAYENNE
STANLEY

8
ASUNCION
BRASILIA
SANTIAGO

10
GEORGETOWN
MONTEVIDEO
PARAMARIBO

11
BUENOS AIRES

Capitals of Australasia and the Pacific Islands

4
APIA
SUVA
VILA

5
AGANA
NAURU

6
NOUMEA
SAIPAN
TARAWA

7
HONIARA
PAPEETE

8
CANBERRA
FAGATOGO
FUNAFUTI
KINGSTON
PAGO PAGO

9
NUKU'ALOFA

10
WELLINGTON

11
PORT MORESBY

Cars (makes and models)

3
AMI
BMW
DAF
IMP
LUX
NSU
TVR

4
ALFA
AUDI
BETA
BORA
CLUB
COLT
FIAT
FORD
GHIA
GOLF
LADA
MAXI
MINI
OPEL
POLO
SAAB
SIVA
STAG
VIVA

5
ASTON
CAPRI
CIVIC
COMBI
COUPE
CROWN
DYANE
ECLAT
EDSEL
ELITE
HONDA
LLAMA
LOTUS
MACH I
MANTA
MAZDA
MERAK
PACER
ROBIN
ROVER
SEDAN
SIMCA
SKODA
SPORT
SUPER

TURBO
VOLVO

6
ALPINE
ASCONA
AUSTIN
CARUNA
CERICA
CHERRY
DATSUN
DE DION
DIESEL
ESCORT
ESPADA
ESPRIT
FALCON
FULVIA
GALANT
HEALEY
HUMBER
HUNTER
JAGUAR
JARAMA
JENSEN
KADETT
KITTEN
LANCER
LANCIA
LAUREL
MAGNUM
MARINA
MEXICO
MIDGET
MORGAN
MORRIS
PACER X
PALLAS
PASSAT
RAPIER
REKORD
SALOON
SHADOW
SPRITE
SPYDER
TOLEDO
TOYOTA
URRACO
VICTOR
VIOLET

7
ALFASUD
ALFETTA
ALLEGRO
AVENGER

BENTLEY
BERLINA
BRISTOL
CAPRICE
CARRERA
CELESTE
CITROEN
CLUBMAN
COROLLA
CORTINA
DAIMLER
FERRARI
GINETTA
GORDINI
GRANADA
HARDTOP
HILLMAN
KHAMSIN
LAGONDA
LINCOLN
MATADOR
MERCURY
MONARCH
MUMFORD
MUSTANG
PACER DL
PANTERA
PEUGEOT
PHANTOM
PONTIAC
PORSCHE
RELIANT
RENAULT
SCEPTRE
SOFT TOP
SPECIAL
SUNBEAM
TRIPPER
TRIUMPH
VENTORA
WEEKEND

8
BLUEBIRD
CADILLAC
CAMARGUE
CATERHAM
CAVALIER
CELICA ST
CHEVETTE
CHRYSLER
CORNICHE
COUNTACH
CRAYFORD

DE TOMASO
DOLOMITE
ELECTRON
FAIRMONT
FIREBIRD
IMP SPORT
LUX COUPE
LUX TARGA
MASERATI
MERCEDES
MG MIDGET
MOSKVICH
PRINCESS
SCIMITAR
SCIROCCO
SPITFIRE
VAUXHALL
WAGONEER
WARTBURG

9
ALFA ROMEO
CHEVROLET
COMMODORE
DEAUVILLE
DOUBLE SIX
LAUREL SIX
LIMOUSINE
LONGCHAMP
SOVEREIGN

10
BERLINETTA
COMBI COUPE
FAIRTHORPE
POLSKI FIAT
RANGE ROVER
ROLLS ROYCE
SUPER ROBIN
TURBO COUPE
VANDEN PLAS

11
ASTON MARTIN
CONTINENTAL
CONVERTIBLE
CROWN ESTATE
INTERCEPTOR
LAMBORGHINI
LANDAULETTE
LAND CRUISER

12
CROWN SPECIAL
FAMILY ESTATE
MERCEDES BENZ
SILVER SHADOW

13
CORNICHE COUPE
REKORD BERLINA
TECH EXPONENTS

14
DOLOMITE SPRINT

15
BERLINETTA BOXER
FIREBIRD TRANSAM

Cathedrals of England and Wales: Anglican

3
ELY

4
YORK

5
DERBY
RIPON
TRURO
WELLS

6
BANGOR
BRECON
DURHAM
EXETER
OXFORD

7
BRISTOL
CHESTER
LINCOLN
NEWPORT
NORWICH
ST ASAPH
ST PAUL'S

8
BRADFORD
CARLISLE
COVENTRY
HEREFORD
LLANDAFF
MONMOUTH
ST ALBANS
ST DAVID'S

9
BLACKBURN
GUILDFORD
LEICESTER
LICHFIELD
LIVERPOOL
NEWCASTLE
ROCHESTER
SALISBURY
SHEFFIELD
SOUTHWARK
SOUTHWELL
WAKEFIELD
WORCESTER

10
BIRMINGHAM
CANTERBURY
CHELMSFORD
CHICHESTER
GLOUCESTER
MANCHESTER
PORTSMOUTH
SAINT ASAPH
SAINT PAUL'S
WINCHESTER

11
SAINT ALBANS
SAINT DAVID'S

12
PETERBOROUGH

13
BURY ST EDMUNDS

Cathedrals of England and Wales: Roman Catholic

5
LEEDS

7
ARUNDEL
CARDIFF
CLIFTON
NORWICH
SALFORD
WREXHAM

8
PLYMOUTH

9
BRENTWOOD
LANCASTER
LIVERPOOL
NEWCASTLE
SOUTHWARK

10
BIRMINGHAM
NOTTINGHAM
PORTSMOUTH
SHREWSBURY

11
NORTHAMPTON
WESTMINSTER

13
MIDDLESBROUGH

Channels and Straits of the British Isles

4
JURA
YELL

5
BARRA
DOVER
ISLAY
MENAI
MINCH
NORTH

6
HARRIS
SANDAY
SOLENT

7
BRISTOL
CUILLIN
ENGLISH
WESTRAY

8
PENTLAND
THE MINCH

9
ST GEORGE'S
THE SOLENT
YELL SOUND

10
KILBRENNAN
NORTH MINCH

11
LITTLE MINCH
MENAI STRAIT
SANDAY SOUND
SOUND OF JURA

12
CUILLIN SOUND
NORTH CHANNEL
SAINT GEORGE'S
SOUND OF BARRA
SOUND OF ISLAY
WESTRAY FIRTH

13
PENTLAND FIRTH
SOUND OF HARRIS

14
BRISTOL CHANNEL
ENGLISH CHANNEL
STRAITS OF DOVER

15
KILBRENNAN SOUND

16
ST GEORGE'S CHANNEL

Channels and Straits of Europe
(excluding the British Isles)

5
KASOS
MALTA
SOUND

7
MESSINA
ORESUND
OTRANTO

8
BOSPORUS
KATTEGAT
KITHIRAI
SICILIAN
THE SOUND

9
BONIFACIO
GIBRALTAR
GREAT BELT
KARPATHOS
SKAGERRAK

10
FEMER BAELT
KALMARSUND
LITTLE BELT

11
DARDANELLES

15
BORNHOLMSGATTET

Channels and Straits of Asia and Australasia

3
KII

4
BASS
COOK
HOYO
PALK
SOYA

5
KERCH
KOREA
SUNDA

6
HORMUZ
TORRES

7
FORMOSA
MAKASAR
MALACCA
TSUGARU

8
MACASSAR

9
SINGAPORE

11
KERCHENSKIY

Channels and Straits of Africa

7
MASSAWA

10
MOZAMBIQUE

11
BAB EL MANDEB

Channels and Straits of North America

5
CABOT
JONES
PEARY

6
HUDSON

9
BELLE ISLE
LANCASTER

10
JUAN DE FUCA
MCCLINTOCK

14
NORTHUMBERLAND

Channels and Straits of Central America and the West Indies

4
MONA

6
CAYMAN

7
FLORIDA
JAMAICA
YUCATAN

8
SOMBRERO
WINDWARD

9
ST VINCENT

10
GUADELOUPE

11
CROOKED ISLE
MONA PASSAGE

12
CAYMAN TRENCH
SAINT VINCENT

15
SOMBRERO PASSAGE
WINDWARD PASSAGE

16
ST VINCENT PASSAGE

17
GUADELOUPE PASSAGE

18
CROOKED ISLE PASSAGE

Channels and Straits of South America

7
BONAIRE

8
FALKLAND
MAGELLAN

13
BONAIRE TRENCH
SERPENT'S MOUTH

Chemical Elements

3
TIN

4
GOLD
IRON
LEAD
NEON
ZINC

5
ARGON
BORON
RADON
XENON

6
BARIUM
CARBON
CERIUM
COBALT
COPPER
CURIUM
ERBIUM
HELIUM
INDIUM
IODINE
NICKEL
OSMIUM
OXYGEN
RADIUM
SILVER
SODIUM

7
ARSENIC
BISMUTH
BROMINE
CADMIUM
CAESIUM
CALCIUM
FERMIUM
GALLIUM
HAFNIUM
HAHNIUM
HOLMIUM
IRIDIUM
KRYPTON
LITHIUM
MERCURY
NIOBIUM
RHENIUM
RHODIUM
SILICON
SULPHUR

TERBIUM
THORIUM
THULIUM
URANIUM
YTTRIUM

8
ACTINIUM
ANTIMONY
ASTATINE
CHLORINE
CHROMIUM
EUROPIUM
FLUORINE
FRANCIUM
HYDROGEN
LUTECIUM
LUTETIUM
NITROGEN
NOBELIUM
PLATINUM
POLONIUM
RUBIDIUM
SAMARIUM
SCANDIUM
SELENIUM
TANTALUM
THALLIUM
TITANIUM
TUNGSTEN
VANADIUM

9
ALUMINIUM
AMERICIUM
BERKELIUM
BERYLLIUM
GERMANIUM
LANTHANUM
MAGNESIUM
MANGANESE
NEODYMIUM
NEPTUNIUM
PALLADIUM
PLUTONIUM
POTASSIUM
RUTHENIUM
STRONTIUM
TELLURIUM
YTTERBIUM
ZIRCONIUM

10
DYSPROSIUM
GADOLINIUM

LAWRENCIUM
MOLYBDENUM
PHOSPHORUS
PROMETHIUM
TECHNETIUM

11
CALIFORNIUM
EINSTEINIUM
MENDELEVIUM

12
KURCHATOVIUM
PRASEODYMIUM
PROTACTINIUM

13
RUTHERFORDIUM

Clothing

3
ABA
ABB
ALB
BIB
BOA
BRA
CAP
FEZ
FIG
FUR
HAT
LID
OBI
TAM
TIE
WIG

STUD
SUIT
TACH
TETE
TILE
TIRE
TOGA
TOGS
TOPI
TRIM
TUTU
VAMP
VEIL
VEST
WEAR
WRAP
ZORI

4
BAGS
BELT
BOOT
CAPE
CEST
CLOG
COAT
COIF
DUDS
GARB
GEAR
GIMP
GOWN
HAIK
HOOD
HOSE
HYKE
JUMP
JUPE
KEPI
KILT
MUFF
MULE
POKE
RAGS
ROBE
RUFF
SACK
SARI
SASH
SCYE
SHOE
SLIP
SLOP
SOCK
SPUR

5
AMICE
AO DAI
APRON
ARRAY
BERET
BLUES
BUSBY
CHAPS
CLOAK
CLOUT
CROWN
CYMAR
DERBY
DHOTI
DICKY
DRESS
DUCKS
EPHOD
FANON
FICHU
FRILL
FROCK
GIPON
GLOVE
GUISE
HABIT
HAICK
JEANS
JUPON
KHAKI
LAMMY
MITRE
MITTS
MUFTI
MUTCH
PAGRI

PANTS
PARKA
PARKI
PILCH
PLAID
PLUME
POLKA
PUMPS
QUOIF
ROMAL
RUMAL
SABOT
SAGUM
SCARF
SHAKO
SHAPS
SHAWL
SHIFT
SHIRT
SHOON
SIMAR
SKIRT
SLOPS
SMOCK
SNOOD
SPATS
STAYS
STOCK
STOLA
STOLE
TACHE
TAILS
TALMA
TAMMY
TERAI
TIARA
TOPEE
TOQUE
TOZIE
TREWS
TUNIC
VISOR
VITTA
WAMUS
WEEDS

6
ABACOT
ABOLLA
ACHKAN
AFGHAN
ANARAK
ANKLET
ANORAK
ATTIRE
BALATA
BANIAN
BARRET

BASHER
BASQUE
BEAVER
BERTHA
BIGGIN
BIKINI
BLAZER
BLOUSE
BOATER
BOBWIG
BODICE
BOLERO
BONNET
BOOTEE
BOWLER
BRACES
BRIEFS
BROGAN
BROGUE
BUCKLE
BUSKIN
BUSTLE
BUTTON
CAFTAN
CALASH
CAPOTE
CASQUE
CASTOR
CESTUS
CHIMER
CHITON
CHOKER
CHOPIN
CILICE
CLOCHE
COATEE
COLLAR
COLLET
CORSET
CRAVAT
CUERPO
DENIMS
DIADEM
DIAPER
DICKEY
DIRNDL
DOLMAN
DOMINO
EAR-CAP
FALLAL
FASCIA
FEDORA
FINERY
GAITER
GALAGE
GALOSH
GARTER
GIRDLE

GOLOSH
HALTER
HELMET
HOGGER
JACKET
JERKIN
JERSEY
JOSEPH
JUMPER
KAFTAN
KIMONO
KIRTLE
LAMMIE
LINING
LIVERY
LOAFER
MANDIL
MANTLE
MANTUA
MITTEN
MOBCAP
MORION
MOTLEY
MUCLUC
MUKLUK
MUNDIL
MUU-MUU
NYLONS
OUTFIT
OXFORD
PANAMA
PANTON
PARKEE
PATTEN
PEPLOS
PEPLUM
PERUKE
PONCHO
PUTTEE
QUERPO
RABATO
RAGLAN
REBATO
REEFER
RIBAND
RIBBON
ROBING
ROCHET
RUFFLE
SACQUE
SALADE
SALLET
SANDAL
SARONG
SEMMIT
SEQUIN
SHORTS
SLACKS

SLEEVE
SLIP-ON
SMALLS
STAMIN
SUNHAT
TABARD
TIGHTS
TIPPET
TOP-HAT
TOPPER
TORQUE
TRILBY
TRUNKS
T-SHIRT
TUCKER
TURBAN
TUXEDO
TWEEDS
ULSTER
VISITE
WADERS
WAMMUS
WEEPER
WESKIT
WHITES
WIMPLE
WOOLLY

7

APPAREL
BABOOSH
BALDRIC
BANDANA
BIRETTA
BLUCHER
BOTTINE
BURNOUS
CALOTTE
CAPOUCH
CAPUCHE
CASSOCK
CHAPEAU
CHEMISE
CHLAMYS
CIVVIES
CLOBBER
CLOTHES
COSTUME
CRACOWE
CUTAWAY
DASHIKI
DOUBLET
DRAWERS
EPAULET
FALLALS
FALSIES
FELT HAT
FILABEG

FILIBEG
FLOUNCE
FROUNCE
FUR COAT
GAITERS
GALAGES
GALOCHE
GAMBADO
GANTLET
GARMENT
GASKINS
GREAVES
HAIRNET
HAIRPIN
HATBAND
HOGGENS
HOMBURG
HOSIERY
LATCHET
LAYETTE
LEGGING
LEGHORN
LOAFERS
MAE WEST
MANTLET
MODESTY
MONTERO
MUFFLER
NECKTIE
NEGLIGE
NIGHTIE
OILSKIN
OVERALL
PAJAMAS
PALETOT
PALLIUM
PANOPLY
PARTLET
PATTENS
PEACOAT
PEGTOPS
PELISSE
PERIWIG
PETASUS
PIERROT
PILLBOX
PITH-HAT
PLUG-HAT
PUTTEES
PYJAMAS
RAIMENT
ROMPERS
RUBBERS
SARAFAN
SILK HAT
SIMARRE
SINGLET
SLICKER

SLIPPER
SMICKET
SNEAKER
SOLA HAT
SPENCER
SPORRAN
SURCOAT
SWEATER
TARBUSH
TEAGOWN
TOGGERY
TOPBOOT
TOPCOAT
TUNICLE
TURNOUT
UNDRESS
UNIFORM
VANDYKE
VESTURE
WHITTLE
WRAPPER
YASHMAK

8

AIGRETTE
BALDRICK
BALMORAL
BATHGOWN
BATHROBE
BAUDRICK
BEARSKIN
BIGGONET
BLOOMERS
BLUCHERS
BOOTIKIN
BREECHES
BRITCHES
BURNOUSE
CAMISOLE
CAPUCCIO
CAPUCHIN
CARDIGAN
CLOTHING
CORSELET
CRACOWES
CULOTTES
DALMATIC
DISGUISE
DRESS TIE
ENSEMBLE
ETON SUIT
FATIGUES
FILLIBEG
FINNESKO
FLANNELS
FLIP-FLOP
FONTANGE
FOOTMUFF

FOOTGEAR
FOOTWEAR
FRIPPERY
FRONTLET
FURBELOW
GAMBESON
GARMENTS
GAUNTLET
GLAD RAGS
HALF-HOSE
HEADBAND
HEADGEAR
HEADWEAR
JACKBOOT
JODHPURS
KAFFIYEH
KERCHIEF
KNICKERS
LEGGINGS
MACKINAW
MANTELET
MANTILLA
MOCASSIN
MOCCASIN
MUCKLUCK
MUFFETEE
NECKBAND
NECKLACE
NEGLIGEE
NIGHTCAP
OILSKINS
OPERA-HAT
OVERALLS
OVERCOAT
OVERSHOE
PANTABLE
PANTOFLE
PEIGNOIR
PELERINE
PHILABEG
PHILIBEG
PIKADELL
PINAFORE
PLUMELET
PRINCESS
PUGGAREE
PULLOVER
RAINCOAT
SACK-COAT
SCAPULAR
SHOE-LACE
SKI-PANTS
SKULLCAP
SLIP-OVER
SNOWBOOT
SNOWSHOE
SOLAR HAT
SOMBRERO

STEPHANE
STOCKING
STRAW HAT
SURPLICE
SWIMSUIT
TAILCOAT
TARBOOSH
TEE-SHIRT
TOILETTE
TRIMMING
TROUSERS
VESTMENT
WOOLLIES
WRISTLET
ZOOT-SUIT

9

AIR-JACKET
ALPARGATA
BALACLAVA
BANDOLEER
BANDOLIER
BEACHWEAR
BEDJACKET
BELLYBAND
BILLYCOCK
BOWLER HAT
BRASSIERE
BUCKSKINS
CHEONG-SAM
COATFROCK
COCKED HAT
COCKLE-HAT
COMFORTER
CORDUROYS
CRINOLINE
DRESS-COAT
DRESS SUIT
DUNCE'S CAP
DUNGAREES
EPAULETTE
FLESHINGS
FORAGE CAP
FORE-SKIRT
FROCK-COAT
FULL DRESS
FUR COLLAR
GABERDINE
GARIBALDI
GAUNTLETS
GLENGARRY
GREATCOAT
HAIR-SHIRT
HEAD-DRESS
HOOP-SKIRT
HOUSECOAT
INVERNESS
JACKBOOTS

KID GLOVES
KILMARNOCK
LOINCLOTH
MILLINERY
NAUTICALS
NECKCLOTH
NEWMARKET
NIGHTGOWN
NIGHTWEAR
OLIVE DRAB
OVERSHOES
PANTALETS
PANTALOON
PEA-JACKET
PEAKED CAP
PETERSHAM
PETTICOAT
PLUS-FOURS
POLONAISE
POURPOINT
PRINCESSE
REDINGOTE
SAILOR-CAP
SAILOR-HAT
SANBENITO
SCAPULARY
SCHOOLCAP
SHOVEL-HAT
SLOPPY JOE
SLOUCH-HAT
SNOWBOOTS
SNOWSHOES
SOU'-WESTER
STEENKIRK
STOCKINGS
STOMACHER
STOVEPIPE
SUNBONNET
SUN-HELMET
SUSPENDER
TRACK-SUIT
TRILBY HAT
TROUSSEAU
UNDERWEAR
UNION SUIT
VESTMENTS
WAISTBAND
WAISTCOAT
WIDEAWAKE

10

BOILER SUIT
CANONICALS
CHAPARAJOS
CORK-JACKET
COURT-DRESS
CRICKET-CAP
CUMMERBUND
DESHABILLE

DRESS-SHIRT
ETON JACKET
FANCY DRESS
GARMENTURE
HABILIMENT
JEISTIECOR
LOUNGE SUIT
MACKINTOSH
NIGHTDRESS
NIGHTSHIRT
OPERA CLOAK
PANTALOONS
PICCADILLY
PICTURE-HAT
POKE-BONNET
PORKPIE HAT
READY-MADES
RIDING-BOOT
RIDING-COAT
ROQUELAURE
SAILOR-SUIT
SCRATCH-WIG
SHIRT-DRESS
SHOE-BUCKLE
SMOCK-FROCK
SPORTS COAT
SPORTSWEAR
SUNDAY BEST
SUSPENDERS
SWEATSHIRT
TRENCH-COAT
WATERPROOF
WRAP-RASCAL

11

AFGHAN SHAWL
BATHING SUIT
BATTLEDRESS
BEDIZENMENT
BELL-BOTTOMS
BOILED SHIRT
CHOLERA BELT
CLODHOPPERS
CRASH HELMET
DIVING DRESS
DOLLY VARDEN
DREADNAUGHT
DREADNOUGHT
FARTHINGALE
HAND-ME-DOWNS
LEATHER COAT
MORNING COAT
MORNING GOWN
MORTAR-BOARD
NECKERCHIEF
NIGHTINGALE
OXFORD SHOES
PHRYGIAN CAP

PILOT-JACKET
REGIMENTALS
RIDING-HABIT
SHELL-JACKET
SLUMBERWEAR
SOUP-AND-FISH
SOUTHWESTER
SWAGGER COAT
SWALLOWTAIL
TAM-O'-SHANTER
TRENCHER-CAP
WELLINGTONS
WIDOW'S WEEDS

12

ANTIGROPELOS
BATHING-DRESS
BIB-AND-TUCKER
BILLYCOCK HAT
CHESTERFIELD
COMBINATIONS
DINNER-JACKET
DRESSING-GOWN
GALLIGASKINS
KNEE-BREECHES
LUMBER JACKET
MONKEY-JACKET
MORNING DRESS
PLAIN CLOTHES
SMALL-CLOTHES
SPORTS JACKET
STOVEPIPE HAT
STRAIT-JACKET
TEN-GALLON HAT
TWO-PIECE SUIT
UNDERCLOTHES
WIDEAWAKE HAT

13

ANTIGROPELOES
BERMUDA SHORTS
FOOTBALL BOOTS
HOOP-PETTICOAT
NORFOLK JACKET
PUDDING-SLEEVE
SHOULDER-STRAP
SMOKING JACKET
SPATTERDASHES
SWADDLING-BAND
UNDERCLOTHING

14

BATHING COSTUME
KNICKERBOCKERS
RIDING-BREECHES
SHOOTING-JACKET
SWADDLING-CLOTH
UNMENTIONABLES

15

SLEEVE-WAISTCOAT
STRAIT-WAISTCOAT

Cambridge Colleges | Oxford Colleges

Cambridge Colleges	Oxford Colleges	
5 CLARE JESUS KING'S	**5** JESUS KEBLE ORIEL	ST CATHERINE'S ST EDMUND HALL
6 DARWIN GIRTON QUEENS' SELWYN	**6** EXETER MERTON QUEEN'S WADHAM	**13** CORPUS CHRISTI
		14 GREYFRIARS HALL
7 CHRIST'S DOWNING NEW HALL NEWNHAM ST JOHN'S TRINITY WOLFSON	**7** BALLIOL LINACRE LINCOLN ST ANNE'S ST CROSS ST HUGH'S ST JOHN'S WOLFSON	**15** SAINT BENET'S HALL SAINT CATHERINE'S SAINT EDMUND HALL **16** LADY MARGARET HALL
8 EMMANUEL PEMBROKE	**8** ALL SOULS HERTFORD MAGDALEN NUFFIELD PEMBROKE ST HILDA'S ST PETER'S	
9 CHURCHILL CLARE HALL MAGDALENE	**9** BRASENOSE MANSFIELD ST ANTONY'S WORCESTER	
10 PETERHOUSE SAINT JOHN'S	**10** NEW COLLEGE SAINT ANNE'S SAINT CROSS SAINT HUGH'S SAINT JOHN'S SOMERVILLE UNIVERSITY	
11 FITZWILLIAM TRINITY HALL	**11** CAMPION HALL REGENT'S PARK SAINT HILDA'S SAINT PETER'S	
12 ST CATHERINE'S SIDNEY SUSSEX	**12** CHRIST CHURCH SAINT ANTONY'S ST BENET'S HALL	
13 CORPUS CHRISTI		
14 ST EDMUND'S HOUSE		
15 SAINT CATHERINE'S		
16 GONVILLE AND CAIUS		
17 SAINT EDMUND'S HOUSE		

Colours and Colourings

3
BAY
DUN
JET
LAC
RED
TAN

4
ANIL
ASHY
BICE
BLUE
BUFF
CYAN
DRAB
EBON
ECRU
FAWN
FLAX
GILT
GOLD
GRAY
GREY
HOAR
INKY
JADE
KOHL
LAKE
NAVY
PIED
PINK
PLUM
PUCE
ROAN
ROSE
ROSY
RUBY
SAND
VERT
WELD
WINE
WOAD

5
AMBER
ASHEN
AZURE
BEIGE
BERYL
BLACK
BLOND
BROWN
CORAL
CREAM

EBONY
EOSIN
FLAME
GREEN
GULES
HAZEL
HENNA
HOARY
INDOL
KHAKI
LEMON
LIARD
LILAC
LIVID
LYART
MAUVE
MILKY
MOUSY
MUREX
OCHRE
OLIVE
ORCIN
ORPIN
PANSY
PEACH
PEARL
ROUGE
RUDDY
SABLE
SANDY
SEPIA
SMOKY
SNOWY
SOOTY
STEEL
STRAW
SWART
TAWNY
TOPAZ
UMBER
VIRID
WHITE

6
ARCHIL
AUBURN
BISTRE
BLONDE
BLUISH
BRONZE
CANARY
CARROT
CERISE
CHERRY
CHROME

CLARET
COBALT
COFFEE
COPPER
CROCUS
DAMASK
DAMSON
ENAMEL
FALLOW
FLAXEN
GOLDEN
INDIGO
INDOLE
ISABEL
KERMES
MADDER
MALLOW
MAROON
MURREY
ORANGE
PURPLE
RESEDA
RUFOUS
RUSSET
SALLOW
SALMON
SIENNA
SILVER
SORREL
STEELY
TITIAN
TYRIAN
VERMIL
VIOLET
VIRENT
YELLOW

7
BISCUIT
CAMBOGE
CARMINE
CARROTY
CELADON
CELESTE
CITRINE
CRIMSON
DAPPLED
EMERALD
GAMBOGE
GRAYISH
GREYISH
GRIZZLY
LOGWOOD
MAGENTA
MAZARIN
MOTTLED
NACARAT
NANKEEN
OLD-GOLD
OLD-ROSE
PIEBALD
PINKISH
PONCEAU
REDDISH
ROSEATE
ROSE-RED
SAFFRON
SCARLET
SEA-BLUE
SILVERY
SKY-BLUE
STAMMEL
SWARTHY
VERDANT
WHITISH
XANTHIC

8
AMARANTH
AMETHYST
ASH-BLOND
BLOOD-RED
BROWNISH
BURGUNDY
CARDINAL
CERULEAN
CHESTNUT
CINNABAR
DOVE-GRAY
DOVE-GREY
EGGSHELL
GUNMETAL
IRON-GRAY
IRON-GREY
JET-BLACK
LAVENDER
MAHOGANY
MARIGOLD
NAVY-BLUE
NUT-BROWN
ORPIMENT
PEA-GREEN
PLATINUM
POPPY-RED
PRIMROSE
PURPLISH
ROSE-HUED
SANGUINE
SAPPHIRE
SEA-GREEN
SKEWBALD
VIRIDIAN

9
ARGENTINE
AUBERGINE
BLUE-BLACK
CARNATION
CARNELIAN
CHAMPAGNE
CHOCOLATE
DANDELION
FIELD-GRAY
FIELD-GREY
JADE-GREEN
KERMESITE
LEAF-GREEN
LILY-WHITE
OLIVE-DRAB
SMOKE-GRAY
SMOKE-GREY
SNOW-WHITE
SOLFERINO
STEEL-GRAY
STEEL-GREY
TANGERINE
TITIAN-RED
TURKEY-RED
VERDIGRIS
VERMILION
YELLOWISH

10
AQUAMARINE
CHARTREUSE
COBALT-BLUE
CORNFLOWER
GRASS-GREEN
HELIOTROPE
OLIVE-GREEN
POWDER-BLUE
QUAKER-GRAY
QUAKER-GREY
ROAN-COLOUR
ROSE-COLOUR
SNOWY-WHITE
STRAWBERRY
TERRA-COTTA

11
BOTTLE-GREEN
BURNT SIENNA
CHROME-GREEN
CRIMSON LAKE
FLAME-COLOUR
FLESH-COLOUR
LIVER-COLOUR
PEACOCK-BLUE
SNUFF-COLOUR
VENETIAN-RED

12
LINCOLN-GREEN
MIDNIGHT-BLUE
PRUSSIAN BLUE
ROSE-COLOURED
SHOCKING PINK

13
FLAME-COLOURED
FLESH-COLOURED
PLATINUM BLOND
SNUFF-COLOURED
STRAW-COLOURED

Composers of Music

3
BAX
CUI

4
ABEL, ADAM, ARNE, BACH, BART, BERG, BOHM, BULL, BYRD, CAGE, GADE, GAUL, GOSS, HABA, IVES, LALO, NERI, NONO, ORFF, PERI, TOCH, WOLF, WOOD

FINCK, FRIML, GATTY, GLUCK, GRIEG, GUNGL, HASSE, HAYDN, HENZE, HOLST, IBERT, ISAAC, JONES, KERLL, LAWES, LEHAR, LISZT, LOTTI, LULLY, MARKS, PROUT, RAVEL, REGER, REYER, ROSSE, ROSSI, SARTI, SATIE, SCOTT, SMYTH, SOUSA, SPOHR, SUPPE, TOSTI, VERDI, WEBER, WEILL, YSAYE

5
ASTON, AURIC, BALFE, BERIO, BIZET, BLISS, BLOCH, BOITO, BRUCH, CARSE, CESTI, COOKE, COSTA, COWEN, DAVID, DEPPE, D'INDY, DUFAY, DUKAS, ELGAR, ESPLA, FALLA, FAURE, FESTA, FIELD

6
ANERIO, ANSELL, ARDITI, ARNOLD, BARBER, BARTOK, BERLIN, BISHOP, BOULEZ, BRAHMS, BRIDGE, BRUHNS, BUSONI, CALKIN, CHAVEZ

CHOPIN, COATES, COWARD, CZERNY, DAVIES, DELIUS, DEMUTH, DE RORE, DUPARC, DVORAK, ENESCO, FOULDS, FRANCK, GADSBY, GERMAN, GILLET, GLINKA, GLOVER, GOUNOD, HANDEL, HARRIS, KADOSA, KEISER, KODALY, KRENEK, KUHNAU, LAMOND, LASSEN, LASSUS, LECOCQ, LESLIE, LIADOV, MAHLER, MERULO, MOERAN, MORLEY, MOZART, MUFFAT, PARKER, PHILIP, PISTON, PLEYEL, QUANTZ, RAMEAU, RONALD, SCHEIN, SCHUTZ, SEIBER, STRAUS, STUART, TALLIS, TAYLOR, THOMAS, TUNDER, VARESE

VITALI, VOGLER, WAGNER, WALLER, WALTON, WEBERN, WILBYE

7
ALBENIZ, BAZZINI, BELLINI, BENNETT, BERLIOZ, BLACHER, BORODIN, BRITTEN, CACCINI, CAMBERT, CAMPION, CAVALLI, CLEAVER, COPLAND, CORELLI, DEBUSSY, DE FALLA, DELIBES, DES PRES, DOWLAND, DUNHILL, FARNABY, FAYRFAX, FRANKEL, FRICKER, GALUPPI, GERHARD, GIBBONS, GODFREY, GOMBERT, HALFTER, HERMANN, HORSLEY, IRELAND, JACKSON, JANACEK, JOACHIM, JOMMELI, JOSQUIN, KETELBY, KNUPFER, LAMBERT, LANDINI, LUTYENS, MACCUNN, MARTINI, MARTINU, MENOTTI, MICHAEL

MILHAUD, MORALES, NICOLAI, NIELSEN, NOVELLO, OBRECHT, OKEGHEM, PINSUTI, POULENC, PUCCINI, PURCELL, QUILTER, REINKER, RODGERS, ROSSINI, SCHEIDT, SINDING, SMETANA, STAINER, STRAUSS, TARTINI, TIPPETT, TORELLI, VIVALDI, WALLACE, WEELKES, ZARLINE

8
ANCLIFFE, ARCADELT, BAUTISTA, BENEDICT, BINCHOIS, BROCKMAN, BRUCKNER, CALLCOTT, CHABRIER, CIMAROSA, COUPERIN, DOHNANYI, FLETCHER, GABRIELI, GERSHWIN, GESUALDO, GIORDANI, GOUDINAL, GRAINGER, GRANADOS, HOLBROOK, HONEGGER, KORSAKOV, KREISLER, LEGRENZI, MARENZIO, MASCAGNI, MASSENET, MESSAGER

MESSIAEN, MONCKTON, PAGANINI, PALMGREN, PETRASSI, PIZZETTI, RAYBOULD, RESPIGHI, SCHNABEL, SCHUBERT, SCHUMANN, SCRIABIN, SESSIONS, SHEBALIN, SIBELIUS, SOMERSET, STANFORD, SULLIVAN, SVENDSEN, TAVERNER, TELEMANN, TOSSELLI, VICTORIA, VITTORIA, VON GLUCK, WAGENAAR, WILLAERT

9
ADDINSELL, BALAKIREV, BEETHOVEN, BERNSTEIN, BUXTEHUDE, CALDICOTT, CALVISIUS, CARISSIMI, CARPENTER, CAVALIERI, CHAMINADE, CHERUBINI, CHEVALIER, CORNELIUS, DE CABEZON, DONIZETTI, DUNSTABLE, FROBERGER, GUGLIELMI, GUILLAUME, HINDEMITH, JANNEQUIN, LOCATELLI, MACDOWELL, MARSCHNER, MAZZINGHI, MEYERBEER, MOSCHELES, OFFENBACH

PACHELBEL	**13**
PAISIELLO	DRAKE-BROCKMAN
PERGOLESI	STAROKADOMSKY
PROKOFIEV	
SCARLATTI	**14**
SCHONBERG	JAQUES-DALCROZE
SPAIN-DUNK	RIMSKY-KORSAKOV
SWEELINCK	VON WALKERSTEIN
TOSCANINI	
	15
10	VAUGHAN WILLIAMS
BOCCHERINI	
CHAIKOVSKY	**16**
CRISTOFORI	STERNDALE BENNETT
KABALEVSKY	
KINDERMANN	**18**
MIASKOVSKY	CASTELNUOVO-TEDESCO
MONTEVERDE	
MONTEVERDI	
MOSZKOWSKI	
MUSSORGSKY	
PADEREWSKI	
PALESTRINA	
PONCHIELLI	
PRAETORIUS	
RAWSTHORNE	
RUBINSTEIN	
SAINT-SAENS	
SCHOENBERG	
SKALKOTTAS	
STRAVINSKY	
VIEUXTEMPS	
VILLA-LOBOS	
WALDTEUFEL	

11
DIMITRIESEN
DITTERSDORF
FRESCOBALDI
HUMPERDINCK
LEONCAVALLO
LUTOSLAWSKI
MENDELSSOHN
MOUSSORGSKY
PIETERSZOON
RACHMANINOV
RHEINBERGER
SCHEIDEMANN
STOCKHAUSEN
TCHAIKOVSKY

12
DALLAPICCOLA
KHACHATURIAN
RACHMANINOFF
SHOSTAKOVICH
TSCHAIKOVSKY

Constellations

3	COLUMBA
ARA	LACERTA
LEO	PEGASUS
	PERSEUS
4	PHOENIX
APUS	SAGITTA
CRUX	SCORPIO
GRUS	SERPENS
LYNX	SEXTANS
LYRA	
PAVO	**8**
VELA	AQUARIUS
	CIRCINUS
5	EQUULEUS
ARIES	ERIDANUS
CETUS	HERCULES
DRACO	LEO MINOR
HYDRA	SCULPTOR
INDUS	
LEPUS	**9**
LIBRA	ANDROMEDA
LUPUS	ARGO NAVIS
MENSA	CENTAURUS
MUSCA	DELPHINUS
NORMA	MONOCEROS
ORION	OPHIUCHUS
PYXIS	RETICULUM
VIRGO	URSA MAJOR
	URSA MINOR
6	VULPECULA
ANTLIA	
AQUILA	**10**
AURIGA	CANIS MAJOR
BOOTES	CANIS MINOR
CAELUM	CASSIOPEIA
CANCER	CHAMAELEON
CARINA	HOROLOGIUM
CORVUS	TRIANGULUM
CRATER	
CYGNUS	**11**
DORADO	CAPRICORNUS
FORNAX	SAGITTARIUS
GEMINI	TELESCOPIUM
HYDRUS	
OCTANS	**12**
PICTOR	CAMELOPARDUS
PISCES	MICROSCOPIUM
PUPPIS	
SCUTUM	**13**
TAURUS	CANES VENATICI
TUCANA	COMA BERENICES
VOLANS	
	14
7	CAMELOPARDALIS
CEPHEUS	CORONA AUSTRINA
	CORONA BOREALIS

15
CORONA AUSTRALIS
PISCIS AUSTRINUS

18
TRIANGULUM AUSTRALE

Constellations, English names

3
CUP
FLY
NET
RAM

4
ARGO
BEAR
BULL
CRAB
CROW
DOVE
FOAL
HARE
KEEL
LION
LYNX
LYRE
POOP
RULE
SAIL
SWAN
WOLF

5
ALTAR
ARROW
CLOCK
CRANE
CROSS
EAGLE
LEVEL
ORION
SAILS
TABLE
TWINS
WHALE

6
ARCHER
CHISEL
DRAGON
FISHES
HUNTER
INDIAN
LIZARD
OCTANT
PLOUGH
SCALES
SHIELD
SQUARE
TOUCAN
VIRGIN

7
AIR-PUMP
BALANCE
CENTAUR
CEPHEUS
DOLPHIN
FURNACE
GIRAFFE
PEACOCK
PEGASUS
PERSEUS
PHOENIX
SEA-GOAT
SERPENT
SEXTANT
UNICORN

8
CHAMPION
GOLDFISH
HERCULES
HERDSMAN
SCORPION
SCULPTOR
TRIANGLE
WATERMAN

9
ANDROMEDA
CHAMELEON
GREAT BEAR
LESSER DOG
LITTLE FOX
SWORDFISH
TELESCOPE

10
CASSIOPEIA
CHARIOTEER
FLYING FISH
GREATER DOG
LESSER LION
LITTLE BEAR
MICROSCOPE
WATER-SNAKE

11
GRAVING TOOL
HUNTING DOGS
LITTLE HORSE
LITTLE SNAKE
WATER-BEARER

12
SOUTHERN FISH

13
BERENICE'S HAIR
NORTHERN CROSS
NORTHERN CROWN
PAINTER'S EASEL
RIVER ERIDANUS
SERPENT-HOLDER
SOUTHERN CROSS
SOUTHERN CROWN

14
BIRD-OF-PARADISE

15
MARINER'S COMPASS
PAIR OF COMPASSES

16
SOUTHERN TRIANGLE

Counties and Regions of the British Isles

English Counties from January 1974

4
AVON
KENT

5
DEVON
ESSEX
SALOP

6
DORSET
DURHAM
SURREY

7
CUMBRIA
NORFOLK
SUFFOLK

8
CHESHIRE
CORNWALL
SOMERSET

9
BERKSHIRE
CLEVELAND
HAMPSHIRE
WILTSHIRE

10
DERBYSHIRE
EAST SUSSEX
HUMBERSIDE
LANCASHIRE
MERSEYSIDE
WEST SUSSEX

11
ISLE OF WIGHT
OXFORDSHIRE
TYNE AND WEAR

12
BEDFORDSHIRE
LINCOLNSHIRE
WARWICKSHIRE
WEST MIDLANDS

13
GREATER LONDON
HERTFORDSHIRE
STAFFORDSHIRE
WEST YORKSHIRE

14
CAMBRIDGESHIRE
LEICESTERSHIRE
NORTHUMBERLAND
NORTH YORKSHIRE
SOUTH YORKSHIRE

15
BUCKINGHAMSHIRE
GLOUCESTERSHIRE
NOTTINGHAMSHIRE

16
NORTHAMPTONSHIRE

17
GREATER MANCHESTER

20
HEREFORD AND WORCESTER

Welsh Counties from January 1974

5
CLWYD
DYFED
GWENT
POWYS

7
GWYNEDD

12
MID GLAMORGAN

13
WEST GLAMORGAN

14
SOUTH GLAMORGAN

Scottish Regions from January 1974

4
FIFE

6
ORKNEY

7
BORDERS
CENTRAL
LOTHIAN
TAYSIDE

8
GRAMPIAN
SHETLAND

9
HIGHLANDS

11
STRATHCLYDE

12
WESTERN ISLES

19
DUMFRIES AND GALLOWAY

Counties of England before 1974

4 KENT	**14** CAMBRIDGESHIRE LEICESTERSHIRE NORTHUMBERLAND WORCESTERSHIRE
5 DEVON ESSEX	
6 DORSET DURHAM LONDON SURREY SUSSEX	**15** BUCKINGHAMSHIRE GLOUCESTERSHIRE HUNTINGDONSHIRE NOTTINGHAMSHIRE
7 NORFOLK RUTLAND SUFFOLK	**16** NORTHAMPTONSHIRE

8
CHESHIRE
CORNWALL
SOMERSET

9
BERKSHIRE
HAMPSHIRE
MIDDLESEX
WILTSHIRE
YORKSHIRE

10
CUMBERLAND
DERBYSHIRE
DEVONSHIRE
LANCASHIRE
SHROPSHIRE

11
DORSETSHIRE
OXFORDSHIRE
WESTMORLAND

12
BEDFORDSHIRE
LINCOLNSHIRE
RUTLANDSHIRE
WARWICKSHIRE

13
HEREFORDSHIRE
HERTFORDSHIRE
STAFFORDSHIRE

Counties of Scotland before 1974

3 AYR	**15** ROSS AND CROMARTY

4
BUTE
FIFE

5
ANGUS
BANFF
MORAY
NAIRN
PERTH

6
ARGYLL
LANARK
ORKNEY

7
BERWICK
KINROSS
PEEBLES
RENFREW
SELKIRK
WIGTOWN

8
ABERDEEN
DUMFRIES
ROXBURGH
SHETLAND
STIRLING

9
CAITHNESS
DUNBARTON
INVERNESS

10
KINCARDINE
MIDLOTHIAN
SUTHERLAND

11
CLACKMANNAN
EAST LOTHIAN
WEST LOTHIAN

13
KIRKCUDBRIGHT

Counties of Wales and Monmouth before 1974

6
BRECON

8
ANGLESEY
MONMOUTH

10
FLINTSHIRE

11
RADNORSHIRE

12
DENBIGHSHIRE

13
CARDIGANSHIRE
MONMOUTHSHIRE
PEMBROKESHIRE

14
BRECKNOCKSHIRE
GLAMORGANSHIRE
MERIONETHSHIRE

15
CAERNARVONSHIRE
CARMARTHENSHIRE
MONTGOMERYSHIRE

Counties of Northern Ireland

4
DOWN

6
ANTRIM
ARMAGH
TYRONE

9
FERMANAGH

11
LONDONDERRY

Counties of the Irish Republic

4
CORK
LEIX
MAYO

5
CAVAN
CLARE
KERRY
LOUTH
MEATH
SLIGO

6
CARLOW
DUBLIN
GALWAY
OFFALY

7
DONEGAL
KILDARE
LEITRIM
WEXFORD
WICKLOW

8
KILKENNY
LAOGHIS
LIMERICK
LONGFORD
MONAGHAN

9
ROSCOMMON
TIPPERARY
WATERFORD
WESTMEATH

Countries of Europe

4
EIRE
USSR

5
ITALY
MALTA
SPAIN
WALES

6
CYPRUS
FRANCE
GREECE
MONACO
NORWAY
POLAND
RUSSIA
SWEDEN
TURKEY

7
ALBANIA
ANDORRA
AUSTRIA
BELGIUM
DENMARK
ENGLAND
FINLAND
GERMANY
HUNGARY
ICELAND
IRELAND
ROMANIA
RUMANIA

8
BULGARIA
PORTUGAL
SCOTLAND

9
GIBRALTAR
LUXEMBURG
SAN MARINO

10
LUXEMBOURG
YUGOSLAVIA

11
NETHERLANDS
SWITZERLAND

13
LIECHTENSTEIN
UNITED KINGDOM

14
CZECHOSLOVAKIA

15
NORTHERN IRELAND

16
VATICAN CITY STATE

24
GERMAN DEMOCRATIC REPUBLIC

31
UNION OF SOVIET SOCIALIST REPUBLICS

Countries of Asia

4
IRAK
IRAN
IRAQ
LAOS
OMAN
USSR

5
BURMA
CHINA
INDIA
JAPAN
KOREA
MACAO
MACAU
NEPAL
QATAR
SYRIA
†TIMOR
YEMEN

6
BHUTAN
BRUNEI
ISRAEL
JORDAN
KUWAIT
†SIKKIM
TAIWAN
TURKEY

7
BAHRAIN
FORMOSA
LEBANON
VIETNAM

8
CAMBODIA
HONG KONG
MALAYSIA
MALDIVES
MONGOLIA
PAKISTAN
SRI LANKA
THAILAND

9
†EAST TIMOR
INDONESIA
SINGAPORE

10
BANGLADESH

NORTH KOREA
SOUTH KOREA
SOUTH YEMEN

11
AFGHANISTAN
PHILIPPINES
SAUDI ARABIA

12
†EASTERN TIMOR
†NORTH VIETNAM
†SOUTH VIETNAM

13
SOUTHERN YEMEN

18
UNITED ARAB EMIRATES

31
UNION OF SOVIET SOCIALIST REPUBLICS

†former country

Countries of Africa

4
CHAD
MALI
TOGO

5
BENIN
CONGO
EGYPT
GABON
GHANA
KENYA
LIBYA
NIGER
SUDAN
ZAIRE

6
ANGOLA
GAMBIA
GUINEA
MALAWI
RWANDA
UGANDA
ZAMBIA

7
ALGERIA
BURUNDI
*DAHOMEY
LESOTHO
LIBERIA
MOROCCO
NAMIBIA
NIGERIA
REUNION
SENEGAL
SOMALIA
TUNISIA

8
BOTSWANA
CAMEROON
CAMEROUN
ETHIOPIA
RHODESIA
ST HELENA
TANZANIA
TRANSKEI

9
*ABYSSINIA
MAURITIUS
SWAZILAND

10
IVORY COAST
MADAGASCAR
MAURITANIA
MOZAMBIQUE
SEYCHELLES
UPPER VOLTA

11
SAINT HELENA
SIERRA LEONE
SOUTH AFRICA

12
GUINEA BISSAU

13
AFARS AND ISSAS
COMORO ISLANDS

15
SOUTH WEST AFRICA

16
CAPE VERDE ISLANDS
EQUATORIAL GUINEA

18
SAO TOME AND PRINCIPE

20
CENTRAL AFRICAN EMPIRE

22
AFARS AND ISSAS TERRITORY
*CENTRAL AFRICAN REPUBLIC

* former name

58 · Countries (contd)

Countries of North and Central America

4 CUBA	**17** ANTIGUA AND BARBUDA DOMINICAN REPUBLIC TRINIDAD AND TOBAGO
5 HAITI	
	19 NETHERLANDS ANTILLES
6 BELIZE CANADA MEXICO PANAMA	ST PIERRE AND MIQUELON **20** BRITISH VIRGIN ISLANDS ST KITTS-NEVIS-ANGUILLA
7 ANTIGUA BAHAMAS BERMUDA GRENADA JAMAICA ST LUCIA	**21** TURKS AND CAICOS ISLANDS UNITED STATES OF AMERICA
8 ANGUILLA BARBADOS DOMINICA HONDURAS TRINIDAD	**22** SAINT PIERRE AND MIQUELON **23** SAINT KITTS-NEVIS-ANGUILLA

9
COSTA RICA
GREENLAND
GUATEMALA
NICARAGUA
ST VINCENT

10
EL SALVADOR
GUADELOUPE
MARTINIQUE
MONTSERRAT
PUERTO RICO
SAINT LUCIA

12
ST KITTS-NEVIS
SAINT VINCENT
UNITED STATES

13
CAYMAN ISLANDS

15
PANAMA CANAL ZONE
SAINT KITTS-NEVIS
US VIRGIN ISLANDS

Countries of South America

4
PERU

5
CHILE

6
BRAZIL
GUYANA
GUYANE

7
BOLIVIA
ECUADOR
SURINAM
URUGUAY

8
COLOMBIA
PARAGUAY

9
ARGENTINA
VENEZUELA

12
FRENCH GUIANA

15
FALKLAND ISLANDS

Countries of Australasia and the Pacific Islands

4
FIJI
GUAM

5
NAURU
SAMOA
TONGA

6
TUVALU

9
AUSTRALIA

10
NEW ZEALAND

11
NEW HEBRIDES

12
NEW CALEDONIA
WESTERN SAMOA

13
AMERICAN SAMOA

14
GILBERT ISLANDS
PAPUA NEW GUINEA
SOLOMON ISLANDS

15
FRENCH POLYNESIA

16
NORTHERN MARIANAS

28
PACIFIC ISLANDS TRUST TERRITORY

Cricket

3
BAT
BYE
CAP
CUT
HIT
LBW
LEG
LOB
OUT
RUN
SIX
TIE
TON

4
BAIL
BALL
BOWL
CLUB
DRAG
DRAW
DROP
DUCK
FOUR
HOOK
NETS
OVER
PADS
PULL
SEAM
SHOT
SLIP
SPIN
TEAM
TOSS
WIDE

5
ASHES
BAILS
BOSIE
CATCH
COVER
EXTRA
GUARD
GULLY
MATCH
MID-ON
PITCH
POINT
RUN-UP
SCORE
SKIER
SLIPS
SNICK
SPOON
STAND
STUMP
SWING
THROW
TOTAL

6
ALL-OUT
APPEAL
BEAMER
BOWLED
BOWLER
BUMPER
CAUGHT
CREASE
ELEVEN
GLOVES
GOOGLY
HITTER
KICKER
LEG-BYE
LONG-ON
MID-OFF
NO BALL
NOT OUT
OPENER
PICK-UP
RABBIT
ROLLER
RUNNER
SCORER
SEAMER
SINGLE
SIX-HIT
SQUARE
STROKE
STUMPS
SWERVE
UMPIRE
WHITES
WICKET
WILLOW
WISDEN
YORKER

7
BATSMAN
BATTING
BOUNCER
BOWLING
CAPTAIN
CENTURY
COW-SHOT
DECLARE

FIELDER
FLY SLIP
HUNDRED
INNINGS
LATE CUT
LEG-SIDE
LONG HOP
LONG-LEG
LONG-OFF
NEW BALL
ON-DRIVE
OVERARM
RETIRED
RUNNING
SCORING
SHOOTER
SPINNER
STRIKER
STUMPED
STUMPER
SWEATER
THROW-IN
TOP-SPIN

8
BACK-LIFT
BODY LINE
BOUNDARY
CHINAMAN
FULL TOSS
HAT TRICK
HOW'S THAT?
LEG-BREAK
LONG STOP
MISFIELD
OFF-BREAK
OFF-DRIVE
ONE SHORT
OUTFIELD
OVER RATE
PAVILION
ROUND-ARM
SHORT-LEG
SHORT RUN
STUMPING
THE ASHES
THIRD MAN
UMPIRING
UNDERARM

9
BLOCK-HOLE
BREAK-BACK
CRICKETER
DEEP FIELD
FIELDSMAN
FIRST SLIP
GAUNTLETS

HIT WICKET
INSWINGER
LEG CUTTER
LEG GLANCE
MID-WICKET
OFF-CUTTER
OVERTHROW
SCOREBOOK
SQUARE CUT
SQUARE LEG
TAIL-ENDER
TELEGRAPH
TEST MATCH
THIRD SLIP
TRIAL GAME

10
BACK STROKE
COVER-DRIVE
COVER-POINT
CRICKET-BAT
DONKEY DROP
EXTRA COVER
FOURTH SLIP
GROUNDSMAN
HALF-VOLLEY
LEG-SPINNER
LONG-HANDLE
NON-STRIKER
OFF-SPINNER
OUTSWINGER
SCOREBOARD
SECOND SLIP
SILLY MID-ON
SILLY POINT
SLOW BOWLER
SPIN BOWLER
SUBSTITUTE
TRIAL MATCH
TWELFTH MAN

11
AWAY SWINGER
CLOSE OF PLAY
COUNTY MATCH
CRICKET-BALL
DAISY-CUTTER
DECK-CRICKET
DECLARATION
GILLETTE CUP
HALF-CENTURY
NET PRACTICE
PARTNERSHIP
RETIRED HURT
SHORT HANDLE
SIGHT SCREEN
SILLY MID-OFF
SLOW BOWLING
SQUARE COVER

STONEWALLER
TEA INTERVAL
VICE-CAPTAIN

12
CHAMPIONSHIP
CRICKET MATCH
DEEP THIRD MAN
FALL OF WICKET
GOOGLY BOWLER
HIT BALL TWICE
RETURN CREASE
SINGLE WICKET
STICKY WICKET
STONEWALLING
WICKETKEEPER

13
BACKWARD POINT
BUTTERFINGERS
CRICKET GROUND
CRICKET STUMPS
DEEP SQUARE LEG
DOUBLE CENTURY
LUNCH INTERVAL
OPENING BOWLER
OVER THE WICKET
POPPING-CREASE
STRAIGHT DRIVE
WICKETKEEPING

14
DEEP EXTRA COVER
HANDLED THE BALL
OPENING BATSMAN
ROUND THE WICKET
SHORT SQUARE LEG

15
HANDLING THE BALL
HIT THE BALL TWICE
SQUARE LEG UMPIRE

Dances

3
BOB
HEY
HOP
JIG
PAS

4
BALL
FRUG
HULA
JIVE
JOTA
JUBA
KOLO
REEL
STEP

5
BOREE
BRAWL
CONGA
FLING
GALOP
GIGUE
GOPAK
LASSU
LOURE
MAMBO
PAVAN
PAVEN
PAVIN
POLKA
RUMBA
SAMBA
TANGO
TWIST
WALTZ

6
BOLERO
BOSTON
BOUREE
BRANLE
CANCAN
CHACHA
CHASSE
COUPEE
FADING
LAVOLT
MAXIXE
MINUET
MORISK
MORRIS
PAVANE
RHUMBA

VALETA
VELETA

7
BEGUINE
BOURREE
BRANSLE
CANTICO
CARIOCA
CORANTO
COURANT
CSARDAS
FARUCCA
FORLANA
FOXTROT
FURLANA
GAVOTTE
HOEDOWN
LANCERS
LANDLER
LAVOLTA
MAZURKA
MORESCO
MORISCO
MORRICE
ONESTEP
PAS SEUL
ROUNDEL
SHUFFLE
TRENISE
TWOSTEP
ZIGANKA

8
CAKEWALK
CANTICOY
CHACONNE
COTILLON
COURANTE
FAN DANCE
FANDANGO
GALLIARD
HABANERA
HIGH LIFE
HORNPIPE
HULA HULA
KANTIKOY
RIGADOON
SARABAND
TAMBURIN
TAP DANCE
TSIGANKA

9
ALLEMANDE
ARABESQUE
BARN DANCE
BOSSA NOVA
BREAKDOWN

CHA-CHA-CHA
CLOG DANCE
COTILLION
ECOSSAISE
FOLKDANCE
GALLOPADE
IRISH REEL
JITTERBUG
KRAKOWIAK
PAS-DE-DEUX
PASODOBLE
PAUL JONES
PIROUETTE
POLONAISE
POUSSETTE
QUADRILLE
QUICKSTEP
RAIN DANCE
ROCK 'N' ROLL
ROUNDELAY
STEPDANCE
TAMBOURIN
TRIPUDIUM
ZAPATEADO

10
CHARLESTON
PASSAMEZZO
ROUND DANCE
SALTARELLO
SKIRT DANCE
SNAKE DANCE
STRATHSPEY
SWORD DANCE
TARANTELLA
TURKEY TROT

11
CONTRA DANCE
CONTRA DANSE
CONTRE DANCE
CONTRE DANSE
CRACOVIENNE
MORRIS DANCE
PAS REDOUBLE
PASSACAGLIA
ROCK AND ROLL
SCHOTTISCHE
SQUARE DANCE
VARSOVIENNE

12
COUNTRY DANCE
HIGHLAND REEL
PASSEMEASURE
PASSYMEASURE
VIRGINIA REEL

13
HIGHLAND FLING

Dogs

3
CUR
LYM
POM
PUG
PUP
YAP

4
CHOW
LIME
LYAM
LYME
MINX
PEKE
RACH
SKYE
TIKE
TYKE

5
BITCH
BOXER
BRACH
CAIRN
CORGI
DHOLE
DINGO
HOUND
HUSKY
KERRY
LAIKA
PUPPY
RACHE
RATCH
SPITZ
WHELP

6
BANDOG
BARBET
BASSET
BEAGLE
BORZOI
BRIARD
COCKER
COLLIE
JOWLER
KELPIE
KENNET
LAPDOG
PARIAH
POODLE
PUGDOG
RANGER
RATTER

SALUKI
SETTER
SHELTY
SHOUGH
TALBOT
TECKEL
YAPPER

7
BULLDOG
BULL-PUP
CLUMBER
DEER-DOG
GRIFFON
HARRIER
LION-DOG
LURCHER
MASTIFF
MONGREL
POINTER
SAMOYED
SAPLING
SHELTIE
SHIH TZU
SPANIEL
STARTER
TARRIER
TERRIER
TUMBLER
VOLPINO
WHIPPET
WILD-DOG
WOLF-DOG
YAPSTER

8
ABERDEEN
AIREDALE
ALSATIAN
BLENHEIM
CHOW-CHOW
COACH-DOG
DEMI-WOLF
ELKHOUND
FOXHOUND
HOUSEDOG
KEESHOND
LABRADOR
LONGTAIL
MALEMUTE
PAPILLON
PEKINESE
SEALYHAM
SHEEPDOG
SPRINGER
TURNSPIT
WATCHDOG
WATER-DOG

9
BADGER-DOG
BOARHOUND
BUCKHOUND
CAIRNGORM
CHIHUAHUA
DACHSHUND
DALMATIAN
DEERHOUND
ESKIMO DOG
GAZEHOUND
GREAT DANE
GREYHOUND
KERRY BLUE
LIMEHOUND
LYAMHOUND
PEKINGESE
POLICE-DOG
POODLE-DOG
RETRIEVER
ST BERNARD
SCHNAUZER
STAGHOUND
TOY POODLE
WOLF-HOUND

10
BEDLINGTON
BLOODHOUND
FOX-TERRIER
MALTESE DOG
OTTER-HOUND
POMERANIAN
SCHIPPERKE
TOY SPANIEL
TOY TERRIER

11
AFGHAN HOUND
BASSET-HOUND
BLACK-AND-TAN
BULL-TERRIER
CARRIAGE-DOG
IRISH SETTER
JACK RUSSELL
LABRADOR DOG
LAND-SPANIEL
SIBERIAN DOG
SKYE TERRIER

12
CAIRN TERRIER
DALMATIAN DOG
DANDY DINMONT
IRISH TERRIER
NEWFOUNDLAND
SAINT BERNARD
SHEPHERD'S DOG
WATER-SPANIEL
WELSH TERRIER

13
AFFENPINSCHER
BORDER TERRIER
BOSTON TERRIER
COCKER SPANIEL
DANDIE DINMONT
ENGLISH SETTER
ST BERNARD'S DOG
SCOTCH TERRIER
SUSSEX SPANIEL

14
CAPE HUNTING DOG
CLUMBER SPANIEL
ENGLISH BULLDOG
IRISH WOLFHOUND

15
ABERDEEN TERRIER
AIREDALE TERRIER
BLENHEIM SPANIEL
BRUSSELS GRIFFON
LABRADOR TERRIER
MINIATURE POODLE
PYRENEAN MASTIFF
SEALYHAM TERRIER

Drinks

3
ALE
BUB
CUP
FIZ
GIN
MUM
NOG
OXO
RUM
RYE
TEA

4
ASTI
BEER
BOCK
BOLS
COKE
COLA
FIZZ
FLIP
GROG
HOCK
KAVA
LIME
MARC
MATE
MEAD
MILD
MILK
MOET
MUMM
MUST
NIPA
OUZO
PORT
PURL
RACK
RAKI
SACK
SAKE
SAKI
SOUR
STUM
TENT
WINE
WORT

5
AIRAN
AYRAN
BLAND
BOHEA
BOOZE
BROTH

CHICA
CIDER
COCOA
CREAM
HOOCH
HYSON
IRISH
JULEP
LAGER
LASSI
MACON
MEATH
MEDOC
MOCHA
NANTZ
NEGUS
NOYAU
OOPAK
PEKOE
PERRY
PLONK
POLLY
PUNCH
SHRUB
SLING
SMASH
SPLIT
STOUT
TAFIA
TODDY
TOKAY
TONIC
VICHY
VODKA

6
ALEGAR
ARRACK
BITTER
BOVRIL
BRANDY
BUBBLY
CANARY
CASSIS
CAUDLE
CHICHA
CLARET
COFFEE
COGNAC
CRUSTA,
EGGNOG
GENEVA
GIMLET
GRAVES
KIRSCH
KUMISS
KUMMEL
LIQUOR
LISBON

MALAGA
MASTIC
MEATHE
MICKEY
MUSCAT
NECTAR
OLD TOM
OOLONG
OOPACK
OULONG
PIMENT
PONTAC
PORTER
POSSET
POTEEN
PTISAN
PULQUE
SAUMUR
SCOTCH
SHANDY
SHERRY
SORBET
SPIRIT
SQUASH
STINGO
SWIPES
TISANE
WHISKY
YAOURT
YOGURT

7
ABSINTH
ALCOHOL
ALE-BREE
ALICANT
ANISEED
BEEF TEA
BITTERS
BOURBON
CATAWBA
CHABLIS
CHIANTI
CHICORY
COBBLER
CORDIAL
CRUSTAE
CURACAO
CURACOA
EGG FLIP
GIN FIZZ
HERB TEA
ICED TEA
JAMAICA
KOUMISS
LIMEADE
LIQUEUR
LOW WINE

MACE-ALE
MADEIRA
MALMSEY
MARSALA
MARTINI
MOSELLE
ORVIETO
PALE ALE
PILSNER
RATAFIA
RED WINE
RETSINA
RHENISH
SANGRIA
SHERBET
SIDECAR
SLOE GIN
SPIRITS
STENGAH
STINGER
SWIZZLE
TEQUILA
TWANKAY
VIN ROSE
WASSAIL
WHISKEY
YOGHURT

8
ABSINTHE
ADVOCAAT
ALEBERRY
AMBROSIA
ANISETTE
APERITIF
ARMAGNAC
BLUE RUIN
BOCK BEER
BORDEAUX
BURGUNDY
CAFE NOIR
CALVADOS
CHARNECO
CHINA TEA
CIDER-AND
CIDER CUP
CIDERKIN
COCKTAIL
DAIQUIRI
DOGSNOSE
DRAMBUIE
EAU-DE-VIE
FLORENCE
FRUIT CUP
GIN AND IT
GIN SLING
GREEN TEA
GUINNESS

HERB BEER	HERMITAGE	BARLEY BROTH	**15**
HIGHBALL	HIPPOCRAS	BARLEY WATER	LACHRYMA CHRISTI
HOLLANDS	HOCKAMORE	BENEDICTINE	LIEBFRAUENMILCH
HYDROMEL	INDIAN TEA	BLACK COFFEE	
ICE-WATER	LAGER BEER	BRISTOL MILK	
LEMONADE	LAMB'S WOOL	CALCAVELLOS	
MUSCADEL	LIME JUICE	COLD-WITHOUT	
MUSCATEL ·	LIME PUNCH	IRISH COFFEE	
NEAR-BEER	MANHATTAN	IRISH WHISKY	
NIGHTCAP	METHEGLIN	LEMON-SQUASH	
PEATREEK	MILK PUNCH	LITHIA WATER	
RED BIDDY	MILK SHAKE	MALT EXTRACT	
RESINATA	MINT JULEP	MOUNTAIN DEW	
RIESLING	MULLED ALE	NIERSTEINER	
ROOT-BEER	MUSCADINE	ORANGE-JUICE	
RUBY PORT	ORANGEADE	PEACH-BRANDY	
RUM PUNCH	RHINE WINE	SAINT JULIEN	
RUM-SHRUB	RYE WHISKY	TOM-AND-JERRY	
SANGAREE	SLIVOVICA	WHISKY-PUNCH	
SAUTERNE	SLIVOVITZ	WHISKY-TODDY	
SCHIEDAM	SMALL BEER	WHITE COFFEE	
SCHNAPPS	SODA-WATER		
SILLABUB	TARRAGONA	**12**	
SKIM MILK	VIN DU PAYS	BRANDY PAWNEE	
SLIVOVIC	WHITE WINE	BRISTOL CREAM	
SMALL-ALE	YERBA MATE	CAFE ESPRESSO	
SOUCHONG		CHERRY-BRANDY	
SOUR MILK	**10**	GRAND MARNIER	
SYLLABUB	BUTTERMILK	GUNPOWDER TEA	
VERJUICE	CAFE-AU-LAIT	ICE-CREAM-SODA	
VERMOUTH	CAFE FILTRE	IRISH WHISKEY	
VIN BLANC	CALCAVELLA	KIRSCHWASSER	
WISHWASH	CHAMBERTIN	MARCOBRUNNER	
YOGHOURT	CHARTREUSE	MINERAL WATER	
	CONSTANTIA	OLDFASHIONED	
9	FRUIT JUICE	PILSENER BEER	
ANGOSTURA	GINGER BEER	SAINT EMILION	
APPETISER	GINGER WINE	SAINT RAPHAEL	
APPETIZER	GRAPE-JUICE	SARSAPARILLA	
APPLEJACK	HOLLAND GIN	SCOTCH WHISKY	
AQUA VITAE	ICED COFFEE	VIN ORDINAIRE	
BIRCH WINE	JAMAICA RUM		
BURNT SACK	LEMON JUICE	**13**	
CAPPUCINO	MALTED MILK	CHATEAU-LAFITE	
CEYLON TEA	MANZANILLA	COBBLER'S PUNCH	
CHAMPAGNE	MARASCHINO	CREME-DE-MENTHE	
CHOCOLATE	MICKEY FINN	GINGER-CORDIAL	
CLARET CUP	MUNICH BEER	FALERNIAN WINE	
COINTREAU	RUMFUSTIAN	LIEBFRAUMILCH	
FALERNIAN	SACK POSSET	LIQUEUR BRANDY	
FIREWATER	SHANDY GAFF	LIQUEUR WHISKY	
GINGERADE	SPRUCE BEER	MOET-ET-CHANDON	
GINGER ALE	TWANKAY TEA	SHERRY COBBLER	
GINGER POP	VICHY WATER	TURKISH COFFEE	
GLENLIVET			
GRENADINE	**11**	**14**	
GUNPOWDER	AGUARDIENTA	CHATEAU-MARGAUX	
HERBAL TEA	AGUARDIENTE	ELDERBERRY WINE	
HERB WATER	AMONTILLADO	PINEAPPLE-JUICE	

Ecclesiastical and Religious Terms

3	POME	DJINN	SUFIC	DEACON
ABA	POPE	DRUID	SUNNA	DECANI
ALB	RAMA	DULIA	SUNNI	DEVOUT
GOD	RITE	DUOMO	TERCE	DHARMA
HEL	ROOD	ELDER	TORAH	DIVINE
LAY	SARK	EPHOD	TRACT	DJINNI
NUN	SECT	FAITH	UNIAT	DOCETE
PEW	SEXT	FAKIR	VEDIC	DONARY
PIE	SHI'A	FRIAR	VICAR	DOSSAL
SEE	SHUL	GENIE	VIGIL	DOSSEL
SIN	SIKH	GLORY	YEZDI	DUNKER
VOW	SIVA	GODLY		EASTER
	SOFI	GRAIL	**6**	ELOHIM
4	SOUL	HADES	ABBACY	ESSENE
ABBA	SUFI	HADJI	ABBESS	FERIAL
ABBE	SURA	HAJJI	ADVENT	FETISH
ALMS	TEXT	HEJRA	ADYTUM	FLAMEN
AMIS	VEDA	HIJRA	AGADAH	FRIARY
APSE	ZEND	HINDU	ALMERY	FRIEND
BAAL		IHRAM	ANOINT	GEMARA
BABI	**5**	IMAGE	ANTHEM	GENTOO
BIER	ABBEY	IMAUM	AUMBRY	GHEBER
CELL	ABBOT	ISLAM	AVESTA	GLORIA
COPE	AISLE	JAINA	AWMRIE	GOPURA
CULT	ALLAH	JINNI	BABISM	GOSPEL
CURE	ALTAR	KALPA	BABIST	GRADIN
DEAN	AMBRY	KORAN	BANNER	GUEBER
EBOR	AMICE	LAUDS	BEADLE	GUEBRE
EDEN	ANGEL	LIMBO	BELIAL	HADITH
FANE	ARIAN	LOGOS	BEGUIN	HALLOW
FAST	ATONE	MANSE	BELIEF	HEAVEN
FONT	AWMRY	MITRE	BETHEL	HEGIRA
HADJ	BABEE	MORSE	BISHOP	HEJIRA
HAJJ	BANNS	NONES	BRAHMA	HERESY
HELL	BIBLE	OBIIT	BUDDHA	HERMIT
HOLI	BIGOT	PAGAN	BURIAL	HOMILY
HOLY	BONZE	PANIM	CANTOR	HOUSEL
HOST	BREVE	PAPAL	CAO DAI	HYMNAL
HYMN	CALPA	PARSI	CENSER	INTONE
IDOL	CANON	PASCH	CHAPEL	ISODIA
IMAM	CAROL	PATEN	CHERUB	JAHVEH
JAIN	CELLA	PIETA	CHIMER	JESUIT
JINN	CERGE	PIETY	CHRISM	JINNEE
JOSS	CHANT	PIOUS	CHRIST	JOSSER
JUJU	CHOIR	PRIOR	CHURCH	KEBLAH
LAIC	CREDO	PSALM	CIERGE	KIBLAH
LAMA	CREED	QURAN	CLERGY	KOSHER
LENT	CROSS	RABBI	CLERIC	K'THIBH
MASS	CRUET	SAINT	CORBAN	LAICAL
MONK	DEIFY	SAKTA	CULDEE	LAMMAS
NAVE	DEISM	SAKTI	CULTIC	LATRIA
OBIT	DEIST	SEKOS	CULTUS	LAVABO
PACE	DEITY	SHEMA	CURACY	LAYMAN
PALL	DEMON	SHIAH	CURATE	LECTOR
PAPA	DEVIL	SIVAN	DATARY	LEGATE

LEVITE	SHAMAN
LITANY	SHIITE
MAHOUN	SHRINE
MARTYR	SHRIVE
MATINS	SINFUL
MIHRAB	SINNER
MISHNA	SOFISM
MISSAL	SPIRIT
MORMON	SUFISM
MOSLEM	SUNDAY
MOSQUE	SUTTEE
MULLAH	TALMUD
MUSLIM	TAOISM
MYSTIC	TE DEUM
NOVICE	TEMPLE
NUNCIO	THEISM
OBITAL	THEIST
OBLATE	THORAH
ORDAIN	TOPHET
ORDERS	TUNKER
OSIRIS	UNIATE
PAINIM	VEDIST
PALMER	VERGER
PAPACY	VESTRY
PAPISH	VISHNU
PAPISM	WAHABI
PAPIST	YEZIDI
PARISH	ZENDIC
PARSEE	
PARSON	**7**
PASTOR	AARONIC
PAYNIM	ABADDON
POPERY	ACOLYTE
PRAYER	ACOLYTH
PREACH	ADAMITE
PRIEST	ADHARMA
PRIMUS	ALCORAN
PROPER	ALFAQUI
PULPIT	ALKORAN
PURANA	AMPULLA
QUAKER	ANCRESS
RECTOR	ANGELIC
REPENT	ANGELUS
RITUAL	ANIMISM
ROCHET	ANIMIST
ROSARY	APOSTLE
RUBRIC	ATHEISM
SABIAN	ATHEIST
SACCOS	BABIISM
SACRED	BAPTISE
SAKKOS	BAPTISM
SANTON	BAPTIST
SCHISM	BAPTIZE
SEDILE	BEATIFY
SERAPH	BEGHARD
SERMON	BEGUINE
SHAKER	BIGOTED
SHAKTI	BIGOTRY

BIRETTA
BRAHMAN
BRAHMIN
CALVARY
CANONIC
CANONRY
CASSOCK
CHALICE
CHANCEL
CHAPLET
CHAPTER
CHARITY
CHIMERE
CHRISOM
CHURCHY
CLUNIAC
COLLECT
CONFIRM
CONVENT
CONVERT
CREEDAL
DARSHAN
DATARIA
DEANERY
DECANAL
DEISTIC
DERVISH
DIOCESE
DIPTYCH
DISSENT
DOCETAE
DOULEIA
ELYSIUM
EPISTLE
ETERNAL
EVANGEL
EXEGETE
FACULTY
FASTING
FRONTAL
GALILEE
GEHENNA
GENEVAN
GENTILE
GLORIFY
GNOSTIC
GODDESS
GODHEAD
GODHOOD
GODLESS
GODLIKE
GRADINE
GRADUAL
GREMIAL
HAGGADA
HALACHA
HEATHEN
HELLISH

HERETIC
HEXAPLA
HOLY DAY
HOSANNA
HUMERAL
HUSSITE
IMAMATE
IMPIETY
IMPIOUS
INCENSE
INFERNO
INFIDEL
ISLAMIC
JAINISM
JEHOVAH
JUDAISE
JUDAISM
JUDAIST
JUDAIZE
KARAITE
LADY DAY
LAICISE
LAICIZE
LAMAISM
LAMAIST
LATERAN
LECTERN
LECTION
LITURGY
LOLLARD
LOW MASS
MADONNA
MAHATMA
MAHOUND
MANIPLE
MATTINS
MESSIAH
MID-LENT
MINSTER
MIRACLE
MISHNAH
MISHNIC
MISSION
MOSAISM
NARTHEX
NIRVANA
NOCTURN
NUNNERY
OBITUAL
ORATORY
ORDINAL
ORDINEE
ORTHROS
OUR LADY
PACE-EGG
PARITOR
PARSISM
PASCHAL

PAULINE
PENANCE
PESHITO
PIETISM
PILGRIM
PISCINA
PONTIFF
POPEDOM
PREBEND
PRELACY
PRELATE
PRESTER
PRIMACY
PROPHET
PSALTER
PURANIC
PURITAN
RABBONI
RAMADAN
REQUIEM
REREDOS
RETABLE
RETREAT
RIGVEDA
ROOD DAY
SABAISM
SABBATH
SACRING
SACRIST
SAINTED
SAINTLY
SANCTUM
SANCTUS
SANKHYA
SARACEN
SATANIC
SAVIOUR
SECTARY
SEDILIA
SERVICE
SHASTER
SHASTRA
SIKHISM
SIVAISM
SIVAITE
SOFIISM
SONNITE
SUNNITE
SYNODIC
TEMPTER
THURIFY
TRINITY
TUNICLE
UNCTION
VATICAN
VEDANTA
VESPERS
VULGATE

WAHABEE
WHITSUN
WORSHIP
YEZIDEE
ZEZIDEE

8
ABLUTION
ACELDAMA
ACOEMETI
ADVOWSON
AGNOSTIC
AGNUS DEI
ALLELUIA
ALMIGHTY
ALMS-DEED
ALMS-DISH
ALTARAGE
ANATHEMA
ANCHORET
ANGLICAN
ANOINTED
ANTIPHON
ANTI-POPE
APOLLYON
APOSTASY
APOSTATE
ARIANISM
ARMINIAN
AVE MARIA
BABEEISM
BEATIFIC
BELIEVER
BENEFICE
BENITIER
BIBLICAL
BREVIARY
BUDDHISM
BUDDHIST
CANONESS
CANONISE
CANONIST
CANONIZE
CANON LAW
CARDINAL
CATHOLIC
CEREMENT
CEREMONY
DALMATIC
DEACONRY
DEVOTION
DIACONAL
DIES IRAE
DIOCESAN
DISCIPLE
DIVINITY
DOCETISM
DOCETIST

DONATIST
DOXOLOGY
DRUIDISM
EBIONITE
EPISTLER
ERASTIAN
ETERNITY
EUSEBIAN
EVENSONG
EXEGESIS
EXEGETIC
FAITHFUL
FAMILISM
FAMILIST
FERETORY
FRONTLET
GENEVESE
GLASSITE
GOD'S ACRE
HAGGADAH
HAGGADIC
HEAVENLY
HELL-FIRE
HEXAPLAR
HIERARCH
HIERATIC
HIERURGY
HIGH MASS
HINDUISE
HINDUISM
HINDUIZE
HOLY LAND
HOLY NAME
HOLY WEEK
HOLY WRIT
HOUSLING
HYMN-BOOK
IDOLATER
IDOLATRY
IMMORTAL
INFERNAL
ISLAMISE
ISLAMISM
ISLAMITE
ISLAMIZE
JAGANATH
JESUITIC
JESUITRY
JUDAISER
JUDAIZER
LAMASERY
LAY VICAR
LAZARIST
LITURGIC
LOLLARDY
LORD'S DAY
LUTHERAN
MANDAEAN

MANICHEE
MARONITE
MASS-BELL
MASS-BOOK
MENOLOGY
MINISTER
MINORESS
MINORITE
MISERERE
MISHNAIC
MODALISM
MODALIST
MONACHAL
MONASTIC
MORAVIAN
MUSULMAN
MYSTICAL
NATIVITY
NAVICULA
NAZAREAN
NAZARENE
NAZARITE
NETHINIM
NOVATIAN
OBITUARY
OBLATION
OFFERING
ORDINAND
ORDINARY
ORTHODOX
PAGANISM
PANTHEON
PAPALISM
PAPISHER
PAPISTRY
PARABEMA
PARSIISM
PASCH-EGG
PASSOVER
PAYNIMRY
PECULIAR
PESHITTA
PESHITTO
PHARISEE
PONTIFEX
POPEHOOD
POPELING
POPESHIP
PREACHER
PREDELLA
PRIESTLY
PRIORESS
PROPHECY
PROPHESY
PSALMIST
PUSEYISM
PUSEYITE
QUAKERLY

QUIETISM
QUIETIST
RABBINIC
RAMADHAN
RAMAYANA
RECTORAL
REDEEMER
RELIGION
RESPONSE
REVEREND
REVERENT
ROGATION
ROMANISE
ROMANISH
ROMANISM
ROMANIST
ROMANIZE
ROOD-BEAM
ROOD-LOFT
ROOD-TREE
SADDUCEE
SANCTIFY
SECTATOR
SHAKTISM
SOCINIAN
STUNDISM
STUNDIST
SUFISTIC
TALAPOIN
TENEBRAE
TEOCALLI
THEOCRAT
THEODICY
THEOGONY
THURIBLE
THURIFER
TRANSEPT
TRIMURTI
UNBELIEF
VEDANTIC
VERSICLE
VESTMENT
VIATICUM
WAHABISM
WAHABITE
WESLEYAN

9

ADVENTIST
ALLELUIAH
ALTAR-TOMB
ALTARWISE
ANCHORAGE
ANCHORESS
ANCHORITE
ANTIPAPAL
ANTIPHONY
APOCRYPHA

APOSTOLIC
APPARITOR
ARCHANGEL
ARCHFIEND
ASCENSION
ASPERSORY
ATHENAEUM
ATONEMENT
BAPTISMAL
BAPTISTRY
BAR MIZVAH
BEATITUDE
BEELZEBUB
BEGUINAGE
BENEDIGHT
BISHOPRIC
BISMILLAH
BLASPHEME
BLASPHEMY
BIBLICISM
BIBLICIST
BRAHMINEE
BRAHMINIC
CALVINISM
CALVINIST
CANDLEMAS
CANONICAL
CARMELITE
CATHEDRAL
CELESTIAL
CHRISTIAN
CHURCHING
CHURCHISM
CHURCHMAN
CITY OF GOD
CO-ETERNAL
COMMUNION
CONFESSOR
CONFUCIAN
CORDELIER
DAMNATION
DEACONESS
DESECRATE
DIACONATE
DISSENTER
DOMINICAL
EASTER DAY
EASTER EVE
EMBER DAYS
EMBER-WEEK
EPISCOPAL
EPISTOLER
EUCHARIST
EUTYCHIAN
EVANGELIC
EXEGETIST
EXPIATION
GENUFLECT

GOSPELISE
GOSPELIZE
GOSPELLER
GREGORIAN
HAGGADIST
HAGIOLOGY
HALLOWE'EN
HEATHENRY
HEXATEUCH
HIEROGRAM
HIEROLOGY
HIGH ALTAR
HOLY WATER
HOMOUSIAN
HOUSELLED
INTERDICT
ISLAMITIC
ISRAELITE
JANSENISM
JANSENIST
JESUITISM
JOSS-HOUSE
JOSS-STICK
LAMASERAI
LAY READER
LAY SISTER
LECTORATE
LITURGICS
LITURGIST
LOLLARDRY
LOW CHURCH
LOW SUNDAY
LUTHERIST
MAHOMETAN
MANICHEAN
MARTYRDOM
MATHURINE
MENDICANT
MENNONITE
METHODISM
METHODIST
MODERATOR
MONACHISM
MONASTERY
MORMONISM
MOSAIC LAW
MOSLEMISM
MUSSULMAN
NAZARITIC
NESTORIAN
NOVITIATE
OBEISANCE
OFFERTORY
ORATORIAN
ORDINANCE
ORTHODOXY
OSTENSORY
PANTHEISM

PANTHEIST
PARACLETE
PARSEEISM
PASSIONAL
PATRIARCH
PAULICIAN
PAULINISM
PAULINIST
PENTECOST
PHARISAIC
PHELONION
PHYSICISM
PIETISTIC
PLAINSONG
PREACHIFY
PREACHING
PREBENDAL
PRECENTOR
PRECISIAN
PRESBYTER
PROSELYTE
PROSEUCHE
PROTHESIS
PROTHETIC
PURGATORY
QUAKERDOM
QUAKERISH
QUAKERISM
QUASIMODO
RABBINATE
RABBINISM
RABBINIST
RECTORATE
RELIGIEUX
RELIGIOSE
RELIGIOUS
REPENTANT
REREDORSE
REREDOSSE
RESPONSES
REVERENCE
RITUALISE
RITUALISM
RITUALIST
RITUALIZE
ROOD-TOWER
RURAL DEAN
SABBATINE
SABBATISM
SABELLIAN
SABIANISM
SACRAMENT
SACRIFICE
SACRILEGE
SALVATION
SANCTUARY
SECTARIAN
SEMI-ARIAN

SEPULCHRE
SHAKERISM
SHAMANISM
SHAMANIST
SIVAISTIC
SOLEMNISE
SOLEMNIZE
SPIRITUAL
SUB-DEACON
SUCCENTOR
SUFFRAGAN
SUFIISTIC
SUTTEEISM
SYNAGOGUE
SYNCRETIC
SYNERGISM
SYNODICAL
TALMUDIST
TELEOLOGY
TESTAMENT
THEOCRACY
THEOCRASY
THEOLOGER
THEOMACHY
THEOPATHY
THEOPHAGY
THEOPHANY
THEOSOPHY
THEOTOKOS
TRIPUDIUM
TRITHEISM
TRITHEIST
UNITARIAN
UPANISHAD
VAISHNAVA
VALDENSES
VENERABLE
VESTMENTS
VICARIATE
VICARSHIP
WAHABIISM
WAHABIITE
WALDENSES

10

ABSOLUTION
ABSTINENCE
ALBIGENSES
ALL-HALLOW
ALTAR-CLOTH
ALTAR-PIECE
ALTAR-RAILS
ALTAR-STONE
ANABAPTISE
ANABAPTISM
ANABAPTIST
ANABAPTIZE
ANCHORETIC

ANOINTMENT
ANTICHRIST
ANTINOMIAN
ANTIPHONAL
ANTIPHONER
ANTIPHONIC
ANTITHEISM
ANTITHEIST
APOCALYPSE
APOSTOLATE
APOTHEOSIS
ARCHBISHOP
ARCHDEACON
ARCHFLAMEN
ARCHPRIEST
ARMAGEDDON
ASSUMPTION
ASTROLATRY
ATHANASIAN
AUTOTHEISM
AUTOTHEIST
BAPTISTERY
BAR MITZVAH
BENEDICITE
BENEDICTUS
BERNARDINE
BLACK FRIAR
CANONICALS
CANONICITY
CANONISTIC
CARTHUSIAN
CATECHUMEN
CEREMONIAL
CHURCH ARMY
CHURCHGOER
CHURCH-RATE
CHURCHYARD
CISTERCIAN
CLEARSTORY
CLERESTORY
CONFESSION
CONSECRATE
CONSISTORY
COSMOLATRY
DEACONSHIP
DEVOTIONAL
DEVITIONAL
DOCETISTIC
DOUAY BIBLE
DRAGONNADE
EASTERTIDE
ECCLESIAST
EPISCOPACY
EPISCOPANT
EPISCOPATE
EVANGELISE
EVANGELISM
EVANGELIST

EVANGELIZE
FREE CHURCH
GENEVANISM
GNOSTICISM
GOOD FRIDAY
GOSPELLISE
GOSPELLIZE
GOSPEL SIDE
HAGIOLATER
HAGIOLATRY
HAGIOSCOPE
HALLELUIAH
HALLELUJAH
HALLOWMASS
HEATHENDOM
HEATHENISE
HEATHENIZE
HEXAPLARIC
HELIOLATER
HELIOLATRY
HENOTHEISM
HENOTHEIST
HEPTATEUCH
HETERODOXY
HIERARCHAL
HIERARCHIC
HIEROCRACY
HIEROGRAPH
HIEROMANCY
HIEROPHANT
HIEROSCOPY
HIGH CHURCH
HIGH PRIEST
HOLY FAMILY
HOLY OFFICE
HOLY ORDERS
HOLY SPIRIT
HOMOOUSIAN
HOUSELLING
HYLOTHEISM
HYLOTHEIST
HYPERDULIA
ICONOCLASM
ICONOCLAST
ICONOLATER
ICONOLATRY
IDOLATROUS
ISRAELITIC
JESUITICAL
JUGGERNAUT
LADY-CHAPEL
LAMMAS-TIDE
LAY BAPTISM
LAY BROTHER
LECTORSHIP
LITURGICAL
LOLLARDISM
LORD'S TABLE

MAGNIFICAT
MAHOMMEDAN
MANICHAEAN
MANICHEISM
MARIOLATER
MASS-PRIEST
MISERICORD
MISSIONARY
MOHAMMEDAN
MONOTHEISM
MONOTHEIST
MONSTRANCE
MUHAMMEDAN
MUHAMMEDAN
NAZARITISM
NUNCIATURE
ORDINATION
PALM SUNDAY
PAPAL CROSS
PASSIONARY
PASSIONIST
PENTATEUCH
PERSUASION
PHAELONION
PHARISAISM
PILGRIMAGE
POLYTHEISM
POLYTHEIST
PREACHMENT
PREBENDARY
PRESBYTERY
PRIESTHOOD
PROSEUCHAE
PROTESTANT
PURITANISM
QUIETISTIC
RABBINICAL
RECTORSHIP
REDEMPTION
REDEMPTIVE
RELIGIEUSE
RELIGIONER
REPENTANCE
REREDORTER
REVELATION
ROOD-SCREEN
SABBATH-DAY
SACERDOTAL
SACROSANCT
SANCTIFIED
SANCTITUDE
SCHISMATIC
SCRIPTURAL
SEPTUAGINT
SEXAGESIMA
SHROVETIDE
SOLEMN MASS
SYNCRETISE

SYNCRETISM
SYNCRETIST
SYNCRETIZE
TABERNACLE
TELEOLOGIC
TEMPTATION
THEOCRATIC
THEOLOGATE
THEOLOGIAN
THEOPNEUST
THEOSOPHER
TRACTARIAN
UNBELIEVER
WALDENSIAN
ZEND-AVESTA

11

ACOLOUTHITE
AGNOSTICISM
ALBIGENSIAN
ALL SOULS' DAY
ANTEPENDIUM
ANTIPHONARY
APOSTLESHIP
APOTHEOSISE
APOTHEOSIZE
ARCHDIOCESE
ARMINIANISM
ASPERSORIUM
AUGUSTINIAN
BENEDICTINE
BENEDICTION
BENEDICTIVE
BENEDICTORY
BIBLIOLATER
BIBLIOLATRY
BIBLIOMANCY
BLASPHEMOUS
BRAHMA SAMAJ
BRAHMO SOMAJ
BROAD CHURCH
CAMPBELLITE
CATHOLICISM
CATHOLICITY
CELEBRATION
CHRISMATORY
CHRISTENDOM
CHURCH-COURT
CHURCHGOING
COMMINATION
COMMINATORY
CONVOCATION
COSMOTHEISM
COSMOTHEIST
CREMATORIUM
CRUCIFIXION
DEIFICATION
DESECRATION

ECCLESIARCH
EPISCOPALIA
ERASTIANISM
ESCHATOLOGY
FREETHINKER
GENEVA BIBLE
GENUFLEXION
HAGGADISTIC
HAGIOGRAPHA
HAGIOGRAPHY
HEATHENESSE
HEXAPLARIAN
HOLY-ROOD DAY
HOMOIOUSIAN
IMMORTALITY
LATIN CHURCH
LORD'S PRAYER
LORD'S SUPPER
LUTHERANISM
MANICHAEISM
MIRACLE PLAY
MISERICORDE
MOHAMMEDISM
MONASTERIAL
MONASTICISM
MORAVIANISM
NICENE CREED
NON-BIBLICAL
NON-CATHOLIC
NOVATIANISM
NOVATIANIST
PARABAPTISM
PARABOLANUS
PARISHIONER
PASCHAL LAMB
PASSING-BELL
PASSION PLAY
PASSIONTIDE
PASSION-WEEK
PATERNOSTER
PATRON SAINT
PENTECOSTAL
PHARISAICAL
PHYSIOLATER
PHYSIOLATRY
PHYSITHEISM
PLYMOUTHISM
PLYMOUTHIST
PONTIFICALS
PONTIFICATE
PRIESTCRAFT
PROSELYTISE
PROSELYTISM
PROSELYTIZE
PROTOMARTYR
REACTIONARY
RELIGIONISE
RELIGIONIST

RELIGIONIZE
RELIGIOSITY
RESERVATION
RITUAL CHOIR
RITUALISTIC
ROMAN CHURCH
ROOD-STEEPLE
SABBATARIAN
SACRAMENTAL
SACRING BELL
SADDUCEEISM
SANCTUARISE
SANCTUARIZE
SANCTUS BELL
SARCOPHAGUS
SOCINIANISE
SOCINIANISM
SOCINIANIZE
THEOMACHIST
THEOMORPHIC
THEOPHAGOUS
THEOSOPHIST
THURIFEROUS
TRINITARIAN
VIA DOLOROSA
VICAR-FORANE
WESLEYANISM
WHITSUNTIDE
ZOROASTRIAN

12

ALL SAINTS' DAY
ANABAPTISTIC
ANCHORETICAL
ANNUNCIATION
ANTICATHOLIC
ANTITHEISTIC
APOSTOLICISM
APOSTOLICITY
ARCHDEACONRY
ASCENSION DAY
ASH WEDNESDAY
CANON REGULAR
CHAPEL OF EASE
CHRISOM-CLOTH
CHRISTIANITY
CHURCHIANITY
CHURCH PARADE
CHURCHWARDEN
CONFESSIONAL
CONFESSORESS
CONFIRMATION
CONFUCIANISM
CONFUCIANIST
CONGREGATION
CONSECRATION
DENOMINATION
DEVIL-WORSHIP

DISCIPLESHIP
DISESTABLISH
DISPENSATION
ECCLESIASTIC
ECCLESIOLOGY
ENTHRONEMENT
EVANGELICISM
FAITH HEALING
GENUFLECTION
HAGIOGRAPHER
HEAVENLY HOST
HENOTHEISTIC
HIEROGRAPHIC
HIEROPHANTIC
HOLY OF HOLIES
HOLY THURSDAY
HOMOLOGUMENA
ICONOMACHIST
INTERDICTION
LAY COMMUNION
LESSER LITANY
LITURGIOLOGY
LOW CHURCHMAN
MANICHEANISM
MARIOLATROUS
MEETING-HOUSE
METROPOLITAN
MUGGLETONIAN
NESTORIANISM
NEW TESTAMENT
NON-CHRISTIAN
NON-SECTARIAN
NUNC DIMITTIS
OLD TESTAMENT
PASQUE-FLOWER
PASSION-MUSIC
PREACHERSHIP
PRECISIANISM
PRECISIANIST
PROSELYTISER
PROSELYTIZER
PSILANTHROPY
PURIFICATION
QUADRAGESIMA
REDEMPTORIST
RED-LETTER DAY
RELIGIONLESS
RITUAL MURDER
ROGATION DAYS
ROGATION WEEK
SABELLIANISM
SALVATIONIST
SECTARIANISM
SEMI-ARIANISM
SPIRITUALISM
SPIRITUALIST
SUNDAY SCHOOL
SUPERFRONTAL

SYNCRETISTIC
THANKSGIVING
THEOLOGASTER
THEOPASCHITE
THEOPATHETIC
TRISMEGISTUS
UNITARIANISM
UNITED GREEKS
UNIVERSALIST
VICAR-GENERAL

13

ALLHALLOWMASS
ALLHALLOWTIDE
ANGLO-CATHOLIC
ANTHROPOLATRY
ANTI-CHRISTIAN
ANTI-EPISCOPAL
ANTINOMIANISM
APOSTLES' CREED
ARCHBISHOPRIC
BEATIFICATION
BENEDICTIONAL
BIBLIOLATROUS
BIDDING-PRAYER
BURNT-OFFERING
CATECHUMENATE
CATECHUMENISM
CEREMONIALISM
CEREMONIALIST
CHURCH SERVICE
CHURCH VISIBLE
CONFESSIONARY
CONFESSORSHIP
EASTERN CHURCH
ECCLESIOLATRY
ELYSIAN FIELDS
EXCOMMUNICATE
FALSE DOCTRINE
GLORIFICATION
HAGIOGRAPHIST
HIGH-CHURCHISM
HIGH-CHURCHMAN
HOMOLOGOUMENA
MANICHAEANISE
MANICHAEANISM
MANICHAEANIZE
MOHAMMEDANISE
MOHAMMEDANISM
MOHAMMEDANIZE
NONCONFORMIST
PAPAPRELATIST
PASCHAL-CANDLE
PASCHAL-FLOWER
PASSION SUNDAY
PASTORAL STAFF
PECTORAL CROSS
PHYSITHEISTIC

PRAYER MEETING
PROTESTANTISM
PSILANTHROPIC
QUINQUAGESIMA
REDEMPTIONIST
REINCARNATION
RELIGIOUSNESS
ROMAN CATHOLIC
SABBATH-BREACH
SACERDOTALISM
SACERDOTALIST
SALVATION ARMY
SHROVE TUESDAY
SWEDENBORGIAN
THEOPASCHITIC
THURIFICATION
TRACTARIANISM
TRINITY SUNDAY
WAY OF THE CROSS
ZARATHUSTRIAN

14
ALBIGENSIANISM
ANTIPHONICALLY
ANTISCRIPTURAL
AUGUSTINIANISM
CELESTIAL GLORY
CHRISTADELPHIAN
CHURCH ASSEMBLY
CHURCH MILITANT
COMMUNION TABLE
CRUTCHED FRIARS
EASTER OFFERING
ECCLESIOLOGIST
EVANGELISATION
EVANGELIZATION
EXTREME UNCTION
FUNDAMENTALISM
FUNDAMENTALIST
GREGORIAN CHANT
HIEROGRAPHICAL
HIGH PRIESTHOOD
HOLY SCRIPTURES
LATERAN COUNCIL
LATTER-DAY SAINT
LITURGIOLOGIST
LORDS SPIRITUAL
MAUNDY THURSDAY
NON-COMMUNICANT
ORTHODOX CHURCH
OXFORD MOVEMENT
PECULIAR PEOPLE
PREACHING-CROSS
PREACHING-FRIAR
PREACHING-HOUSE
PONTIFICAL MASS
PSILANTHROPISM
PSILANTHROPIST

REFORMED CHURCH
RELIGIOUS ORDER
RELIGIOUS TRUTH
ROGATION SUNDAY
ROSICRUCIANISM
SABBATARIANISM
SABBATH-BREAKER
SACRAMENTARIAN
SANDEMANIANISM
SIGN OF THE CROSS
THEOPASCHITISM
TRINITARIANISM
UNITED BRETHREN
VICAR-APOSTOLIC
ZOROASTRIANISM

15
ANTIEVANGELICAL
ANTITRINITARIAN
ATHANASIAN CREED
CARDINAL VIRTUES
CHURCH INVISIBLE
CHURCH UNIVERSAL
ECCLESIASTICISM
EPISCOPALIANISM
EVERLASTING FIRE
EXCOMMUNICATION
HARVEST FESTIVAL
JEHOVAH'S WITNESS
LAY IMPROPRIATOR
METROPOLITANATE
MORAL REARMAMENT
PASCH OF THE CROSS
PLYMOUTH BROTHER
PRESBYTERIANISM
SABBATH-BREAKING
SUFFRAGAN BISHOP
TRANSFIGURATION

Education

3
ART
DON
FAG
GYP
POP

4
ARTS
CRAM
CRIB
DEAN
DEMY
FORM
GATE
GOWN
GURU
HALL
HEAD
HOOD
PREP
SWOT
TERM
VIVA

5
BEDEL
CLASS
COACH
DRILL
GAUDY
GRADE
GRIND
HOUSE
KHOJA
LATIN
LEARN
LINES
LOGIC
LYCEE
MUSIC
PUPIL
SCOUT
SIZAR
SLOID
SLOYD
STUDY
TAWSE
TUTOR
WELSH

6
BEADLE
BURSAR
COURSE

DEGREE
DOCENT
DOCTOR
EXAMEN
FELLOW
FRENCH
GERMAN
GRADUS
GREATS
INCEPT
INFANT
JUNIOR
KHODJA
LECTOR
LESSON
LOCALS
LOCKER
LYCEUM
MASTER
MATRON
MENTOR
MOLLAH
MOOLAH
MULLAH
NOVICE
OPTIME
PEDANT
PUNDIT
READER
RECTOR
REMOVE
SCHOOL
SCONCE
SENATE
SMALLS
TRIPOS
TUTRIX
WARDEN

7
ACADEMY
BATTELS
BIOLOGY
BOOKISH
BULLDOG
BURSARY
COLLEGE
CRAMMER
DICTION
DIPLOMA
DOMINIE
DRAWING
ENGLISH
EXAMINE
EXAMPLE

FACULTY
FAMULUS
FRESHER
GRAMMAR
GRINDER
HEAD BOY
HISTORY
HONOURS
ITALIAN
LEARNER
LECTURE
MONITOR
MOOTMAN
PHYSICS
PREFECT
PRELECT
PRIMARY
PROCTOR
PROVOST
READING
RUSSIAN
SCHOLAR
SCIENCE
SEMINAR
SPANISH
STUDENT
TEACHER
THEOREM
TRIVIUM
TUCK-BOX
TUITION
TUTRESS

8
ACADEMIC
APTITUDE
CLASSICS
CLASSMAN
COACHING
COLLEGER
COMMERCE
DIVINITY
DIVISION
DRILLING
EDUCABLE
ENCAENIA
EXAMINEE
EXAMINER
EXAMPLAR
EXEMPLAR
EXERCISE
FRESHMAN
GRADUATE
HEAD GIRL
HOMEWORK
HUMANISM
INSTRUCT
LANGUAGE

LEARNING
LECTURER
LITERACY
LITERATE
LITTLE-GO
MANCIPLE
MISTRESS
REGISTER
ROLL-CALL
SEMESTER
SEMINARY
SEND DOWN
STATUTES
TABERDAR
TEACHING
TEXT-BOOK
THEOLOGY
TUCK-SHOP
TUTELAGE
TUTORAGE
TUTORESS
TUTORIAL
TUTORISM
VACATION
VIVA-VOCE
WRANGLER

9
ALMA MATER
ART SCHOOL
BILATERAL
CHEMISTRY
CLASSBOOK
CLASSMATE
CLASSROOM
COLLEGIAL
COLLEGIAN
DAY SCHOOL
DIDACTICS
DORMITORY
ECONOMICS
EDUCATION
EXAMINANT
EXAMINATE
GEOGRAPHY
GREAT HALL
GYMNASIUM
INCEPTION
INCULCATE
IN-SERVICE
LECTORATE
NOVITIATE
PEDAGOGIC
PEDAGOGUE
PRECEPTOR
PRELECTOR
PRESIDENT
PRINCIPAL

PROFESSOR
REGISTRAR
RUDIMENTS
RUSTICATE
SCHOOLBAG
SCHOOLBOY
SCHOOLERY
SCHOOLING
SCHOOLMAN
SIXTH FORM
SOCIOLOGY
SPEECH DAY
SUB-RECTOR
SURMASTER
SURVEYING
TUTORSHIP

10
APPRENTICE
ARITHMETIC
BLACKBOARD
CHALKBOARD
CHANCELLOR
CHAUTAUQUA
CLASSICISM
CLASSICIST
COLLEGIATE
COUNSELLOR
DAME SCHOOL
DICTIONARY
DINING-HALL
DISCIPLINE
ELEVEN-PLUS
EXAMINABLE
EXAMINATOR
EXHIBITION
EXPOSITION
EXTRA-MURAL
FELLOWSHIP
FORM-MASTER
FREE-SCHOOL
FRESHERDOM
FROEBELISM
GYMNASTICS
HEADMASTER
HIGH SCHOOL
HUMANITIES
ILLITERACY
ILLITERATE
INNUMERACY
INNUMERATE
INSTRUCTOR
INTRA-MURAL
INVIGILATE
JUNIOR-HIGH
LABORATORY
LECTORSHIP
LICENTIATE

MANUAL ARTS
MONTESSORI
NEEDLEWORK
NIGHT-CLASS
PEDAGOGICS
POSTMASTER
QUADRANGLE
QUADRIVIUM
READERSHIP
REAL'SCHULE
SCHOLASTIC
SCHOOLBELL
SCHOOLBOOK
SCHOOLBRED
SCHOOLDAME
SCHOOLGIRL
SCHOOLMAID
SCHOOL TERM
SCHOOLTIDE
SCHOOLTIME
SCHOOLWARD
SCHOOLWORK
STATISTICS
SUBPREFECT
UNIVERSITY

11
ABECEDARIAN
ACADEMICIAN
BOOKISHNESS
BOOK-KEEPING
CLASSFELLOW
CO-EDUCATION
COLLEGIANER
CONVOCATION
EDUCATIONAL
EURHYTHMICS
EXAMINATION
GAMES-MASTER
HOLIDAY TASK
HOUSEMASTER
INCULCATION
INSTRUCTION
INVIGILATOR
LIBERAL ARTS
MATHEMATICS
MATRICULATE
MODERN GREEK
MORTAR-BOARD
MUSIC-MASTER
NIGHT-SCHOOL
PEDAGOGUERY
POLYTECHNIC
PROGRESSIVE
RESPONSIONS
SCHOLARSHIP
SCHOOLCHILD
SCHOOLCRAFT

SCHOOLGOING
SCHOOLHOUSE

12
BOOK-LEARNING
CALISTHENICS
CHALK-AND-TA[..]
CONSERVATOR[Y]
COUNTY SCHOO[L]
DISCIPLINARY
EXHIBITIONER
FORM-MISTRES[S]
FRESHMANSHIP
HEADMISTRESS
HUMAN BIOLOG[Y]
INDOCTRINATE
INFANT SCHOOL
JUNIOR SCHOOL
KINDERGARTEN
MASTER OF ART[S]
MIDDLE SCHOOL
MODERN GREAT[..]
MODERN HEBRE[W]
POST-GRADUAT[E]
PRIVAT-DOZENT
PRIVATE STUDY
PROPAEDEUTIC
PUBLIC ORATOR
PUPIL TEACHER
SCHOOLBOYISH
SCHOOL-DIVINE
SCHOOLFELLOW
SCHOOLFRIEND
SCHOOL-LEAVER
SCHOOLMASTER
SENIOR MASTER
SUNDAY SCHOO[L]

13
ARTS-AND-CRAF[T]
BASIC TRAINING
CALLISTHENICS
COEDUCATIONAL
COMPREHENSIVE
CONSERVATOIRE
CONVENT SCHOO[L]
COUNCIL SCHOO[L]
COURSE OF STUD[Y]
EVENING-SCHOO[L]
FACULTY MEMBE[R]
GRAMMAR SCHO[OL]
KINDERGARTNER
MATRICULATION
MEDICAL SCHOO[L]
PHYSICAL JERKS
PRIMARY SCHOO[L]
PROPAEDEUTICS
QUALIFICATION

Etchers and Engravers

3	6	DE LAUNE	MAZZUOLI
BOL	AUDRAN	FLAMENG	NANTEUIL
PYE	BACHER	FLIPANT	PIRANESI
	BARRAS	GILLRAY	PISSARRO
4	BERVIC	GOODALL	RAIMONDI
BONE	BEWICK	HOGARTH	RICKETTS
COCK	CALLOT	HOLBEIN	ROBINSON
COPE	CANALE	HOLROYD	TEMPESTA
CORT	COCHIN	LEPICIE	VAN SOMER
EAST	DREVET	LORRAIN	WHISTLER
GILL	DUPONT	MACBETH	WILLMORE
GRAF	FARRER	MORGHEN	WOEIRIOT
GRUN	FOSTER	NATOIRE	WOOLLETT
HOLE	GEDDES	PARRISH	WORLIDGE
HUET	GOODEN	PENNELL	
RENI	HARVEY	PERELLE	9
WARD	HOLLAR	PONTIUS	ALTDORFER
ZORN	JACQUE	PRUD'HON	ARMINGTON
	LEGROS	RETZSCH	DROESHOUT
5	LEPERE	ROBETTA	ELSTRACKE
BEHAM	LEYDEN	ST AUBIN	FAITHORNE
BINCK	MASSON	SCHELTA	FRAGONARD
BLAKE	MATHAM	SCHMIDT	HOUBRAKEN
BOWYS	MELLAN	SHANNON	LABOUREUR
BRILL	MERYON	SHERWIN	NICHOLSON
CAMPI	MILLER	SIMMONS	REMBRANDT
COOKE	MILLET	SOUTMAN	SAENREDAM
COPIA	MOREAU	STRANGE	SUYDERHOF
COROT	MULLER	TARDIEU	VAN LEYDEN
CRAIG	PALMER	TENIERS	VILLAMENA
CROME	PARIGI	TIEPOLO	VON SIEGEN
DE LEU	PERHAM	VOLPATO	
DURER	POTTER	WALTNER	10
DUVET	ROGERS	WATTEAU	ALDEGREVER
EISEN	STRANG		CAMPAGNOLA
GHISI	TAYLOR	8	CRUIKSHANK
GREEN	THOMAS	BALECHOU	FINIGUERRE
HADEN	TURNER	BRANGWYN	JACQUEMART
HIRST	VERTUE	BRIDGMAN	ROWLANDSON
KEENE	WALKER	BROSAMER	SAINT AUBIN
LASNE	WALLIS	CALAMATA	SCHONGAUER
LEWIS	WILKIE	CARRACCI	VORSTERMAN
LUCAS		DOUBIGNY	
MCBEY	7	DUVNEECK	11
MAROT	BALDUNG	EDELINCK	MARCANTONIO
MOORE	BARBARI	FARLEIGH	VAN RUISDAEL
MORAN	BECKETT	GAILLARD	
MORIN	BETTINI	GAULTIER	12
PLACE	BOETIUS	GOLTZIUS	VAN DER HEYDEN
PLATT	BOYDELL	GOURMONT	
PRATT	BRUEGEL	GRAVELOT	13
SHARP	CAMERON	JOULLAIN	HUGHES-STANTON
SHORT	CHARLET	LANDELLS	
SMITH	COUSINS	LA TOUCHE	
WHITE	DANIELL	LEIGHTON	
WILLE	DELARAM	MANTEGNA	

Fish (including shellfish; see also Food)

2
ID

3
BAR
BIB
COD
EEL
GAR
GED
IDE
PAR
RAY
ROE
SAR
TAI

4
BASS
BLAY
BLEY
BRIT
CARP
CHAD
CHAR
CHUB
CLAM
COHO
CRAB
CUSK
DACE
DART
DORY
DRUM
GADE
GOBY
GRIG
HAKE
HUSO
JACK
KELT
KETA
LING
LUCE
MASU
MORT
OPAH
ORFE
PARR
PEAL
PEEL
PIKE
POPE
POUT
RUDD

RUFF
SCAD
SCAR
SCUP
SHAD
SNIG
SOLE
SPAT
TOPE
TUNA
TUSK

5
ABLET
ALLIS
BASSE
BLEAK
BREAM
BRILL
CHARR
CISCO
COBIA
COHOE
COLEY
DOREE
DORSE
ELOPS
ELVER
FLUKE
GAPER
GIBEL
GRUNT
GUPPY
LANCE
LOACH
MORAY
MURRY
NERKA
NURSE
PADLE
PERCH
PIPER
POGGE
PORGY
POWAN
PRAWN
ROACH
ROKER
RUFFE
SAITH
SARGO
SAURY
SEWEN
SEWIN
SHARK

SKATE
SMELT
SMOLT
SNOEK
SNOOK
SPRAT
SPROD
TENCH
TOGUE
TORSK
TROUT
TUNNY
WHELK
WHIFF
WITCH

6
ALEVIN
ALLICE
ANABAS
ANGLER
BARBEL
BELUGA
BLENNY
BONITO
BOWFIN
BRASSY
BUCKIE
BUMALO
BURBOT
CAPLIN
CHEVEN
CHEVIN
COCKLE
COMBER
CONGER
CONNER
CUNNER
DARTER
DENTEX
DIPNOI
DOCTOR
DORADO
DUN-COW
ELLOPS
FINNAC
FINNAN
FINNER
GADOID
GANOID
GARVIE
GORAMY
GRILSE
GROPER
GUNNEL
GURAMI

GURNET
KIPPER
LAUNCE
MAHSIR
MAIGRE
MARLIN
MEAGRE
MEGRIM
MILTER
MINNOW
MORGAY
MUDCAT
MULLET
MURENA
MURRAY
MURREY
MUSSEL
OYSTER
PADDLE
PAIDLE
PLAICE
POLLAN
PORGIE
RED-EYE
REMORA
ROBALO
RUFFIN
SAITHE
SALMON
SAMLET
SANDER
SARDEL
SAUGER
SAUREL
SEA-APE
SEA-BAT
SEA-CAT
SEA-DOG
SEA-FOX
SEA-OWL
SEEDER
SEPHEN
SHANNY
SHINER
SHRIMP
SUCKER
TARPON
TAUTOG
TRYGON
TURBOT
TWAITE
WEEVER
WINKLE
WRASSE
ZANDER
ZINGEL

7
ACALEPH
ALEWIFE
ANCHOVY
BERGYLT
BLOATER
BLUECAP
BLUE-EYE
BRASSIE
BUMMALO
CAPELIN
CATFISH
CAVALLY
CHIMERA
CICHLID
CLUPEID
CODFISH
CRUCIAN
CRUSIAN
DOGFISH
DOLPHIN
DUN-FISH
EELFARE
EEL-POUT
FANTAIL
FINDRAN
FINNACK
FINNOCK
GARFISH
GARPIKE
GARVOCK
GOURAMI
GROUPER
GRUNTER
GUDGEON
GURNARD
GWINIAD
GWYNIAD
HADDOCK
HALIBUT
HERLING
HERRING
HIRLING
HOGFISH
HOMELYN
JEWFISH
KEELING
LOBSTER
MAHSEER
MERLING
MORWONG
MUDFISH
MURAENA
OAR-FISH
OLD-WIFE

OSSETER
PEGASUS
PIGFISH
POLLACK
POLLOCK
POMFRET
POMPANO
POUTING
QUINNAT
ROCK-COD
SARDINE
SAWFISH
SEA-BASS
SEA-COCK
SEA-DACE
SEA-FISH
SEA-PIKE
SEA-WIFE
SEA-WOLF
SNAPPER
SUN-FISH
TIDDLER
TOHEROA
TOPKNOT
TORGOCH
TORPEDO
WALL-EYE
WHITING

8
ACALEPHA
ACALEPHE
ALBACORE
ALBICORE
ARAPAIMA
BAND-FISH
BLUEFISH
BOARFISH
BONY PIKE
BUCKLING
BULLHEAD
CHIMAERA
CLUPEOID
COALFISH
CRAWFISH
CRAYFISH
DEALFISH
DRAGONET
DRUMFISH
EAGLE-RAY
FILE-FISH
FLAT-FISH
FLOUNDER
FORKTAIL
FOX-SHARK
FROGFISH
GILLAROO
GILTHEAD

GOATFISH
GOLDFISH
GRAINING
GRAYLING
HAIRTAIL
HORNBEAK
HORNPOUT
JOHN DORY
KABELJOU
KINGFISH
LUMPFISH
LUNGFISH
MACKEREL
MAN-OF-WAR
MENHADEN
MOONFISH
PICKEREL
PILCHARD
PIPEFISH
PIRARUCU
POOR JOHN
ROCK-FISH
ROCKLING
SAILFISH
SALMONET
SALMONID
SARDELLE
SAW-SHARK
SCARFISH
SCUPPAUG
SEA-ADDER
SEA-BREAM
SEA-DEVIL
SEA-HORSE
SEA-LOACH
SEA-PERCH
SEA-ROBIN
SEA-SNAIL
SEA-SNIPE
SEEDFISH
STINGRAY
STURGEON
TARWHINE
THRASHER
THRESHER
TOAD-FISH
TREVALLY
TROUTLET
WOLF-FISH

9
AMBERFISH
ANGEL-FISH
ARGENTINE
BARRACUDA
BLACK BASS
BLACKFISH
BLACK GOBY

BULL-TROUT
BUMMALOTI
CONGER-EEL
CORYPHENE
CRAMP-FISH
DEVIL-FISH
DOLPHINET
GASPEREAU
GLOBE-FISH
GOLOMYNKA
HENPAIDLE
HIPPODAME
HOUNDFISH
JACULATOR
JOHN DOREE
KABELJOUW
MENOMINEE
PILOT-FISH
ROUNDFISH
SAIL-FLUKE
SAND-LANCE
SCHNAPPER
SEA-DRAGON
SEA-LAWYER
SEA-SALMON
SHEAT-FISH
SNIPE-FISH
SPEARFISH
STARGAZER
STINGAREE
STINGBULL
STINGFISH
SURMULLET
SWORDFISH
THORNBACK
TITTLEBAT
TROUTLING
TRUMPETER
WHITEBAIT
WHITEBASS
WHITE FISH

10
AMBLYOPSIS
ARCHER-FISH
BARRACOOTA
BARRACOUTA
BARRAMUNDA
BOMBAY DUCK
BOTTLE-FISH
BOTTLENOSE
BUTTERFISH
CANDLEFISH
COCKPAIDLE
COELACANTH
CRAIG-FLUKE
DEMOISELLE
DRAGONFISH

FIVE-FINGER
FLYING-FISH
HAMMERFISH
HAMMERHEAD
HORNED POUT
LUMPSUCKER
MILLER'S-DOG
MORRIS-PIKE
PARROT-FISH
PERIWINKLE
RABBIT-FISH
RIBBON-FISH
RUDDERFISH
SAND-LAUNCE
SEA-POACHER
SEA-SURGEON
SHEATH-FISH
SHOVELHEAD
TIGER-SHARK
TWAITE SHAD
WHALE-SHARK

11
BELLOWS-FISH
DOLLY VARDEN
ELECTRIC EEL
ELECTRIC RAY
FIVE-FINGERS
HIPPOCAMPUS
LAKE-HERRING
LEPIDOSIREN
OXYRHYNCHUS
PEACOCK-FISH
PRICKLE-BACK
SALMON-TROUT
SEA-HEDGEHOG
SEA-SCORPION
STICKLEBACK
SUCKING-FISH
TRUMPET-FISH
WHISTLE-FISH

12
BASKING-SHARK
FATHER-LASHER
FIGHTING-FISH
MILLER'S-THUMB
PARROT-WRASSE
RAINBOW-TROUT
SEA-PORCUPINE
SERGEANT-FISH
SILVER SALMON

13
BURNETT SALMON
BUTTERFLY-FISH
FINDON-HADDOCK
FINNAN-HADDOCK

LEATHER-JACKET
MACKEREL-GUIDE
MACKEREL-MIDGE
MACKEREL-SHARK
THRESHER-SHARK

Flowers (see also Plants)

3
MAY

4
ALOE
BALM
FLAX
GEUM
GOOL
GULE
IRIS
IXIA
LILY
LOTE
MUSK
PINK
PINY
ROSE
SEGO

5
AJUGA
ASTER
BLOOM
BLUET
BROOM
BUGLE
DAISY
ERICA
GOOLD
HEATH
LILAC
LINUM
LOTUS
LUPIN
MURVA
ORPIN
ORRIS
OXEYE
OXLIP
PADMA
PAGLE
PANSY
PEONY
PHLOX
PIONY
POKER
POPPY
STOCK
TORCH
TULIP
VIOLA
YUCCA
YULAN

6
ACACIA
AZALEA
BELLIS
BORAGE
CACTUS
CISTUS
CLOVER
COLEUS
CORNEL
COSMEA
COSMOS
DAHLIA
IBERIS
KOCHIA
MIMOSA
MOORVA
ORCHID
ORCHIS
ORRICE
PAEONY
PAIGLE
PIONEY
PROTEA
RESEDA
ROCKET
SALVIA
SCILLA
SILENE
THRIFT
VIOLET
WATTLE
YARROW
ZINNIA

7
ACONITE
ALYSSUM
ANCHUSA
ANEMONE
BEGONIA
BLAWORT
BLOSSOM
BOUQUET
BUGLOSS
CAMPION
CANDOCK
CATALPA
CATTAIL
CHAPLET
CLARKIA
COWSLIP
CUP-ROSE
DAY-LILY
DOG-ROSE
DOGWOOD
ERODIUM
FESTOON
FREESIA
FUCHSIA
GAZANIA
GENTIAN
GERBERA
GODETIA
HEATHER
HYACINE
JASMINE
JESSAMY
JONQUIL
KINGCUP
LANTANA
LINARIA
LOBELIA
LUPINUS
MARYBUD
MAY-LILY
MELILOT
MELISSA
MILFOIL
MIMULUS
MUSCARI
NELUMBO
NEMESIA
NIGELLA
NOSEGAY
PAPAVER
PETUNIA
PICOTEE
PRIMULA
RAMBLER
ROSE-BAY
SPIRAEA
STATICE
SYRINGA
TAGETES
TEA-ROSE
TRITOMA
VERBENA

8
ABUTILON
ACANTHUS
AGERATUM
AMARANTH
ARUM LILY
ASPHODEL
AUBRETIA
AURICULA
BEDSTRAW
BERGENIA
BIGNONIA
BLUEBELL
BUDDLEIA
CALAMINT
CAMELLIA
CLEMATIS
DAFFODIL
DIANTHUS
DICENTRA
FIREWEED
FOXGLOVE
GARDENIA
GERANIUM
GLOXINIA
HAREBELL
HAWTHORN
HELENIUM
HEPATICA
HIBISCUS
HOTTONIA
HYACINTH
JAPONICA
LARKSPUR
LAVENDER
MAGNOLIA
MARIGOLD
MARTAGON
MOSSROSE
MYOSOTIS
NENUPHAR
NOISETTE
NYMPHAEA
OLEANDER
PHORMIUM
PLUMBAGO
PRIMROSE
ROCK-ROSE
SCABIOUS
SNOWBALL
SNOWDROP
STARWORT
SWEET-PEA
TIGRIDIA
TRILLIUM
TRITONIA
TUBEROSE
TURNSOLE
VALERIAN
VERONICA
VIBURNUM
VICTORIA
WILD ROSE
WISTARIA
WISTERIA
WOODBIND
WOODBINE

9
AARON'S ROD
ACHIMINES
AMARYLLIS
AQUILEGIA
ARTEMISIA
BLOODWORT
BRIAR ROSE
BRIER ROSE
BUTTERCUP
CALENDULA
CAMPANULA
CANDYTUFT
CANNA LILY
CARNATION
CELANDINE
CHERRY-PIE
CHINA ROSE
CINERARIA
CLOVE PINK
COCKSCOMB
COLTSFOOT
COLUMBINE
COREOPSIS
CORNPOPPY
DANDELION
DEVIL'S-BIT
DIGITALIS
DOG VIOLET
DORONICUM
DOVE'S FOOT
EDELWEISS
EGLANTINE
FORSYTHIA
GLADIOLUS
GOLDEN ROD
HELLEBORE
HOLLYHOCK
HYBRID TEA
HYDRANGEA
HYPERICUM
IMPATIENS
JESSAMINE
KNIPHOFIA
LOTUS LILY
MAYFLOWER
MEDAEWART
MONKSHOOD
NAKED LADY
NARCISSUS
NEMOPHILA
PIMPERNEL
PORTULACA
PYRETHRUM
SAXIFRAGE
SPEARWORT
SPEEDWELL
SUNFLOWER

TIGER LILY
TORCH LILY
TWAY-BLADE
VERBASCUM
WATERFLAG
WATERLILY

10
AGAPANTHUS
AMARANTHUS
BELLFLOWER
BUSY LIZZIE
CALLIOPSIS
CHINA-ASTER
CHIONODOXA
CINQUEFOIL
CORNFLOWER
DAMASK ROSE
DELPHINIUM
EASTER LILY
FLEUR-DE-LIS
FRITILLARY
HEARTSEASE
HELIANTHUS
HELIOTROPE
IMMORTELLE
LADY'S SMOCK
MARGUERITE
MIGNONETTE
MOCK ORANGE
MOTHERWORT
NASTURTIUM
ORANGE LILY
OXEYE DAISY
PENTSTEMON
PERIWINKLE
POINSETTIA
POLYANTHUS
POTENTILLA
RAGGED-LADY
RANUNCULUS
SNAPDRAGON
WALLFLOWER
WELSH POPPY
WHITE POPPY
WILLOW HERB
WINDFLOWER

11
ADAM'S NEEDLE
ANTIRRHINUM
BLOODFLOWER
CABBAGE ROSE
CALCEOLARIA
CHEIRANTHUS
CONVOLVULUS
COTONEASTER
FIG-MARIGOLD

FIVE-FINGERS
FORGET-ME-NOT
GILLYFLOWER
HONEYFLOWER
HONEYSUCKLE
KIDNEY VETCH
LADY'S MANTLE
LONDON-PRIDE
LOOSESTRIFE
LOVE-IN-A-MIST
MADONNA LILY
MEADOWSWEET
PELARGONIUM
PEPPER-ELDER
PHEASANT-EYE
POPPY-MALLOW
RAGGED-ROBIN
RAMBLER-ROSE
RED-HOT-POKER
SCHIZANTHUS
SEA-LAVENDER
SWEET ROCKET
SWEET SULTAN
TIGER-FLOWER
WATER VIOLET
WOOD ANEMONE
XERANTHEMUM

12
CENTURY-PLANT
CUCKOO-FLOWER
DEVIL-IN-A-BUSH
FLOWER-DE-LUCE
HEATHERBELLS
HORN-OF-PLENTY
JACOBEAN-LILY
JACOB'S LADDER
LADY'S CUSHION
LADY'S SLIPPER
MIDDAY-FLOWER
MORNING-GLORY
PASQUE-FLOWER
PHILADELPHUS
RHODODENDRON
ROSE OF SHARON
SALPIGLOSSIS
SHIRLEY POPPY
SHOOTING STAR
SOLOMON'S SEAL
SWEET-WILLIAM

13
AFRICAN VIOLET
APPLEBLOSSOM
BLEEDING-HEART
CHERRY-BLOSSOM
CHRISTMAS-ROSE
CHRYSANTHEMUM

CREEPING JENNY
CROWN IMPERIAL
ESCHSCHOLTZIA
GRAPE-HYACINTH
MARSH MARIGOLD
ORANGE-BLOSSOM
PASSION-FLOWER
ROSE-BAY LAUREL
ROSE-OF-JERICHO
SWEET-CALABASH
TRUMPET-FLOWER
VIRGINIA STOCK

14
BACHELOR-BUTTON
BLACK-EYED-SUSAN
CANTERBURY-BELL
CARDINAL-FLOWER
LOVE-IN-IDLENESS
MOCCASIN-FLOWER

15
BACHELORS-BUTTON
CALIFORNIA POPPY
CHRISTMAS FLOWER
LILY-OF-THE-VALLEY
MICHAELMAS-DAISY
STAR-OF-BETHLEHEM

16
BACHELORS-BUTTONS
CALIFORNIAN POPPY
INDIAN-PAINTBRUSH
LOVE-LIES-BLEEDING

17
RESURRECTION-PLANT

Food (see
also **Fish**;
Fruit;
Plants)

3
BAP
BUN
EGG
FAT
FRY
GUM
HAM
ICE
JAM
KAI
LEG
PIE
POI
ROE
SOY

4
BEEF
BERE
BIGG
BISK
BRAN
BRIE
CAKE
CHOP
CHOW
COLE
CURD
DISH
DUCK
EATS
EDAM
FARE
FARL
FEED
FLAN
FOWL
GAME
GHEE
GRAM
GRUB
HARE
HASH
JOWL
JUNK
KEEP
KESP
LAMB
LARD
LEAN
LOAF

LOIN	CHUCK	ROAST	DUNLOP	RAGOUT	CAYENNE
MACE	CHUET	ROUND	ECLAIR	RASHER	CHAPATI
MALT	COOKY	SALAD	ENTREE	RELISH	CHARQUI
MASH	CREAM	SALMI	FAGGOT	SADDLE	CHEDDAR
MEAL	CRUST	SAUCE	FARINA	SALAMI	CHICKEN
MEAT	CUPID	SCOFF	FLITCH	SCAMPI	CHUPATI
MUSH	CURDS	SCONE	FODDER	SEA-PIE	CHUTNEY
OLIO	CURRY	SENVY	FONDUE	SHORTS	COMMONS
OLLA	DOUGH	SHANK	FORAGE	SIMNEL	COMPOTE
PATE	FARCE	SLOPS	FROISE	SINKER	CONFECT
PEAS	FLANK	SPICE	FUMADO	SORBET	CORNCOB
PECK	FLAWN	STEAK	GAMMON	SOWANS	CRACKER
PONE	FLESH	STOCK	GATEAU	SOWENS	CROWDIE
PORK	FLOUR	SUGAR	GINGER	SQUISH	CRULLER
PROG	FRIER	SWEET	GIRKIN	STAPLE	CRUMPET
PUFF	FRUIT	SWILL	GREENS	STARCH	CUISINE
ROCK	FRYER	SYRUP	GROUSE	SUCKET	CUSTARD
ROLL	FUDGE	TABLE	HACHIS	SUNDAE	DARIOLE
ROUX	GARUM	TAFFY	HAGGIS	SUPAWN	FARCING
RUMP	GIGOT	TANSY	HOMINY	SUPPER	FIG-CAKE
RUSK	GOODY	TOAST	HOT-DOG	SWEETS	FONDANT
SAGO	GOOSE	TOFFY	HOTPOT	TAMALE	FRITTER
SALT	GOUDA	TOMMY	HUMBUG	TIDBIT	FURMETY
SAMP	GRAVY	TRIPE	JUJUBE	TIFFIN	FURMITY
SASS	GRILL	TRUCK	JUMBAL	TITBIT	GAME-PIE
SLAW	GRUEL	VIAND	JUMBLE	TOFFEE	GHERKIN
SOJA	GUMBO	VIFDA	JUNKET	TONGUE	GIZZARD
SOUP	HALVA	VIVDA	LARDON	TRIFLE	GLUCOSE
SOYA	HEART	WAFER	LEAVEN	TUCKER	GNOCCHI
STEW	HONEY	YEAST	LIEBIG	TURKEY	GRISTLE
SUET	HOOSH		MARROW	VIANDS	GROCERY
TART	ICING	**6**	MASLIN	WAFFLE	GRUYERE
TUCK	INGAN	BATTER	MATZAH	WASTEL	GUMDROP
VEAL	JELLY	BIFFIN	MATZOH	YAOURT	HIGH TEA
WHET	JOINT	BISQUE	MEALIE	YOGURT	HOE-CAKE
WHEY	KABAB	BONBON	MESLIN		INCHPIN
WING	KABOB	BORSCH	MORSEL	**7**	JAM ROLL
YOLK	KEBAB	BREAST	MOUSSE	ALCORZA	JAM TART
	KEBOB	BRUNCH	MUFFIN	ALIMENT	KEBBUCK
5	KEECH	BUTTER	MUSSEL	BANNOCK	KETCHUP
ASPIC	LIVER	CANAPE	MUTTON	BANQUET	KIDNEYS
BACON	MAIZE	CATSUP	NOODLE	BATH-BUN	KNUCKLE
BEANS	MANNA	CAVIAR	NOUGAT	BEEF-HAM	LARDOON
BEVER	MATZO	CECILS	OLIVER	BILTONG	LASAGNE
BOARD	MELBA	CEREAL	OMELET	BISCUIT	LOZENGE
BOMBE	MINCE	CHEESE	OXYMEL	BOTARGO	MANCHET
BREAD	NAVEW	CHEWET	PANADA	BOUILLI	MANNOSE
BROMA	OLIVE	CHILLI	PARKIN	BRIOCHE	MATZOTH
BROSE	PASTA	COLLOP	PASTRY	BRISKET	MEATPIE
BROTH	PASTE	COMFIT	PEPPER	BROCHAN	MEAT TEA
BULLY	PASTY	COMPOT	PICKLE	BROILER	MUSTARD
CABOB	PATTY	COOKIE	PILAFF	BURGOUT	NOODLES
CABOC	PEASE	CROWDY	PILLAU	CALIPEE	NURTURE
CANDY	PILAU	CRUMBS	POLONY	CANELLA	OATCAKE
CAPON	PILAW	CULLIS	POSSET	CARAMEL	OATMEAL
CATES	PULSE	CUTLET	POTAGE	CARCAKE	OLYCOOK
CHEER	PUREE	DAINTY	PULLET	CATCHUP	OLYKOEK
CHIPS	QUAIL	DINNER	RABBIT	CAVIARE	PABULUM

PANCAKE	BAKEMEAT	MEAT STEW	CREAM-PUFF	BAKED BEANS
PANOCHA	BARBECUE	MERINGUE	CROQUETTE	BATH OLIVER
PAPRIKA	BECHAMEL	MINCEPIE	EASTER EGG	BECHE-DE-MER
PARFAIT	BLACKCAP	MISHMASH	EMMENTHAL	BEEF-BREWIS
PEA-SOUP	BOUILLON	MOLASSES	ENTREMETS	BLANCMANGE
PICKLES	CHAPATTI	OMELETTE	ERVALENTA	BLANQUETTE
PIKELET	CHESHIRE	PANDOWDY	EWE-CHEESE	BLUE CHEESE
PLUM-JAM	CHOP-SUEY	PARMESAN	FLESH-MEAT	BOILED EGGS
PLUM-PIE	CHOW-CHOW	PASTRAMI	FORCEMEAT	BOILED MEAT
POLENTA	CHOW-MEIN	PEMMICAN	FORETASTE	BREADBERRY
POPADUM	CHUPATTI	PHEASANT	FRICASSEE	BREADSTUFF
POPCORN	CLAMBAKE	PIECRUST	FRIEDCAKE	BRIDESCAKE
PORK-PIE	COLESLAW	PLUM-CAKE	FRIED FISH	BROWN BREAD
POTTAGE	CONFETTI	PLUM-DUFF	FRIED RICE	CALF'S LIVER
POULTRY	CONSERVE	POPPADUM	FRUITCAKE	CALVES'-FOOT
PRALINE	CONSOMME	PORK CHOP	GALANTINE	CHEESECAKE
PRETZEL	CORN-BEEF	PORRIDGE	GENOA CAKE	CHELSEA BUN
PUDDING	CORN-CAKE	POT-ROAST	GINGERNUT	CHERRY CAKE
RAMAKIN	CORN-PONE	PRESERVE	GRAVY-SOUP	CHERRY TART
RAMEKIN	COUSCOUS	QUENELLE	GROCERIES	COCKYLEEKY
RAREBIT	CRACKNEL	QUIDANNY	HAMBURGER	COMESTIBLE
RATAFIA	CREAM-BUN	RACAHOUT	HONEYCOMB	CONFECTION
RATIONS	CROSS-BUN	RAMEQUIN	IRISH STEW	CORN-DODGER
RAVIOLI	DELICACY	RHUM-BABA	KICKSHAWS	CORNED BEEF
RISOTTO	DOUGHBOY	RICE-SOUP	KIDNEY PIE	CORNFLAKES
RISSOLE	DOUGHNUT	ROCK-CAKE	LEG OF LAMB	COTTAGE-PIE
ROASTER	DRESSING	ROLY-POLY	LIQUORICE	CURRANT-BUN
RUM-BABA	DRIPPING	RYE-BREAD	LIVER-WING	EDAM CHEESE
SAPSAGO	DUCKLING	SALT BEEF	LOAF-SUGAR	EMMENTALER
SAUSAGE	DUMPLING	SALT-JUNK	ROQUEFORT	FIG-PUDDING
SAVELOY	EMMENTAL	SALT PORK	SALT BACON	FLESH-BROTH
SAVOURY	FISH-MEAL	SANDWICH	SCOTCH EGG	FOOD SUPPLY
SEAFOOD	FLAPJACK	SEEDCAKE	SEASONING	FRANGIPANE
SHERBET	FLUMMERY	SEMOLINA	SHORTCAKE	FRANGIPANI
SIRLOIN	FROSTING	SHOULDER	SODA-SCONE	FRENCH LOAF
SOUFFLE	FRUIT-PIE	SILLABUB	SOURDOUGH	FRICANDEAU
STILTON	FRUMENTY	SLAPJACK	SPAGHETTI	FRUIT-SALAD
STRUDEL	FURMENTY	SPARE RIB	SPLIT PEAS	GINGERSNAP
SUCCADE	HARDBAKE	SQUAB-PIE	SPOON-FOOD	GIRDLE-CAKE
SUCROSE	HARDTACK	STUFFING	SPOON-MEAT	GORGONZOLA
SUPPAWN	HODGEPOT	SUPPLIES	STIRABOUT	GRAPE-SUGAR
TAPIOCA	HOTCHPOT	SYLLABUB	SUCCOTASH	GREEN SALAD
TARTLET	ICE-CREAM	TEA-BREAD	SUGARLOAF	GROUND-RICE
TEACAKE	JULIENNE	TORTILLA	SUGARPLUM	GUAVA JELLY
TREACLE	KEDGEREE	TROTTERS	SWEETMEAT	HAM-AND-EGGS
TREHALA	KICKSHAW	TURNOVER	SWISS ROLL	HAMBURGHER
TRUFFLE	KOUSKOUS	UNDERCUT	TASTY DISH	HEADCHEESE
VENISON	LICORICE	VICTUALS	TIPSY-CAKE	HODGE-PODGE
YOGHURT	LOAFCAKE	WHITE-POT	VOL-AU-VENT	HOTCH-POTCH
ZAKUSKA	LOBLOLLY	YOGHOURT	WHITE MEAT	ICING-SUGAR
ZAKUSKI	LOLLIPOP	ZWIEBACK	WHOLE MEAL	JERKED BEEF
	LUNCHEON		WILD-HONEY	JOHNNY-CAKE
8	MACARONI	**9**		JUGGED HARE
ALLSPICE	MACAROON	APPETISER	**10**	LAMB CUTLET
AMBROSIA	MAIN DISH	APPETIZER	ALMOND-CAKE	LAVER BREAD
ANTEPAST	MARINADE	CAMEMBERT	APPLE-JELLY	MAPLE-SUGAR
APPLE-JAM	MARZIPAN	CHOCOLATE	APPLE-SAUCE	MAPLE-SYRUP
APPLE-PIE	MEAT LOAF	CREAM-CAKE	APRICOT JAM	MARROWBONE

MAYONNAISE
MINCED MEAT
MINESTRONE
MOCK-TURTLE
MOZZARELLA
MUTTON-CHOP
PATISSERIE
PEASE-BROSE
PEPPER-CAKE
PEPPERMINT
PICCALILLI
POACHED EGG
POTTED MEAT
PROVISIONS
PUDDING-PIE
PUFF-PASTRY
RAISIN-LOAF
RHUBARB-PIE
SACCHARINE
SALMAGUNDI
SALT BUTTER
SAUERKRAUT
SEA-BISCUIT
SHEEP'S HEAD
SHISH KEBAB
SHORTBREAD
SIMNEL-CAKE
SPITCHCOCK
SPONGE-CAKE
STEWED MEAT
SUGAR-CANDY
SUSTENANCE
SWEETBREAD
SWISS CHARD
TENDERLOIN
TOMATO-SOUP
TURTLE-SOUP
VEAL CUTLET
VERMICELLI
WATER-GRUEL
WHITE BREAD

11

BAKED POTATO
BANANA-SPLIT
BANBURY CAKE
BARLEY-SUGAR
BONNE-BOUCHE
CHICKEN-SOUP
CHITTERLING
CLAM-CHOWDER
COCKALEEKIE
CREAM-CHEESE
CURRANT-CAKE
CURRANT-LOAF
CURRY-POWDER
DUTCH CHEESE
EMMENTHALER

FRANKFURTER
FRENCH BREAD
GALAM BUTTER
GINGERBREAD
GOLDEN SYRUP
GOUDA CHEESE
HAM SANDWICH
HORS D'OEUVRE
HOT CROSS BUN
IRON RATIONS
JAM SANDWICH
LEG OF MUTTON
MADEIRA CAKE
MARSHMALLOW
MEAT-PUDDING
MEDLAR JELLY
MILK-PUDDING
NOURISHMENT
OLLA-PODRIDA
OYSTER-PATTY
PETITS FOURS
PLUM-PUDDING
QUINCE JELLY
RAISIN-BREAD
REFRESHMENT
RHUBARB-TART
RICE-PUDDING
ROAST TURKEY
SAGO PUDDING
SAUSAGE-ROLL
SHORT PASTRY
SIDE OF BACON
SIMNEL BREAD
SMORGASBORD
SOUTER'S CLOD
STEWED FRUIT
SUET PUDDING
TAGLIATELLE
TUTTI-FRUTTI
TWELFTH-CAKE
WEDDING-CAKE
WELSH MUTTON
WELSH RABBIT
WENSLEYDALE
WHEATEN LOAF

12

APPLE-FRITTER
APPLE-PUDDING
BIRTHDAY-CAKE
BLOOD-PUDDING
BREAST OF LAMB
BREAST OF VEAL
BURNT ALMONDS
BUTCHER'S MEAT
BUTTERSCOTCH
CHOICE MORSEL
CLOTTED CREAM

CLUB SANDWICH
COCKIELEEKIE
COMMISSARIAT
CORN-ON-THE-COB
CURDS AND WHEY
CURRANT-BREAD
CURRANT-JELLY
EGGS-AND-BACON
FILLET OF SOLE
FISH AND CHIPS
FRUIT-PUDDING
GARAM MASSALA
GUARANA BREAD
HAMBURG STEAK
HASTY PUDDING
HODGE-PUDDING
JULIENNE SOUP
KISSING-CRUST
LIVER-SAUSAGE
LOBSTER PATTY
MAID-OF-HONOUR
MULLIGATAWNY
MUTTON-CUTLET
PEASE-BANNOCK
PEASE-PUDDING
PIGS' TROTTERS
PLUM-PORRIDGE
PUMPERNICKEL
QUARTERN-LOAF
REFRESHMENTS
SCRAMBLED EGG
SHEPHERD'S PIE
SHIP'S BISCUIT
SHORT COMMONS
TRIPE DE ROCHE
WELSH RAREBIT

13

APPLE-DUMPLING
BATTER-PUDDING
BOUILLABAISSE
CHEDDAR CHEESE
CHRISTMAS CAKE
CONFECTIONERY
COTTAGE CHEESE
CUSTARD-COFFIN
DOUBLE-GLOSTER
FLITCH OF BACON
GERMAN SAUSAGE
GIGOT-DE-MOUTON
GRUYERE CHEESE
PETIT DEJEUNER
RASHER OF BACON
ROLL-AND-BUTTER
SCOTCH COLLOPS
SIRLOIN OF BEEF
STILTON CHEESE
VEAL-AND-HAM PIE

14

APPLE CHARLOTTE
BOLOGNA SAUSAGE
BREAD-AND-BUTTER
CHARLOTTE RUSSE
CHESHIRE CHEESE
CRAB-APPLE JELLY
GOOSEBERRY-FOOL
HAUNCH OF MUTTON
MASHED POTATOES
MOCK-TURTLE SOUP
PARMESAN CHEESE
PATE-DE-FOIE-GRAS
SADDLE OF MUTTON
TOASTED TEACAKE
TURKISH DELIGHT
WHOLEMEAL BREAD
WORCESTERSHIRE

15

BAKED SHEEP'S HEAD
BUBBLE-AND-SQUEAK
CHOCOLATE ECLAIR
DEVONSHIRE CREAM
HAUNCH OF VENISON
ROQUEFORT CHEESE
WIENER SCHNITZEL

Football

3
CUP
NET
TRY

4
BACK
CLUB
DRAW
FOUL
GAME
GATE
GOAL
HEEL
KICK
MARK
PLAY
PUNT
SAVE
SHOT

5
FA CUP
FIELD
MATCH
RUGBY
SCORE
SCRUM
SHOOT
TOUCH

6
CENTRE
CORNER
CUP-TIE
HEADER
KICKER
LEAGUE
ON-SIDE
PLAYER
RUGGER
SCORER
SOCCER
TACKLE

7
CAPTAIN
CONVERT
DRIBBLE
FORWARD
FOULING
HEADING
KICK-OFF
KNOCK-ON
MANAGER

OFFSIDE
PENALTY
REFEREE
STADIUM
STRIKER
TACTICS
THROW-IN
TRAINER
UPRIGHT

8
ATTACKER
CROSSBAR
CUP-FINAL
DEAD BALL
DEFENDER
DIVISION
DROP-KICK
FOUL PLAY
FRIENDLY
FULL-BACK
GOAL AREA
GOAL-LINE
GOALPOST
HALF-BACK
HALF-TIME
HAND BALL
HANDLING
LINESMAN
SHOOTING
SIX-A-SIDE
TACKLING
TRAINING
TRANSFER
TRIPPING
UPRIGHTS

9
DRAWN GAME
FIVE-A-SIDE
GATE-MONEY
GOALMOUTH
GOALPOSTS
PLACE-KICK
RUGBY BALL
SCRUM-HALF
SCRUMMAGE
TOUCHLINE

10
CENTRE-HALF
CONVERSION
CORNER-FLAG
CORNER-KICK
GOALKEEPER
GOAL-SCORER
GRAND STAND
INSIDE-LEFT

RUGBY UNION
RUGGER BALL
SEVEN-A-SIDE
SOCCER BALL
TOUCH-JUDGE
W-FORMATION

11
ASSOCIATION
DROPPED GOAL
HALFWAY-LINE
INSIDE-RIGHT
OFFSIDE RULE
OUTSIDE-LEFT
PENALTY AREA
PENALTY GOAL
PENALTY KICK
PENALTY SPOT
RUGBY LEAGUE
TRANSFER FEE

12
CENTRE CIRCLE
DEAD BALL LINE
INTERNATIONAL
OUTSIDE-RIGHT
THREE-QUARTER
WING HALF-BACK

13
CENTRE-FORWARD
DEFENSIVE PLAY
FRIENDLY MATCH
HALF-TIME SCORE
INSIDE-FORWARD

14
CAMBRIDGE RULES
GAELIC FOOTBALL

15
AUSTRALIAN RULES

French Departments

3
AIN
LOT
VAR

4
AUBE
AUDE
CHER
EURE
GARD
GERS
JURA
NORD
OISE
ORNE
TARN

5
AISNE
DOUBS
DROME
INDRE
ISERE
LOIRE
MARNE
MEUSE
PARIS
RHONE
SOMME
YONNE

6
ALLIER
ARIEGE
CANTAL
CREUSE
LANDES
LOIRET
LOZERE
MANCHE
NIEVRE
SARTHE
SAVOIE
VENDEE
VIENNE
VOSGES

7
ARDECHE
AVEYRON
BAS-RHIN
BELFORT
CORREZE

COTE-D'OR
ESSONNE
GIRONDE
HERAULT
MAYENNE
MOSELLE

8
ARDENNES
CALVADOS
CHARENTE
DORDOGNE
HAUT-RHIN
MORBIHAN
VAL-D'OISE
VAUCLUSE
YVELINES

9
FINISTERE
PUY-DE-DOME

10
CORSE-DU-SUD
DEUX-SEVRES
EURE-ET-LOIR
HAUTE-CORSE
HAUTE-LOIRE
HAUTE-MARNE
HAUTE-SAONE
LOIR-ET-CHER
VAL-DE-MARNE

11
COTES-DU-NORD
HAUTES-ALPES
HAUTE-SAVOIE
HAUTE-VIENNE
PAS-DE-CALAIS

12
HAUTE-GARONNE
HAUTS-DE-SEINE
INDRE-ET-LOIRE
LOT-ET-GARONNE
MAINE-ET-LOIRE
SAONE-ET-LOIRE
SEINE-ET-MARNE

13
ILLE-ET-VILAINE
SEINE-MARITIME
TARN-ET-GARONNE

14
ALPES-MARITIMES
BOUCHES-DU-RHONE
HAUTES-PYRENEES

15
LOIRE-ATLANTIQUE
SEINE-SAINT-DENIS

16
CHARENTE-MARITIME
MEURTHE-ET-MOSELLE

18
PYRENEES-ORIENTALES

19
PYRENEES-ATLANTIQUES

20
ALPES-DE-HAUTE-PROVENCE

Fruit (see also Plants)

3
COB
FIG
HAW
HEP
HIP
NUT
UVA

4
AKEE
COLA
CRAB
DATE
GAGE
GEAN
KAKI
KOLA
LIME
MAST
PEAR
PEPO
PILI
PLUM
POME
RASP
SLOE
UGLI

5
ANANA
APPLE
ASSAI
BERRY
CUBEB
DRUPE
GOURD
GRAPE
GUAVA
JAFFA
LEMON
MANGO
MELON
MERRY
MOREL
MORUS
NARAS
NELIS
OLIVE
PAPAW
PEACH
PECAN
PINON
PROIN
PROYN
PRUNE

6
ACHENE
ALMOND
ANANAS
BANANA
BEN-NUT
BIFFIN
CHERRY
CITRON
COB-NUT
CODLIN
DAMSON
DRUPEL
DURIAN
DURION
GROSER
GROSET
JUJUBE
LITCHI
LONGAN
LOQUAT
LYCHEE
MAGUEY
MAMMEE
MAYPOP
MAZARD
MEDLAR
MUSCAT
MUSSEL
NARRAS
NELIES
NUTMEG
ORANGE
PAPAYA
PAWPAW
PEANUT
PIPPIN
POMELO
PREWYN
PROINE
PROYNE
PRUINE
QUINCE
RAISIN
RENNET
RUSSET
SAMARA
SECKEL
SOUARI
WALNUT
WAMPEE
WARDEN

7
APRICOT

AVOCADO
BABASSU
BUCKEYE
BULLACE
CATAWBA
CEDRATE
CHESNUT
COCONUT
CODLING
COLANUT
COSTARD
CUMQUAT
CURRANT
EGG-PLUM
FILBERD
FILBERT
GENIPAP
GROSERT
HAUTBOY
HOGPLUM
KOLA-NUT
KUMQUAT
LEECHEE
MALMSEY
MAY-DUKE
MAZZARD
MORELLO
PILI-NUT
PINGUIN
PLUMCOT
POMEROY
POMPELO
PUPUNHA
RIBSTON
SAOUARI
SATSUMA
SOURING
SOURSOP
TANGELO
WILDING

8
ABRICOCK
ALLSPICE
APRICOCK
ARECA-NUT
BARBERRY
BAYBERRY
BEECHNUT
BERGAMOT
BETEL-NUT
BILBERRY
BOGBERRY
CALABASH
CAPRI FIG

CHESTNUT
CITRANGE
COCOANUT
COCOPLUM
COKERNUT
COQUILLA
COWBERRY
CREAM-NUT
DATE-PLUM
DEWBERRY
DOGBERRY
DRUPELET
GROSSART
HANEPOOT
HASTINGS
HAZELNUT
HONEYPOT
JAPONICA
JONATHAN
KALUMPIT
MALVESIE
MANDARIN
MAY-APPLE
MULBERRY
MUSCADEL
MUSCATEL
MUSK-PEAR
MUSK-PLUM
NISBERRY
PEARMAIN
PECAN-NUT
PLANTAIN
PRUNELLO
QUANDANG
QUANDONG
QUANTONG
QUEENING
RAMBUTAN
RIBSTONE
SHADDOCK
SWEETING
SWEET-SOP
TAMARIND
VICTORIA

9
ALGARROBA
APPLE-JOHN
BEARBERRY
BEECH-MAST
BLAEBERRY
BLUEBERRY
BRAZIL NUT
BUTTERNUT
CANDLENUT
CANTALOUP
CARMELITE
CASHEW NUT

CHERIMOYA
CHINCAPIN
CHINKAPIN
CHIRIMOYA
CHOKE-PEAR
COROZO-NUT
CRAB-APPLE
CRANBERRY
CROWBERRY
DAMASCENE
GREENGAGE
GROUNDNUT
HAANEPOOT
HINDBERRY
INDIA FIG
JACK-FRUIT
JENNETING
JOHN-APPLE
KING-APPLE
LOVE-APPLE
MALVOISIE
MANDARINE
MANGOSTAN
MELOCOTON
MUSCADINE
MUSK-MELON
MYROBALAN
NASEBERRY
NECTARINE
NEESBERRY
PERSIMMON
PHYSIC-NUT
PINEAPPLE
PISTACHIO
PLUMDAMAS
POKE BERRY
QUARENDEN
QUARENDER
RASPBERRY
ROSEAPPLE
RUSSETING
SAPODILLA
SOUARI NUT
STAR-APPLE
TANGERINE
VICTORINE
WALLFRUIT
WHINBERRY

10
BIRD-CHERRY
BLACKBERRY
BLACKHEART
BREADFRUIT
BROWN JOLLY
CHERIMOYER
CHINQUAPIN
CHOKEBERRY

CLEMENTINE
CLOUDBERRY
CRAKEBERRY
DAMASK PLUM
ELDERBERRY
GOOSEBERRY
GRANADILLA
GRAPEFRUIT
GRENADILLA
HICKORY-NUT
JARGONELLE
LOGANBERRY
MANGOSTEEN
MARASCHINO
MARKING NUT
MELICOTTON
MELOCOTOON
MUSSEL PLUM
PHILIPPINA
PHILIPPINE
PHILOPOENA
POME CITRON
POMPELMOUS
PUMPLENOSE
QUARANTINE
QUARRENDER
RED-CURRANT
SAOUARI NUT
SOUR CHERRY
STONE-FRUIT
STRAWBERRY
SUGAR-APPLE
SWEET-WATER
WATER-LEMON
WATER-MELON
WILD-CHERRY

11
ACHAENOCARP
ANCHOVY PEAR
AVOCADO PEAR
BITTER-APPLE
BITTER-SWEET
BLACK WALNUT
BON CHRETIEN
BOYSENBERRY
CANDLE-BERRY
CASHEW-APPLE
CHOKE-CHERRY
FRENCH BERRY
HESPERIDIUM
HUCKLEBERRY
HURTLEBERRY
INDIAN-BERRY
JAFFA ORANGE
LEATHERCOAT
MAGNUM BONUM
MALAKATOONE

MAMMEE APPLE
MONKEY-BREAD
MULBERRY-FIG
NAVEL ORANGE
PAMPELMOOSE
PAMPELMOUSE
POMEGRANATE
POMPELMOOSE
POMPELMOUSE
PRICKLY-PEAR
QUANDONG-NUT
QUARRINGTON
QUEENE-APPLE
QUEEZ-MADDAM
RUSSET APPLE
SCUPPERNONG
WINTER-APPLE

12
AMERICAN ALOE
BLACKCURRANT
BUFFALO-BERRY
CENTURY PLANT
CHECKERBERRY
CITRUS FRUITS
CUSTARD-APPLE
MAMMEE SAPOTA
PASSION-FRUIT
PERSIAN BERRY
SASSAFRAS-NUT
VICTORIA PLUM
WHORTLEBERRY
WINTER-CHERRY

13
ALLIGATOR PEAR
CATHERINE PEAR
HONEYDEW-MELON
HORSE-CHESTNUT
QUEENSLAND NUT
RIBSTON-PIPPIN
SAPODILLA-PLUM

14
ALLIGATOR APPLE
BARBADOS CHERRY
CAPE-GOOSEBERRY

15
BARBADOES CHERRY
SPANISH CHESTNUT

Games and Sports (see also **Cricket**; **Football**)

3
CAT
GIN
LOO
NAP
PIT
PUT
TAG
TAW
TIG

4
BALL
BRAG
CRIB
DIBS
DICE
FARO
GOLF
GRAB
JUDO
LUDO
MORA
POLO
POOL
PUTT
RUFF
SKAT
SNAP
SUMO

5
BANDY
BINGO
BLUFF
BOWLS
CHESS
CRAPS
FIVES
HALMA
KENDO
LOTTO
MARLS
MONTE
MORRA
OMBRE
POKER
RUGBY
RUMMY
WHIST

6

AIKIDO
BANKER
BASSET
BOSTON
BOXING
BRIDGE
CAVING
COBNUT
CRAMBO
DISCUS
ECARTE
EUCHRE
FAN-TAN
FLYING
GAMMON
GOBANG
HAZARD
HOCKEY
HURLEY
LOGGAT
MERELS
MERILS
MORALS
MORRIS
PELOTA
PIQUET
QUINZE
QUOITS
RACING
RIDING
RUGGER
SHINNY
SHINTY
SKI-ING
SOCCER
SQUASH
TENNIS
TIPCAT

7

ARCHERY
BATHING
BEZIQUE
BOWLING
CANASTA
CASSINO
CHARADE
COON-CAN
CRICKET
CROQUET
CURLING
DIABOLO
FENCING
GLIDING
HACKING
HURLING
JAI ALAI

JU-JITSU
LOGGATS
LOTTERY
MAHJONG
MARBLES
MARRELS
MERELLS
NETBALL
OLD MAID
PALLONE
PATBALL
PINOCLE
PONTOON
PRIMERO
PUSH-PIN
RACKETS
REVERSI
SAILING
SHOT-PUT
SKATING
SNOOKER
SURFING
TENPINS
TILTING
TOMBOLA
WAR-GAME

8

ALL-FOURS
BACCARAT
BASEBALL
CHARADES
CHECKERS
CLIMBING
CONTRACT
CRIBBAGE
DECK-GAME
DOMINOES
DRAUGHTS
FIVE-PINS
FOOTBALL
FORFEITS
GIN RUMMY
HANDBALL
HURDLING
JIU-JITSU
KIM'S GAME
KORFBALL
LACROSSE
LEAPFROG
MAHJONGG
MIRACLES
NAPOLEON
NINEPINS
PALL-MALL
PATIENCE
PING-PONG
PINOCHLE

POPE JOAN
PUSHBALL
PYRAMIDS
RACQUETS
REVERSIS
ROLY-POLY
ROULETTE
ROUNDERS
SARDINES
SCRABBLE
SHOOTING
SKITTLES
SLEDDING
SOFTBALL
TICK-TACK
TRAPBALL
TRAY-TRIP
TRIC-TRAC
TUG-OF-WAR
WALL-GAME

9

AUNT SALLY
BADMINTON
BAGATELLE
BILLIARDS
BLACKJACK
BOB-CHERRY
CHERRY-PIT
CLOCK-GOLF
FIVE-A-SIDE
HOPSCOTCH
ICE-HOCKEY
MATRIMONY
NEWMARKET
NINE-HOLES
POT-HOLING
QUADRILLE
SOLITAIRE
STOOLBALL
STUD-POKER
VINGT-ET-UN
WATER-POLO
WRESTLING

10

BACKGAMMON
BASKETBALL
CRISS-CROSS
DECK-QUOITS
DECK-TENNIS
HANDY-DANDY
HOT-COCKLES
ICE-SKATING
JACKSTRAWS
KETTLEPINS
KITTLEPINS
KRIEGSPIEL

LANSQUENET
LAWN TENNIS
PAPER-CHASE
REAL TENNIS
SHOVE-GROAT
SHUFFLE-CAP
SKI-JUMPING
SNAPDRAGON
SPILLIKINS
SURF-RIDING
TRICK-TRACK
TROU-MADAME
VOLLEYBALL

11

BARLEY-BRAKE
BUMBLE-PUPPY
FOX-AND-GEESE
GENERAL POST
HIDE-AND-SEEK
KRIEGSSPIEL
ROUGE-ET-NOIR
ROYAL TENNIS
SANCHO-PEDRO
SHOVELBOARD
SPAN-COUNTER
SPECULATION
TABLE-TENNIS
TENT-PEGGING
TIDDLYWINKS
TOBOGANNING
TROLL-MY-DAME

12

BOBSLEIGHING
CONSEQUENCES
HOODMAN-BLIND
HOUSEY-HOUSEY
KNUR AND SPELL
PITCH-AND-TOSS
SHOVE-HA'PENNY
SHUFFLEBOARD
SINGLE-WICKET
SPAN-FARTHING
TROLL-MY-DAMES

13

AUCTION BRIDGE
BLINDMAN'S BUFF
CHUCK-FARTHING
HARE-AND-HOUNDS
KISS-IN-THE-RING
MUSICAL CHAIRS
PITCH-FARTHING
POSTMAN'S KNOCK
PRISONERS'-BASE
ROLLER-SKATING
SHOOTING CRAPS

SQUASH RACKETS
WEIGHT-LIFTING

14
ALL-IN WRESTLING
CONTRACT BRIDGE
DUCKS-AND-DRAKES
HUNT-THE-SLIPPER
MOUNTAINEERING
NINE MEN'S MORRIS
PUTTING THE SHOT
SHOVE-HALFPENNY
SNIPSNAPSNORUM

15
CATCH-AS-CATCH-CAN
CHINESE CHECKERS
FIVEPENNY MORRIS
NINEPENNY MORRIS

Government

3
ACT
BAR
GAG
LAW
SIT
TAX

4
AYES
BILL
DAIL
DIET
DUMA
LORD
MACE
NAZI
NOES
OATH
PACT
PASS
PEER
POLL
RAAD
RUMP
SEAT
TORY
VOTE
VULI
WHIG
WHIP
WRIT
YUAN

5
AGENT
AMEND
BENCH
BOULE
BY-LAW
CABAL
CHAIR
CLERK
COUNT
DRAFT
EDICT
ELECT
ENACT
HOUSE
IRADE
JUNTA
LOBBY
MAJLI
ORDER
PAPER

PARTY
PLAID
PORTE
RALLY
SOKOL
THING
UKASE
VALID
VOTER
WITAN

6
ASSENT
BACKER
BALLOT
BUDGET
CAUCUS
CENTRE
CIRCAR
CLAUSE
CORTES
DECREE
DIVIDE
ENOSIS
FABIAN
FIRMAN
GOVERN
GRILLE
HECKLE
LABOUR
LEADER
MEMBER
MOTION
PAPACY
POLICY
QUORUM
RECESS
RECORD
REFORM
REGIME
REPORT
RULING
SECEDE
SENATE
SIRCAR
SIRKAR
SOVIET
SPEECH
SUMMON
SWARAJ
TARIFF
TELLER
TYRANT

7
ADJOURN
ALTHING
BARRACK
BOROUGH
BURGESS
CABINET
CANVASS
CAPITOL
CENSURE
CLOSURE
COMMONS
COUNCIL
DEFICIT
DETENTE
DIARCHY
DISSENT
DUARCHY
ELECTOR
ESTATES
FUEHRER
FASCISM
FASCIST
FEDERAL
FINANCE
GALLERY
HANSARD
HECKLER
KNESSET
KREMLIN
LAGTING
LANDTAG
LIBERAL
MANDATE
MARXISM
MARXIST
MUGWUMP
NAZI-ISM
NEW DEAL
OUTVOTE
PASSAGE
PREMIER
RADICAL
RECOUNT
RED TAPE
RE-ELECT
RE-ENACT
REGENCY
RIGSDAG
RIKSDAG
SENATOR
SERKALI
SESSION
SPEAKER
STATISM
TORYISM
TYRANNY
VACANCY

ZIONISM
ZIONIST

8
ASSEMBLY
AUTARCHY
AUTONOMY
BLACK ROD
CAUDILLO
CHAIRMAN
CONGRESS
COMMONER
DEMOCRAT
DICTATOR
DIPLOMAT
DISSOLVE
ELECTION
FELSOHAZ
FREE VOTE
GEROUSIA
HOME RULE
HUSTINGS
LAGTHING
LEFT WING
LOBBYING
MAJORITY
MINISTER
MINISTRY
MINORITY
MONARCHY
OFFICIAL
POLITICO
POLITICS
PROROGUE
REFORMER
REPUBLIC
SCHEDULE
SOBRANJE
SOBRANYE
STORTING
TANAISTE
THEARCHY
TREASURY
TRIARCHY
UNIONISM
UNIONIST
WHIGGERY
WOOLSACK

9
AMENDMENT
AUTOCRACY
BALLOT-BOX
BI-CAMERAL
BUNDESRAT
CANDIDATE
COALITION
COMMISSAR

COMMITTEE
COMMUNISM
COMMUNIST
DEMOCRACY
DESPOTISM
DETERRENT
DIPLOMACY
EDUSKUNTA
EXTREMISM
EXTREMIST
FABIANISM
FIRST LORD
FOLKETING
LANDSTING
LEGISLATE
LOGROLLER
MONOCRACY
ODELSTING
OLIGARCHY
OMBUDSMAN
PARTY WHIP
PATRONAGE
POLITBURO
POUJADIST
PRESIDENT
RED-TAPISM
RED-TAPIST
REICHSTAG
RIGHT WING
SECRETARY
SHIRE MOOT
SKUPSTINA
SOCIALISM
SOCIALIST
STANDERAT
STATESMAN
TAOISEACH
TERRORISM
THEOCRACY

10
ABSOLUTISM
ABSOLUTIST
ARISTARCHY
BLOCK GRANT
BY-ELECTION
CAPITALISM
CAPITALIST
CHANCELLOR
COLLECTIVE
CONFERENCE
CROSS BENCH
DEVOLUTION
DUUMVIRATE
FEDERALISM
FEDERALIST
FEDERATION
GOVERNMENT

GUILLOTINE
HETERONOMY
INVALIDATE
LOGROLLING
LOWER HOUSE
MARTIAL LAW
MATRIARCHY
MILITARISM
MILITARIST
MUGWUMPERY
NEO-FASCISM
NEO-FASCIST
OPPOSITION
OPPRESSION
ORDER PAPER
PARLIAMENT
PATRIARCHY
PLAID CYMRU
POLITICIAN
PSEPHOLOGY
RADICALISM
REPUBLICAN
RESOLUTION
SCRUTINEER
UNI-CAMERAL
UPPER HOUSE
WHITE PAPER

11
ADJOURNMENT
ARISTOCRACY
BACK-BENCHER
BACK BENCHES
BALLOT-PAPER
BOURGEOISIE
BUREAUCRACY
BYE-ELECTION
CASTING VOTE
CO-EXISTENCE
COLONIALISM
CONGRESSMAN
CONSTITUENT
DAIL EIREANN
DEMARCATION
DISSOLUTION
FINANCE BILL
INDEPENDENT
IRON CURTAIN
LEGISLATION
LEGISLATIVE
LEGISLATURE
MCCARTHYISM
MERITOCRACY
NATIONALISM
NATIONALIST
NATIONALRAT
PACKAGE DEAL
PARTY LEADER

POLICE STATE
PREROGATIVE
PRIVATE BILL
PROGRESSIVE
STATUTE BOOK
SYNDICALISM
SYNDICALIST
TECHNOCRACY
THE CHAMBERS
TRIUMVIRATE
WITENAGEMOT
YEOMAN USHER

12
CIVIL SERVICE
COMMISSIONER
COMMON MARKET
COMMONWEALTH
CONSERVATISM
CONSERVATIVE
CONSTITUENCY
CONSTITUTION
CORTES GERAES
CROSSBENCHER
CROSS BENCHES
DICTATORSHIP
DOMINION RULE
FEDERAL UNION
FIRST CHAMBER
HOUSE OF LORDS
HOUSE OF PEERS
IMPERIAL DIET
INVALIDATION
JURISDICTION
KEPVISELOHAZ
LOWER CHAMBER
PANTISOCRACY
PATRIARCHATE
POPULAR FRONT
SNAP DIVISION
SUBLIME PORTE
TOTALITARIAN
UNION COUNCIL
UPPER CHAMBER
WAYS AND MEANS
WELFARE STATE

13
ANDRA KAMMAREN
CONFEDERATION
DEPUTY SPEAKER
DOWNING STREET
FILIBUSTERING
FREE TRADE AREA
GARRISON STATE
HOME SECRETARY
LORD PRESIDENT
LORD PRIVY SEAL

PRESSURE GROUP
PRIME MINISTER
REIGN OF TERROR
REVOLUTIONARY
REVOLUTIONIST
SEANAD EIREANN
SECOND CHAMBER
SINGLE CHAMBER
STATES-GENERAL
SUPREME SOVIET
UNITED NATIONS
VOTE OF CENSURE

14
ADMINISTRATION
BALANCE OF POWER
DEPUTY CHAIRMAN
DEPUTY SERGEANT
DEPUTY SERJEANT
ELDER STATESMAN
FORSTA KAMMAREN
GOVERNMENT WHIP
HOUSE OF COMMONS
LORD CHANCELLOR
MATRIARCHALISM
OPPOSITION WHIP
REPRESENTATIVE
SELF-GOVERNMENT
SERGEANT-AT-ARMS
SERJEANT-AT-ARMS
UNDER-SECRETARY

15
ATTORNEY GENERAL
CIVIL GOVERNMENT
CLERK OF THE HOUSE
GENERAL ASSEMBLY
GENERAL ELECTION
LEGISLATIVE BODY
MINISTER OF STATE
PERSONALITY CULT
ROYAL COMMISSION
SELECT COMMITTEE
SENATE COMMITTEE
SUPER-GOVERNMENT
TOTALITARIANISM

Heraldry

2
OR

3
BAR
FUR

4
ANKH
ARMS
BASE
BEND
BOAR
BRAY
DELF
FESS
FRET
GAMB
GARB
GULY
ORLE
PALE
PALL
PALY
PILE
ROSE
SEME
SEMY
UNDY
URDE
URDY
VAIR
VERT
WAVY

5
ARMED
AZURE
BADGE
BARRY
BATON
BELEF
BELIC
BENDY
BOUGE
BOWED
CHAMP
CHIEF
COSTE
CROSS
DANCE
DWALE
EAGLE
FESSE
FIELD

FLORY
FUSIL
GARBE
GEMEL
GIRON
GULES
GYRON
LABEL
PARTY
PHEON
POINT
REBUS
SABLE
SCARP
SEMEE
TENNE
TORSE
TRICK
TYGER
URDEE
VAIRE
VAIRY
WAVED

6
ARCHED
ARGENT
ARMORY
AT GAZE
BARBED
BASTON
BEZANT
BILLET
BLAZON
BORDER
BOSOUN
BOTONE
BOUGET
CANTON
CHARGE
CHECKY
CLECHE
COTISE
COUPED
COWARD
CRINED
CRONEL
DEXTER
DRAGON
ERASED
ERMINE
ESCROL
ETOILE
FILFOT
FITCHY

FLANCH
FLEURY
FRETTY
FYLFOT
GOBONY
GORGED
GOUTTY
GURGES
HAMEDE
HELMET
HERALD
JESSED
LIONEL
LODGED
MANCHE
MASCLE
MULLET
NAIANT
NEBULY
POTENT
PROPER
RAGULY
REBATE
RUSTRE
SEEDED
SEJANT
SHIELD
UNGLED
VOIDED
VOIDER
VOLANT
VORANT
WIVERN
WREATH
WYVERN

7
ALERION
ANNULET
ATTIRED
ATTIRES
BATTLED
BEARING
BENDLET
BERNAKE
BEZANTY
BILLEKE
BORDURE
BOTTONY
CADENCY
CHAPEAU
CHAPLET
CHEVRON
CLARION
COMPONY
CORONAL
COURANT
CRUSULY

DORMANT
EMBELIF
EMBLAZE
ENARMED
ENDORSE
ENGRAIL
ERMELIN
ESCROLL
ESTOILE
FRETTED
FRUCTED
GARDANT
GARLAND
GRIFFIN
ISSUANT
JESSANT
LEOPARD
LIONCEL
LOZENGE
LOZENGY
MARTLET
MAUNCHE
MONSTER
NOMBRIL
OVERALL
PASSANT
PATONCE
POTENCE
POTENTY
PURPURE
QUARTER
RAGULED
RAMPANT
RAYONNY
ROUNDEL
ROUNDLE
SALIENT
SALTANT
SALTIER
SALTIRE
SCUCHEON
SCUCHIN
SEA-LION
SLIPPED
STATANT
TORTEAU
TREFOIL
UNGULED
UNICORN

8
AFFRONTE
ALLERION
ANTELOPE
ARMORIST
BANDEROL
BARNACLE
BARRULET
BASILISK

BEVILLED
BIRDBOLT
BLAZONED
BLAZONRY
CABOCHED
CABOSHED
COUCHANT
CRESCENT
CROSSLET
CUBIT ARM
DANCETTE
DANCETTY
DRAGONNE
EMBLAZON
ENDORSED
ENGOULED
ESCALLOP
FLANCHED
FLANCHES
FOUNTAIN
GONFALON
GONFANON
GUARDANT
HAURIANT
HAURIENT
INDENTED
INSIGNIA
INVECKED
INVECTED
MANTLING
MASCALLY
MILLRIND
NAISSANT
OPINICUS
ORDINARY
PALEWISE
POWDERED
ROUNDLET
SCUCHEON
SCUCHION
SINISTER
STANDARD
TINCTURE
TRESSURE
TRISKELE

9
AFFRONTEE
BANDEROLE
BARRYPILY
BEVILWAYS
BLAZONING
CHESS-ROOK
COMBATANT
CONTOURNE
CROSS PATY
DANCETTEE
DIMIDIATE

DISPLAYED
EMBATTLED
ENGRAILED
ENVELOPED
ESCUCHEON
FESSE-WISE
HATCHMENT
LIONCELLE
LYON COURT
QUARTERLY
REGARDANT
SCUTCHEON
SPUR REVEL
SUPPORTER
TRESSURED

10
BAR-GEMELLE
BARRYBENDI
BARRY-BENDY
BARS GEMELS
CINQUEFOIL
COAT-OF-ARMS
COCKATRICE
CROSS FLORY
CROSS FORMY
DIFFERENCE
DIFFERENCY
EMBLAZONRY
ESCUTCHEON
FESSEE-WISE
FESSE-POINT
FIMBRIATED
FLEUR-DE-LIS
FLEUR-DE-LYS
LAMBREQUIN
LEOPARDESS
MURAL CROWN
NAVAL CROWN
QUARTERING
REBATEMENT
SURMOUNTED
THROUGHOUT
TRISKELION

11
ACHIEVEMENT
BICAPITATED
BICORPORATE
COMPARTMENT
CROSS FITCHY
CROSS FLEURY
CROSS MALINE
CROSS VOIDED
DIMIDIATING
DISMEMBERED
ENGRAILMENT
ESCARBUNCLE

ESCUCHEONED
HONOUR-POINT
INESCUCHEON
SPREAD-EAGLE
SUBORDINARY
WATER BOUGET
WATER BUDGET

12
ANIMAL CHARGE
BEND-SINISTER
COUNTER-PALED
CROSS BOTTONY
CROSS FLEURTY
CROSS MATELEY
DIFFERENCING
EASTERN CROWN
EMBLAZONMENT
ESCUTCHEONED
INESCUTCHEON

13
BENDY-SINISTER
COLLEGE OF ARMS
CROSS-CROSSLET
QUEUE FOURCHEE

14
COUNTERCHARGED
COUNTER-PASSANT
PARTITION LINES

Horses

3
BAY
COB
NAG
PAD
RIG
RIP
TAT
TIT

4
ARAB
BARB
COLT
FOAL
GREY
HACK
JADE
MARE
PONY
ROAN
TURK

5
BIDET
CAPLE
CAPUL
FILLY
PUNCH
SCREW
SHIRE
STAIG
STEED
WALER

6
BAYARD
BRONCO
BRUMBY
CAYUSE
DOBBIN
GARRAN
GARRON
GINNET
HUNTER
JENNET
KELPIE
ROARER
SHELTY
SORREL
TARPAN
TRACER

7
ARABIAN

BLEEDER
BRONCHO
COURSER
GELDING
HACKNEY
MUSTANG
PALFREY
PIEBALD
SHELTIE
SUMPTER
THILLER
WHEELER

8
BAT-HORSE
CART-JADE
CHESTNUT
GALLOWAY
GIN-HORSE
LED-HORSE
PALOMINO
POLO PONY
SHETLAND
SKEWBALD
STALLION
WARHORSE

9
BROOD-MARE
CART-HORSE
DRAYHORSE
MALT-HORSE
PACKHORSE
PERCHERON
POST-HORSE
RACEHORSE
STUD-HORSE
WILD HORSE

10
BLOOD-HORSE
BUCEPHALUS
CLYDESDALE
COACH-HORSE
DRAFT-HORSE
SHIRE HORSE
THILL-HORSE
WHEEL-HORSE

11
SADDLE-HORSE

12
DRAUGHT-HORSE
HUNTING HORSE
QUARTER HORSE
SHETLAND PONY
THOROUGHBRED

13
CARRIAGE-HORSE

16
PRZEWALSKI'S HORSE

Islands of the British Isles

3
EWE
HOY
MAN
MAY
MEW
SOA

4
ARAN
BERE
BUTE
CARA
COLL
DANA
EDDY
EIGG
GOLA
HERM
HOLY
IONA
JURA
LOOE
MUCK
MULL
RHUM
RONA
SARK
SEIL
SKYE
SOAY
TEXA
TORY
ULVA
UNST
WIAY
YELL

5
ANNET
ARRAN
BARRA
CAHER
CALDY
CANNA
CLARE
CLEAR
ENSAY
EORSA
FARNE
FOULA
FUDAY
GIGHA
HANDA
ISLAY

LEWIS
LONGA
LUING
LUNDY
LUNGA
NEAGH
RONAY
SANDA
SCARP
SHEEP
SHUNA
WIGHT

6
ACHILL
BURHOU
CANVEY
DURSEY
FETLAR
HARRIS
JERSEY
JETHOU
LAMBAY
MUTTON
OLDANY
ORKNEY
PABBAY
PLADDA
PRIEST
PUFFIN
RAASAY
RAMSEY
ROUSAY
SALTEE
SANDAY
SCARBA
SCILLY
SHIANT
SKOMER
STAFFA
STROMA
SUMMER
WHIDDY

7
BARDSEY
BORERAY
BRESSAY
CROWLIN
EASDALE
ERISKAY
FLANNAN
GORUMNA
HAYLING
KERRERA

LISMORE
MULLION
RATHLIN
ST KILDA
ST MARY'S
SANDRAY
SCARIFF
SHERKIN
WESTRAY
ZETLAND

8
ALDERNEY
ANGLESEY
BERNERAY
BRECQHOU
BROWNSEA
CARDIGAN
CASQUETS
FAIR ISLE
FLAT HOLM
FOULNESS
GUERNSEY
INISHARK
INISHEER
INISHKEA
MAINLAND
SHETLAND
SKOKHOLM
STRONSAY
VALENTIA
VATERSAY

9
BENBECULA
EILEAN MOR
GRASSHOLM
HAVERGATE
INCHKEITH
INISHMAAN
INISHMORE
INISHTURK
INNISFREE
ISLE OF EWE
ISLE OF MAN
ISLE OF MAY
NORTH UIST
PAPA STOUR
ST GEORGE'S
ST MARTIN'S
ST TUDWAL'S
SOUTH UIST
WEST BURRA

10
AILSA CRAIG
DUBH ARTACH
DUBH EILEAN
INISHBOFIN
ISLE MARTIN
ISLE OF SKYE
SAINT KILDA
SAINT MARY'S
STEEP HOLME

11
EILEAN SHONA
INCHMARNOCK
INISHMURRAY
ISLE OF WIGHT
PAPA WESTRAY

12
EILEAN NAN RON
GREAT BLASKET
GREAT CUMBRAE
INISHTRAHULL
SAINT GEORGE'S
SAINT MARTIN'S
SAINT TUDWAL'S

13
EILEAN TRODDAY
LITTLE CUMBRAE

14
LITTLE COLONSAY
SOUTH RONALDSAY

15
EILEAN AN ROIN MOR

Islands of the World
(outside the British Isles)

2
RE

3
ARU
COS
DIU
GAN
IOS
IZU
KAI
KEA
KOS
KRK
OBI
OKI
TSU
YAP
YEU

4
ALOR
AYON
BALI
BATU
BATZ
BEAR
BELY
BIWA
BRAC
BURU
COOK
CRES
CUBA
ELBA
FIJI
GOZO
GUAM
HOOK
HVAR
JAVA
JOLO
LAUT
LINE
LONG
MAHE
MAUI
MILL
MUNA
NIAS

NIUE	MAFIA	BIKINI	MALDEN	CORCYRA	PALMYRA
OAHU	MALTA	BINTAN	MALUKU	CORSICA	PARACEL
OENO	MANUS	BISCOE	MARAJO	COULMAN	PHOENIX
PALM	MATSU	BORDEN	MARCUS	CURACAO	REDONDA
ROCK	MELOS	BORKUM	MASIRA	CYTHERA	RENNELL
ROSS	MILOS	BORNEO	MIDWAY	CYTHNOS	REUNION
ROTI	MITRE	BOUNTY	MISOOL	DIOMEDE	RISHIRI
SABA	NAURU	BOUVET	NANSEI	DOUGLAS	ROCKALL
SADO	NAXOS	BOWMAN	NATUNA	ENGGANO	ST CROIX
SAWU	NEVIS	BREHAT	NEGROS	ESTADOS	ST KITTS
SEPT	NIHAU	BUTUNG	OLERON	FANNING	ST LUCIA
SHAW	NIHOA	CAICOS	PANTAR	FARASAN	SAO TOME
SULA	NORTH	CANARY	PATMOS	FEHMARN	SHIKOKU
SULU	OCEAN	CANTON	PHUKET	FORMOSA	SOCIETY
TAKE	OLAND	CAYMAN	†PIGALU	FRISIAN	SOCOTRA
TRUK	OSUMI	CERIGO	PONAPE	GAMBIER	SOLOMON
WAKE	PALAU	CEYLON	QUEMOY	GARDNER	SPETSAI
	PAROS	CHAGOS	RHODES	GILBERT	STEWART
5	PARRY	CHAVES	RYUKYU	GOTLAND	SUMATRA
ALAND	PEMBA	CHERRY	ST PAUL	GRENADA	SUMBAWA
ARUBA	PERCY	CHILOE	SAIPAN	GRIMSEY	TERNATE
BABAR	PERIM	COMINO	SCYROS	ICELAND	THERMIA
BANKS	RHODE	COMORO	SICILY	ISABELA	TOKELAU
BATAN	RUGEN	CRUZEN	SKIROS	JAMAICA	TUAMOTU
BELLE	SABLE	CYPRUS	STATEN	KABAENA	VANGUNU
BOHOL	SAMAR	DJERBA	TAHITI	KAMARAN	VULCANO
BONIN	SAMOA	EASTER	TAIWAN	KEELING	WATLING
BYLOT	SAMOS	ELLICE	TALAUD	KERKIRA	WRANGEL
CAPRI	SANTO	EUBOEA	TARAWA	KHIUMAA	ZEALAND
CERAM	SCOTT	EUROPA	THASOS	KITHIRA	
CHEJU	SENJA	FAEROE	TIDORE	KITHNOS	8
CHIOS	SERAM	FLORES	TOBAGO	KORCULA	ADELAIDE
COCOS	SOLTA	FRASER	TUBUAI	LA PALMA	AITUTAKI
CORFU	SOUTH	FUTUNA	USHANT	LASTOVO	ALEUTIAN
CRETE	SUMBA	HAINAN	VANNOY	LEEWARD	ANGUILLA
DEVON	TELOS	HAWAII	VIRGIN	LOFOTEN	ANTILLES
DISKO	TENOS	HEARST	WALLIS	LOLLAND	ARAGUAIA
DJAWA	TEXEL	HIVA OA		LOMBLEN	AUCKLAND
DUCIE	THERA	HONSHU	7	LOYALTY	BALEARIC
EFATE	THIRA	IKARIA	ALDABRA	LYAKHOV	BARBADOS
EGADI	TILOS	IMBROS	AMBOINA	MADEIRA	BATHURST
FUNEN	TIMOR	IONIAN	ANDAMAN	MAJORCA	BORNHOLM
GROIX	TINOS	ISCHIA	ANEGADA	MALAITA	BROTHERS
IBIZA	TONGA	ITHACA	*ANNOBON	MALDIVE	BUNGURAN
IMROZ	TURKS	ITHAKI	ANTIGUA	MALPELO	CALYMNOS
IVIZA	ULAWA	ITURUP	AUSTRAL	MAYOTTE	CAROLINE
JAPEN	WETAR	JARVIS	BAHRAIN	MENORCA	CHOISEUL
JUIST	WIESE	KODIAK	BALLENY	MINDORO	CLARENCE
KASOS	ZANTE	KYUSHU	BALTRUM	MINORCA	CORNWALL
KAUAI		LABUAN	BARBUDA	MOROTAI	CYCLADES
KAULA	6	LAURIE	BASILAN	NANUMEA	DESIRADE
KHARK	ANDROS	LEMNOS	BERMUDA	NICOBAR	DOLLEMAN
KHIOS	ANVERS	LESBOS	BONAIRE	NISIROS	DOMINICA
KRITI	AZORES	LINGGA	CELEBES	NISYROS	D'URVILLE
KURIL	BAFFIN	LIPARI	CHARCOT	NORFOLK	ELEPHANT
LEROS	BAHAMA	LOMBOK	CHATHAM	NUNIVAK	FALKLAND
LEYTE	BANABA	MADAME	CHAUSEY	OKINAWA	FRANKLIN
LUZON	BANGKA	MADURA	CHEDUBA	PALAWAN	FUNAFUTI

GANONGGA
HERSCHEL
HILIUMAA
HOKKAIDO
HONG KONG
JAN MAYEN
JOHNSTON
KALIMNOS
KERKENNA
KERMADEC
KUNASHIR
LANGEOOG
MAGDALEN
MAGNETIC
MALEKULA
MALLORCA
MARIANAS
MARSHALL
MELVILLE
MENTAWAI
MINDANAO
MIQUELON
MOLUCCAS
MONTAGUE
NUKU HIVA
OKUSHIRI
PITCAIRN
PRIBILOF
PRINCIPE
QUELPART
ROTTNEST
SAAREMAA
ST HELENA
ST MARTIN
ST PIERRE
ST THOMAS
SAN FELIX
SARDINIA
SEPT ILES
SHIKOTAN
SKOPELOS
SOMBRERO
SOMERSET
SPORADES
STJERNOY
SULAWESI
SVERDRUP
TANIMBAR
TASMANIA
TAWITAWI
TENERIFE
THOUSAND
THURSDAY
TRINIDAD
ULLUNG DO
WINDWARD
ZANZIBAR

9

ABD AL KURI
ADMIRALTY
ANTICOSTI
ANTIPODES
ASCENSION
BELLE ISLE
CAPE VERDE
CHICHAGOF
CHRISTMAS
DECEPTION
DRYGALSKI
ELLESMERE
ERROMANGA
GALAPAGOS
GREENLAND
HALMAHERA
JAMES ROSS
JOINVILLE
KARPATHOS
LACCADIVE
LAMPEDUSA
LANZAROTE
LISIANSKI
LOUISIADE
MACQUARIE
MADELEINE
MANHATTAN
MARGARITA
MARQUESAS
MAURITIUS
NANTUCKET
NEW GUINEA
NORDERNEY
RAKAHANGA
RAROTONGA
ROBERTSON
ROOSEVELT
ST MATTHEW
SAINT PAUL
ST VINCENT
SANTA CRUZ
SHORTLAND
SINGAPORE
STILLWELL
STROMBOLI
WALCHEREN
WANGEROOG
WELLESLEY
ZACYNTHOS
ZAKINTHOS

10

ASTIPALAIA
ASTYPALAEA
CEPHALONIA
CLIPPERTON
CORNWALLIS

CORONATION
DODECANESE
FORMENTERA
GREAT SANDY
GRENADINES
GUADELOUPE
HELIGOLAND
HISPANIOLA
KALIMANTAN
KEFALLINIA
KING GEORGE
KURIA MURIA
LADY ELLIOT
LES SAINTES
LIVINGSTON
MADAGASCAR
MANITOULIN
MARTINIQUE
MONTE BELLO
MONTSERRAT
NEW BRITAIN
NEW GEORGIA
NEW IRELAND
PARECE VELA
PHILIPPINE
POSSESSION
PUERTO RICO
RESOLUTION
SAINT CROIX
SAINT KITTS
ST LAWRENCE
SAINT LUCIA
SEYCHELLES
SPIEKEROOG
THREE KINGS
WASHINGTON
WHITSUNDAY

11

AXEL-HEIBERG
CEPHALLENIA
DIRK HARTOGS
*FERNANDO POO
GRAN CANARIO
GRAND CANARY
GREAT KEPPEL
GUADALCANAL
ILIODHROMIA
KING WILLIAM
MONTE CRISTO
MOUNT DESERT
NEW HEBRIDES
PANTELLERIA
ST EUSTATIUS
SAINT HELENA
SAINT MARTIN
SAINT PIERRE
SAINT THOMAS

SAN SALVADOR
SANTA ISABEL
SANTA YSABEL
THE BROTHERS

12

BOUGAINVILLE
GREAT BARRIER
†MACIAS NGUEMA
MARIE GALANTE
MICHIPICOTEN
NEW AMSTERDAM
NEW CALEDONIA
NEWFOUNDLAND
NORTH FRISIAN
NOVAYA ZEMLYA
PRINCE EDWARD
PROCLAMATION
ST BARTHELEMY
SAINT MATTHEW
SAINT VINCENT
SAN CRISTOBAL
SOUTH GEORGIA

13

ESPIRITO SANTO
ESPIRITU SANTO
FUERTEVENTURA
INDEFATIGABLE
JUAN FERNANDEZ
PRINCE OF WALES
PRINCE PATRICK
SAINT LAWRENCE
SOUTH SANDWICH
SOUTH SHETLAND

14

QUEEN CHARLOTTE
QUEEN ELIZABETH
SAINT EUSTATIUS
TRISTAN DA CUNHA

15

NORTH STRADBROKE
SAINT BARTHELEMY

† new name
* former name

Kings and Queens of England, AD 827–1603

Kings
4
CNUT
EDWY
JOHN

5
EDGAR
EDRED
HENRY

6
ALFRED
CANUTE
EDMUND
EDWARD
EGBERT
HAROLD

7
RICHARD
STEPHEN
WILLIAM

8
ETHELRED

9
ATHELSTAN
ETHELBALD
ETHELBERT
ETHELWULF

10
HARTHACNUT

11
HARDICANUTE

14
EDMUND IRONSIDE

Queens
4
JANE
MARY

7
MATILDA

9
ELIZABETH

British Kings and Queens from 1603

Kings
4
JAMES

6
EDWARD
GEORGE

7
CHARLES
WILLIAM

Queens
4
ANNE
MARY

8
VICTORIA

9
ELIZABETH

Kings of Scotland, AD 843–1603

4
AEDH
DUBH

5
DAVID
EDGAR
EOCHA
GIRIC
JAMES

6
DONALD
DUNCAN
INDULF
LULACH
ROBERT

7
CUILEAN
CULLEAN
EOCHAID
KENNETH
MACBETH
MALCOLM
WILLIAM

9
ALEXANDER

10
DONALD BANE
JOHN BALIOL

11
CONSTANTINE
JOHN BALLIOL

Queens of Scotland

4
MARY

8
MARGARET

Lakes of Europe

3
REE
ZUG

4
ARVO
COMO
DERG
ERNE
IDRO
ISEO
JOUX
MASK
NESS
ORTA
SHIN
THUN
VICO
VOZE
WURM

5
ASNEN
ELTON
FERTO
FOYLE
GARDA
ILMEN
INARI
INDER
LEMAN
MAMRI
MJOSA
NEAGH
OHRID
ONEGA
SALTO
VORTS

6
ALBANO
ANNECY
BELOYE
BRIENZ
CECITA
CORRIB
DUMMER
FEMUND
GENEVA
GULPER
LADOGA
LANGER
LESINA
LOMOND
LUGANO

PEIPUS
PLAUER
PRESPA
SAIMAA
SALKAR
SILJAN
VANERN
VARANO
VARESE
ZURICH

7
ALSERIO
ARALSOR
BALATON
CERESIO
DRAGGAN
IMANDRA
LUCERNE
MALAREN
ORIVESI
PALADRU
PUSIANO
SIMSSEE
TEGELER
UDDJAUR
VATTERN
WORTHER

8
AMMERSEE
BODENSEE
HORNAVAN
KALLSJON
KRAKOWER
MAGGIORE
PAIJANNE
PIELINEN
SNIARDWY
STORSJON
STORUMAN
TOLLENSE
TOP OZERO
VELIKOYE
WALENSEE
YLIKITKA

9
AMPOLLINO
BASKUNCAK
BIELERSEE
CONSTANCE
GRUNDLSEE
HAUKIVESI
HELGASJON

JIESJARVI
KEMIJARVI
KOLPINSEE
LEKS OZERO
MALCHINER
NASIJARVI
NEUCHATEL
OULUJARVI
PUULAVESI
PYHAJARVI
PYHASELKA
SCHAALSEE
TEGERNSEE
TRASIMENO

10
HARKORTSEE
IJSSELMEER
ITMURYNKOL
KUBENSKOYE
KUMMEROWER
PSKOVSKOYE
RURSTAUSEE
SCHWERINER
STAFFELSEE
WINDERMERE

11
BALDENEYSEE
HALLSTATTER
HENGSTEYSEE
KIANTAJARVI
PORTTIPAHTA
SAN GIULIANO
SPEICHERSEE
STARNBERGER

12
AUSSENALSTER
HALLWILERSEE
MOHNE-STAUSEE
PIHLAJARVESI

13
GORKO-SOLENOYE
SANTA GIUSTINA
TREMPLINERSEE

14
STEINHUDER MEER

15
STORA LULEVATTEN

Lakes of Asia

3
SAP
TAI
TUZ
UVS
VAN

4
CHAO
POSO
SALT
TOBA

5
ANLIN
ELING
KAOYU
LANAO
URMIA

6
BAIKAL
BAYKAL
BUMUHU
CHAHAN
CHANKA
CHILKA
KHANKA
LOP NOR
MAYYIT
NAM TSO
NAMU HU
NANHAI
POYANG
TAIMYR
TAYMYR
TOWUTI
ZAISAN
ZAYSAN

7
ASAHI-KO
BUKECHI
CHUKEHU
DEAD SEA
HUNGTZE
KOKO NOR
NANYANG
SAMBHAR
SHAYANG
SHIFUHU
SONGHUA
SULUCHI
TOGO-IKE
WEISHAN

8
BALKHASH
CHILIN HU
CHONGHAI
DALAI NOR
HAMANA-KO
HUAI YANG
ISSYK-KUL
KINNERET
SHINJI-KO
TIBERIAS
TONLE SAP
TOYOTA-KO
TSING HAI
TUNGPING
TUNGTING

9
HULUN CHIH
KOYAMA-IKE
KUNMINGHU
TASHIBUHU
TENGRI NOR

10
HA MELAH YAM
TANGKULA HU

11
ANGLALING HU

13
YANGCHOYUNG HU

15
KIJIMA-CHOSUICHI

Lakes of Africa

3
DOW

4
CHAD
KIVU
TANA

5
ABAYA
EYASI
KYOGA
MWERU
NGAMI
QARUN
RUKWA
VOLTA
ZIWAY

6
*ALBERT
BOTKUL
CHILWA
*EDWARD
IKIMBA
KARIBA
MALAWI
NASSER
NATRON
RUDOLF
SHIRWA
SIBAYA

7
BARINGO
MANYARA
PEOLELA
VAALDAM

8
NAIVASHA
STEFANIE
VICTORIA

9
BANGWEULU
FAGUIBINE
*LEOPOLD II
MACKILLOP
†MAI NDOMBE
SALISBURY

10
TANGANYIKA

11
 BIRKAT QARUN
GREAT BITTER
†IDI AMIN DADA

14
†MOBUTU SESE SEKO

* former name

† new name

Lakes of North and Central America

3
DRY
HAY
MUD
RED

4
BURT
DALY
ERIE
JUNE
KNEE
KNOB
MEAD
MONO
RICE
ROSS
SEAL
SEUL
SODA
SWAN
TULE
UTAH
WACO
WOLF
YALE

5
ABERT
ADAMS
AMISK
ATLIN
BANKS
BLACK
BURNT
CADDO
CADIZ
CEDAR
CHINA
CROSS
CRUMP
DANBY
DEASE
EAGLE
EVANS
FABER
GATUN
GAUER
GOOSE
GRAND
GREEN

HONEY	GEORGE	SUMMER	MISSISA	HARDISTY
HORSE	GUZMAN	TAGISH	MULLETT	HARRISON
HURON	HARNEY	TESTIN	MUSKOKA	HIGHROCK
KASBA	HARPER	TEXOMA	NIPIGON	HOUGHTON
KEMPT	HODGES	THORPE	NONACHO	IROQUOIS
KEUKA	HOTTAH	TULARE	NORFOLK	JEANNINE
LOCHE	IMURUK	TURNER	NUELTIN	KAMLOOPS
LOWER	INDIAN	VERRET	NUYAKUK	KENTUCKY
MILLS	ISLAND	WABUSH	ONTARIO	KESAGAMI
MINTO	JOSEPH	WALKER	OSSIPEE	LILLOOET
MOOSE	KAKAGI	WALLED	PENNASK	MANITOBA
MOSES	KAKISA	WILLOW	PLETIPI	MATAGAMI
OOSTA	KELLER	WILSON	POMPTON	MAUREPAS
OTTER	KIPAWA	WINISK	PYRAMID	MEELPAEG
PALEN	KLUANE		QUESNEL	MESGOUEZ
QUILL	KOTCHO	**7**	RED DEER	MESQUITE
RAINY	KUSAWA	ABITIBI	ST CLAIR	MICHIGAN
RONGE	LARDER	AGASSIZ	ST LOUIS	MONTREAL
ROUND	MAGPIE	ALBANEL	ST LUCIA	MOULTRIE
SANDY	MAGUSE	ALMANOR	SARANAC	OKANAGAN
SETON	MARIAN	BARKLEY	SASAMAT	OLD WIVES
SPLIT	MARION	BIG BEAR	SCHROON	OUACHITA
STAVE	MARTIN	BISTCHO	SEARLES	PATIENCE
STONY	MARTRE	BRAS D'OR	SELAWIK	PICKWICK
STUMP	MERCED	BROCHET	SEYMOUR	PREISSAC
TACHE	MERWIN	BUFFALO	SHUSWAP	PRIMROSE
TAHOE	MIRAGE	BURNABY	SUCCESS	PUCKAWAY
TAKLA	MOLSON	CALUMET	SUNAPEE	QUINAULT
TAZIN	MUNCHO	CENTRAL	TADOULE	RAQUETTE
TOPAZ	MURRAY	CHAPALA	TALQUIN	REINDEER
TROUT	MYSTIC	CHATUGE	TEXCOCO	ROSAMOND
TUDOR	NAKNEK	CRYSTAL	THUTADE	ST JOSEPH
TYLER	NELSON	CUITZEO	TORONTO	ST MARTIN
UNION	NICOLA	CYPRESS	UMBAGOG	ST PIERRE
UPPER	NORRIS	DEADMAN	UTIKUMA	SINCLAIR
WHITE	ONEIDA	DOWNTON	WATAUGA	SIPIWESK
WOODS	OTSEGO	DUBAWNT	WAWASEE	SNOWBIRD
	OWASCO	EABEMET	WHEELER	SULLIVAN
6	OXFORD	ELLIOTT	WHITNEY	SUPERIOR
ALKALI	OZARKS	ENNADAI	WINDIGO	TATHLINA
ALLARD	OZETTE	ETAWNEY		TAWAKONI
AYLMER	PLACID	EUFAULA	**8**	TRAMPING
BABINE	POWELL	FONTANA	AISHIHIK	UPPER RED
BALSAM	POYGAN	FRANCES	AMADJUAK	WATERHEN
BENSON	RIDEAU	FRANCIS	ANDERSON	WHOLDAIA
BERMAN	ROGERS	GRANDIN	ASSINICA	WINNIPEG
BORGNE	ST JOHN	HIGGINS	ATIKONAK	
BOWRON	SAKAMI	HUBBARD	AZISCOOS	**9**
CAYUGA	SCUGOG	ILIAMNA	BACHELOR	ALGONQUIN
CHABOT	SELWYN	KAMINAK	BECHAROF	ALLATOONA
CHIPAI	SENECA	KENNEDY	BIG TROUT	ASHUANIPI
CHISEL	SEVIER	LABERGE	BOMOSEEN	ATHABASCA
COYOTE	SHASTA	LUCERNE	CAMPBELL	BERRYESSA
CRATER	SHAVER	MCCLURE	CHIPPEWA	BISKOTASI
DUNCAN	SILVER	MALHEUR	CRESCENT	BISTINEAU
EDEHON	SIMCOE	MENDOTA	FLATHEAD	CALCASIEU
EUTSUK	SPROAT	MENIHEK	FRANCOIS	CATAHOULA
GASTON	STUART	MERRITT	HAMILTON	CHAMPLAIN

CHEROKEES
CHURCHILL
CRANBERRY
CUDDEBACK
GRANVILLE
GREAT BEAR
GREAT SALT
IBERVILLE
MILLE LACS
MOOSEHEAD
NAOCOCANE
NICARAGUA
NIPISSING
PETER POND
PILLSBURG
PINEHOUSE
PIPMUACAN
PLAYGREEN
ROSSIGNOL
SAKAKAWEA
SALTON SEA
SAMMAMISH
SHIBOGAMA
TESHEKPUK
VERMILION
WHITEGULL
WINNEBAGO
WISCONSIN
WOLLASTON
WUNNUMMIN

10
BEAVERHILL
BUENA VISTA
CHAUTAUQUA
CHESUNCOOK
CLAIR ENGLE
CLEARWATER
CUMBERLAND
FAVOURABLE
GREAT SLAVE
HILL ISLAND
KISSISSING
KOSHKONING
LOWER ARROW
MASSABESIC
MICHIKAMAU
MISTASSINI
NETTILLING
NORTH KNIFE
OKEECHOBEE
PIKANGIKUM
SAINT CLAIR
ST FRANCOIS
SAINT LOUIS
SAINT LUCIA
SAN ANDREAS
SOUTH HENIK

THREE LAKES
UPPER ARROW
WASHINGTON
WINNEMUCCA
XOCHIMILCO

11
ATTIKAMAGEN
CANANDAIGUA
CHAMBERLAIN
CHICKAMAUGA
DIEFENBAKER
FRANCIS CASE
INDIAN HOUSE
INFIERNILLO
KANIAPISKAU
LESSER SLAVE
MANICOUAGAN
MAXINKUCKEE
PEND OREILLE
SAINT JOSEPH
SAINT MARTIN
SAINT PIERRE
SKANEATELES
TIMISKAMING
TSALA APOPKA
YELLOWSTONE

12
ATTAWAPISKAT
GUNTERSVILLE
ILE-A-LA-CROSSE
LAST MOUNTAIN
MEMPHREMAGOG
NORTH CARIBOU
PETITSIKAPAU
POISSON BLANC
SANTIAGUILLO
SOUTH HOLSTON
UPPER KLAMATH
WINNIPEGOSIS

13
FRENCHMAN FLAT
PONTCHARTRAIN
SAINT FRANCOIS
WINNIPESAUKEE

14
SOUTHERN INDIAN

16
TRENTE-ET-UN MILLES

18
FRANKLIN D ROOSEVELT

Lakes of South America

4
LUNA

5
IBERA
ITATI
MIRIM
PATOS
PEIXE
POOPO

6
BARROS
IZABAL
MEDINA
PARANA

7
ROGAGUA
SAN LUIS

8
TITICACA
VALENCIA

9
ARGENTINO
MANGUEIRA
MARACAIBO
PETEN ITZA

10
ROGOAGUADO

Lakes of Australasia

4
EYRE

5
CAREY
COWAL
MASON
MOORE
TAUPO

6
AUSTIN
BARLEE
GEORGE
LEFROY
MACKAY
PUKAKI
TANDOU
TEKAPO

7
BALLARD
RAESIDE
REBECCA
TORRENS
TYRRELL

8
WAKATIPU

9
EUCUMBENE
HINDMARSH
JOHNSTONE
MACHATTIE

10
TRAVELLERS
YAMMA YAMMA

11
ALEXANDRINA

Materials

3
ABA
ABB
FUR
KID
NET
REP
RUG
SAY

4
ABBA
BAFT
DOWN
DUCK
FELT
GIMP
GROS
HIDE
JANE
JEAN
JUTE
KELT
LACE
LAME
LAWN
LENO
MESH
MINK
MULL
PELT
PULU
REPP
RAMI
SACK
SHAG
SILK
TAPE
TICK
WOOL
YARN
YUFT

5
ABACA
ABAYA
ARRAS
ATLAS
BAIZE
BAUGE
BEIGE
BRAID
BUDGE
CAPOC
CHINO

CLOTH
CRAPE
CRASH
CREPE
DENIM
DRILL
ERMIN
FLOSS
GAUZE
GUNNY
INKLE
KAPOK
KHAKI
LINEN
LISLE
MOIRE
MUNGO
NINON
NYLON
ORRIS
PIQUE
PLAID
PLUSH
PRINT
RAMEE
RAMIE
RAYON
SABLE
SATIN
SCRIM
SERGE
SHEER
STRAW
STUFF
SUEDE
SURAT
TABBY
TAMIN
TAMIS
TASAR
TERRY
TIBET
TOILE
TULLE
TWEED
TWILL
VOILE
WEEDS
WIGAN

6
ALPACA
ANGORA
ARDASS
BAREGE

BEAVER
BERLIN
BOUCLE
BURLAP
BYSSUS
CALICE
CAMLET
CANVAS
CASTOR
CHINTZ
CILICE
COBURG
COTTON
COUTIL
CREPON
CUBICA
CYPRUS
DACRON
DAMASK
DIAPER
DIMITY
DOMETT
DOSSAL
DOSSEL
DOWLAS
DUFFEL
DURANT
DURRIE
ERMINE
FABRIC
FAILLE
FERRET
FLEECE
FRIEZE
GURRAH
HODDEN
JERSEY
KERSEY
KINCOB
LINSEY
LUSTRE
MADRAS
MELTON
MERINO
MOHAIR
MOREEN
MURREY
MUSLIN
NANKIN
NEBRIS
NUTRIA
PELTRY
PONGEE
POPLIN
RIBBON
RUSSEL
RUSSET
RUSSIA

SAMITE
SATARA
SATEEN
SEMMIT
SHALLI
SHAMMY
SHODDY
SOMERI
STAMIN
TAMINE
TARTAN
TISSUE
TOISON
TRICOT
TUSSAH
TUSSEH
TUSSER
VELOUR
VELURE
VELVET
WINCEY

7
ACRILAN
ALEPINE
BARACAN
BATISTE
BLANKET
BOCKING
BROCADE
BUCKRAM
BUNTING
CAMBLET
CAMBRIC
CARACUL
CHALLIS
CHAMOIS
CHEVIOT
CHIFFON
COATING
COWHIDE
CYPRESS
DELAINE
DOESKIN
DOGSKIN
DORNICK
DRABBET
DRUGGET
ERMELIN
FELTING
FINGRAM
FLANNEL
FOULARD
FUSTIAN
GALLOON
GENAPPE
GINGHAM

GROGRAM
GUIPURE
HOGSKIN
HOLLAND
HOPSACK
JACONET
KIPSKIN
LEATHER
LOCKRAM
MALINES
MATTING
MECHLIN
MINEVER
MINIVER
MOROCCO
NACARAT
NANKEEN
NETTING
OILSILK
OILSKIN
ORGANZA
ORLEANS
PAISLEY
PERCALE
PIGSKIN
RATTEEN
SACKING
SAFFIAN
SAGATHY
SARSNET
SATINET
SCARLET
STAMMEL
SUITING
TABARET
TABINET
TAFFETA
TAFFETY
TATTING
TICKING
TIFFANY
TUSSORE
VEILING
VELOURS
VESTING
WEBBING
WORSTED

8
ARRASENE
BARATHEA
BARRACAN
BAUDEKIN
BEDLINEN
BLANCARD
BONELACE
BROCATEL
BUCKSKIN

CASHMERE
CEREMENT
CHENILLE
CLOAKING
CONY-WOOL
CORDOVAN
CORDUROY
CORDWAIN
COTELINE
COUTILLE
CRETONNE
DAMASSIN
DEERSKIN
DRILLING
DUNGAREE
FLORENCE
FLOX-SILK
GAMBROON
GOSSAMER
HOMESPUN
JACQUARD
JEANETTE
KNITWEAR
KOLINSKY
LUSTRINE
LUSTRING
MARCELLA
MAROCAIN
MARSELLA
MATERIAL
MOLESKIN
MUSLINET
MUSQUASH
NAINSOOK
NEAR-SILK
OIL-CLOTH
ORGANDIE
OSNABURG
PADUASOY
PONYSKIN
PRUNELLA
PRUNELLO
QUILTING
SARCENET
SARSENET
SHAGREEN
SHALLOON
SHANTUNG
SHEETING
SHIRTING
SPUNSILK
SWANSKIN
TABBINET
TAFFETAS
TARLATAN
TERYLENE
TOILINET
VALENCIA

VALENTIA
WOODPULP

9
ARDASSINE
ASTRAKHAN
BALDACHIN
BALDAQUIN
BENGALINE
BLONDLACE
BOMBASINE
BOMBAZINE
CALAMANCO
CASSIMERE
CERECLOTH
CHARMEUSE
COURTELLE
CRINOLINE
DRABBETTE
FARANDINE
FILOSELLE
FINGERING
FLOSS-SILK
GABARDINE
GABERDINE
GEORGETTE
GOLD-CLOTH
GRENADINE
GROSGRAIN
HAIRCLOTH
HORSEHAIR
HUCKABACK
INSERTION
LAMBSWOOL
LEVANTINE
LONGCLOTH
MACINTOSH
MARCELINE
ORGANZINE
PARAMATTA
PETERSHAM
PINA-CLOTH
SACKCLOTH
SAILCLOTH
SATINETTE
SHARKSKIN
SHEEPSKIN
STOCKINET
STROUDING
SWANSDOWN
THREEPILE
TOWELLING
VELVETEEN

10
BALBRUGGAN
BEAVERTEEN
BERLINWOOL

BLANKETING
BLONDE-LACE
BOOKMUSLIN
BROADCLOTH
BROCATELLE
CAMBRASINE
CAMBRESINE
CANDLEWICK
CASSINETTE
CHINCHILLA
COLBERTINE
FARRANDINE
FEARNOUGHT
FERRANDINE
FLORENTINE
GOLD-THREAD
GRASS-CLOTH
HODDEN GREY
HOPSACKING
KENTE CLOTH
KERSEYMERE
LUTESTRING
MACKINTOSH
MARCELLINE
MARSEILLES
MOUSELLINE
PILOTCLOTH
PINA-MUSLIN
SEERSUCKER
THROWN-SILK
TOILENETTE
TOILINETTE
TROUSERING
TUSSER-SILK

11
CHEESECLOTH
DRAP-DE-BERRY
DREADNOUGHT
FLANNELETTE
HONITON-LACE
KENDAL-GREEN
LEATHERETTE
MARQUISETTE
NARROWCLOTH
NETTLECLOTH
NUN'S VEILING
STOCKINETTE

12
CREPE-DE-CHINE
LEATHERCLOTH
MOIRE ANTIQUE
STOCKINGETTE
VALENCIENNES
WELSH FLANNEL

13
CASEMENT-CLOTH
COVERT COATING
FRENCH MOROCCO
LEVANT MOROCCO
LINSEY-WOOLSEY
PEPPER-AND-SALT
RUSSIA-LEATHER
SATIN-SHEETING
SHAMMY-LEATHER

14
ARTIFICIAL SILK
PERSIAN MOROCCO

Military Leaders, Generals, Field Marshals

3	WHITE	MCMAHON	LYTTELTON
NEY	WOLFE	MACMUNN	MACDONALD
NYE		MASSENA	NICHOLSON
	6	MAURICE	POLE CAREW
4	BARROW	MAXWELL	RAWLINSON
ADAM	BULLER	METHUEN	ROBERTSON
BOLS	BUTLER	MORTIER	VON HAUSEN
BRAY	CAESAR	NIVELLE	WELLESLEY
BYNG	CAPPER	O'CONNOR	WILLCOCKS
DUFF	CREAGH	OUDINOT	
DYER	CRERAR	ROBERTS	10
FOCH	CRONJE	SHERMAN	ALANBROOKE
GIAP	DAVONT	SIMPSON	AUCHINLECK
GORT	DUNDAS	STEWART	BERNADOTTE
HAIG	FRENCH	TURENNE	CHELMSFORD
HART	FULLER	WEYGAND	CORNWALLIS
JODL	GIRAUD	WINGATE	EISENHOWER
PECK	GORDON		FALKENHAYN
PILE	GRAHAM	8	HINDENBURG
SHEA	HARRIS	ANDERSON	KEILERMANN
SLIM	HUNTER	AUGEREAU	KELLY-KENNY
WOOD	JOFFRE	BIRDWOOD	KESSELRING
	KEITEL	BROWNING	KUROPATKIN
5	KONIEV	CAMPBELL	LUDENDORFF
BAIRD	LANNES	CHETWODE	MANNERHEIM
BLOOD	MANGIN	CROMWELL	MONTGOMERY
BOTHA	MURRAY	DE GAULLE	RICHARDSON
BRUCE	NAPIER	FREYBERG	VOROSHILOV
BRUNE	OUTRAM	GALLIENI	WELLINGTON
CLARK	PATTON	GLEICHEN	
CLIVE	PETAIN	HAMILTON	11
CONDE	PLUMER	HANNIBAL	MARLBOROUGH
CRAIG	POMPEY	HAVELOCK	
DAWES	RAGLAN	HEWETSON	
DE WET	ROMMEL	IRONSIDE	
GOUGH	RUNDLE	LOCKHART	
GRANT	SCIPIO	MONTCALM	
HORNE	VICTOR	MONTROSE	
ISMAY	WILSON	NAPOLEON	
JACOB	ZHUKOV	PERSHING	
JONES		TOWNSEND	
JUNOT	7	STIRLING	
LEESE	ALLENBY	URQUHART	
MAUDE	BLUCHER	VON BULOW	
MILNE	BRADLEY	VON KLUCK	
MONRO	CADORNA	WOLSELEY	
MOORE	CAPELLO		
MURAT	DEMPSEY	9	
NEILL	GAMELIN	ALEXANDER	
PAGET	GASELEE	BERTHELOT	
PATCH	GATACRE	BOULANGER	
RABAN	GOURAND	GARIBALDI	
SMUTS	HALDANE	HARINGTON	
SOULT	JACKSON	HASDRUBAL	
WEEKS	LYAUTEY	KITCHENER	

Money, Past and Present

2	DAUM
AS	DAWM
AT	DIME
SY	DOIT
	DONG
3	DUIT
BIT	DURO
BOB	GELD
COB	HWAN
DAM	JOEY
ECU	KICK
FAR	KOBO
FEN	KRAN
FIL	KYAT
FIN	LAKH
KIP	LIRA
LAT	LIRE
LEI	MARK
LEK	MERK
LEU	MILL
LEV	MITE
MAG	OBOL
MEG	PARA
MIL	PENI
MOY	PESO
PAI	PICE
PIE	PLUM
PUL	PONY
PYA	PULA
RAG	QUID
RAP	RAND
REE	REAL
REI	REIS
SEN	RIAL
SHO	RIEL
SOL	RYAL
SOU	TAEL
WON	TAKA
YEN	TALA
ZUZ	UNIK
	YUAN
4	ZACK
ANNA	
BAHT	5
BANI	ACKEY
BEAN	ANGEL
BIRR	ASPER
BONE	AUREI
BUCK	BELGA
CASH	BERRY
CEDI	BETSO
CENT	BOFFO
CHIP	BRASS

BUTUT
CHIAO
COLON
CONTO
COPEC
CROWN
DARIC
DINAR
DUCAT
EAGLE
FIVER
FRANC
GRAND
GROAT
KRONA
KRONE
LEPTA
LIARD
LIBRA
LITAS
LIVRE
LOCHO
LOUIS
MAILE
MEDIO
MOHAR
MOHUR
MONGO
MOPUS
NAIRA
NGWEE
NOBLE
OBANG
ONCER
PAISA
PENCE
PENGO
PENNI
PENNY
PLACK
POUND
QURSH
RIYAL
RUBLE
RUPEE
SAUDI
SCRIP
SCUDI
SCUDO
SEMIS
SOLDI
SOLDO
STICA
STYCA
SUCRE
SYCEE
TICCY
TICEY

TICCY
TOMAN
UNCIO
UNITE
ZAIRE
ZLOTY

6
AMANIA
AZTECA
BALBOA
BAUBEE
BAWBEE
BEZANT
BUKSHA
CONDOR
COPANG
COPECK
COPPER
DALASI
DEANER
DECIME
DENIER
DIRHAM
DOBLON
DOLLAR
ESCUDO
FLORIN
FORINT
FUORTE
GOURDE
GROSZY
GUINEA
GULDEN
HELLER
JITNEY
KOPECK
KORUNA
KURUSH
KWACHA
LEPTON
MAGPIE
MARKHA
MAWPUS
MONKEY
NICKEL
PA'ANGA
PAGODA
PAGODE
PESETA
PESEWA
PRUTAH
RAPPEN
ROUBLE
SATANG
SCEATT
SEQUIN
SHEKEL

SOMALO
SOVRAN
STATER
STIVER
TALARI
TALENT
TANNER
TENNER
TESTER
THALER
TICKEY
TOMAUN
TUGRIK
VELLON
ZECHIN

7
AFGHANI
ANGELOT
ANGOLAR
BOLIVAR
CAROLUS
CENTAVO
CENTIME
CENTIMO
CENTURY
CORDOBA
CRUSADO
DENARII
DRACHMA
GUARANI
GUILDER
HA'-PENNY
JACOBUS
LEMPIRA
MILREIS
MOIDORE
NGUSANG
PFENNIG
PIASTER
PIASTRE
PISTOLE
QUARTER
QUETZAL
QUINTAR
SAWBUCK
SEXTANS
SMACKER
STOOTER
TEN-SPOT
TESTOON
TESTRIL
TUGHRIK
XERAFIN

8
CRUZEIRO
DIDRACHM

DOUBLOON
DUCATOON
FARTHING
FIVE-SPOT
FLORENCE
GROSCHEN
HALF-ANNA
HALF-MARK
JOHANNES
KREUTZER
LOUIS D'OR
MARAVEDI
MARIGOLD
NAPOLEON
PICAYUNE
PORTAGUE
PORTIGUE
QUADRANS
SESTERCE
SHILLING
SIXPENCE
XERAPHIN

9
CENTESIMO
CUARTILLO
DANDIPRAT
DANDYPRAT
DIDRACHMA
DUPONDIUS
FOURPENCE
FOURPENNY
GOLD-BROAD
GOLD-NOBLE
GOLD-PENNY
HALF-ACKEY
HALF-ANGEL
HALF-BROAD
HALF-CROWN
HALF-GROAT
HALFPENNY
LILANGENI
PISTAREEN
RIX DOLLAR
ROSE-NOBLE
SCHILLING
SESTERTII
SOVEREIGN
SPUR-ROYAL
STOTINKAS
YELLOW-BOY

10
CROWN PIECE
DOUBLE-PICE
EASTERLING
GOLD-STATER
HALF-A-CROWN

HALF-FLORIN
HALF-GUINEA
PORTCULLIS
QUADRUSSIS
REICHSMARK
SESTERTIUM
SILVERLING
STOUR-ROYAL
TRIPONDIUS
VENEZOLANO

11
DEUTSCHMARK
DOUBLE-CROWN
DOUBLE-EAGLE
GEORGE-NOBLE
GUINEA-PIECE
HALF-GUILDER
HALF-THISTLE
SILVER-PENNY
SPADE-GUINEA
TETRADRACHM

12
DOUBLE-SEQUIN
HALF-FARTHING
MILL-SIXPENCE
PIECE-OF-EIGHT
QUARTER-ANGEL
QUARTER-NOBLE
SILVER-STATER
TRIBUTE-PENNY

13
HALF-ROSE-NOBLE
HALF-SOVEREIGN
QUARTER-DOLLAR
QUARTER-FLORIN
QUARTER-LAUREL

14
HONG-KONG DOLLAR
QUARTER-GUILDER

The Muses

4
CLIO

5
ERATO

6
THALIA
URANIA

7
EUTERPE

8
CALLIOPE

9
MELPOMENE

10
POLYHYMNIA

11
TERPSICHORE

Musical instruments

3
KIT
LUR

4
BASS
BELL
DRUM
FIFE
GONG
HARP
HORN
LURE
LUTE
LYRE
OBOE
PIPE
TUBA
VIOL

5
AULOS
BANJO
BRASS
BUGLE
CELLO
CHENG
CRWTH
FLUTE
LOURE
NAKER
ORGAN
PIANO
REBEC
SHALM
SHAWM
SITAR
TABOR
TIBIA
VIOLA

6
CITHER
CORNET
CYMBAL
FIDDLE
GUITAR
POMMER
RACKET
RUBEBE
SHOFAR
SPINET
TABOUR
TABRET
TUCKET

VIOLIN
ZITHER

7
BAGPIPE
BANDORA
BANDORE
BARYTON
BASSOON
BUCCINA
CELESTA
CEMBALO
CHEKKER
CITHARA
CITHERN
CITTERN
CLAVIER
CORNETT
GAMELAN
GITTERN
HAUTBOY
KITHARA
MANDORE
MARIMBA
MUSETTE
OCARINA
PANDORA
PANDORE
PAN-PIPE
PIANOLA
PIBGORN
PICCOLO
RIBIBLE
SACKBUT
SAMISEN
SAXHORN
SERPENT
TABORIN
THEORBO
TIMBREL
TIMPANI
TRUMPET
UKULELE
VIHUELA

8
ARCHLUTE
CASTANET
CIMBALOM
CLARINET
CLAVECIN
CRUMHORN
DULCIMER
HARP LUTE
JEW'S HARP

KEY BUGLE
PHAGOTUS
PIANETTE
POCHETTE
POST HORN
PSALTERY
RECORDER
TABOURIN
TENOR COR
THEREMIN
TRIANGLE
TROMBONE
VAMP HORN
VIRGINAL
WALDHORN
WOODWIND
ZAMBOMBA

9
ACCORDION
BALALAIKA
BANDURRIA
BOMBARDON
CELESTINA
CHALUMEAU
DULCITONE
EUPHONIUM
FLAGEOLET
HARMONICA
HARMONIUM
HYDRAULUS
KENT BUGLE
MANDOLINE
OCTO BASSE
SAXOPHONE
SERAPHENE
SERINETTE
STOCKHORN
TENOR DRUM
TUBAPHONE
WURLITZER
XYLOPHONE

10
BASSET HORN
CHITARRONE
CONCERTINA
COR ANGLAIS
DOUBLE BASS
FRENCH HORN
GRAND PIANO
HAND BASSEL
HURDYGURDY
KETTLEDRUM
LYRE-GUITAR
MOUTH ORGAN
MUSICAL BOW
NAIL VIOLIN

OPHICLEIDE
PERCUSSION
PIANOFORTE
SAXOTROMBA
SOUSAPHONE
TAMBOURINE
VIBRAPHONE
WATER ORGAN

11

AEOLIAN HARP
BARREL ORGAN
DOUBLE FLUTE
FIPPLE FLUTE
GERMAN FLUTE
HARPSICHORD
KEYED GUITAR
PANDEAN PIPE
PLAYER-PIANO
VIOLINCELLO

12

BASS CLARINET
CEMBAL D'AMORE
CHAMBER ORGAN
CHEST OF VIOLS
CLAVICEMBALO
COMB AND PAPER
CONCERT GRAND
GLOCKENSPIEL
GRAVICEMBALO
HARMONICHORD
REGENT'S BUGLE
SARRUSOPHONE
UPRIGHT PIANO

13

AMERICAN ORGAN
CLAVICYTHERUM
DOUBLE BASSOON
MARINE TRUMPET
ONDES MARTENOT
PHYSHARMONICA
POSITIVE ORGAN
SHEPHERD'S PIPE
UILLEANN PIPES

14

GLASS HARMONICA
PORTATIVE ORGAN

15

LUTE-HARPSICHORD
MOOG SYNTHESIZER

Musical terms

2

DO
FA
LA
ME
MI
RE
SI
SO
TE
TI
UT

3

BAR
BEN
BIS
BOW
CUE
DOH
DUO
FAH
JIG
KEY
LAH
NUT
PES
SOH
SOL
SUB
TIE

4

ALTO
ARIA
BAND
BASS
BEAT
BRIO
CLEF
CODA
DUET
FADO
FINE
FLAT
FORM
FRET
GLEE
HYMN
JACK
KEEN
LIED
MASS
MODE
MOOD

MUTE
NEUM
NODE
RANK
REED
REST
ROLL
ROOT
ROTA
SLUR
SOLO
SONG
STOP
TIME
TONE
TRIO
TUNE
TURN
VIVO
VOCE
WOLF

5

ANIMA
BRACE
BREVE
BURLA
CANON
CATCH
CHANT
CHOIR
CHORD
DIRGE
DOLCE
DRONE
ETUDE
FORTE
FUGUE
FUOCO
GAMBA
GAMUT
GRAVE
GUSTO
GYMEL
JODEL
LARGE
LARGO
LENTO
LYRIC
MAJOR
MARCH
METRE
MEZZO
MINIM
MINOR

MOSSO
MOTET
MOTIF
NEUME
NONET
OCTET
OSSIA
PAUSE
PEDAL
PIANO
PITCH
PLENO
PLICA
POINT
PRESA
PRIMO
QUINT
RONDO
ROTTE
ROUND
SCALE
SCORE
SEGNO
SEGUE
SHAKE
SHARP
SIXTH
SLIDE
STAFF
STAVE
SUITE
SWELL
TABLE
TACET
TEMPO
TENOR
THEME
THIRD
TONIC
TOUCH
TRIAD
TRILL
TROPE
TUTTI
UP BOW
VALVE
VOICE
VOLTA
VOLTI
YODEL

6

ACCENT
ADAGIO
ANTHEM
ARIOSO
A TEMPO
ATONAL

AUBADE
BALLAD
BALLET
BOWING
BRIDGE
BURDEN
CANTOR
CAOINE
CHORAL
CHORUS
COPULA
DA CAPO
DAMPER
DECANI
DOODLE
DULCET
ENCORE
ENTREE
FLORID
FUGATO
GEIGEN
GIUSTO
GRACES
GRAZIA
HAMMER
HOCKET
LAMENT
LEGATO
LIEDER
MAGGOT
MANUAL
MAXIMA
MELODY
MINORE
NOBILE
OCTAVE
PHRASE
PISTON
PRESTO
QUAVER
REPEAT
RHYTHM
RIGORE
RUBATO
SEMPRE
SEPTET
SEXTET
SHANTY
SIMILE
SONATA
STRING
SUBITO
TAMPON
TENUTO
TERZET
TREBLE
TROPPO
TUNING

UNISON	RESPOND	GEMSHORN	UNA CORDA	QUINTATON
UP BEAT	RIPIENO	HALF NOTE	WIND BAND	QUODLIBET
VAGANS	ROSALIA	HALF TONE	ZARZUELA	RESONANCE
VIVACE	SALICET	HARMONIC		RICERCARE
VOLUME	SCHERZO	INTERVAL	9	SCHNELLER
	SCIOLTO	KEYBOARD	A CAPPELLA	SEMIBREVE
7	SCORING	LEGGIERO	AD LIBITUM	SFORZANDO
AGITATO	SECONDO	LIBRETTO	AFFETUOSO	SICILIANA
ALLEGRO	SEVENTH	LIEBLICH	ALLA BREVE	SIGNATURE
ANDANTE	SOPRANO	LIGATURE	ALLA ZOPPA	SMORZANDO
ANIMATO	SORDINO	MADRIGAL	ALLEMANDE	SOLFEGGIO
ARIETTA	STRETTO	MAESTOSO	ANDAMENTO	SOLO ORGAN
ATTACCA	STRINGS	MAGGIORE	ANDANTINO	SOSTENUTO
ATTACCO	TANGENT	MEANTONE	BAGATELLE	SOTTO VOCE
BASS-BAR	TOCCATA	MODERATO	BRASS BAND	SOUND POST
BELLOWS	TRACKER	NEO-MODAL	BRILLANTE	SPIRITOSO
BRAVURA	TREMOLO	NOCTURNE	CANTABILE	SUCCENTOR
CADENCE	TRIPLET	NOTATION	CANTILENA	TABLATURE
CADENZA	TRITONE	ORATORIO	CAPRICCIO	TENOR CLEF
CALANDO	TWELFTH	OSTINATO	CASSATION	TESSITURA
CANTATA	VIBRATO	OVERTURE	CHORISTER	TREMULANT
CANZONA	WIND WAY	PARLANDO	CHROMATIC	VOLUNTARY
CHORALE		PARLANTE	COLLA VOCE	VOX HUMANA
CLARION	8	PARTIALS	COME SOPRA	WHOLE NOTE
CODETTA	A BATTUTA	PART SONG	CONTRALTO	WHOLE TONE
COMPASS	ALTO CLEF	PASTORAL	CRESCENDO	WINDCHEST
CONCORD	ANTIPHON	PLECTRUM	DITHYRAMB	WIND TRUNK
CON MOTO	A PIACERE	POINTING	DOUBLE BAR	WREST-PINS
CONSOLE	ARPEGGIO	POSITION	FINGERING	
COUPLER	BARITONE	POSTLUDE	FULL ORGAN	10
DESCANT	BASS CLEF	PSALMODY	GLISSANDO	A CAPRICCIO
DISCORD	BERCEUSE	REED STOP	HALF-CLOSE	ACCIDENTAL
DOWN BOW	BURLESCA	REGISTER	HARMONICS	ALLARGANDO
FANFARE	BURLETTA	RESPONSE	HEXACHORD	ALLEGRETTO
GIOCOSO	CANTICLE	RHAPSODY	HUMORESKE	BARCAROLLE
GRADUAL	CASTRATO	RICOCHET	INFLEXION	BASSE DANSE
HARMONY	CASTRATI	RITENUTO	INTERLUDE	BINARY FORM
INTRADA	CAVATINA	ROMANTIC	INVERSION	CANTO FERMO
KEY NOTE	CHACONNE	SAUTILLE	LARGHETTO	CANZONETTA
MARCATO	COL LEGNO	SEMITONE	LEITMOTIV	CHAIR ORGAN
MEASURE	CONCERTO	SEMPLICE	MEDIATION	CHIME-BELLS
MEDIANT	CONTINUO	SEQUENCE	METRONOME	CHOIR ORGAN
MELISMA	CROTCHET	SERENADE	MEZZA VOCE	COLLA PARTE
MIXTURE	DAL SEGNO	SERENATA	MONOCHORD	COLORATURA
MORDENT	DIAPASON	SEXTOLET	OBBLIGATO	COMMON TIME
MORENDO	DIATONIC	SINFONIA	OPEN NOTES	CONSONANCE
NATURAL	DOLOROSO	SOGGETTO	ORCHESTRA	CON SORDINI
PASSAGE	DOMINANT	SOLO STOP	PASTICCIO	DIMINUENDO
PESANTE	DOWN BEAT	SONATINA	PEDAL NOTE	DISSONANCE
PIACERE	DULCIANA	SPIANATO	PIACEVOLE	DOUBLE FLAT
PIBROCH	ENSEMBLE	SPICCATO	PIANGENDO	ENHARMONIC
PIETOSO	FABURDEN	STACCATO	PIZZICATO	EXPOSITION
POMPOSO	FALSETTO	STOPPING	PLAINSONG	EXPRESSION
PRELUDE	FANTASIA	SWELL BOX	POLYPHONY	FORTEPIANO
QUINTET	FLOURISH	SYMPHONY	PRECENTOR	FORTISSIMO
REPORTS	FLUE-WORK	TONALITY	PRICKSONG	GRACE NOTES
REPRISE	FOLK SONG	TONGUING	PRINCIPAL	GREAT STAVE
REQUIEM	FUGHETTA	TRE CORDE	PROLATION	GROUND BASS

HUMORESQUE
INTERMEZZO
LEGER LINES
MODULATION
MOUTHPIECE
PEDAL BOARD
PEDAL ORGAN
PEDAL POINT
PENTATONIC
PERDENDOSI
PIANISSIMO
PLAINCHANT
PONTICELLO
PORTAMENTO
PROPRIETAS
RECITATIVE
REMOTE KEYS
REPETITION
RITARDANDO
RITORNELLO
SALICIONAL
SALTARELLO
SCHERZANDO
SCORDATURA
SCOTCH SNAP
SEGUIDILLA
SEMICHORUS
SEMIQUAVER
SONATA FORM
SOUND BOARD
SOUND HOLES
SPEAKER KEY
STRINGENDO
SUABE FLUTE
SUBMEDIANT
SUPERTONIC
SUSPENSION
SWELL ORGAN
SWELL PEDAL
TETRACHORD
TONIC SOL-FA
TRANQUILLO
TRANSITION
TREBLE CLEF
TUNING FORK
TWELVE-NOTE
TWELVE-TONE
TYROLIENNE
VARIATIONS
VILLANELLA
WREST-PLANK

11
ACCELERANDO
AFFRETTANDO
ALLA TEDESCA
ALTERNATIVO
COMMON CHORD

CONCERTANTE
CONSECUTIVE
DAMPER PEDAL
DECRESCENDO
DIVIDED STOP
DOUBLE FUGUE
DOUBLE SHARP
DOUBLE TOUCH
FAUX BOURDON
FIGURED BASS
FINGER BOARD
FUNDAMENTAL
LEADING NOTE
MESSA DI VOCE
MUSICA FICTA
PART PLAYING
PASSING NOTE
PLAGAL MODES
PRESTISSIMO
PROGRESSION
QUARTER NOTE
QUARTER-TONE
RALLENTANDO
RELATED KEYS
SCOTCH CATCH
SHORT OCTAVE
SINFONIETTA
SOLMISATION
SOLMIZATION
SOPRANO CLEF
STOPPED PIPE
STRING PLATE
SUBDOMINANT
SYNCOPATION
TEMPO GIUSTO
TENERAMENTE
TERNARY FORM
THROUGH BASS
TONIC ACCENT
TUNING SLIDE
VEILED VOICE
VOIX CELESTE

12
ACCIACCATURA
ACOUSTIC BASS
AGOGIC ACCENT
APPASSIONATA
APPOGGIATURA
CHAMBER MUSIC
CHANGING NOTE
COUNTERPOINT
COUNTER-TENOR
DIVERTIMENTO
HIDDEN FIFTHS
KEY SIGNATURE
MELODIC MINOR
MUTATION STOP

NOTA CAMBIATA
PASTORAL OBOE
POLYTONALITY
PRALLTRILLER
RECITING NOTE
RELATIVE KEYS
RHYTHMIC MODE
SLOW MOVEMENT
SPEAKING STOP
THOROUGH BASS
UPPER PARTIAL

13
ABSOLUTE PITCH
ACCOMPANIMENT
AUXILIARY NOTE
CLARABEL FLUTE
DYNAMIC ACCENT
FALSE RELATION
HAMMERKLAVIER
HARMONIC FLUTE
HARMONIC MINOR
HIDDEN OCTAVES
IMPROVISATION
L'ISTESSO TEMPO
MEDESIMO TEMPO
MEISTERSINGER
ORCHESTRATION
RESULTANT TONE
SUL PONTICELLO
SUMMATION TONE
SUPERDOMINANT
SYMPHONIC POEM
TIME SIGNATURE
TRANSCRIPTION
TRANSPOSITION
UNEQUAL VOICES
VENETIAN SWELL

14
CHROMATIC SCALE
CONTRARY MOTION
DEMISEMIQUAVER
DOUBLE DIAPASON
DOUBLE STOPPING
DOUBLE TONGUING
EIGHT-FOOT PITCH
ESSENTIAL NOTES
GREGORIAN CHANT
GREGORIAN MUSIC
GREGORIAN TONES
HARMONIC SERIES
MUSICA FIGURATA
SINGLE TONGUING
SPEAKING LENGTH
TEMPO ORDINARIO
WHOLE TONE SCALE

15
DOMINANT SEVENTH
INCIDENTAL MUSIC
MUSICA MENSURATA
OCCASIONAL MUSIC
OVERSPUN STRINGS
PENTATONIC SCALE
RECITATIVO SECCO
SYMPATHETIC TONE
UNESSENTIAL NOTE

Boys' Names

2
CY
ED

3
ABE
ABY
ALF
ALI
ASA
BEN
BOB
DAI
DAN
ERN
GIL
GUS
GUY
HAL
IAN
IKE
IRA
JAY
JEM
JIM
JOB
JOE
JON
JOS
KAY
KEN
KIT
LEN
LEO
LEW
LOU
MAT
MAX
NAP
NED
PAT
RAY
REX
ROB
ROD
ROY
SAL
SAM
SID
SIM
SOL
TAM
TED
TIM
TOM

VIC
WAT

4
ABEL
ADAM
AGAR
ALAN
ALEC
ALEX
ALGY
AMOS
ANDY
AXEL
BART
BEAU
BEDE
BERT
BILL
BUCK
CAIN
CARL
CARY
CLAY
DAVE
DAVY
DICK
DION
EARL
EDDY
EDEN
EMIL
ERIC
EROS
ESAU
ESME
ESRA
EUAN
EVAN
EZRA
FRED
GARY
GENE
GLEN
GLYN
GWYN
HANS
HUGH
HUGO
IFOR
IKEY
IOAN
IVAN
IVOR
JACK

JAKE
JEAN
JOAB
JOCK
JOEL
JOEY
JOHN
JOSE
JOSH
JUAN
JUDE
KARL
KAYE
LEON
LEVI
LUKE
MARC
MARK
MATT
MICK
MIKE
NEAL
NEIL
NICK
NOAH
NOEL
OTHO
OTTO
OWEN
PAUL
PETE
PHIL
PIUS
REES
RENE
RHYS
RORY
ROSS
SAUL
SEAN
SETH
STAN
THEO
TOBY
TONY
VERE
WALT
WILL
WYNN
ZACH
ZEKE

5
AARON
ABDUL
ABNER
ABRAM
ALBAN

ALECK
ALGIE
ALICK
ALLAN
ALRED
ALROY
ALVAR
ALVES
ALWIN
ALWYN
AMAND
ANDRE
ANGUS
ANTON
ARCHY
BARRY
BASIL
BENNY
BERTY
BEVIS
BILLY
BOBBY
BRIAN
BRUCE
CAIUS
CALEB
CAREW
CECIL
CHRIS
CHUCK
CLAUD
CLIVE
COLIN
COSMO
CRAIG
CYRIL
CYRUS
DANNY
DARBY
DARCY
DAVID
DENIS
DENYS
DEREK
DICKY
EARLE
EDDIE
EDGAR
EDWIN
EDWYN
ELIAB
ELIAS
ELLIS
EMERY
ENOCH
ERNIE
ERNST
ERROL

EWART
FELIX
FRANK
FRANZ
FRITZ
GARTH
GAVIN
GEOFF
GILES
GLYNN
GRANT
GUIDO
HARRY
HENRI
HENRY
HIRAM
HOSEA
HYMAN
INIGO
INNES
IRWIN
ISAAC
IZAAK
JABEZ
JACKY
JACOB
JAIME
JAMES
JAMIE
JARED
JASON
JERRY
JESSE
JIMMY
JONAH
JULES
KEITH
KENNY
LARRY
LEWIS
LOUIS
MEYER
MICKY
MILES
MONTE
MONTY
MOSES
MYLES
NEDDY
NEILL
NEVIL
NEVIN
NIGEL
OSCAR
OSMAN
OSWYN
OWAIN
PADDY

PEDRO
PERCY
PERRY
PETER
PIERS
RALPH
RAMON
RAOUL
REMUS
ROBIN
ROGER
ROLLO
ROMEO
RUFUS
SANDY
SCOTT
SERGE
SHANE
SHAUN
SILAS
SIMON
STEVE
TEDDY
TIMMY
TITUS
TOMMY
TUDOR
ULICK
ULRIC
URIAH
WALLY
WILLY
WYNNE

6
ADOLPH
ADRIAN
AENEAS
ALARIC
ALBERT
ALEXIS
ALFRED
ANDREW
ANGELO
ANSELM
ANTONY
ARCHIE
ARMAND
ARNOLD
ARTHUR
AUBREY
AUSTIN
AYLMER
BALBUS
BARNEY
BENITO
BENNIE
BERTIE

BRUTUS
CAESAR
CARLOS
CEDRIC
CERDIC
CICERO
CLAUDE
CONRAD
DAMIAN
DANIEL
DENNIS
DERMOT
DERRIC
DICKIE
DICKON
DONALD
DOUGAL
DUDLEY
DUGALD
DUGGIE
DUNCAN
DWIGHT
EDMOND
EDMUND
EDWARD
EGBERT
ELDRED
ELIJAH
ELISHA
ERNEST
ERROLL
ERVINE
ESMOND
EUGENE
EVELYN
FABIAN
FERGUS
FINLAY
FREDDY
GARNET
GASTON
GEORGE
GERALD
GERARD
GIDEON
GORDON
GRAEME
GRAHAM
GWILYM
GWYNNE
HAMISH
HAMLET
HAROLD
HECTOR
HENRYK
HERMAN
HERVEY
HORACE

HOWARD	OSWALD	ARTEMAS	LINDSEY	ZEBEDEE	LAURENCE
HOWELL	PHILIP	ARTEMUS	LUDOVIC		LAWRENCE
HUBERT	PIERRE	AUGUSTE	MALACHI	**8**	LEONIDAS
HUGHIE	RAFAEL	BALDWIN	MALCOLM	ACHILLES	LLEWELYN
ILLTYD	RAMSAY	BARNABY	MARCIUS	ADOLPHUS	LLYWELYN
INGRAM	RAMSEY	BARNARD	MATTHEW	ALASDAIR	MATTHIAS
IRVINE	RAPHEL	BERNARD	MAURICE	ALASTAIR	MEREDITH
IRVING	REGGIE	BERTRAM	MAXWELL	ALGERNON	MONTAGUE
ISAIAH	REUBEN	CHARLES	MAYNARD	ALISTAIR	MORTIMER
ISRAEL	ROBBIE	CHARLIE	MICHAEL	ALOYSIUS	NAPOLEON
JACKIE	ROBERT	CHESTER	MONTAGU	ALPHONSE	NEHEMIAH
JAIRUS	RODGER	CLEMENT	NEVILLE	ALPHONSO	NICHOLAS
JAPHET	RODNEY	CONNELL	NICOLAS	ANTONIUS	OCTAVIUS
JASPER	ROLAND	CRISPIN	OBADIAH	ARISTIDE	ODYSSEUS
JEROME	RONALD	CRISPUS	ORLANDO	AUGUSTIN	PAULINUS
JERVIS	ROWLEY	CYPRIAN	PATRICK	AUGUSTUS	PERCEVAL
JOHANN	RUDOLF	DERRICK	PERSEUS	BARNABAS	PERCIVAL
JOHNNY	RUPERT	DESMOND	PHINEAS	BAPTISTE	PEREGRIN
JOSEPH	ST JOHN	DIAMOND	QUENTIN	BENEDICT	PHILEMON
JOSHUA	SAMSON	DOMINIC	QUINTIN	BENJAMIN	POTIPHAR
JOSIAH	SELWYN	DOUGLAS	RANDALL	BERTRAND	RANDOLPH
JULIAN	SIDNEY	EMANUEL	RANULPH	BEVERLEY	RANDULPH
JULIUS	SIMEON	EPHRAIM	RAPHAEL	BONIFACE	REGINALD
JUSTIN	SINBAD	ERASMUS	RAYMOND	CHRISTIE	RODERICK
KERSEY	STEVEN	EUSTACE	RAYMUND	CLARENCE	SECUNDUS
LAURIE	STUART	EZEKIEL	REYNARD	CLAUDIUS	SEPTIMUS
LESLIE	SYDNEY	FRANCIS	RICHARD	CLIFFORD	SHADRACH
LESTER	THOMAS	FREDDIE	RODERIC	CRISPIAN	SIEGMUND
LIONEL	TOBIAH	GABRIEL	ROMULUS	CUTHBERT	SILVANUS
LUCIAN	TOBIAS	GASPARD	ROWLAND	DOMINICK	SYLVANUS
LUCIEN	TREFOR	GEOFFRY	RUDOLPH	EBENEZER	THEOBALD
LUCIUS	TREVOR	GEORGIE	RUDYARD	EMMANUEL	THEODORE
LUDWIG	VERNON	GERVAIS	RUSSELL	ETHELRED	TRISTRAM
LUTHER	VICTOR	GERVASE	SERGIUS	FLORIZEL	VLADIMAR
MANSEL	VIVIAN	GILBERT	SEYMOUR	FRANCOIS	VLADIMIR
MARCEL	VIVIEN	GLADWYN	SHELDON	FRANKLIN	ZACCHEUS
MARCUS	VYVYAN	GODFREY	SIGMUND	FREDERIC	ZEBADIAH
MARTIN	WALTER	GRAHAME	SOLOMON	GAMALIEL	ZEDEKIAH
MARTYN	WARREN	GREGORY	SPENCER	GEOFFERY	
MERLIN	WESLEY	GUSTAVE	SPENSER	GEOFFREY	**9**
MERVYN	WILBUR	HADRIAN	STANLEY	GIUSEPPE	ALAISTAIR
MICKIE	WILLIE	HERBERT	STEPHEN	GREVILLE	ALEXANDER
MILTON	WILMER	HERMANN	STEUART	GRIFFITH	ALPHONSUS
MORGAN	XAVIER	HILAIRE	STEWART	GUSTAVUS	ARCHIBALD
MORRIS		HORATIO	SWITHIN	HANNIBAL	AUGUSTINE
NAPIER	**7**	HUMBERT	TERENCE	HERCULES	BARTIMEUS
NATHAN	ABRAHAM	HUMFREY	TERTIUS	HEREWARD	CHRISTIAN
NELSON	ABSALOM	IBRAHIM	TIMOTHY	HEZEKIAH	CORNELIUS
NEVILE	ALADDIN	JACQUES	ULYSSES	HORATIUS	DEMETRIUS
NEVILL	ALFONSO	JAPHETH	UMBERTO	HUMPHREY	ETHELBERT
NICKOL	ALISTER	JEFFERY	VAUGHAN	IGNATIUS	FERDINAND
NINIAN	ALMERIC	JOCELYN	VINCENT	IMMANUEL	FRANCISCO
NORMAN	ALSAGER	KENNETH	WALLACE	JEREMIAH	FREDERICK
NOWELL	AMBROSE	LAMBERT	WILFRED	JEREMIAS	HONORATUS
OLIVER	ANATOLE	LAZARUS	WILFRID	JERVOISE	JOSCELINE
OSBERT	ANTHONY	LEANDER	WILHELM	JONATHAN	LLEWELLYN
OSMOND	ANTOINE	LEONARD	WILLIAM	JOSEPHUS	LLYWELLYN
OSMUND	ANTONIO	LINDSAY	WINSTON	LANCELOT	MARMADUKE

NATHANIEL
PATRICIUS
PEREGRINE
RUDOLPHUS
SAINT JOHN
SALVATORE
SEBASTIAN
SIEGFRIED
SIGISMUND
SILVESTER
SYLVESTER
VALENTINE
VALENTINO
ZACHARIAH
ZECHARIAH

10
ATHANASIUS
ATHELSTANE
BARRINGTON
MAXIMILIAN
THEOPHILUS

11
BARTHOLOMEW
CHRISTOPHER
CONSTANTINE

Girls' Names

3
ADA
AMY
ANN
BAB
BEA
BEE
BET
CIS
DOT
ENA
EVA
EVE
FAN
FAY
FLO
IDA
INA
ISA
IVY
JOY
KAY
KIT
LIZ
LOU
LYN
MAE
MAI
MAY
MEG
MIN
NAN
PAM
PAT
PEG
PEN
SAL
SIS
SUE
TIB
UNA
ZIA
ZOE

4
AGAR
AGGY
ALBA
ALMA
ANNA
ANNE
ANNY
AVIS
BABA
BABS

BEBE
BESS
BETH
CATH
CLEA
CLEO
CORA
DAWN
DIDO
DODO
DORA
EDIE
EDNA
ELLA
ELSA
EMMA
EMMY
ENID
ERNA
ESME
ETTA
FAYE
FIFI
GABY
GAIL
GENE
GIGI
GWEN
HEBE
HERA
HOPE
INEZ
IONE
IRIS
IRMA
ISLA
ISMA
JANE
JEAN
JESS
JILL
JOAN
JOSE
JUDY
KATE
KATY
LALA
LEAH
LENA
LILA
LILY
LINA
LISA
LITA
LIZA

LOIS
LOLA
LUCY
LULU
LYNN
MAIR
MARY
MAUD
META
MIMI
MINA
MOLL
MONA
MYRA
NELL
NENA
NEST
NINA
NITA
NORA
POLA
POLL
PRUE
RITA
ROSA
ROSE
ROSY
RUBY
RUTH
SARA
SIAN
SITA
SUSY
SUZY
TESS
THEA
TINA
VERA
VIDA
VITA
ZENA
ZITA

5
ABBIE
ADELA
ADELE
AGGIE
AGNES
AILIE
AILSA
AIMEE
ALICE
ALINE
ANGEL
ANITA
ANNIE
APRIL

ARBEL
AVICE
AVRIL
BECKY
BELLA
BELLE
BERTA
BERYL
BESSY
BETSY
BETTE
BETTY
BIDDY
BRIDE
BUNTY
CAROL
CARYL
CATHY
CECIL
CELIA
CHLOE
CHRIS
CISSY
CLAIR
CLARA
CLARE
DAISY
DELIA
DIANA
DILYS
DINAH
DODIE
DOLLY
DORIS
DULCE
EDITH
EFFIE
ELENA
ELERI
ELFIE
ELISA
ELISE
ELIZA
ELLEN
ELSIE
EMILY
EMMIE
ERICA
ESSIE
ETHEL
ETTIE
FAITH
FANNY
FIONA
FLORA
FREDA
GABIE
GERTY

GRACE
GRETA
HATTY
HAZEL
HELEN
HENNY
HETTY
HILDA
HONOR
HYLDA
IRENE
JACKY
JANET
JANEY
JANIE
JENNY
JESSY
JOYCE
JULIA
JULIE
KAREN
KATEY
KATIE
KEZIA
KITTY
LAILA
LAURA
LEILA
LELIA
LETTY
LILLY
LIZZY
LORNA
LOTTA
LOTTE
LOTTY
LUCIA
LUCIE
LYDIA
LYNNE
MABEL
MADGE
MAGGY
MAMIE
MANDY
MANYA
MARIA
MARIE
MATTY
MAUDE
MAVIS
MEGAN
MERCY
MERLE
MERRY
MILLY
MOIRA
MOLLY

MOYRA	AMANDA	FATIMA	MARINA	URSULA	FELICIA
MYRLE	AMELIA	FELICE	MARION	VERENA	FENELLA
NADIA	AMELIE	GAYNOR	MARTHA	VERONA	FEODORA
NANCE	ANABEL	GERTIE	MATTIE	VIOLET	FLORRIE
NANCY	ANDREA	GLADYS	MAXINE	VIVIAN	FLOSSIE
NANNY	ANGELA	GLORIA	MERCIA	WINNIE	FRANCES
NANSI	ANTHEA	GODIVA	MERIEL	YVONNE	GILLIAN
NAOMI	ASTRID	GRACIE	MELITA	ZILLAH	GWENNIE
NELLY	ATHENA	GRIZEL	MIGNON		GWENYTH
NESTA	AUDREY	GUSSIE	MILLIE	7	GWLADYS
NORAH	AURORA	GWENDA	MINNIE	ABIGAIL	GWYNETH
NORMA	AWDREY	GWYNNE	MIRIAM	ADELINE	HARRIET
OLIVE	BABBIE	HANNAH	MOLLIE	ALBERTA	HEATHER
PANSY	BEATIE	HELENA	MONICA	ALETHEA	HESTHER
PATSY	BENITA	HESTER	MURIEL	ALFREDA	HONORIA
PATTY	BERTHA	HILARY	MYRTLE	ANNABEL	HORATIA
PAULA	BESSIE	HONORA	NADINE	ANNETTE	HYPATIA
PEARL	BETTIE	HONOUR	NANCIE	ANSTICE	ISIDORA
PEGGY	BIBBIE	IMELDA	NELLIE	ANTONIA	JANETTE
PHEBE	BIDDIE	IMOGEN	NESSIE	ARIADNE	JEANNIE
PIXIE	BINNIE	ISABEL	NETTIE	AUGUSTA	JESSICA
POLLY	BIRDIE	ISHBEL	NOREEN	BABETTE	JILLIAN
POPPY	BLANCH	ISOBEL	OLIVIA	BARBARA	JOCELIN
PRUDY	BLONDE	JACKIE	PAMELA	BEATRIX	JOCELYN
RENEE	BRIDIE	JANICE	PATTIE	BELINDA	JULIANA
RHODA	BRIGID	JANINE	PEGGIE	BERNICE	KATRINA
RHONA	BRIONY	JEANIE	PHOEBE	BETTINA	KATRINE
ROSIE	CARRIE	JEANNE	PORTIA	BETTINE	LAVINIA
SADIE	CASSIE	JEMIMA	RACHEL	BLANCHE	LEONORA
SALLY	CATHIE	JENNIE	RAMONA	BLOSSOM	LETITIA
SANDY	CECILE	JESSIE	RAQUEL	BRIDGET	LILLIAN
SARAH	CECILY	JOANNA	REGINA	CAMILLA	LILLIAS
SASIE	CELINA	JUDITH	ROBINA	CECILIA	LIZBETH
SONIA	CHERRY	JULIET	ROSINA	CHERRIE	LUCILLE
SOPHY	CICELY	LALAGE	ROWENA	CLARICE	LUCINDA
SUSAN	CISSIE	LALLIE	SABINA	CLAUDIA	MABELLE
SUSIE	CLAIRE	LASSIE	SABINE	COLETTE	MARGERY
SUZIE	CONNIE	LEONIE	SALLIE	COLLEEN	MARJORY
SYBIL	DAPHNE	LESLEY	SALOME	CORINNE	MATILDA
TANIA	DAVINA	LETTIE	SANDRA	CYNTHIA	MAUREEN
THORA	DORCAS	LILIAN	SAPPHO	DEBORAH	MELANIE
TILDA	DOREEN	LILIAS	SELINA	DEIRDRE	MILDRED
TRUDY	DULCIE	LILLAH	SERENA	DOLORES	MINERVA
UNITY	EDITHA	LILLIE	SHARON	DORINDA	MIRANDA
VESTA	EDWINA	LIZZIE	SHEILA	DOROTHY	NATALIA
VICKI	EDYTHE	LOLITA	SOPHIA	ELEANOR	NATALIE
VICKY	EILEEN	LOTTIE	SOPHIE	ELFREDA	NIGELLA
VIOLA	ELAINE	LOUISA	STELLA	ELFRIDA	NINETTE
WANDA	ELINOR	LOUISE	SYLVIA	ELSPETH	OCTAVIA
WENDY	ELOISA	LUCILE	TAMSIN	EMELINE	OPHELIA
WILMA	ELOISE	MAGGIE	TERESA	EMERALD	PANDORA
	ELVIRA	MAIMIE	TERTIA	ESTELLE	PAULINA
6	EMILIE	MAISIE	TESSIE	EUGENIA	PAULINE
AGATHA	ESTHER	MARCIA	THALIA	EUGENIE	PHYLLIS
AILEEN	EUNICE	MARGEY	THELMA	EULALIA	QUEENIE
ALICIA	EUPHIE	MARGIE	THIRZA	EVALINE	REBECCA
ALISON	EVELYN	MARGOT	TRIXIE	EVELINA	RICHMAL
ALTHEA	FANNIE	MARIAN	ULRICA	EVELINE	ROBERTA

ROSALIE
ROSELLA
ROSETTA
ROSETTE
SHELAGH
SUSANNA
SUSANNE
SUSETTE
SUZANNE
SUZETTE
SYBILLA
TABITHA
TATIANA
THERESA
THERESE
TITANIA
VALERIA
VALERIE
VANESSA
VENETIA
YOLANDE

8
ADELAIDE
ADRIENNE
ALBERTHA
ANGELICA
ANGELINA
ANGELINE
ARABELLA
ARAMINTA
ATLANTA
BEATRICE
BERENICE
CARLOTTA
CAROLINA
CAROLINE
CATHLEEN
CHRISSIE
CHRYSTAL
CLARIBEL
CLARISSA
CLEMENCE
CLEMENCY
CLOTILDE
CONSUELA
CONSUELO
CORDELIA
CORNELIA
DOROTHEA
DRUSILLA
DULCINIA
ELEANORA
ELEANORE
ELFRIEDA
ELFRIEDE
ELLALINE
EMMELINA

EMMELINE
EUPHEMIA
EVELINDA
FELICITY
FILOMENA
FLORENCE
GEORGINA
GERMAINE
GERTRUDE
GRIZELDA
HERMIONE
HORTENSE
HYACINTH
ISABELLA
ISABELLE
JEANETTE
JENNIFER
JULIETTA
JULIETTE
KATHLEEN
LAETITIA
LAVENDER
LUCRETIA
MADELINE
MAGDALEN
MARCELLA
MARCELLE
MARGARET
MARIANNE
MARIETTE
MARIGOLD
MARJORIE
MATHILDA
MIREILLE
MORWENNA
MURIELLE
NATHALIE
PATIENCE
PATRICIA
PENELOPE
PHILIPPA
PHILLIDA
PHILLIPA
PRIMROSE
PRUDENCE
PRUNELLA
RAYMONDE
REBECCAH
ROSALIND
ROSAMOND
ROSAMUND
ROSEMARY
SAMANTHA
SAPPHIRE
SUSANNAH
TALLULAH
THEODORA
VERONICA

VICTORIA
VIRGINIA
VIVIENNE
WINIFRED

9
ALBERTINE
ALEXANDRA
AMBROSINE
ANASTASIA
ANNABELLA
ANNABELLE
BRITANNIA
CASSANDRA
CATHERINE
CELESTINE
CHARLOTTE
CHRISTINA
CHRISTINE
CLEOPATRA
CLOTHILDE
COLUMBINE
CONSTANCE
CORISANDE
DESDEMONA
EGLANTINE
EGLANTYNE
ELISABETH
ELIZABETH
ERNESTINE
ESMERALDA
FRANCESCA
FREDERICA
GABRIELLE
GEORGETTE
GEORGIANA
GERALDINE
GWENDOLEN
GWENLLIAN
HARRIETTE
HENRIETTA
HENRIETTE
HORTENSIA
IPHIGENIA
JEANNETTE
JOSEPHINE
KATHARINE
KATHERINE
MADELEINE
MAGDALENE
MARGARITA
MEHITABEL
MELISANDE
MILLICENT
PIERRETTE
PRISCILLA
ROSABELLA
ROSABELLE

STEPHANIE
THOMASINA
THOMASINE
VALENTINA
VALENTINE
WINEFRIDE

10
ANTOINETTE
CHRISTIANA
CHRISTABEL
CHRISTOBEL
CINDERELLA
CLEMENTINA
CLEMENTINE
CONSTANTIA
ERMINTRUDE
ERMYNTRUDE
ETHELWYNNE
EVANGELINA
EVANGELINE
GWENDOLINE
HILDEGARDE
JACQUELINE
MARGARETTA
MARGARETTE
MARGHERITA
MARGUERITE
WILHELMINA
WILHELMINE

11
ALEXANDRINA
ALEXANDRINE

Painters

3
ARP
COX
DOU
DOW
LEE

4
BOTH
CANO
CIMA
COLE
COPE
CUYP
DAHL
DALI
DIAZ
DODD
DUCK
DUFY
DYCE
DYKE
ETTY
EYCK
FAED
GOES
GOYA
GRIS
GROS
HALS
HART
HOLE
HOLL
HOOK
HUNT
JOHN
KENT
KLEE
LEAR
LELY
MARC
MIRO
NEER
OPIE
REID
RENI
ROSS
WINT
WOOD
WYON
ZORN

5
ABBEY
ALLAN

BACON	PROUT	GEDDES	SANDBY	DANIELL	MORLAND
BEHAM	PUGET	GIBSON	SEDDON	DA PONTE	MURILLO
BOUGH	PUVIS	GIOTTO	SEURAT	DAUMIER	ORCAGNA
BRETT	REDON	GIRTIN	SEVERN	DA VINCI	PARSONS
BROWN	ROSSI	GIULIO	SIGNAC	DECAMPS	PHILLIP
CAMPI	RYDER	GLEYRE	SISLEY	DE HONDT	PICABIA
CARRA	SMART	GLOVER	STREET	DICKSEE	PICASSO
COLLE	SMITH	GORDON	STUART	DOUGLAS	PINWELL
COROT	STEEN	GRAHAM	STUBBS	DUCHAMP	POLLOCK
COSTA	STEER	GREUZE	TADEMA	EDWARDS	POUSSIN
COXIE	STONE	GUARDI	THOMAS	EL GRECO	POYNTER
CRANE	UWINS	HACKER	TITIAN	FORREST	PRINSEP
CREDI	WATTS	HAYDON	TURNER	FOUQUET	PRUDHON
CROME	WELLS	HENNER	VANLOO	FRANCIA	RACKHAM
DANBY	WYATT	HILTON	VARLEY	GAUGUIN	RAEBURN
DAVID		HODLER	VASARI	GENDRON	RAPHAEL
DEGAS	6	HOLMES	VEDDER	GIFFORD	RETZSCH
DIETZ	ANDREA	INGRES	VERNET	GILBERT	RIBALTA
DURER	BAUDRY	JACQUE	VERRIO	GLEIZES	ROBERTS
ENSOR	BENOIS	JORDAN	WALKER	GOODALL	ROUAULT
ERNST	BENTON	KEYSER	WEYDEN	GOSSART	RUSSELL
FOPPA	BONNAT	KNIGHT	WILBYE	GREGORY	SARGENT
FRIPP	BOXALL	LA TOUR	WILKIE	GUTHRIE	SCHETKY
FRITH	BRAQUE	LAUDER	WILSON	HACKERT	SEGUIER
FURSE	BRAUER	LAVERY	WRIGHT	HERBERT	SICKERT
GADDI	BRETON	LAWSON	WYNANT	HERDMAN	SIMPSON
GATTI	BRIGHT	LEADER	YEAMES	HERRERA	SNYDERS
GENGA	BROUER	LE BRUN		HERRING	SOLARIO
GRANT	BURTON	LEPERE	7	HOBBEMA	SOLOMON
GUIDO	CARTER	LESLIE	ARETINO	HODGSON	SOUTINE
HOARE	CESARI	LINTON	BALDUNG	HOFMANN	TENNIEL
HOMER	CHALON	LIZARS	BASSANO	HOGARTH	TERBURG
JONES	CIGOLI	LOVINO	BEECHEY	HOKUSAI	THOMSON
KLIMT	CLAUDE	MABUSE	BELCHER	HOLBEIN	TIEPOLO
LANCE	CLOUET	MANSON	BELLOWS	HONDIUS	UCCELLO
LEECH	COELLO	MASSON	BERNINI	HOPPNER	UTRILLO
LEGER	COLMAN	MATSYS	BOCKLIN	HORSLEY	VAN DYCK
LEGRO	CONDER	MEDINA	BONNARD	ISRAELS	VANDYKE
LIPPI	COOPER	MESDAG	BOUCHER	JACKSON	VAN EYCK
LOTTO	COPLEY	MEULEN	BROUWER	KNELLER	VAN GOGH
LUCAS	COSWAY	MILLET	BRUEGEL	KOONING	VAN VEEN
LUINI	COTMAN	MORONI	CALVERT	LAMBERT	VERMEER
MANET	COZENS	MORRIS	CAMERON	LANCRET	WATTEAU
MARIN	COWELL	MULLER	CARACCI	LE HAVRE	WEELKES
MARIS	DAVIES	MURRAY	CARUCCI	LENBACH	WIJNANT
MASON	DAWSON	PALMER	CASSATT	LINNELL	ZOFFANY
MAUVE	DERAIN	PETTIE	CEZANNE	LORENZO	
METSU	DEWINT	PIOMBO	CHAGALL	MACBETH	8
MONET	DOBSON	POTTER	CHARDIN	MACLISE	ANGELICO
MOORE	DUCCIO	RENOIR	CHARLET	MARQUET	ARMITAGE
MUNCH	EAKINS	RIBERA	CHIRICO	MARTINI	BEAUMONT
NICOL	EGMONT	RIGAUD	CIMABUE	MATEJKO	BOCCIONI
NOLDE	ELMORE	RIVERA	CLAUSEN	MATISSE	BOUGHTON
ORPEN	EWORTH	ROBERT	COGNIET	MEMLINC	BRABAZON
PALMA	FILDES	ROMANO	COLLIER	MESSINA	BRANGWYN
PATER	FORBES	ROMNEY	COLLINS	M'GREGOR	BREUGHEL
PATON	FRIESZ	RONALD	COURBET	MILLAIS	BRIDGMAN
POOLE	FUSELI	RUBENS	CRANACH	MORISOT	CALDERON

CALVAERT
CARRIERE
CHALMERS
CHAMBERS
CHISHOLM
CIPRIANI
CONSTANT
CORBOULD
CRESWICK
DAGUERRE
DAUBIGNY
DE LA PENA
DEL SARTO
DETAILLE
DRUMMOND
EASTLAKE
EECKHOUT
FIELDING
FRANCAIS
GAILLARD
GARAFALO
GIORDANO
HERKOMER
JANSSENS
JONGKIND
JORDAENS
KAUFFMAN
KIRCHNER
LANDSEER
LA TOUCHE
LAURENCE
LEIGHTON
LIMOUSIN
LORRAINE
MAGRITTE
MANTEGNA
MARSHALL
MASOLINO
M'CULLOCH
MONDRIAN
MULREADY
MUNNINGS
NEVINSON
OZENFANT
PATENIER
PERUGINO
PISSARRO
PONTORMO
REDGRAVE
REYNOLDS
RICHMOND
ROMANINO
ROSSETTI
ROUSSEAU
RUISDAEL
RUNCIMAN
SANDRART
SERUSIER

SEVERINI
SPINELLO
STOTHARD
TER BORCH
VANNUCCI
VERONESE
VLAMINCK
VUILLARD
WATERLOW
WHISTLER
ZURBARAN

9

BAKHUIZEN
BENDEMANN
BONINGTON
CALDECOTT
CAMUCCINI
CANALETTO
CARPACCIO
CONSTABLE
CORREGGIO
DEFREGGER
DE KOONING
DE LA CROIX
DE LA MOTTE
DE LA ROCHE
ELSHEIMER
FARINGTON
FEININGER
FRAGONARD
FRANCESCA
GASTINEAU
GERICAULT
GIORGIONE
GRUNEWALD
HONTHORST
HORSCHELT
HOUBRAKEN
JOHNSTONE
KANDINSKY
KAUFFMANN
KOKOSCHKA
LANFRANCO
LANGUERRE
MCTAGGART
NICHOLSON
NORTHCOTE
REMBRANDT
SCHALCKEN
STANFIELD
STEENWIJK
THORNHILL
VALLOTTON
VELASQUEZ
VENEZIANO

10

ALMA TADEMA
BACKHUYSEN
BOTTICELLI
BURNE-JONES
CARAVAGGIO
CATTERMOLE
HARPIGNIES
LIEBERMANN
LORENZETTI
MACWHIRTER
MEISSONIER
MODIGLIANI
MONTICELLI
ORCHARDSON
PARMIGIANO
POELENBURG
POLLAIUOLO
SIGNORELLI
SUTHERLAND
TINTORETTO
VAN DER GOES
VAN DER NEER
VERROCCHIO

11

DELLA ROBBIA
FARQUHARSON
FRA ANGELICO
FRANCIABIGO
GHIRLANDAIO
MANSUR USTAD
PACCHIORATO
PICKERSGILL
THORNYCROFT
VAN DER VELDE
VAN RUISDAEL

12

FANTIN LATOUR
GAINSBOROUGH
LINDENSCHMIT
MICHELANGELO
PARMIGIANINO
PINTURICCHIO
SASSOFERRATO
VAN DER WEYDEN

13

BASTIEN-LEPAGE
VERBOECKHOVEN

14

ANDREA DEL SARTO

15

LEONARDO DA VINCI
TOULOUSE-LAUTREC

The Major Planets

4
MARS

5
EARTH
PLUTO
VENUS

6
SATURN
URANUS

7
JUPITER
MERCURY
NEPTUNE

Plants (see also Flowers; Fruit)

3
BOX, COS, ERS, HOP, IVY, KAT, NEP, OAT, PEA, PIA, POA, RUE, RYE, SEG, TEF, YAM, ZEA

4
ALFA, ALGA, ALOE, ANIL, ARUM, BEAN, BEET, BENT, BIGG, COCA, COLE, CORN, DILL, DISS, DOCK, DOOB, FERN, FLAG, FLAX, GALE, HEMP, HERB, ILEX, IRID, JUTE, KAIL, KALE, KALI, KANS, KELP, LEEK, LING, MATE, MINT, MOLD, MOSS, MUSA, NABK, OATS, OKRA, PEAT, PIPI, POKE, RACE, RAGI, RAMI, RAPE, REED, RHEA, RICE, ROOT, RUSH, RUST, RUTA, SAGE, SMUT, SOLA, TARA, TARE, TARO, TEFF, THEA, TULE, TUTU, ULEX, VINE, WALD, WEED, WELD, WHIN, WOAD, WORT

5
AGAVE, AJUGA, ALANG, ALDER, ALGAE, ANISE, AVENS, BASIL, BLITE, BRAKE, BRANK, BRIAR, BRIER, BROOM, BUTEA, CACTI, CAMAS, CANNA, CAPER, CAREX, CHARA, CHAYA, CHIVE, CHUFA, CIBOL, CLARY, CLOTE, CLOVE, COUCH, CRESS, CUMIN, DULSE, DURRA, DWALE, ELDER, ERICA, ERUCA, FICUS, FITCH, FUCUS, FUNGI, FURZE, GLAUX, GOMBO, GORSE, GOSSE, GRAMA, GRASS, GUMBO, HALFA, HENNA, HOLLY, LIANA, LIANE, LINUM, LOOFA, LOUFA, LUFFA, MAIZE, MEDIC, MOREL, MOULD, MUCOR, MUSCI, NAIAS, NAVEW, NOPAL, ORACH, ORRIS, OSHAC, OSIER, PADDY, PANIC, PULSE, RAMEE, RAMIE, RUBIA, RUBUS, RUNCH, SALAL, SAVIN, SAVOY, SCROG, SEDGE, SENNA, SHRUB, SISAL, SOLAH, SOLAR, SPIKE, SUMAC, TANSY, THORN, THYME, VETCH, VITIS, WAHOO, WHEAT, WHORT, WITHY, WRACK, YEAST, YUPON

6
ACORUS, AGARIC, ALHAGI, ARALIA, ARBUTE, ARNICA, BALSAM, BAMBOO, BARLEY, BATATA, BENNET, BORAGE, BRYONY, BURNET, CACTUS, CAMASH, CAMASS, CARROT, CASSIA, CATNEP, CATNIP, CELERY, CICELY, CICUTA, CLOVER, COCKLE, COFFEE, COTTON, COWPEA, CROTON, DAPHNE, DARNEL, DATURA, DODDER, ELODEA, ENDIVE, ERYNGO, FENNEL, FERULA, FESCUE, FIMBLE, FIORIN, FRUTEX, FUNGUS, FUNKIA, FUSTEL, GARLIC, GNETUM, GOMBRO, HENBIT, HYSSOP, INDIGO, JUNCUS, KALMIA, KARITE, KIEKIE, KNAWEL, LALANG, LAUREL, LICHEN, LOLIUM, LOOFAH, LOVAGE, LUPINE, MADDER, MAGUEY, MALLOW, MANIOC, MARRAM, MARROW, MARRUM, MATICO, MESCAL, MILLET, MYRICA, MYRTLE, NARDOO, NERIUM, NETTLE, NUTMEG, ORACHE, ORCHID, ORCHIS, ORIGAN, ORRICE, OXALIS, PACHAK, PEPPER, POTATO, PRIVET, QUINOA, QUITCH, RADISH, RAGGEE, RAMSON, RATTAN, RUSCUS, SAVINE, SAVORY, SENEGA, SESAME, SESELI, SMILAX, SORREL, SPURGE, SPURRY, SQUASH, SQUILL, STYRAX, SUMACH, SUNDEW, TEASEL, TEAZEL, TEAZLE, TOMATO, TURNIP, TUTSAN, URTICA, YARROW, YAUPON

7
ABSINTH, ACONITE, ALECOST, ALFALFA, ALKANET, ALL-GOOD, ALL-HEAL, ALTHAEA, AMANITA, ARBUTUS, AWLWORT, BENTHON, BISTORT, BOG-BEAN, BRACKEN, BRAMBLE, BRINJAL, BUGWORT, BULBULE, BULRUSH, BURDOCK, BUR-REED, CABBAGE, CALAMUS, CARAWAY, CARDUUS, CARLINE, CASSAVA, CATMINT, CEREALS, CHERVIL, CHICORY, CLIVERS, COMFREY, COWBANE, COWHAGE, COWITCH, COW-WEED, CREEPER, CUDBEAR, CUDWEED, CUP-MOSS, CURCUMA, CYTISUS, DIONAEA, DITTANY, DOGBANE, DOG'S-RUE, EAR-WORT, EPACRID, ESPARTO, EUGENIA, EUTERPE, FELWORT, FEMITER, FENITAR, FIGWORT, FLY-TRAP, FOXTAIL, FROGBIT, FUMARIA, GALANGA, GENISTA, GINGILI, GINSENG, GIRASOL, GRADDAN, GUAYULE, HEATHER, HELODEA, HEMLOCK, HENBANE, HERBAGE

HONESTY
HOP-VINE
IPOMOEA
ISOETES
JEW'S-EAR
JINJILI
JUNIPER
LATAKIA
LETTUCE
LUCERNE
LYCHNIS
MANDIOC
MANIHOC
MATWEED
MAYWEED
MUGWORT
MULLEIN
MUSTARD
OLITORY
OPUNTIA
ORIGANE
OSMUNDA
PANICUM
PAPYRUS
PAREIRA
PARELLA
PARELLE
PARSLEY
PARSNIP
PIMENTO
PUMPION
PUMPKIN
PUTCHUK
QUAMASH
RAGWEED
RAGWORT
RAMBLER
RAMPION
RHATANY
RHUBARB
ROBINIA
SAFFRON
SALIGOT
SALSAFY
SALSIFY
SANICLE
SAW-WORT
SEAWEED
SENECIO
SERINGA
SETUALE
SETWALL
SOLANUM
SPINACH
SPURREY
STATICE
SUCCORY
TALIPAT

TALIPOT
TARWEED
THISTLE
TOBACCO
TRAILER
TREFOIL
TRUFFLE
TURBITH
TURPETH
VANILLA
VERBENA
VERVAIN
WARATAH
WITLOOF
ZEDOARY
ZIZANIA

8

ACANTHUS
AGRIMONY
AMBROSIA
AMELCORN
ANGELICA
ANTHEMIA
ASPHODEL
ASPIDIUM
BANEWORT
BAROMETZ
BEARBINE
BEAR'S-EAR
BELLWORT
BERBERIS
BINDWEED
BOG-GRASS
BOGWHORT
BRASSICA
BRUNELLA
BULLWEED
BULLWORT
CAMOMILE
CANNABIS
CAPSICUM
CARDAMOM
CARL-HEMP
CARRAWAY
CASH CROP
CATCHFLY
CAT'S-TAIL
CENTAURY
CHARLOCK
CHICKPEA
CINCHONA
CINNAMON
CLEAVERS
CLEMATIS
CLUBMOSS
CLUBRUSH
COCCULUS

COCKSPUR
COCKWEED
COLESEED
CONFERVA
CORNFLAG
CORNROSE
COSTMARY
COWGRASS
COW-WHEAT
CUCUMBER
CYCLAMEN
DANEWORT
DIANDRIA
DOG-BRIAR
DOG-BRIER
DOG-GRASS
DOLICHOS
DROPWORT
DUCKWEED
DUMBCANE
EARTHNUT
EARTH-PEA
ECHINOPS
EGG-PLANT
EGLATERE
EPIPHYTE
ERIGERON
EUONYMUS
FEMETARY
FEVERFEW
FLEABANE
FLIXWEED
FRAGARIA
FUMITORY
GALANGAL
GARCINIA
GINGELLY
GIRASOLE
GOATWEED
GOUTWEED
GOUTWORT
GROMWELL
GULFWEED
HARE'S-EAR
HAWKWEED
HAWTHORN
ICE-PLANT
KNAPWEED
KNOTWEED
LECANORA
LICORICE
LUNGWORT
MALE-FERN
MANDIOCA
MANDRAKE
MARATTIA
MARJORAM
MARSILEA

MAT-GRASS
MAY-BLOOM
MESQUITE
MEZEREON
MILKWEED
MILKWORT
MOONSEED
MOONWORT
MOUSE-EAR
MUSHROOM
NUTGRASS
OLEANDER
OLEASTER
PATIENCE
PEAT-MOSS
PINKROOT
PLANTAIN
PLANTLET
PLANTULE
POKEWEED
PRUNELLA
PUFFBALL
PURSLANE
PUTCHOCK
RATSBANE
REED-MACE
RIB-GRASS
ROCCELLA
ROCKROSE
ROCKWEED
ROSEMARY
RYE-GRASS
SAINFOIN
SALTWORT
SAMNITIS
SARGASSO
SCAMMONY
SEA-WRACK
SEEDLING
SENGREEN
SHAMROCK
SIMARUBA
SKULLCAP
SMALLAGE
SOAPROOT
SOAPWORT
SOWBREAD
STARWORT
TAMARISK
TARA-FERN
TARRAGON
TEA-PLANT
TOAD-FLAX
TOAD-RUSH
TREE-FERN
TREE-MOSS
TREMELLA
TRITICUM

TURK'S-CAP
TURMERIC
TURNSOLE
VALERIAN
VERATRUM
VIBURNUM
WALLMOSS
WARTWORT
WITHWIND
WOODBIND
WOODBINE
WOODROOF
WOODRUFF
WOODRUSH
WOODSAGE
WORMWOOD
XANTHIUM
ZINGIBER

9

ADDERWORT
ANACHARIS
ARROWHEAD
ARROWROOT
ARTEMISIA
ARTICHOKE
ASCLEPIAD
ASCLEPIAS
ASPARAGUS
AUBERGINE
BALSAMINA
BEAN-CAPER
BEECH-FERN
BENT-GRASS
BIRD'S-FOOT
BLOODROOT
BLUEGRASS
BLUE-JOINT
BRIAR-ROOT
BRIER-ROOT
BRIARWOOD
BRIERWOOD
BROOKLIME
BROOKMINT
BROOKWEED
BROOMCORN
BROOMRAPE
BUCKTHORN
BUCKWHEAT
BUTTERBUR
CAPERBUSH
CAPRIFOLE
CARDAMINE
CARRAGEEN
CATCHWEED
CHAMOMILE
CHAPPARAL
CHICKWEED

CHINAROOT
CLOVE-TREE
COLCHICUM
COLOCYNTH
COLTSFOOT
CORAL-ROOT
CORAL-TREE
CORIANDER
CORN-SALAD
COTYLEDON
COURGETTE
CRAMP-BARK
CRATAEGUS
CUCKOO-BUD
CULVER-KEY
DANDELION
DIGITALIS
DITTANDER
DOCK-CRESS
DUCK'S-FOOT
DUCK'S-MEAT
DULCAMARA
DYER'S-WEED
DYER'S-WELD
EQUISETUM
EUPHORBIA
EVERGREEN
EYEBRIGHT
FENUGREEK
GALENGALE
GALINGALE
GAMA-GRASS
GERMANDER
GLASSWORT
GOOSEFOOT
GOSSYPIUM
GREENWEED
GROUND-IVY
GROUND-NUT
GROUNDSEL
HAIR-GRASS
HARE'S-FOOT
HELLEBORE
HERD-GRASS
HAORHOUND
HOARHOUND
HORSEFOOT
HORSETAIL
KNEE-HOLLY
KNOTGRASS
LARK'S-HEEL
LASERWORT
LIQUORICE
LIVERWORT
LYME GRASS
MANDIOCCO
MANZANITA
MARIHUANA

MARIJUANA
MEADOW-RUE
MILK-VETCH
MISTLETOE
MONKSHOOD
MOSCHATEL
MOUSETAIL
NEPENTHES
NICOTIANA
PATCHOULI
PATCHOULY
PELLITORY
POISON-IVY
POISON-OAK
PYRACANTH
PYRETHRUM
RAFFLESIA
RED CLOVER
ROCAMBOLE
ROCK-BRAKE
ROCK-CRESS
SAFFLOWER
SAGEBRUSH
SAINTFOIN
SAPONARIA
SARGASSUM
SASKATOON
SAXIFRAGE
SCALE-FERN
SCALE-MOSS
SEA-LENTIL
SISAL-HEMP
SMARTWEED
SNAKEROOT
SNAKEWEED
SNOWBERRY
SPEARMINT
SPIKENARD
STELLARIA
STONECROP
STONEWORT
SUGAR-BEET
SUGAR-CANE
SUN-SPURGE
SWEET-FLAG
SWEETGALE
SWEETWOOD
TARAXACUM
THEOBROMA
THORNBUSH
TOADGRASS
TOADSTOOL
TONGA-BEAN
TONKA-BEAN
TOOTHWORT
TORMENTIL
TRIFOLIUM
WAKE-ROBIN

WALL-CRESS
WATER-WEED
WAX-MYRTLE
WIDOW-WAIL
WILD THYME
WINCOPIPE
WINK-A-PEEP
WOLFSBANE
WOLF'S-CLAW
WOLF'S-FOOT
WORM-GRASS
WOUNDWORT

10

ADDER'S-FERN
ADDER'S-WORT
ALEXANDERS
AMPELOPSIS
BEARD-GRASS
BELLADONNA
BITTER-ROOT
BLACKTHORN
BROME-GRASS
BUFFALO-NUT
BUNCHGRASS
BUTTERDOCK
BUTTERWORT
CANADA RICE
CARRAGHEEN
CASSUMUNAR
CHERRY-BEAN
CHINA GRASS
CINQUEFOIL
CORNCOCKLE
COTTONWEED
COUCH-GRASS
COW-CHERVIL
COW-PARSLEY
CRAKEBERRY
CRANESBILL
CURLY GRASS
DEADNETTLE
DOG'S-FENNEL
DOG'S-TONGUE
DRACONTIUM
DRAGONHEAD
ELECAMPANE
ESCOLLONIA
FRANGIPANI
FRIAR'S-COWL
FURROW-WEED
GARDEN-MINT
GAULTHERIA
GLOBE-DAISY
GOLDEN-HAIR
GOLDEN-SEAL
GOLDY-LOCKS
GOOSE-GRASS

GRAMA-GRASS
GRASS-WRACK
GREASEWOOD
GREENBRIER
GROUND PINE
HEMPNETTLE
HERD'S-GRASS
HOP-TREFOIL
INDIAN CORN
INDIAN-POKE
INDIAN-SHOT
ITALIAN RYE
JEW'S-MALLOW
JIMSON-WEED
KAFFIR CORN
KING'S-SPEAR
KNAPBOTTLE
LADY'S-THUMB
LAURUSTINE
LYCOPODIUM
MAIDENHAIR
MANILA-HEMP
MAYBLOSSOM
MOCK-PRIVET
NIGHTSHADE
NIPPLEWORT
OPIUM PLANT
OPIUM POPPY
PARKLEAVES
PASSIFLORA
PENNYROYAL
PEPPERMINT
PEPPERWORT
PERIWINKLE
PIMPINELLA
POTENTILLA
PYRACANTHA
RANUNCULUS
RED JASMINE
REST-HARROW
ROSE-LAUREL
ROSE-MALLOW
SAPROPHYTE
SARRACENIA
SEA-LETTUCE
SETTERWORT
SHAVEGRASS
SHIELD-FERN
SILVERWEED
SISAL-GRASS
SNAKE'S-HEAD
SNEEZEWORT
SOW-THISTLE
SPEARGRASS
SPIKE-GRASS
SPLEEN-WORT
STAVESACRE
STITCHWORT

STONE-BREAK
STORK'S-BILL
SWEETBRIAR
SWEETBRIER
SWORD-GRASS
THORN-APPLE
THORN-HEDGE
THROATWORT
TOUCH-ME-NOT
TRAGACANTH
TROPAEOLUM
TUMBLEWEED
VENUS'S-COMB
WALLPEPPER
WATERCRESS
WATER-PLANT
WHITETHORN
WILD INDIGO
WILLOW-WEED
WITCH-HAZEL
WOLF'S-PEACH
WOOD-SORREL
YELLOWROOT
YELLOW-WEED
YELLOW-WORT

11

BEAR'S-BREECH
BISHOP'S-WEED
BITTERSWEET
BLACK-MEDICK
BLADDER-FERN
BOTTLE-GOURD
BOULDER-FERN
BRANK-URSINE
CANARY-GRASS
CAULIFLOWER
CHANTERELLE
COFFEE-PLANT
CONTRAYERVA
CONVOLVULUS
CORN-PARSLEY
COTONEASTER
COTTON-GRASS
COTTON-PLANT
DAME'S-VIOLET
DOG'S-MERCURY
DRACUNCULUS
DRAGON'S-HEAD
DUTCH-CLOVER
DYER'S ROCKET
FESCUE-GRASS
FIELD MADDER
FINGER-GRASS
FULLER'S-HERB
GIANT FENNEL
GUINEA-GRASS
HART'S-TONGUE

ICELAND-MOSS
INDIAN-CRESS
IPECACUANHA
JIMPSON-WEED
KIDNEY-VETCH
LADY'S-FINGER
LASERPICIUM
LAURUSTINUS
LEATHERLEAF
MARRAM-GRASS
MARRUM-GRASS
MARSH MALLOW
MEADOWGRASS
MILK-THISTLE
MILLET-GRASS
OYSTER-PLANT
PAMPAS GRASS
PARSLEY-FERN
PELARGONIUM
PEPPER-GRASS
POISON-SUMAC
QUITCH-GRASS
REINDEER MOSS
RIBBON-GRASS
SEA-PURSLANE
SNAIL-FLOWER
STAR-THISTLE
SULPHUR-ROOT
SULPHURWORT
SWEET-CICELY
SWEET-POTATO
SWINE'S-CRESS
THOROUGH-WAX
TONQUIN-BEAN
TUSSAC-GRASS
TWITCH-GRASS
VIPER'S-GRASS
WHITE BRYONY
WHITE CLOVER
WHITLOW-WORT
WINTERBLOOM
WINTER-CRESS
WINTERGREEN
XANTHOXYLUM
ZYGOPHYLLUM

12

ADDER'S-TONGUE
AUTUMN CROCUS
BERMUDA GRASS
BLACK SALSAFY
BLACK SALSIFY
BUFFALO-GRASS
CHRIST'S-THORN
COLOQUINTIDA
COMMON SORREL
COMPASS-PLANT
CORN-MARIGOLD

ECHINOCACTUS
FEATHER-GRASS
FENNEL-FLOWER
FOOL'S-PARSLEY
GLOBE-THISTLE
HEDGE-MUSTARD
HOUND'S-TONGUE
INDIAN MILLET
INDIAN TURNIP
LADY'S-THISTLE
MANGEL-WURZEL
MONK'S-RHUBARB
NONE-SO-PRETTY
PADDOCK-STOOL
PALMA-CHRISTI
PATIENCE-DOCK
PICKEREL-WEED
PITCHER-PLANT
POISON-SUMACH
QUAKING GRASS
REINDEER MOSS
SARSAPARILLA
SEA-BUCKTHORN
SNOW-IN-SUMMER
SOLOMON'S-SEAL
SPANISH BROOM
SPANISH CRESS
SPANISH GRASS
SPEAR-THISTLE
SPURGE-LAUREL
STAGHORN MOSS
TIMOTHY-GRASS
TOBACCO-PLANT
TORCH-THISTLE
VIRGIN'S-BOWER
WATER-PARSNIP
WATER-SOLDIER
WHITLOW-GRASS
YELLOW-RATTLE

13

BUTCHER'S BROOM
CAT'S-TAIL GRASS
COTTON-THISTLE
DOG'S-TAIL GRASS
ELEPHANT-GRASS
ELEPHANT'S-FOOT
FLOWERING RUSH
GARLIC-MUSTARD
GOOD-KING-HENRY
INDIAN TOBACCO
JAMESTOWN-WEED
MANGOLD-WURZEL
MEADOW-SAFFRON
RASPBERRY-BUSH
ROSE-BAY LAUREL
SCOTCH-THISTLE
SPIKE-LAVENDER

TRAVELLER'S-JOY
VENUS'S-FLYTRAP
VIPER'S-BUGLOSS
WATER-HYACINTH
WATER-STARWORT
WAYFARING TREE
WILD LIQUORICE
WOOD-GERMANDER

14

BLACKBERRY-BUSH
CARLINE-THISTLE
CASTOR-OIL PLANT
CHINESE LANTERN
GOOSEBERRY-BUSH
HOTTENTOT BREAD
LORDS-AND-LADIES
MOUNTAIN LAUREL
MOUNTAIN SORREL
PRINCE'S-FEATHER
SENSITIVE PLANT
SHEPHERD'S-PURSE
SPANISH BAYONET
SPANISH NEEDLES
STARCH-HYACINTH
TREACLE-MUSTARD
WHITE HELLEBORE
WOOD-NIGHTSHADE
YELLOW-CENTAURY

15

BLACK NIGHTSHADE
BRUSSELS SPROUTS
BURNET SAXIFRAGE
DYER'S-YELLOW-WEED
GOLDEN SAXIFRAGE
INDIAN LIQUORICE
JACK-IN-THE-PULPIT
MEADOW-SAXIFRAGE
MUSTARD-AND-CRESS
SENEGA SNAKEROOT
SHEPHERD'S-NEEDLE
VIRGINIA CREEPER
WOODY NIGHTSHADE

Poets

3
GAY
KEN
POE

4
CATO
CORY
GRAY
HOGG
HOOD
HUNT
LANG
LEAR
LI PO
NASH
OVID
OWEN
POPE
RHYS
TATE
TU FU
VAUX

5
AIKEN
ARANY
BASHO
BLAIR
BLAKE
BLOOM
BLUNT
BOWEN
BROWN
BRUCE
BURKE
BURNS
BYRON
CINNA
CLARE
CROCE
DANTE
DONNE
ELIOT
FROST
GOSSE
GOULD
GOWER
HARDY
HEINE
HOMER
KEATS
KEBLE
LEWIS
LUCAN

MONRO
MOORE
NEALE
NOYES
POUND
PRIOR
SCOTT
SMART
SMITH
TASSO
VAZOV
VIGNY
WATTS
WILDE
WOLFE
WYATT
YEATS

6
ALCMAN
ARNOLD
AUSTIN
AYTOUN
BAILEY
BARHAM
BARING
BARNES
BASHOH
BELLOC
BIALIK
BINYON
BRONTE
BROOKE
CAMOES
CIBBER
CLOUGH
COWLEY
COWPER
CRABBE
DAVIES
DEKKER
DOBELL
DOBSON
DOWSON
DRYDEN
DUNBAR
GOETHE
GORDON
GREENE
HEMANS
HENLEY
HOLMES
HORACE
LANDOR
MASSEY
MILTON
MORRIS
NERUDA

PINDAR
RACINE
RAMSAY
SAPPHO
SAVAGE
SEAMAN
SEDLEY
SIDNEY
SQUIRE
STEELE
SURREY
TAGORE
THOMAS
TUPPER
UHLAND
VALERY
VERGIL
VILLON
VIRGIL
WALLER
WATSON
WESLEY
WOTTON

7
ADDISON
ALCAEUS
ARIOSTO
BAILLIE
BARBOUR
BLUNDEN
BRIDGES
BULLETT
CAEDMON
CAMPION
CANNING
CHAUCER
COLLINS
CRASHAW
DE VIGNY
DOUGHTY
DOUGLAS
DRAYTON
DUNSANY
EMERSON
FLECKER
FREEMAN
GAUTIER
GOGARTY
HERBERT
HERRICK
HEWLETT
HODGSON
HOFFMAN
HOPKINS
HOUSMAN
INGELOW
JUVENAL

KIPLING
LINDSAY
LYDGATE
MANZONI
MARLOWE
MARTIAL
MARVELL
MASTERS
MEYNELL
MISTRAL
NEWBOLT
PALAMAS
PASCOLI
PATMORE
PEACOCK
PLAUTUS
PUSHKIN
RIMBAUD
RUSSELL
SASSOON
SERVICE
SHELLEY
SITWELL
SOUTHEY
SPENDER
SPENSER
TERENCE
THOMSON
VALLEJO
VAUGHAN
WHITMAN

8
AKENSIDE
BEECHING
BETJEMAN
BROWNING
BUCHANAN
CAMPBELL
CATULLUS
CONQUEST
CROMPTON
CYNEWULF
DAVIDSON
DAY LEWIS
DRUMMOND
FLETCHER
GRENFELL
KINGSLEY
LANGLAND
LAWRENCE
LOVELACE
MACAULAY
MACLEISH
MACNEICE
MAITLAND
MALLARME
MEREDITH

PALGRAVE
PETRARCH
ROSSETTI
SCHLEGEL
SHADWELL
SUCKLING
TENNYSON
THOMPSON
VERLAINE
VOLTAIRE
WHITTIER

9
ALDINGTON
BOCCACCIO
CALVERLEY
COLERIDGE
D'ANNUNZIO
DICKINSON
GOLDSMITH
LAMARTINE
MASSINGER
MONTAIGNE
NIETZSCHE
ROCHESTER
SACKVILLE
SWINBURNE
WYCHERLEY

10
CHATTERTON
CHESTERTON
DRINKWATER
FITZGERALD
HEIDENSTAM
LONGFELLOW
MONTGOMERY
PROPERTIUS
THEOCRITUS
VOGELWEIDE
WORDSWORTH

11
ABERCROMBIE
LE GALLIENNE
MONTGOMERIE
SHAKESPEARE
WATTS-DUNTON

12
O'SHAUGHNESSY

13
SACKVILLE-WEST

14
ALMEIDA GARRETT

Poets Laureate

3
PYE

4
ROWE
TATE

5
LEWIS

6
AUSTIN
CIBBER
DRYDEN
EUSDEN
JONSON
WARTON

7
BRIDGES
SOUTHEY

8
BETJEMAN
D'AVENANT
DAY LEWIS
SHADWELL
TENNYSON

9
MASEFIELD
WHITEHEAD

10
WORDSWORTH

Politicians and Statesmen

3
FOX
HUA
ITO
KIM
KUN
LEE
MAO
PYM
U NU

4
AMIN
BENN
BLUM
BOSE
BROZ
CARR
CATO
CHOU
COKE
DIAZ
DIEM
EDEN
FOOT
FORD
FREI
GREY
HESS
HOLT
HOME
HYDE
KHAN
KING
KNOX
LONG
MEIR
MORE
NAGY
PEEL
PITT
REES
RHEE
RUSK
TAFT
TENG
TITO
TODD

5
ADAMS
AGNEW
AZANA
BANDA
BENES

BERIA
BEVAN
BEVIN
BOTHA
BURKE
CASEY
CECIL
CIANO
CLIVE
DAYAN
DRACO
DRAGO
ELIOT
ESSEX
GOWON
GRANT
HAYES
HEATH
HENRY
HOXHA
KADAR
KEMAL
LAVAL
LENIN
MALAN
MARAT
MASON
MBOYA
NEHRU
NENNI
NIXON
NORTH
PERON
PRIOR
SADAT
SHORT
SMITH
SMUTS
SOLON
SULLA
SULLY
TISZA
WITTE

6
ATTLEE
BARBER
BARRAS
BRIAND
BRIGHT
BRUTUS
CAESAR
CARSON
CASTRO
CAVOUR

CICERO
COBDEN
CRIPPS
CURZON
DANTON
DE WITT
DJILAS
DUBCEK
DUBOIS
DULLES
EUGENE
FOUCHE
FRANCO
FRASER
GANDHI
GIEREK
GORTON
GRIVAS
GUIZOT
HEALEY
HITLER
HOOVER
JAURES
JUAREZ
KAUNDA
KRUGER
LOUBET
MEDICI
MOBUTU
MOSLEY
NASSER
ORSINI
PANDIT
PETAIN
POWELL
PRASAD
RAHMAN
RHODES
RIPPON
RIVERA
SIEYES
STALIN
THIERS
TRUMAN
U THANT
WILKES
WILSON
WOLSEY

7
ACHESON
AGRIPPA
ASQUITH
ATTWOOD
AZIKIWE

BALDWIN
BALFOUR
BATISTA
BOLIVAR
CANNING
CHATHAM
COBBETT
COLBERT
COLLINS
DE SULLY
FORSTER
GOERING
GOGARTY
GOMULKA
GRATTAN
GROMYKO
GUEVARA
HALDANE
HALIFAX
HAMPDEN
HIMMLER
HOUSTON
IDI AMIN
JENKINS
JOHNSON
KENNEDY
KOZYGIN
LAURIER
LINCOLN
LUMUMBA
MASARYK
MAZARIN
MAZZINI
MENZIES
MIKOYAN
MINTOFF
MOLOTOV
NEVILLE
NKRUMAH
NYERERE
OBREGON
O'CONNOR
O'MALLEY
PARNELL
PEARSON
RAPACKI
RUSSELL
SALAZAR
SARAGAT
SCHACHT
SENGHOR
SHASTRI
SHOTOKU
SNOWDEN
SUKARNO
TROTSKY
TRUDEAU
TSHOMBE

VORSTER
WALLACE
WALPOLE
WHITLAM
YOSHIDA

8
ADENAUER
BEN BELLA
BISMARCK
BREZHNEV
BUKHARIN
COOLIDGE
CROMWELL
CROSLAND
CROSSMAN
DALADIER
DE GAULLE
DELCASSE
DE VALERA
DISRAELI
DOLLFUSS
DUVALIER
FRANKLIN
FUJIWARA
GAMBETTA
GOEBBELS
GOTTWALD
HAILSHAM
HAMILTON
HARRIMAN
HEYDRICH
HUMPHREY
KEKKONEN
KENYATTA
KRUSCHEV
LANSBURY
LITVINOV
MCCARTHY
MCGOVERN
MCNAMARA
MAKARIOS
MALENKOV
MARSHALL
MAUDLING
MIRABEAU
MONTFORT
PERICLES
PLIMSOLL
POINCARE
POMPIDOU
QUISLING
SCHUMANN
SIKORSKI
THATCHER
TRUMBULL
ULBRICHT
VERWOERD

WEIZMANN
WHITELAW
WILLIAMS
ZINOVIEV

9
ARISTIDES
BEN GURION
BONDFIELD
BOULANGER
BOURGUIBA
BRADLAUGH
CALLAGHAN
CHOU EN-LAI
CHURCHILL
CONDORCET
DIONYSIUS
GAITSKELL
GARIBALDI
GLADSTONE
GLANVILLE
HO CHI MINH
JEFFERSON
KIM IL SUNG
KISSINGER
LAFAYETTE
LIVERPOOL
MACDONALD
MAGSAYSAY
MATTEOTTI
MELBOURNE
MOSSADEGH
MUSSOLINI
PAASIKIVI
PILSUDSKI
RICHELIEU
ROOSEVELT
SALISBURY
SAN MARTIN
STEVENSON
STREICHER
STRUENSEE
SUN YAT-SEN
TOGLIATTI
VENIZELOS
VYSHINSKY

10
BIRKENHEAD
BUSTAMENTE
CLEMENCEAU
DE MONTFORT
EISENHOWER
HINDENBURG
HUA KUO-FENG
KARAMANLIS
KHRUSHCHEV
LA FOLLETTE

LEE KUAN YEW
MANNERHEIM
MAO TSE-TUNG
METTERNICH
PALMERSTON
RIBBENTROP
SCHUMACHER
SEKOU TOURE
STRESEMANN
TALLEYRAND
WASHINGTON
WELLINGTON

11
BOUMEDIENNE
CASTLEREAGH
CHAMBERLAIN
CHARLEMAGNE
DEMOSTHENES
DOUGLAS-HOME
NGO DINH DIEM
PISISTRATUS
ROBESPIERRE
SCHUSCHNIGG
STAMBOLISKY

12
BANDARANAIKE
SEYSS-INQUART
THEMISTOCLES

13
CHIANG KAI-SHEK
TENG HSIAO-PING

15
HOUPHOUET-BOIGNY

17
CAMPBELL-BANNERMAN

Ports of Europe

4
BARI
CORK
HULL
KIEL
OSLO
RIGA

5
BREST
CADIZ
DOVER
EMDEN
GENOA
MALMO
TURKU

6
BERGEN
BREMEN
CALAIS
DANZIG
DIEPPE
DUBLIN
GDANSK
GDYNIA
LISBON
LONDON
LUBECK
MALAGA
NANTES
NAPLES
NARVIK
ODESSA
OPORTO
OSTEND
TOULON
TROMSO

7
AJACCIO
ANTWERP
BELFAST
BRISTOL
CARDIFF
GLASGOW
HAMBURG
HARWICH
IPSWICH
LEGHORN
LE HAVRE
LIVORNO
MESSINA
PALERMO
PIRAEUS
ROSTOCK

SWANSEA
TARANTO
TRIESTE

8
ABERDEEN
BORDEAUX
BOULOGNE
BRINDISI
CAGLIARI
CUXHAVEN
FLUSHING
GOTEBORG
HELSINKI
HOLYHEAD
ISTANBUL
NEWHAVEN
PLYMOUTH
ST HELIER
SALONIKA
VALENCIA

9
AMSTERDAM
AVONMOUTH
BARCELONA
CHERBOURG
EDINBURGH
LENINGRAD
LIVERPOOL
NEWCASTLE
ROTTERDAM
SANTANDER
STOCKHOLM
ZEEBRUGGE

10
COPENHAGEN
FOLKESTONE
GOTHENBURG
MARSEILLES
PORTSMOUTH

11
BREMERHAVEN
SAINT HELIER
ST PETER PORT
SOUTHAMPTON

12
SAN SEBASTIAN

13
HOOK OF HOLLAND
MIDDLESBROUGH

14
SAINT PETER PORT

Ports of Asia

4
ADEN
AMOY
BAKU
CEBU
LU-TA

5
AQABA
DAVAO
EILAT
GALLE
HAIFA
IZMIR
JIDDA
KERCH
KOCHI
OSAKA
OTARU
PUSAN

6
ASHDOD
BATUMI
BEIRUT
BOMBAY
CANTON
CHEFOO
GURIEV
GUR'YEV
HAIKOW
HOIHOW
INCHON
KUWAIT
†LUSHUN
MADRAS
MANAMA
MANILA
PENANG
SAMSUN
SWATOW
YENTAI

7
BANGKOK
COLOMBO
CUTTACK
FUKUOKA
JAKARTA
KARACHI
KOWLOON
KUCHING
MAGADAN
MURORAN
RANGOON
SOVETSK

8
AL-KUWAIT
ALLEPPEY
CALCUTTA
DJAKARTA
HAIPHONG
HAKODATE
HONG KONG
ISTANBUL
KANÁZAWA
NAGASAKI
SHANGHAI
SURABAJA
SURABAYA
TAGANROG
TSINGTAO
YOKOHAMA
YOKOSUKA

9
KOZHIKODE
KWANGCHOW
MANGALORE
SINGAPORE
TAKAMATSU
YOKKAICHI

10
CHITTAGONG
GEORGE TOWN
*PORT ARTHUR
PORT SOVIET
SEBASTOPOL
SEVASTOPOL
TRIVANDRUM

11
CHINWANGTAO
SHIMONOSEKI
TRINCOMALEE
VLADIVOSTOK

12
CHINGWANGTAO
†LUSHUN-TALIEN

13
SOVIET HARBOUR

* former name
† new name

Ports of Africa

4
*BONE
LOME
ORAN
SUEZ

5
ACCRA
*BEIRA
DAKAR
LAGOS
RABAT
TANGA
TUNIS

6
†ANNABA
DOUALA
DURBAN
JIBUTI
LOBITO
LUANDA
†MAPUTO
†SOFALA
TETUAN
TOBRUK

7
ABIDJAN
ALGIERS
BENGASI
*KENITRA
MAJUNGA
MASSAWA
MOMBASA
SEKONDI
TANGIER
TRIPOLI

8
BENGHAZI
BENGUELA
CAPE TOWN
DJIBOUTI
FREETOWN
PORT SAID
TAMATAVE
ZANZIBAR

9
BENGUELLA
PORT-BOUET
PORT SUDAN
WALVIS BAY

10
ALEXANDRIA
CASABLANCA
EAST LONDON
LIBREVILLE
MOCAMBIQUE
MOZAMBIQUE

11
DAR ES SALAAM

12
PORT HARCOURT

13
PORT ELIZABETH

14
†MINA HASSAN TANI

15
*LOURENCO MARQUES
SEKONDI-TAKORADI

* former name
† new name

Ports of North and Central America

5
TAMPA

6
BELIZE
BOSTON
DULUTH
HAVANA
NASSAU
QUEBEC
ST JOHN
TOLEDO

7
DETROIT
HALIFAX
HOUSTON
NEW YORK
NORFOLK
OAKLAND
ST JOHN'S
SAN JUAN
SEATTLE
TAMPICO

8
MONTREAL
NEW HAVEN
PORTLAND
SAN DIEGO
SAVANNAH
VERACRUZ
VICTORIA

9
BALTIMORE
CHURCHILL
GALVESTON
LONG BEACH
PENSACOLA
SAINT JOHN
VANCOUVER

10
CHARLESTON
NEW ORLEANS
PORT ARTHUR
PROVIDENCE
QUEBEC CITY
SAINT JOHN'S
THUNDER BAY
WILMINGTON

11
BROWNSVILLE
NEW YORK CITY

12
JACKSONVILLE
PHILADELPHIA
POINTE-A-PITRE
PORT-AU-PRINCE
PRINCE RUPERT
SAN FRANCISCO
SANTO DOMINGO

13
CORPUS CHRISTI
SAULT STE MARIE

14
SANTIAGO DE CUBA

Ports of South America

5
ARICA
*BAHIA
BELEM
NATAL

6
CALLAO
CUMANA
ILHEUS
MACEIO
RECIFE
SANTOS

7
ARACAJU
CAYENNE
IQUIQUE
SAO LUIS
VITORIA

8
LA GUAIRA
†SALVADOR

9
CARTAGENA
FORTALEZA
MARACAIBO

10
GEORGETOWN
JOAO PESSOA
MONTEVIDEO
PARAMARIBO
SANTA MARTA
TALCAHUANO
VALPARAISO

11
ANTOFAGASTA
BAHIA BLANCA
BUENOS AIRES

12
BARRANQUILLA
BUENAVENTURA
NEW AMSTERDAM
RIO DE JANEIRO

13
FLORIANOPOLIS

* former name
† new name

Ports of Australasia

4
SUVA

5
PERTH

6
ALBANY
DARWIN
HOBART
NOUMEA
OAMARU
SYDNEY
TIMARU

7
BUNBURY
DUNEDIN

8
ADELAIDE
AUCKLAND
BRISBANE
GISBORNE
WANGANUI

9
GERALDTON
MELBOURNE
NEWCASTLE
WHANGAREI

10
WELLINGTON

11
NEW PLYMOUTH
PORT HEDLAND

12
CHRISTCHURCH

Presidents of the USA

4
FORD
POLK
TAFT

5
ADAMS
GRANT
HAYES
NIXON
TYLER

6
ARTHUR
CARTER
HOOVER
MONROE
PIERCE
TAYLOR
TRUMAN
WILSON

7
HARDING
JACKSON
JOHNSON
KENNEDY
LINCOLN
MADISON

8
BUCHANAN
COOLIDGE
FILLMORE
GARFIELD
HARRISON
MCKINLEY
VAN BUREN

9
CLEVELAND
JEFFERSON
ROOSEVELT

10
EISENHOWER
WASHINGTON

British Prime Ministers

4
BUTE
EDEN
GREY
PEEL
PITT

5
DERBY
HEATH
NORTH

6
ATTLEE
PELHAM
WILSON

7
ASQUITH
BALDWIN
BALFOUR
CANNING
CHATHAM
GRAFTON
RUSSELL
WALPOLE

8
ABERDEEN
BONAR LAW
DISRAELI
GODERICH
PERCEVAL
PORTLAND
ROSEBERY

9
ADDINGTON
CALLAGHAN
CHURCHILL
GLADSTONE
GRENVILLE
LIVERPOOL
MACDONALD
MACMILLAN
MELBOURNE
NEWCASTLE
SALISBURY
SHELBURNE

10
DEVONSHIRE
PALMERSTON
ROCKINGHAM
WELLINGTON

WILMINGTON

11
CHAMBERLAIN
DOUGLAS-HOME
LLOYD GEORGE

17
CAMPBELL-BANNERMAN

Reptiles

3
ASP
BOA
BOM
EFT

4
BOMA
EMYS
EVET
GILA
WORM

5
ABOMA
ADDER
AGAMA
ASPIC
COBRA
DRACO
ELAPS
GECKO
GUANA
HYDRA
KRAIT
MAMBA
SNAKE
VARAN
VIPER

6
AGAMID
ANOLIS
BOYUNA
CAIMAN
CAYMAN
DABOIA
DABOYA
DIPSAS
DRAGON
GAVIAL
GOANNA
GOPHER
IGUANA
JIBOYA
KARAIT
LIZARD
MOLOCH
MUGGER
PYTHON
TRITON
TURTLE
WORRAL
WORREL
ZONURE

7
ANOURIS
COLUBER
HICATEE
HOGNOSE
MONITOR
RATTLER
SERPENT
TESTUDO
TUATARA
TUATERA

8
ANACONDA
BASILISK
CERASTES
DINOSAUR
DRAGONET
HICCATEE
JARARACA
JARARAKA
MOCASSIN
MOCCASIN
OPHIDIAN
RAT-SNAKE
SAND-WORM
SEA-SNAKE
STELLION
TERRAPIN
TORTOISE
WATER-DOG

9
ALLIGATOR
BEAD-SNAKE
BOOMSLANG
CHAMELEON
CHELONIAN
CROCODILE
DART-SNAKE
HAMADRYAD
HAWKSBILL
HORN-SNAKE
IGUANODON
KING-COBRA
KING-SNAKE
PINE-SNAKE
PUFF-ADDER
RING-SNAKE
RIVER-JACK
ROCK-SNAKE
SEA-TURTLE
TREE-SNAKE

10
COCKATRICE
CONGO SNAKE
COPPERHEAD

DEATH-ADDER
DINOSAURUS
DIPLODOCUS
GLASS-SNAKE
GRASS-SNAKE
HELLBENDER
LOGGERHEAD
MEGALOSAUR
MOSASAUROS
MOSASAURUS
PONDTURTLE
ROCK-PYTHON
SEA-SERPENT
TREE-LIZARD
WALL-LIZARD
WATER-SNAKE

11
COTTONMOUTH
DART SERPENT
GILA MONSTER
ICHTHYOSAUR
RATTLESNAKE
RINGED SNAKE
ROCK SERPENT
STEGOSAURUS
TREE SERPENT
TRICERATOPS
TYRANNOSAUR

12
BRONTOSAURUS
DIAMOND SNAKE
DRAGON-LIZARD
HYLAEOSAURUS
MEGALOSAURUS
POND-TORTOISE
WATER-SERPENT

13
AQUATIC LIZARD
BEARDED LIZARD
DOLICHOSAURUS
ICHTHYOSAURUS
PAINTED TURTLE
TYRANNOSAURUS

14
BOA CONSTRICTOR
COACHWHIP-SNAKE
COBRA-DE-CAPELLO
RAT-TAILED SNAKE
SNAPPING TURTLE

15
ALLIGATOR LIZARD
HAWKSBILL TURTLE
PAINTED TORTOISE

16
RAT-TAILED SERPENT
TYRANNOSAURUS REX

Rivers of the British Isles

3	4
ADD	ADUR
ALN	AIRE
ALT	ALAW
ASH	ALDE
AXE	ALED
AYR	ALNE
CAM	ALUN
CAN	ARAY
DEE	AROS
DON	ARUN
EAU	AVAN
ELY	AVON
ESK	BAIN
EXE	BANN
EYE	BARR
FAL	BRAN
GAM	BRAY
IRT	BRIT
ISE	BRUE
JED	BURE
KYM	BURN
LEA	BUSH
LEE	CAIN
LEW	CALE
LOY	CARY
MOY	CERI
NAR	CHAR
NOE	CHET
OCK	CHEW
ORE	CLAW
RAY	CLUN
REA	COLE
REE	COLN
RIB	CONA
ROY	CREE
RYE	CULM
SOW	DANE
TAF	DART
TAS	DEAN
TAW	DOON
TAY	DORE
TER	DORN
TUD	DOVE
URE	DYFI
URR	DYKE
USK	EARN
VER	EBBW
WEY	EDEN
WID	EHEN
WYE	ELAN
YAR	ELWY
YEO	ERCH

ERME
ERNE
EWES
FINN
FONT
FOSS
FYNE
GADE
GALA
GELT
GLEN
GOWY
HART
HULL
IDLE
INNY
ISIS
ISLA
ISLE
IVEL
KALE
KENT
KING
LARK
LEAM
LERI
LING
LLIW
LUCE
LUGG
LUNE
LYNE
LYON
MAIN
MAUN
MEIG
MEON
MILK
MOLE
NENE
NIDD
NITH
NORE
OUSE
PANT
PENK
PLYM
REDE
RHIW
RUEL
SARK
SCAR
SEPH
SHEE
SLEA
SOAR
SOWE
SPEY

SUCK
SUIR
TAFF
TAME
TARF
TAVY
TAWE
TEES
TEME
TEST
THAW
THET
TILL
TILT
TONE
TOVE
TYNE
TYWI
UGIE
URIE
WEAR
WENT
WEST
WICK
WYRE
YARE

5

AERON
AFTON
ALHAM
ALLAN
ALLEN
AMMAN
ANKER
ANNAN
ARDLE
ARROW
ARTRO
AWBEG
BANWY
BARLE
BEANE
BEELA
BEULT
BLACK
BLANE
BLYTH
BOGIE
BOVEY
BOYNE
BRAIN
BRANT
BREDE
BRETT
BRIDE
BROCK
BRORA

CAIRN
CAMEL
CAREY
CEIRW
CERNE
CHESS
CHURN
CLARE
CLWYD
CLYDE
CLYST
COLNE
CORVE
COTHI
COVER
CRAKE
CYNIN
CYNON
CYWYN
DEBEN
DEVON
DRYFE
EBBLE
ELLEN
ETIVE
FEALE
FEUGH
FLEET
FORTH
FOYLE
FROME
GAIRN
GARNO
GARRY
GRETA
GWASH
GWAUN
GWILL
HAYLE
IRFON
!THEN
KINGS
KNAIK
LEITH
LEVEN
LOCHY
MANOR
MEASE
MEDEN
MEESE
MORDA
MUICK
NAIRN
NAVER
NEATH
OGWEN
ORCHY
ORRIN

OTTER
OUZEL
PERRY
RODEN
ROMAN
RYTON
SENCE
SEVEN
SHEAF
SHIRA
STORT
STOUR
STRAT
SULBY
SWALE
SWIFT
TAMAR
TANAT
TEIFI
TEIGN
TEISE
TEITH
THAME
TIRRY
TORNE
TRENT
TWEED
TWRCH
WAVER
WNION
WYLYE
YARTY
YEALM
YSCIR
YTHAN

6

AFFRIC
ALMOND
ANNICK
BALDER
BANDON
BARROW
BARVAS
BEAULY
BILBOA
BLITHE
BLYTHE
BORGIE
BOURNE
BRAINT
BROSNA
CALDER
CALDEW
CAMOGE
CARRON
CHATER
CLETWR

CLUNIE
CONWAY
COQUET
CRERAN
CROUCH
DARENT
DARVEL
DARWEN
DEARNE
DEVILS
DIGHTY
DUDDON
ENRICK
ERICHT
EVELIX
EWENNY
FARRAR
FERGUS
HONDDU
HUMBER
IRVINE
IRWELL
ITCHEN
KELTIE
KENNET
KINGIE
KINNEL
KIRTLE
LIFFEY
LLYNFI
LOCHAY
LOSSIE
LYNHER
MAIGUE
MARTEG
MEDWAY
MERSEY
MOFFAT
MONNOW
NADDER
NEFERN
NENAGH
ORWELL
OTTERY
OYKELL
PARRET
PIDDLE
PRYSOR
RIBBLE
RODING
ROTHER
SAWDDE
SEVERN
SLANEY
SPRINT
STRULE
SWILLY
TEVIOT

THAMES
THURSO
TUMMEL
TWYMYN
VYRNWY
WALDON
WEAVER
WENSUM
WHARFE
WISSEY
WITHAM
WREAKE
YARROW
YSTRAD

7

AHERLOW
BROWNEY
CANNICH
CASSLEY
CEIRIOG
CHELMER
CHURNET
CHWEFRU
CROGLIN
DERWENT
DEVERON
DOCHART
DOUGLAS
DUCHRAY
DYSYNNI
ENBORNE
ETTRICK
FALLOCH
GIPPING
GWYRFAI
IRTHING
KENMARE
LEANNAN
LOUGHOR
MUNSTER
OLD HOWE
OLD NENE
POULTER
ROUGHTY
SHANNON
STRATHY
WAVENEY
WELLAND
WENNING
YSTWYTH

8

ALLADALE
ANCHOLME
BEAULIEU
BLACK ESK
BLADNOCH

BREAMISH
CHERWELL
CLAERWEN
CLYWEDOG
CUCKMERE
DUNBEATH
EVENLODE
EYE WATER
FINDHORN
FOULNESS
GREAT EAU
HART BURN
JED WATER
NORTH ESK
SKIRFACE
STEEPING
STIFFKEY
STINCHAR
THRUSHEL
URR WATER
WANSBECK
WASHBURN
WHITE ESK
WINDRUSH

9
ALLAGHAUN
AVON WATER
BALNAGOWN
BARR WATER
DEAN WATER
EAST ALLEN
EAST STOUR
EDDLESTON
EWES WATER
GALA WATER
GWYDDERIG
HALLADALE
KALE WATER
KING WATER
NORTH BECK
NORTH TYNE
SHEE WATER
TARF WATER
WATER OF AE
WEST ALLEN
WEST WATER

10
AFTON WATER
ALLEN WATER
BERRIEDALE
BLACKWATER
BLACK WATER
BLANE WATER
CAIRN WATER
DRYFE WATER
GYPSEY RACE

LITTLE DART
LITTLE OUSE
MANOR WATER
STRATHMORE

11
ANNICK WATER
CLUNIE WATER
DEVILS WATER
DIGHTY WATER
KELTIE WATER
KINNEL WATER
KIRTLE WATER
LITTLE STOUR
WATER OF LUCE
WATER OF MILK
WEST CLEDDAU
YARROW WATER

12
CROGLIN WATER
DOUGLAS WATER
DUCHRAY WATER
ETTRICK WATER
WATER OF FEUGH
WATER OF FLEET
WATER OF LEITH

13
DUNBEATH WATER

14
EDDLESTON WATER

15
BERRIEDALE WATER
STRATHMORE WATER

Rivers of Europe
(excluding the British Isles and the USSR)

2
PO

3
EMS
INN
LEK
LOT
LYS
MUR
SIL

4
AARE
ADDA
ARNO
AUBE
AUDE
CHER
DORE
DRAU
EBRO
EGER
ELBE
ENNS
EURE
GAIL
GARD
GERS
GOTA
ISAR
KEMI
LABE
LAHN
LECH
LOIR
LOUE
MAAS
MAIN
MINO
ODER
ODRA
OHRE
OISE
ORNE
OUST
PRUT
SAAR
SAVA
SAVE
SIEG
TARN

THUR
WAAL

5
ADIGE
ADOUR
AISNE
DONAU
DOUBS
DOURO
DRAVA
DRAVE
DROME
FULDA
GENIL
ISERE
JUCAR
LAGEN
LEYRE
LOIRE
MARCH
MARNE
MESTA
MEUSE
MINHO
MOSEL
OGLIO
PIAVE
REUSS
RHINE
RHONE
SAALE
SAONE
SEGRE
SEINE
SERIO
SIRET
SOMME
SPREE
TAGUS
THORE
TIBER
TISZA
TORNE
VESLE
WESER
WISLA
YONNE

6
ALLIER
ARIEGE

BLAVET
CAVADO
DANUBE
GLOMMA
IJSSEL
ISARCO
ISONZO
LJUNGA
MOLDAU
MORAVA
MUONIO
NEISSE
NESTOS
ORNAIN
OURTHE
SAMBRE
SARTHE
SEGURA
STRUMA
THEISS
TICINO
VIENNE
VINDEL
VLTAVA
ZEZERE

7
AVEYRON
BEUVRON
DURANCE
GARONNE
GHAGHRA
GIRONDE
MARITSA
MAYENNE
MIJARES
MOSELLE
NERETVA
SALZACH
SCHELDT
VILAINE
VISTULA

8
DORDOGNE
GUADIANA

9
SKELLEFTE

12
GUADALQUIVIR

13
SEVRE NANTAISE

14
SEVRE NIORTAISE

Rivers of the USSR

2	7
OB	DNIEPER
	MURGHAB
3	PECHORA
BUG	SELENGA
CHU	YENISEY
DON	
ILI	8
OKA	AMU DAR'YA
PUR	DNIESTER
TAZ	JAXARTES
UFA	SYR DAR'YA
USA	VYCHEGDA

4	9
AMGA	INDIGIRKA
AMUR	WEST DVINA
KAMA	
LENA	11
OXUS	BLACK IRTYSH
SVIR'	
TURA	13
URAL	NORTHERN DVINA
VAKH	

5
ALDAN
AMGUN
DVINA
IZHMA
KUBAN
NEMAN
TAVDA
TOBOL'
VITIM
VOLGA

6
ANABAR
ANADYR'
ANGARA
BELAYA
CHULYM
DONETS
IRTYSH
KOLYMA
OLENEK
PRIPET
SAMARA
SHILKA
TURGAY
USSURI
VILYUY

Rivers of Asia
(outside the USSR)

2	MANJRA
LO	MEKONG
LU	PENNAR
SI	SUTLEJ
WU	TIGRIS
	USSURI
3	YAMUNA
FEN	YELLOW
HAB	
HAN	7
MIN	CHAMBAL
NAL	DAMODAR
PEH	HOOGHLY
SAI	KALADAN
SON	KERULEN
TAO	KRISHNA
WEI	MALSANG
	NARBADI
4	PARBATI
AMUR	SAKARYA
BEAS	SELENGO
HARI	SHINANO
KOSI	SITTANG
LIAO	SUNGARI
RAVI	TSANGHO
TONE	YANGTZE
TSAI	YARKAND
YUAN	
	8
5	BEYSEHIR
ARAKS	BRAHMANI
ATRAK	CHINDWIN
BETWA	GODAVARI
BHIMA	ISHIKARI
CORUH	MAHANADI
DASHT	MENDERES
GANGA	PENGANGA
HWANG	
INDUS	9
ISHIM	IRRAWADDY
SIANG	
TAPTI	10
TARIM	KIZIL IRMAK
TISTA	
	11
6	BLACK IRTYSH
CHENAB	BRAHMAPUTRA
GANDAK	
GANGES	
GOMATI	
JHELUM	
JORDAN	
KHOTAN	
KINSHA	

Rivers of Africa

3
DRA
JUR

4
JUBA
NILE
TANA
UELE
VAAL

5
BENUE
CHARI
CONGO
CUITO
KAFUE
KASAI
KEBBI
NIGER
SHIRE
ZAIRE

6
ATBARA
GALANA
GAMBIA
KUNENE
LUKUGA
MODDER
MOLOPO
ORANGE
RUFIJI
RUVUMA
UBANGI

7
CHELIFF
LIMPOPO
LUALABA
SANYATI
SEMLIKI
SENEGAL
SHIBELI
ZAMBEZI

8
BLUE NILE
MEDJERDA
OKAVANGO
OUBANGUI
RED VOLTA
SHANGANI

9
WHITE NILE

10
BLACK VOLTA
WHITE VOLTA

11
BAHR EL JEBEL

12
BAHR EL GHAZAL

Rivers of North and Central America

4
DUCK
GILA
MILK
OHIO

5
GREEN
JAMES
LIARD
PEACE
PECOS
SLAVE
SNAKE
YAQUI
YUKON

6
BALSAS
BRAZOS
FRASER
GRANDE
HUDSON
MAUMEE
OTTAWA
PLATTE
POWDER
ST JOHN
SKEENA
WABASH

7
ALABAMA
CONCHOS
KANAWHA
POTOMAC
ST CLAIR
ST CROIX
SEGOVIA

8
ARKANSAS
CANADIAN
COLORADO
COLUMBIA
DELAWARE
ILLINOIS
KENTUCKY
MISSOURI
OKANOGAN
SAGUENAY
SAQUENAY

9
ALLEGHENY
ATHABASCA

CHURCHILL
MACKENZIE
MERRIMACK
PENOBSCOT
SAINT JOHN
WISCONSIN

10
CUMBERLAND
SAINT CLAIR
SAINT CROIX
ST LAWRENCE
SAN JOAQUIN
WILLAMETTE

11
CONNECTICUT
MISSISSIPPI

12
SASKATCHEWAN

13
SAINT LAWRENCE

Rivers of South America

4
BENI
PARA

5
CAUCA
CHICO
DULCE
JURUA
NEGRO
PLATE
PURUS
XINGU

6
AMAZON
BRANCO
CARONI
CHUBUT
MORONA
PARANA
SALADO
VAUPES

7
JURUENA
MADEIRA
MARANON
ORINOCO
TAPAJOS
UCAYALI

8
COLORADO
DEMERARA
GALLEGOS
HUALLAGA
PARAGUAY
SOLIMOES

9
ESSEQUIBO
MAGDALENE
PILCOMAYO
TOCANTINS

10
CASIQUIARE

Rivers of Australasia

3
FLY
ORD

4
DALY
HUME
SWAN

5
BLAND
BOYNE
NAMOI
OVENS
TUMUT
WAIAU
YARRA

6
BARCOO
BARWON
BULLER
CLUTHA
DAWSON
HUNTER
MURRAY
NORMAN
SEVERN
WAIRAU
WILSON

7
DARLING
FITZROY
GILBERT
GLENELG
HURUNUI
MACLEAY
MATAURA
WAIKATO
WAITAKI
WARREGO

8
BEYLANDO
BURDEKIN
CLARENCE
FLINDERS
MITCHELL
VICTORIA
WANGANUI

9
BLACKWOOD

CONDAMINE
FORTESCUE
GREENOUGH
MACINTYRE
MACKENZIE
MACQUARIE
MURCHISON

10
SHOALHAVEN

Saints

3
ABO
ANN
BEE
FOY
GUY
ITA
IVO
LEO
ODO

4
AFRA
ANNE
BARR
BAVO
BEDE
CEDD
CHAD
CUBY
CYBI
DEWI
EDME
ELMO
ELOI
ENDA
ERIC
FARO
GALL
GLEB
HUGH
JOAN
JOHN
JUDE
LUCY
LUKE
MALO
MARK
MARO
MARY
NEOT
OLAF
OMER
OTTO
OUEN
PAUL
PIUS
REMI
RITA
ROCH
ROCK
ROSE
SAVA
YVES
ZENO
ZITA

5
AARON
ADDAI
AEDAN
AGAPE
AGNES
AIDAN
ALBAN
AMAND
ASAPH
BASIL
BEGGA
BEUNO
BLAAN
BLANE
BORIS
BRICE
BRIDE
BRUNO
BUDOC
CADOC
CLARE
CLOUD
CYRIL
CYRUS
DAVID
DENIS
DIEGO
EDITH
EDWIN
EGWIN
ELIAS
EMILY
ESKIL
FAITH
FELIX
FINAN
FLORA
GILES
HELEN
HENRY
HILDA
IRENE
ISAAC
JAMES
JONAH
JUTTA
KEVIN
LIOBA
LOUIS
LUPUS
MENAS
ODILO
PAULA
PETER
PIRAN

SABAS	HELIER	CAJETAN	MILDRED	GELASIUS
SILAS	HILARY	CASIMIR	NORBERT	GENESIUS
SIMON	HUBERT	CASSIAN	PANCRAS	GEOFFREY
STURM	ILLTYD	CECILIA	PATRICK	GERMANUS
TEILO	ISABEL	CHARITY	PELAGIA	GERTRUDE
TITUS	JEROME	CHARLES	PHILEAS	GODELIVE
ULRIC	JOSEPH	CHIONIA	PHOTIUS	HALLVARD
VITUS	JULIAN	CLEMENT	PIONIUS	HILARION
	JULIUS	COLETTE	RAPHAEL	HONORIUS
6	JUSTIN	COLUMBA	RAYMUND	HYACINTH
ADRIAN	JUSTUS	COMGALL	RICHARD	IGNATIUS
AELRED	KENELM	CRISPIN	ROMANUS	LADISLAS
AGATHA	LOUISE	CUTHMAN	ROMUALD	LAWRENCE
AILRED	LUCIAN	CYPRIAN	SERGIUS	MARCELLA
ALBERT	MAGNUS	CYRICUS	SIGFRID	MARGARET
ALEXIS	MARTHA	DAMASUS	STEPHEN	MATTHIAS
ANDREW	MARTIN	DEINIOL	SULPICE	MAUGHOLD
ANGELA	MONICA	DIDACUS	SWITHIN	MELLITUS
ANSELM	NARSES	DOMINIC	SWITHUN	MERIADOC
ANSKAR	NINIAN	DONATUS	THORLAC	MONTANUS
ANTONY	ODILIA	DOROTHY	TIMOTHY	NICETIUS
ARNULF	OSMUND	DUNSTAN	TORIBIO	NICHOLAS
AUBERT	OSWALD	EDBURGA	VINCENT	NOTBURGA
AUBREY	PEDROG	ELIGIUS	WILFRID	OLYMPIAS
AUDREY	PERRAN	ERASMUS	WILLIAM	PAULINUS
AUSTIN	PETROC	EUGENIA	WULFRIC	PERPETUA
BERARD	PHILIP	EULALIA	ZACHARY	POLYCARP
BLAISE	ROBERT	EUSTACE		PORPHYRY
BRIAUC	RUPERT	EYSTEIN	**8**	RADEGUND
BRIGID	SAMSON	FABIOLA	ADALBERT	SERAPHIM
CANICE	SIMEON	FINBARR	ADELAIDE	SERAPION
CANUTE	TERESA	FINNIAN	ALOYSIUS	THEODORE
CARPUS	THOMAS	FLAVIAN	ANTONINO	THORFINN
CECILY	TIKHON	FOILLAN	ARSENIUS	VERONICA
CELSUS	UBALDO	FRANCES	ATTRACTA	WILLIGIS
CIARAN	VIRGIL	FRANCIS	AURELIUS	WINIFRED
COLMAN		GABRIEL	BALDHILD	WOLFGANG
CONRAD	**7**	GILBERT	BARNABAS	WULFSTAN
COSMAS	ABRAHAM	GODFREY	BENEDICT	
DAMIAN	ADAMNAN	GOTHARD	BENIGNUS	**9**
DANIEL	ALBERIC	GREGORY	BERNWARD	ACHILLEUS
DIDIER	ALDHELM	GUTHLAC	BERTHOLD	ALEXANDER
DONNAN	ALPHEGE	HADRIAN	BLANDINA	ALMACHIUS
DYFRIG	AMADOUR	HERBERT	BONIFACE	ALPHONSUS
DYMPNA	AMBROSE	ISIDORE	CAMILLUS	ANASTASIA
EDMUND	ANTHELM	JOACHIM	CARTHAGE	APOLLONIA
EDWARD	BACCHUS	JULIANA	COLUMBAN	AUGUSTINE
ELZEAR	BARBARA	KENNETH	CRISPINA	CAESARIUS
FIACRE	BARLAAM	LAMBERT	CUNEGUND	CALLISTUS
FINTAN	BATHILD	LEANDER	CUTHBERT	CATHERINE
FURSEY	BERNARD	LEONARD	CYNEHELM	CELESTINE
GEORGE	BIBIANA	LUTGARD	CYRIACUS	CHRISTINE
GERALD	BIRINUS	MALACHY	ETHELRED	CORNELIUS
GERARD	BOTOLPH	MATILDA	EUGENIUS	CUTHBURGA
GILDAS	BRAULIO	MATTHEW	EUPHEMIA	CYNEBURGA
GODRIC	BRENDAN	MAXIMUS	EUSEBIUS	DEMETRIUS
HARVEY	BRIDGET	MEINRAD	FEBRONIA	DIONYSIUS
HEDWIG	BROCARD	MICHAEL	FELICITY	DUBRICIUS

ELIZABETH
ENGELBERT
ERCONWALD
ETHELBERT
ETHELWOLD
EUPHRASIA
EUTHYMIUS
FERDINAND
GENEVIEVE
GWENFREWI
HILDEGARD
HOMOBONUS
JANUARIUS
KATHERINE
KENTIGERN
MADELEINE
MARCELLUS
METHODIUS
MILTIADES
NICODEMUS
PAMPHILUS
PHILIBERT
SEVERINUS
SILVESTER
SPIRIDION
STANISLAS
VALENTINE
WENCESLAS
WILLIBALD

10
ANASTASIUS
ATHANASIUS
BARBA'SHMIN
BERNADETTE
BERNARDINE
CHRODEGANG
CRISPINIAN
DESIDERIUS
ETHELBURGA
EUSTOCHIUM
FRIDESWIDE
FRUCTUOSUS
FRUMENTIUS
FULGENTIUS
GAUDENTIUS
JOHN FISHER
MARCELLIAN
MARY DI ROSA
MAXIMILIAN
PAMMACHIUS
PHILIP NERI
RENE GOUPIL
SIMON STOCK
SOPHRONIUS
THEODOSIUS
THOMAS MORE
VICTRICIUS

WILLIBRORD

11
APOLLINARIS
BARTHOLOMEW
BONAVENTURE
CHRISTOPHER
CHRYSANTHUS
CHRYSOGONUS
ISAAC JOGUES
JOHN LALANDE
JOHN NEPOMUK
MARCELLINUS
PETER CHANEL
PETER CLAVER
PETER DAMIAN

12
BURGONDAFARA
MARGARET MARY
MARY MAGDALEN
NOEL CHABANEL
PETER FOURIER
PETER NOLASCO

13
JEAN DE BREBEUF
THOMAS AQUINAS
VINCENT DE PAUL

14
MARTIN DE PORRES

Scientists

3
OHM

4
BAIN
BALL
BELL
BOHR
BOSE
BURT
COUE
DAVY
DORN
FUNK
GALL
GREW
HAHN
HALL
HAUY
HEAD
HESS
HOFF
HULL
HUNT
JOLY
JUNG
KOCH
LANG
LAUE
LENZ
LOEB
MACH
MEAD
OWEN
ROSS
POPE
SALK
SWAN
UREY
WATT
WENT

5
BACON
BAIRD
BAKER
BAUME
BINET
BLACK
BOWER
BOYLE
BRAGG
BRAHE
BRETT
BROWN

BRUSH
CHAIN
COOKE
COUCH
CRICK
CROLL
CROSS
CURIE
DEWAR
DIRAC
DIXON
DUMAS
EVANS
EWINS
FABRE
FERMI
FRANZ
FREUD
FROMM
GAUSS
GIBBS
HABER
HALES
HERTZ
HOOKE
JABIR
JAMES
JANET
JEANS
JOULE
KLEIN
KOLBE
KROGH
LANGE
LE BEL
LEBON
LEWIN
LIBBY
LINNE
LODGE
LOWRY
MASON
MAYOW
MEYER
MONGE
NEMEC
NOBEL
PAPIN
PAULI
PROUT
RHINE
ROSSE
RUSKA
SACHS
SCOTT

SIMON
SMITH
SODDY
STAHL
STAMP
VOLTA
WAAGE
WEBER
WELCH
WHITE
WUNDT
WURTZ

6
AMAGAT
AMPERE
AYRTON
BECHER
BALMER
BORDET
BOUGER
BUNSEN
COUPER
CUVIER
CZAPEK
DALTON
DARWIN
DE BARY
DOMAGK
DRAPER
EDISON
ENDERS
EOTVOS
FIZEAU
FRASCH
FRAZER
GEIGER
GESELL
GLINKA
GMELIN
GRAEBE
GRAHAM
HALLER
HALLEY
HARVEY
HOFMAN
HOOKER
HORNEY
HUGHES
HUNTER
HUXLEY
JENNER
KEKULE
KELVIN
KEPLER
KIRWAN
KNIGHT
KOFFKA

KORNER	FECHNER	SIEMENS	SIDGWICK	HEISENBERG
LANDAU	FEYNMAN	SKINNER	STARLING	HOFMEISTER
LEAKEY	FISCHER	STANLEY	STEVINUS	INGEN-SOUSZ
LEMERY	FITTING	THOMSEN	VAN'T HOFF	KOELREUTER
LIEBIG	FLEMING	THOMSON	WEISMANN	LIEBERMANN
LISTER	FRESNEL	VINCENT	WEIZMANN	MAXIMOWICZ
LORENZ	FRIEDEL	VIRCHOW	WELSBACH	MENDELEYEV
LOVELL	GALILEO	VON MOHL	WILHELMY	PEREGRINUS
MARBUT	GALVANI	WALLACE	WOODWARD	RUTHERFORD
MENDEL	GARTNER	WARMING		VAN BENEDEN
MORGAN	GASSEND	WHEELER	**9**	VAN HELMONT
MULDER	GILBERT	WIELAND	ARRHENIUS	VAN TIEGHEN
MULLER	GLAUBER	WINKLER	BECQUEREL	WATSON-WATT
NAGELI	GODDARD		BERTHELOT	WHEATSTONE
NERNST	HAECKEL	**8**	BERTILLON	
NEWTON	HERBART	ANGSTROM	BERZELIUS	**11**
OBERTH	HOFMANN	ASKENASY	CAVENDISH	HERTZSPRUNG
ODLING	HOPKINS	AVOGADRO	COCKCROFT	LANDSTEINER
OLBERS	HUGGINS	BJERKNES	DESCARTES	LE CHATELIER
OLIVER	HUYGENS	BLACKMAN	DUTROCHET	LEEUWENHOEK
PASCAL	KARSTEN	BRENTANO	EDDINGTON	OPPENHEIMER
PAVLOV	KHORANA	BREWSTER	EMMERLING	SCHRODINGER
PERKIN	KIDSTON	CHADWICK	FALLOPIUS	VAN DE GRAAFF
PIAGET	KIPPING	CHEVREUL	FLAMSTEED	VAN DER WAALS
PLANCK	KREMERS	CLAUSIUS	FRANKLAND	WILLSTATTER
PROUST	KUNCKEL	COURTOIS	GAY-LUSSAC	
RAMSAY	LAENNEC	CROMPTON	GLADSTONE	**12**
RAOULT	LAMARCK	DUCHESNE	GRISEBACH	BOUSSINGAULT
RITTER	LASHLEY	EINSTEIN	HEAVISIDE	BOYSON-JENSEN
RIVERS	LAURENT	ERLANGER	HELMHOLTZ	MITSCHERLICH
STOKES	LECLUSE	FOUCAULT	HORSTMANN	THEOPHRASTUS
SWARTZ	LENSSEN	FRANKLIN	KIRCHHOFF	
TELLER	LOCKYER	GASSENDI	KURCHATOV	**13**
TERMAN	MALTHUS	GEISSLER	LAVOISIER	MUSSCHENBROEK
TSWETT	MARCONI	GEOFFROY	LOMONOSOV	VON STRADOWITZ
TURNER	MAXWELL	GERHARDT	MACDOUGAL	
WATSON	MEDAWAR	GULDBERG	MACINTOSH	**14**
WENZEL	MEITNER	HARSCHEL	MICHELSON	ALBERTUS MAGNUS
YERKES	MESSIER	HISINGER	MOSSBAUER	
YUKAWA	MOISSAN	HUMBOLDT	PRIESTLEY	
	MORISON	JOHNSTON	SCHONHEIN	
7	OERSTED	KLAPROTH	TACHYNIUS	
ANDREWS	OSTWALD	LANGEVIN	THORNDIKE	
BENTLEY	PASTEUR	LIBAVIUS	TSCHERMAK	
BERGMAN	PAULING	LINNAEUS	WHINFIELD	
BERNARD	PFEFFER	MCMILLAN	WHITWORTH	
BROGLIE	PICCARD	MALPIGHI		
CALVERT	POTONIE	MILLIKAN	**10**	
CHAPTAL	POULSEN	MYNSICHT	ARCHIMEDES	
COMPTON	RASPAIL	NEWLANDS	BERTHOLLET	
COULOMB	REAUMUR	PLUNKETT	CANNIZZARO	
CROOKES	RICHTER	PURKINJE	CHARDONNET	
DAUBENI	RONTGEN	RAYLEIGH	COPERNICUS	
DE VRIES	ROTHERT	REGNAULT	DOBEREINER	
DOPPLER	RUMFORD	RICHARDS	ERLENMEYER	
EHRLICH	RUNCORN	ROBINSON	FAHRENHEIT	
EYSENCK	SCHEELE	ROENTGEN	FRAUNHOFER	
FARADAY	SEMENOV	SHOCKLEY	HABERLANDT	

Sculptors

4
ADAM
ASAM
BAHR
BERG
BIRD
BURN
CARR
COLT
DICK
FORD
GABO
GILL
HOLL
JUNI
KENT
NASH
POST
RUDE
SHAW
THOM
TUBY
WEBB
WOOD
WREN
ZORN
ZURN

5
BACON
BAILY
BANKS
BARRY
BARYE
BOEHM
BROCK
BROWN
BRUCE
CAMPI
CRAIG
DALOU
DAMER
DANCE
DAVID
DRAKE
DUDOK
EGELL
FOLEY
FRINK
GEEFS
GENGA
GIBBS
JONES
KRAFT
LEONI

LE VAU
LUCAS
MOORE
MYRON
PAINE
PAJOU
PETEL
PILON
PREST
PUGET
PUGIN
RAUCH
RODIN
ROSSO
SCOTT
SOANE
STONE
STOSS
TATTI
THEED
WYATT

6
ARCHER
AUSTEN
BEHNES
BROKER
BURNET
CALDER
CANINA
CANOVA
CHEERE
CIBBER
CIGOLI
COOLEY
COUSIN
DA COMO
D'ARRAS
DERAIN
DONNER
DUMONT
GANDON
GEORGE
GIBSON
GIOTTO
GIULIO
GOUJON
HOUDON
JAGGER
JANSEN
LEDOUX
LEGROS
LESCOT
MICHEL
MILLES

NICOLA
PARLER
PISANO
POWERS
ROBBIA
ROMANO
SLODTZ
SMIRKE
SOLARI
STRAUB
STREET
STRONG
STUART
TATLIN
TAYLOR
VASARI
WAGNER
WRIGHT

7
ALGARDI
BALDWIN
BARLACH
BECERRA
BEHRENS
BELLING
BERLAGE
BERNINI
BOLOGNA
BURNARD
CELLINI
CHAUDET
CLODION
CORDIER
COUSTOU
CUYPERS
D'ANGERS
DA VINCI
DE BAZEL
DEERING
DE L'ORME
DESPIAU
DE SWART
DE VRIES
EL GRECO
EPSTEIN
FERRATA
FLAXMAN
FRAIKIN
GABRIEL
GERHARD
GIBBONS
GILBERT
GRASSER
GUARINI
GUNTHER
HOETGER
HOLLAND

JACKSON
JANSSEN
JOHNSON
KRUMPER
LAMBERT
LAURANA
LAURENS
LEMAIRE
LEMOYNE
LE SUEUR
LUTYENS
MADERNA
MAILLOL
MANSARD
MANSART
MANSHIP
MAZZONI
MEUNIER
NEUMANN
NICCOLO
ORCAGNA
PEVSNER
PHIDIAS
PICASSO
PIGALLE
POUSSIN
PRADIER
REICHLE
SCHADOW
SCHLAUM
STAMMEL
STEVENS
THOMSON
VIGARNI
VISCHER
WILKINS
WOOLMER

8
ARMSTEAD
BOCCIONI
BONTEMPS
BRAMANTE
BRANCUSI
BUSHNELL
BUSTELLI
CAMPBELL
CARPEAUX
CATTANEO
CHADWICK
CHAMBERS
CHANTREY
CIVITALI
COCHRANE
COYSEVOX
CRAWFORD
DI CAMBIO
DI DUCCIO

FALCONET
FANCELLI
FILARETE
FRAMPTON
GHIBERTI
GIOVANNI
GIRARDON
HARRISON
HEPWORTH
LIPCHITZ
LYSIPPUS
MARSHALL
PALLADIO
PERMOSER
PERRAULT
PIRANESI
POELAERT
QUEIROLO
RYSBRACK
SARRAZIN
SCAMOZZI
SCHINKEL
SCHLUTER
SERPOTTA
SKEAPING
VAN AELST
VANBRUGH
VITTORIA

9
ABLEITNER
AGESANDER
BORROMINI
BOURDELLE
COCKERELL
CORNEILLE
CORRADINI
CUVILLIES
DANNECKER
DONALDSON
DONATELLO
DU CERCEAU
DUQUESNOY
FERNANDEZ
FLITCROFT
GREENOUGH
GUILLAUME
HAWKSMORE
LA DAURADE
LEHMBRUCK
LETHABURY
MESTROVIC
NICHOLSON
NOLLEKENS
REGNAUDIN
RIEDINGER
RODCHENKO
ROUBILIAC

SANSOVINO
VINGBOONS
VON BANDEL
VON ERLACH

10
ARCHIPENKO
BERRUGUETE
BOUCHARDON
DA CAMPIONE
GIACOMETTI
LEINBERGER
MACKINTOSH
MAROCHETTI
POLYCLITUS
PRAXITELES
RICHARDSON
SANMICHELE
VECCHIETTA
VERROCCHIO
WATERHOUSE
WESTMACOTT
WINSTANLEY

11
BUTTERFIELD
DELLA ROBBIA
GISLEBERTUS
KELDERMANNS
PRIMATICCIO
SCHEEMAKERS
VON ENSINGEN

12
DELLA QUERCIA
FRANCHEVILLE
MICHELANGELO
SAINT-GAUDENS
SCHWANTHALER
VANTONGERLOO

13
DUCHAMP-VILLON
FAISTENBERGER
GUGGENBICHLER
WILLIAM OF SENS

14
VON HILDEBRANDT

15
CARRIER-BELLEUSE
LEONARDO DA VINCI
RIEMENSCHNEIDER

Shakespeare's Men and Women

Key to abbreviations

AC = Antony and Cleopatra; *AW* = All's Well that Ends Well; *AY* = As You Like It; *C* = Coriolanus; *CE* = Comedy of Errors; *Cym* = Cymbeline; *H* = Hamlet; *1H4* = King Henry the Fourth, Pt 1; *2H4* = King Henry the Fourth, Pt 2; *H5* = King Henry the Fifth; *1H6* = King Henry the Sixth, Pt 1; *2H6* = King Henry the Sixth, Pt 2; *3H6* = King Henry the Sixth, Pt 3; *H8* = King Henry the Eighth; *J* = King John; *JC* = Julius Caesar; *KL* = King Lear; *L* = Love's Labour's Lost; *M* = Macbeth; *MA* = Much Ado about Nothing; *MM* = Measure for Measure; *MN* = Midsummer Night's Dream; *MV* = Merchant of Venice; *MW* = Merry Wives of Windsor; *O* = Othello; *P* = Pericles; *R2* = King Richard the Second; *R3* = King Richard the Third; *RJ* = Romeo and Juliet; *T* = The Tempest; *TA* = Titus Andronicus; *TC* = Troilus and Cressida; *TG* = Two Gentlemen of Verona; *Tim* = Timon of Athens; *TN* = Twelfth Night; *TS* = Taming of the Shrew; *WT* = Winter's Tale.

Shakespeare's Men

3
ELY *R3, H5*
NYM *H5,MW*
SAY *2H6*
SLY *TS*

4
ADAM *AY*
AJAX *TC*
CADE *2H6*
CATO *JC*
DAVY *2H4*
DICK *2H6*
DION *WT*
DULL *L*
EROS *AC*
FANG *2H4*
FORD *MW*
GREY *H5,R3*
HUME *2H6*
IAGO *O*
IDEN *2H6*
JAMY *H5*
JOHN *MA,R2,1,2H4,J,RJ*
KENT *KL*
LEAR *KL*
LUCY *1H6*

MOTH *L,MN*
PAGE *MW*
PETO *1,2H4*
PUCK *MN*
ROSS *M,R2*
SNUG *MN*
TIME *WT*
VAUX *2H6,H8*
WART *2H4*
YORK *R2,1,2H4,H5,2H6,R3*

5
AARON *TA*
ABRAM *RJ*
ANGUS *M*
ARIEL *T*
BAGOT *R2*
BATES *H5*
BELCH *TN*
BEVIS *2H6*
BIGOT *J*
BLUNT *1,2H4*
BOULT *P*
BOYET *L*
BUSHY *R2*
BUTTS *H8*
CAIUS *MW,TA*

CASCA *JC*
CINNA *JC*
CLEON *P*
CORIN *AY*
COURT *H5*
CUPID *Tim*
CURAN *KL*
CURIO *TN*
DENNY *H8*
DERBY *R3*
EDGAR *KL*
EGEUS *MN*
ELBOW *MM*
ESSEX *J*
EVANS *MW*
EXTON *R2*
FESTE *TN*
FLUTE *MN*
FROTH *MM*
GOBBO *MV*
GOFFE *2H6*
GOWER *2H4,H5,P*
GREEN *R2*
HENRY *J,R2,1,2H4,H5,*
    1,2,3H6,R3,H8
HYMEN *AY*
LAFEU *AW*
LEWIS *J,H5,3H6*
LOVEL *R3*
LUCIO *MM*
MARCH *1H4,3H6*
MELUN *J*
MENAS *AC*
MILAN *TG*
OSRIC *H*
PARIS *RJ,TC*
PEDRO *MA*
PERCY (Northumberland)
    1,2H4,R2
PETER *J,2H6,MM,RJ*
PHILO *AC*
PINCH *CE*
POINS *1,2H4*
PRIAM *TC*
ROBIN *MW*
ROMEO *RJ*
RUGBY *MW*
SANDS *H8*
SMITH *2H6*
SNARE *2H4*
SNOUT *MN*
SPEED *TG*
TIMON *Tim*
TITUS *TA,Tim*
TUBAL *MV*
VARRO *JC*

6

ADRIAN *C,T*
AEGEON *CE*
AENEAS *TC*
ALBANY *KL*
ALEXAS *AC*
ALONSO *T*
AMIENS *AY*
ANGELO *CE,MM*
ANTONY *JC,AC*
ARMADO *L*
ARTHUR *J*
BANQUO *M*
BASSET *1H6*
BLOUNT *R3*
BOTTOM *MN*
BRUTUS *C,JC*
CAESAR *JC*
CAPHIS *Tim*
CASSIO *O*
CHIRON *TA*
CICERO *JC*
CIMBER *JC*
CLITUS *JC*
CLOTEN *Cym*
COBWEB *MN*
CURTIS *TS*
DECIUS *JC*
DENNIS *AY*
DORSET *R3*
DROMIO *CE*
DUNCAN *M*
EDMUND *R2,3H6,KL*
EDWARD *2,3H6,R3*
EXETER *H5,3H6*
FABIAN *TN*
FEEBLE *2H4*
FENTON *MW*
FRANCE (King) *AW,KL*
GALLUS *AC*
GEORGE *3H6,R3*
GREMIO *TS*
GRUMIO *TS*
GURNEY *J*
HAMLET *H*
HECTOR *TC*
HORNER *2H6*
HUBERT *J*
JAQUES *AY*
JOSEPH *TS*
LAUNCE *TG*
LE BEAU *AY*
LENNOX *M*
LOVELL *H8*
LUCIUS *Cym,JC,TA,Tim*
MARCUS *TA*
MORTON *2H4,R3*
MOULDY *2H4*

MUTIUS *TA*
NESTOR *TC*
OBERON *MN*
OLIVER *AY*
ORSINO *TN*
OSWALD *KL*
OXFORD *3H6,R3*
PHILIP *J,TS*
PIERCE *R2*
PISTOL *2H4,H5,MW*
POMPEY *AC,MM*
QUINCE *MN*
RIVERS *3H6,R3*
RUMOUR *2H4*
SCALES *2H6*
SCARUS *AC*
SCROOP *R2,1,2H4,H5*
SEYTON *M*
SHADOW *2H4*
SILIUS *AC*
SIMPLE *MW*
SIWARD *M*
STRATO *JC*
SURREY *R2,2H4,R3,H8*
TALBOT *1H6*
TAURUS *AC*
THOMAS *2H4,MM*
THURIO *TG*
TRANIO *TS*
TYBALT *RJ*
TYRREL *R3*
VENICE *MV,O*
VERGES *MA*
VERNON *1H4,1H6*
WOLSEY *H8*

7

ABRAHAM *RJ*
AGRIPPA *AC*
ALARBUS *TA*
ALENCON *1H6*
ANTENOR *TC*
ANTONIO *MA,MV,T,TG,TN*
ARRAGON *MV*
AUMERLE *R2*
AUSTRIA *J*
BEDFORD *H5,1H6*
BEROWNE *L*
BERTRAM *AW*
BOURBON *H5*
BRANDON *R3,H8*
CALCHAS *TC*
CALIBAN *T*
CAMILLO *WT*
CAPULET *RJ*
CASSIUS *JC*
CATESBY *R3*
CERIMON *P*

CHARLES *AY,H5,1H6*
CLAUDIO *MA,MM*
CONRADE *MA*
COSTARD *L*
CRANMER *H8*
DE BURGH *J*
DOUGLAS *1H4*
DUMAINE *L*
ESCALUS *MM,RJ*
ESCANES *P*
FLAVIUS *JC,Tim*
FLEANCE *M*
FRANCIS *1H4,MA*
GONZALO *T*
GREGORY *RJ*
HELENUS *TC*
HERBERT *R3*
HOLLAND *2H6*
HORATIO *H*
HOTSPUR *R2,1H4*
IACHIMO *Cym*
LAERTES *H*
LARTIUS *C*
LAVACHE *AW*
LEONATO *MA*
LEONINE *P*
LEONTES *WT*
LEPIDUS *JC,AC*
LINCOLN *H8*
LORENZO *MV*
LYMOGES *J*
MACBETH *M*
MACDUFF *M*
MALCOLM *M*
MARCADE *L*
MARCIUS *C*
MARDIAN *AC*
MARTEXT *AY*
MARTIUS *TA*
MERCADE *L*
MESSALA *JC*
MICHAEL *1H4,2H6*
MONTANO *O*
MONTJOY *H5*
MOROCCO *MV*
MOWBRAY *R2,2H4*
NICANOR *C*
NORFOLK *R2,3H6,R3,H8*
ORLANDO *AY*
ORLEANS *H5,1H6*
OTHELLO *O*
PISANIO *Cym*
PROTEUS *TG*
PUBLIUS *JC,TA*
QUINTUS *TA*
RICHARD *R2,2,3H6,R3*
RUTLAND *3H6*
SALANIO *MV*

SALERIO *MV*
SAMPSON *RJ*
SHALLOW *2H4,MW*
SHYLOCK *MV*
SILENCE *2H4*
SILVIUS *AY*
SIMPCOX *2H6*
SLENDER *MW*
SOLANIO *MV*
SOLINUS *CE*
STANLEY *2,3H6,R3*
SUFFOLK *1,2H6,H8*
THESEUS *MN*
THYREUS *AC*
TRAVERS *2H4*
TRESSEL *R3*
TROILUS *TC*
TYRRELL *R3*
ULYSSES *TC*
URSWICK *R3*
VARRIUS *AC,MM*
VAUGHAN *R3*
WARWICK *2H4,H5,1,2,3H6*
WILLIAM *AY*

8

ABHORSON *MM*
ACHILLES *TC*
AEMILIUS *TA*
AUFIDIUS *C*
BAPTISTA *TS*
BARDOLPH *1,2H4,H5,MW*
BARNARDO *H*
BASSANIO *MV*
BEAUFORT *1,2H6*
BELARIUS *Cym*
BENEDICK *MA*
BENVOLIO *RJ*
BERKELEY *R2,R3*
BERNARDO *H*
BORACHIO *MA*
BULLCALF *2H4*
BURGUNDY *H5,1H6,KL*
CAMPEIUS *H8*
CANIDIUS *AC*
CAPUCIUS *H8*
CARLISLE *R2*
CLARENCE *2H4,3H6,R3*
CLAUDIUS *H,JC*
CLIFFORD *2,3H6*
COLEVILE *2H4*
COMINIUS *C*
CORNWALL *KL*
CROMWELL *H8*
DERCETAS *AC*
DIOMEDES *AC,TC*
DOGBERRY *MA*
EGLAMOUR *TG*

FALSTAFF *1,2H4,MW*
FASTOLFE *1H6*
FLORENCE *AW*
FLORIZEL *WT*
FLUELLEN *H5*
GADSHILL *1H4*
GARDINER *H8*
GARGRAVE *1H6*
GRANDPRE *H5*
GRATIANO *MV,O*
GRIFFITH *H8*
HARCOURT *2H4*
HASTINGS *2H4,3H6,R3*
HUMPHREY *2H4,2H6*
JACK CADE *2H6*
LAURENCE *RJ*
LEONARDO *MV*
LEONATUS *Cym*
LIGARIUS *JC*
LODOVICO *O*
LUCENTIO *TS*
LUCILIUS *JC,Tim*
LUCULLUS *Tim*
LYSANDER *MN*
MALVOLIO *TN*
MARULLUS *JC*
MECAENAS *AC*
MENELAUS *TC*
MENENIUS *C*
MENTEITH *M*
MERCUTIO *RJ*
METELLUS *JC*
MONTAGUE *3H6,RJ*
MORTIMER *1H4,1,3H6*
NICHOLAS *TS*
OCTAVIUS *JC,AC*
OLD GOBBO *MV*
PANDARUS *TC*
PANDULPH *J*
PANTHINO *TG*
PAROLLES *AW*
PEMBROKE *J,3H6*
PERICLES *P*
PHILARIO *Cym*
PHILEMON *P*
PHILOTUS *Tim*
PINDARUS *JC*
POLONIUS *H*
POMPEIUS *AC*
POPILIUS *JC*
PROSPERO *T*
RAMBURES *H5*
RATCLIFF *R3*
REIGNIER *1H6*
REYNALDO *H*
RICHMOND *3H6,R3*
RODERIGO *O*
SALARINO *MV*

SELEUCUS *AC*
SICINIUS *C*
SOMERSET *1,2,3H6*
STAFFORD *2,3H6*
STEPHANO *MV,T*
THALIARD *P*
TITINIUS *JC*
TOM SNOUT *MN*
TRESSELL *R3*
TRINCULO *T*
WHITMORE *2H6*
WILLIAMS *H5*
WOODVILE *1H6*

9

AGAMEMNON *TC*
AGUECHEEK *TN*
ALEXANDER *TC*
ANTIGONUS *WT*
ANTIOCHUS *P*
APEMANTUS *Tim*
ARCHIBALD *1H4*
ARVIRAGUS *Cym*
AUTOLYCUS *WT*
BALTHASAR *RJ*
BALTHAZAR *CE,MA,MV*
BASSIANUS *TA*
BIONDELLO *TS*
BOURCHIER *R3*
BRABANTIO *O*
CAITHNESS *M*
CAMBRIDGE *H5*
CHATILLON *J*
CLEOMENES *WT*
CORNELIUS *Cym,H*
CYMBELINE *Cym*
DARDANIUS *JC*
DEIPHOBUS *TC*
DEMETRIUS *AC,MN,TA*
DOLABELLA *AC*
DONALBAIN *M*
ENOBARBUS *AC*
ERPINGHAM *H5*
FERDINAND *L,T*
FITZWATER *R2*
FLAMINIUS *Tim*
FRANCISCO *H,T*
FREDERICK *AY*
GLANSDALE *1H6*
GLENDOWER *1H4*
GUIDERIUS *Cym*
GUILDFORD *H8*
HELICANUS *P*
HORTENSIO *TS*
HUGH EVANS *MW*
LANCASTER *R2,1,2H4*
MACMORRIS *H5*
MAMILLIUS *WT*

MARCELLUS *H*
NATHANIEL *L,TS*
PATROCLUS *TC*
PETRUCHIO *TS*
POLIXENES *WT*
POSTHUMUS *Cym*
ROTHERHAM *R3*
SALISBURY *J,R2,H5,1,2H6*
SEBASTIAN *T,TN*
SERVILIUS *Tim*
SIMONIDES *P*
SOUTHWELL *2H6*
THERSITES *TC*
TOBY BELCH *TN*
TREBONIUS *JC*
VALENTINE *TA,TG,TN*
VENTIDIUS *AC,Tim*
VINCENTIO *MM,TS*
VOLTIMAND *H*
VOLUMNIUS *JC*
YOUNG CATO *JC*

10

ALCIBIADES *Tim*
ANDRONICUS *TA*
ANTIPHOLUS *CE*
ARCHIDAMUS *WT*
BARNARDINE *MM*
BRAKENBURY *R3*
BUCKINGHAM *2H6,R3,H8*
CANTERBURY *H5,R3,H8*
EUPHRONIUS *AC*
FORTINBRAS *H*
GLOUCESTER *2H4,H5,
    1,2,3H6,R3,KL*
HENRY PERCY *R2,1H4*
HOLOFERNES *L*
HORTENSIUS *Tim*
JOHN TALBOT *1H6*
LONGAVILLE *L*
LYSIMACHUS *P*
MARGARELON *TC*
MARK ANTONY *JC,AC*
MENECRATES *AC*
MONTGOMERY *3H6*
NICK BOTTOM *MN*
PROCULEIUS *AC*
SATURNINUS *TA*
SEMPRONIUS *TA,Tim*
SOMERVILLE *3H6*
STARVELING *MN*
TOUCHSTONE *AY*
WILLOUGHBY *R2*
WINCHESTER *1,2H6,H8*

11

ABERGAVENNY *H8*
ARTEMIDORUS *JC*

BOLINGBROKE *R2,2H6*
CAIUS LUCIUS *Cym*
GEORGE BEVIS *2H6*
JAMES GURNEY *J*
JAMES TYRREL *R3*
JOHN HOLLAND *2H6*
JOHN OF GAUNT *R2*
MUSTARDSEED *MN*
OLD CLIFFORD *2H6*
PETER QUINCE *MN*
PHILOSTRATE *MN*
PLANTAGENET *1,2,3H6*
ROSENCRANTZ *H*
WESTMINSTER *R2*
WILLIAM PAGE *MW*
YOUNG LUCIUS *TA*
YOUNG SIWARD *M*
YOUNG TALBOT *1H6*

12

ANTHONY DENNY *H8*
CAIUS MARCIUS *C*
DECIUS BRUTUS *JC*
FRANCIS FLUTE *MN*
GUILDENSTERN *H*
HUGH MORTIMER *3H6*
JAMES TYRRELL *R3*
JOHN COLEVILE *2H4*
JOHN FALSTAFF *1,2H4,MW*
JOHN FASTOLFE *1H6*
JOHN MORTIMER *3H6*
JULIUS CAESAR *JC*
JUNIUS BRUTUS *C*
MARCUS BRUTUS *JC*
MATTHEW GOFFE *2H6*
NICHOLAS VAUX *H8*
PEASEBLOSSOM *MN*
POPILIUS LENA *JC*
THOMAS HORNER *2H6*
THOMAS LOVELL *H8*
TITUS LARTIUS *C*
WESTMORELAND
    1,2H4,H5,3H6
YOUNG MARCIUS *C*

13

ALEXANDER IDEN *2H6*
FAULCONBRIDGE *J*
HUBERT DE BURGH *J*
JOHN SOUTHWELL *2H6*
OLIVER MARTEXT *AY*
OWEN GLENDOWER *1H4*
PIERCE OF EXTON *R2*
RICHARD SCROOP *1,2H4*
RICHARD VERNON *1H4*
STEPHEN SCROOP *R2*
YOUNG CLIFFORD *2H6*

14

CHRISTOPHER SLY *TS*
EDMUND MORTIMER *1H4,1H6*
LAUNCELOT GOBBO *MV*
MARCUS ANTONIUS *JC*
METELLUS CIMBER *JC*
NORTHUMBERLAND *R2,1,2H4,3H6*
SAUNDER SIMPCOX *2H6*
SEXTUS POMPEIUS *AC*
TULLUS AUFIDIUS *C*

15

ADRIANO DE ARMADO *L*
AEMILIUS LEPIDUS *JC,AC*
ANDREW AGUECHEEK *TN*
EDMUND OF LANGLEY *R2*
MENENIUS AGRIPPA *C*
ROBIN STARVELING *MN*
SICINIUS VELUTUS *C*
THOMAS ROTHERHAM *R3*
TITUS ANDRONICUS *TA*

Shakespeare's Women

4

ANNE *R3*
BONA *3H6*
FORD (Mistress) *MW*
GREY (Lady) *3H6*
HERO *MA*
IRAS *AC*
IRIS *T*
JOAN *1H6*
JUNO *T*
LUCE *CE*
PAGE (Mistress) *MW*
YORK (Duchess) *R2,R3*

5

ALICE *H5*
CELIA *AY*
CERES *T*
DIANA *AW,P*
HELEN *Cym,TC*
JULIA *TG*
MARIA *L,TN*
MOPSA *WT*
PERCY (Lady) *1,2H4*
PHEBE *AY*
REGAN *KL*
VIOLA *TN*

6

AUDREY *AY*
BIANCA *O,TS*
BLANCH *J*
DORCAS *WT*
ELINOR *J*
EMILIA *O,WT*
HECATE *M*
HELENA *AW,MN*
HERMIA *MN*
IMOGEN *Cym*
ISABEL *H5*
JULIET *MM,RJ*
MARINA *P*
OLIVIA *TN*
PORTIA *JC,MV*
SILVIA *TG*
TAMORA *TA*
THAISA *P*
URSULA *MA*

7

ADRIANA *CE*
AEMILIA *CE*
CAPULET (Lady) *RJ*
DIONYZA *P*
ELEANOR *2H6*

GONERIL *KL*
JESSICA *MV*
LAVINIA *TA*
LUCETTA *TG*
LUCIANA *CE*
MACBETH (Lady) *M*
MACDUFF (Lady) *M*
MARIANA *AW,MM*
MIRANDA *T*
NERISSA *MV*
OCTAVIA *AC*
OPHELIA *H*
PAULINA *WT*
PERDITA *WT*
PHRYNIA *Tim*
QUICKLY (Mistress)
    1,2H4,MW,H5
TITANIA *MN*
VALERIA *C*

8

ANNE PAGE *MW*
AUVERGNE (Countess)
    1H6
BEATRICE *MA*
CHARMIAN *AC*
CORDELIA *KL*
CRESSIDA *TC*
GERTRUDE *H*
HERMIONE *WT*
ISABELLA *MM*
MARGARET *MA,*
    1,2,3H6,R3
MONTAGUE (Lady) *R*
MORTIMER (Lady) *1H*
OVERDONE (Mistress)
    MM
PATIENCE *H8*
ROSALIND *AY*
ROSALINE *L*
TIMANDRA *Tim*
VIOLENTA *AW*
VIRGILIA *C*
VOLUMNIA *C*

9

CASSANDRA *TC*
CLEOPATRA *AC*
CONSTANCE *J*
DESDEMONA *O*
ELIZABETH *3H6,R3*
FRANCISCA *MM*
HIPPOLYTA *MN*
KATHARINA *TS*
KATHARINE *H5,H8,L*

LYCHORIDA *P*
ROUSILLON (Countess) *AW*

10
ANDROMACHE *TC*
ANNE BULLEN *H8*
CALPHURNIA *JC*
GLOUCESTER (Duchess) *R2,2H6*
JAQUENETTA *L*

13
DOLL TEARSHEET *2H4*
FAULCONBRIDGE (Lady) *J*
JOAN LA PUCELLE *1H6*

14
NORTHUMBERLAND (Lady) *2H4*

15
MARGERY JOURDAIN *2H6*

Speakers of the House of Commons

3
SAY
ONSLOW
PELHAM
POPHAM
4
BELL
BRAY
COKE
CUST
DYER
HARE
HUNT
KING
LONG
MORE
PEEL
RICH
ROUS
WODE
WOOD
WRAY

5
ABBOT
BAKER
BOWES
BRAND
BUSSY
CHUTE
CREWE
CROKE
DRURY
FINCH
FOLEY
GREEN
GULLY
LLOYD
MOYLE
POWLE
SMITH
SNAGG

6
AUDLEY
BROOKE
BURLEY
CHENEY
CHEYNE
DUDLEY
EMPSON
FLOWER
HANMER
HARLEY
LOVELL
NORTON

SAVAGE
SAWYER
SNAGGE
THOMAS
THORPE
TREVOR
TYRREL
VERNON
WALTON
WAUTON

7
BAYNARD
BROMLEY
CATESBY
CHALTON
CHAUCER
COMPTON
CORDELL
DENISON
ESTURMY
FITZROY
GREGORY
HEIGHAM
LEFEVRE
LOWTHER
MITFORD
NEVILLE
OLDHALL
PHELIPS
POLLARD
REDFORD
RUSSELL
SEYMOUR
TIPTOFT
TRESHAM
TURNOUR
TYRRELL
WENLOCK
WHITLEY

8
ALINGTON
BAMFYLDE
CHARLTON
CORNWALL
DE LA MARE
DOREWOOD
GARGRAVE
GRIMSTON
LENTHALL

MORDAUNT
MORRISON
REDMAYNE
STOURTON
WILLIAMS

9
ADDINGTON
BAMPFYLDE
BEAUCHAMP
GLANVILLE
GRENVILLE
GRIMSTONE
LITTLETON
PICKERING
PUCKERING
SHEFFIELD
WINGFIELD
YELVERTON

10
ABERCROMBY
ENGLEFIELD
HUNGERFORD
RICHARDSON
WALDEGRAVE
WHITELOCKE

11
FITZWILLIAM
GOLDSBROUGH
SHAW-LEFEVRE
STRANGEWAYS
WIDDRINGTON

12
CLIFTON-BROWN
HYLTON-FOSTER
STRANGEWAIES

13
MANNERS-SUTTON

14
GUILDESBOROUGH

Stars (a few of the 71,000,000 stars observed by astronomers)

3			SHAULA
SUN			SIRIUS
			SUHAIL
4			
CAPH			7
ENIF			ALCYONE
MIRA			ALNILAM
SADR			ALNITAK
VEGA			ALPHARD
			ANTARES
5			CANOPUS
ACRUX			CAPELLA
AGENA			DOG-STAR
ALGOL			ELTANIN
ANKAA			MENKENT
ATRIA			MINTAKA
AVIOR			PEACOCK
DENEB			POLARIS
DUBHE			PROCYON
HADAR			REGULUS
HAMAL			RUCHBAH
MERAK			SCHEDAR
MIZAR			
NUNKI			8
RIGEL			ACHERNAR
RIGIL			ALPHECCA
SAIPH			ARCTURUS
SPICA			CANICULA
			CYNOSURE
6			DENEBOLA
ACAMAR			LOADSTAR
ADHARA			LODESTAR
ALIOTH			POLE STAR
ALKAID			
ALMAAK			9
ALMACH			ALDEBARAN
ALNAIR			ALPHERATZ
ALTAIR			BELLATRIX
BECRUX			BETELGEUX
CASTOR			COR CAROLI
DIPHDA			FOMALHAUT
ELNATH			RIGEL KENT
GACRUX			
GIENAH			10
KOCHAB			BETELGEUSE
MARKAB			RASALHAGUE
MEGREZ			
MENKAR			11
MIMOSA			MIAPLACIDUS
MIRACH			
MIRFAK			13
PHECDA			KAUS AUSTRALIS
POLLUX			ZUBENELGENUBI
SCHEAT			
			14
			ZUBENELCHEMALE

Swiss Cantons

3
URI
ZUG

4
VAUD

5
BASEL
BERNE

6
AARGAU
GENEVA
GLARUS
ST GALL
SCHWYZ
TICINO
VALAIS
ZURICH

7
GRISONS
LUCERNE
THURGAU

8
FRIBOURG
ST GALLEN

9
APPENZELL
NEUCHATEL
SAINT GALL
SOLOTHURN

10
GRAUBUNDEN

11
SANKT GALLEN
UNTERWALDEN

12
SCHAFFHAUSEN

Cities, Towns and some villages of England

3		BLYTH
ASH		BRIGG
CAM		CALNE
ELY		CATON
EYE		CHARD
HAY		CHEAM
LEE		CLARE
RYE		CORBY
WEM		COWES
		CREWE
4		CROOK
ACLE		DERBY
BATH		DOVER
BEER		EGHAM
BRAY		EPSOM
BUDE		ERITH
BURY		ESHER
DEAL		FILEY
DISS		FLEET
HOLT		FLINT
HOOK		FOWEY
HOVE		FROME
HULL		GOOLE
HYDE		GRAYS
LEEK		HAXBY
LISS		HAYES
LOOE		HEDON
LYDD		HYTHE
LYMM		LEEDS
MERE		LEIGH
PENN		LEVEN
ROSS		LEWES
RYDE		LOUTH
SALE		LUTON
SEAL		MARCH
SHAP		ONGAR
STOW		POOLE
SWAY		RIPON
WARE		RUGBY
WOOL		SANDY
YARM		SARRE
YATE		SELBY
YORK		STEEP
		STOKE
5		THAME
ALTON		TRING
AMBLE		TRURO
ASCOT		UPTON
ASTON		VANGE
AYTON		WELLS
BACUP		WIGAN
BLABY		

6
ALBURY
ALFORD
ALSTON
ARKLEY
ARNOLD
ASKERN
AUDLEM
AUDLEY
AVELEY
BADDOW
BARHAM
BARLBY
BARNET
BASING
BATLEY
BATTLE
BAWTRY
BEDALE
BELPER
BENSON
BEXLEY
BIBURY
BODMIN
BOGNOR
BOLTON
BOSHAM
BOSTON
BOTLEY
BOURNE
BUNGAY
BURLEY
BURTON
BUXTON
COBHAM
COSHAM
DARWEN
DEDHAM
DENHAM
DENTON
DIDCOT
DISLEY
DUDLEY
DUNMOW
DURHAM
ELLAND
EPPING
EXETER
FAWLEY
FINDON
FORMBY
HARLOW
HARROW
HAVANT
HEANOR
HELSBY
HENLEY
HEXHAM

HISTON
HORLEY
HURLEY
ILFORD
ILKLEY
KENDAL
KENTON
KIRKLY
KNOWLE
LACEBY
LACOCK
LODDON
LOFTUS
LONDON
LUDLOW
LYDNEY
LYNTON
LYTHAM
MALDON
MALTBY
MALTON
MARLOW
MILLOM
MILTON
NELSON
NEWARK
NEWENT
NEWLYN
OAKHAM
OAKLEY
OCKLEY
ODIHAM
OFFLEY
OLDHAM
ORSETT
OSSETT
OTFORD
OULTON
OUNDLE
OXFORD
PAGHAM
PENRYN
PROBUS
PURLEY
RAMSEY
REDCAR
RIPLEY
ROMSEY
ROWLEY
ROYTON
RUBERY
ST BEES
ST IVES
ST JUST
SAWTRY
SCALBY
SCAWBY
SEAMER

SEATON
SELSEY
SETTLE
SIDCOT
SIDCUP
SLOUGH
STREET
STROOD
STROUD
SUTTON
SYSTON
THEALE
THIRSK
THORNE
TIPTON
TOTNES
TURVEY
UPAVON
WALMER
WALTON
WATTON
WEEDON
WEELEY
WELWYN
WESTON
WHITBY
WIDNES
WIGTON
WILTON
WITHAM
WOBURN
WOKING
WOOLER
YEOVIL

7
AINTREE
ALNWICK
ALREWAS
ANDOVER
APPLEBY
ARNSIDE
ARUNDEL
ASHFORD
ASHOVER
ASHTEAD
ASHWELL
AUGHTON
AVEBURY
AYLSHAM
BAGSHOT
BAILDON
BALDOCK
BAMFORD
BAMPTON
BANBURY
BANWELL
BARDNEY

BARKING
BARNTON
BARWELL
BECCLES
BEDFORD
BEESTON
BENTHAM
BENTLEY
BERWICK
BEWDLEY
BEXHILL
BICKLEY
BILLING
BINGLEY
BLAGDON
BLAYDON
BOURTON
BRAMLEY
BRANDON
BRISTOL
BRIXHAM
BRIXTON
BROMLEY
BROTTON
BUCKDEN
BURFORD
BURNHAM
BURNLEY
BURWASH
CANNOCK
CHAILEY
CHARING
CHATHAM
CHEADLE
CHEDDAR
CHENIES
CHESTER
CHORLEY
CLAPHAM
COLD ASH
CONSETT
COOKHAM
CORSHAM
COWLING
CRAWLEY
CROYDON
DANBURY
DARENTH
DAWLISH
DENMEAD
DEREHAM
DEVIZES
DORKING
DOWNTON
DURSLEY
DUXFORD
ELSTREE
ENFIELD

EVESHAM
FAREHAM
FARNHAM
FERRING
FLIXTON
FRINTON
GARSTON
GLOSSOP
GOSPORT
GRIMSBY
HALIFAX
HARSTON
HARWICH
HELSTON
HEYSHAM
HEYWOOD
HIGHLEY
HINDLEY
HITCHIN
HONITON
HORSHAM
HOYLAKE
IPSWICH
KELSALL
KESWICK
KINETON
KINGTON
KIRKHAM
LAINDON
LEDBURY
LEYBURN
LEYLAND
LINCOLN
LOWDHAM
LYDFORD
LYNEHAM
MALVERN
MARGATE
MARTOCK
MATLOCK
MAULDEN
MERIDEN
MITCHAM
MODBURY
MORETON
MORPETH
MOSELEY
MOULTON
MULLION
NEWBURY
NEWNHAM
NEWPORT
NEWQUAY
NORTHAM
NORWICH
OLDBURY
OVERTON
PADIHAM

PADSTOW
PENRITH
PINXTON
PORLOCK
PRESTON
RADLETT
RAINHAM
READING
REDHILL
REDRUTH
REIGATE
RETFORD
ROMFORD
ROTHLEY
ROXWELL
ROYSTON
RUGELEY
RUISLIP
RUNCORN
RUSHDEN
ST AGNES
ST ANNES
ST MARY'S
ST MAWES
ST NEOTS
SALFORD
SALTASH
SANDOWN
SEAFORD
SEDGLEY
SHALDON
SHIFNAL
SHILDON
SHIPLEY
SHIRLEY
SIDFORD
SILLOTH
SKIPTON
SONNING
SOUTHAM
STAINES
STALHAM
STANLEY
STANTON
STILTON
SUDBURY
SWANAGE
SWANLEY
SWINDON
SWINTON
TAUNTON
TETBURY
TEYNHAM
TILBURY
TOPSHAM
TORQUAY
TUTBURY
TUXFORD

VENTNOR
WALFORD
WALMLEY
WALSALL
WANTAGE
WARBOYS
WAREHAM
WARWICK
WATCHET
WATFORD
WATNALL
WEDMORE
WELLING
WEMBLEY
WESTHAM
WICKHAM
WIGSTON
WINDSOR
WISBECH
WORKSOP
WRITTLE
WROTHAM
WROXHAM
YATELEY
YELDHAM

8
ABINGDON
ACKWORTH
AINSDALE
ALCESTER
ALFRETON
ALVESTON
AMBERLEY
AMERSHAM
AMESBURY
AMPTHILL
ARDLEIGH
ASPATRIA
ATHERTON
AXBRIDGE
BAKEWELL
BALCOMBE
BANSTEAD
BARNSLEY
BEARSTED
BEAUFORT
BEAULIEU
BEDWORTH
BENENDEN
BENFLEET
BERKELEY
BEVERLEY
BICESTER
BIDEFORD
BINFIELD
BLOCKLEY
BOSCOMBE

BOUGHTON
BRACKLEY
BRADFORD
BRADWELL
BRAMHALL
BRAMPTON
BRANSTON
BRAUNTON
BRIDPORT
BRIGHTON
BROADWAY
BROMYARD
BRUNDALL
CAMBORNE
CARLISLE
CATERHAM
CHAGFORD
CHARTHAM
CHERTSEY
CHESHUNT
CHIGWELL
CLAYGATE
CLEVEDON
CODICOTE
COLEFORD
CONISTON
COULSDON
COVENTRY
CRANFORD
CREDITON
DARTFORD
DAVENTRY
DEBENHAM
DEWSBURY
DRYBROOK
DUFFIELD
EASTWOOD
EMSWORTH
EVERSLEY
EYNSFORD
FAIRFORD
FAKENHAM
FALMOUTH
FLITWICK
GARFORTH
GLAPWELL
GODSHILL
GODSTONE
GOLBORNE
GOSFORTH
GRANTHAM
HADFIELD
HAILSHAM
HAINAULT
HALSTEAD
HANSLOPE
HARBORNE
HARTFORD

HARTLAND
HASSOCKS
HASTINGS
HATFIELD
HAY-ON-WYE
HELMSLEY
HEREFORD
HERNE BAY
HERTFORD
HINCKLEY
HINDHEAD
HOLBEACH
HOLYHEAD
HOLYWELL
HORNDEAN
HOUGHTON
HOUNSLOW
HUCKNALL
HUNMANBY
ILKESTON
INGLETON
KEGWORTH
KEIGHLEY
KELVEDON
KEYNSHAM
KINGSTON
KNIGHTON
KNOWSLEY
LAMBOURN
LARKHILL
LAVENHAM
LISKEARD
LOUGHTON
LULWORTH
LYDBROOK
MARAZION
MARNHULL
MARYPORT
MAYFIELD
MELKSHAM
MIDHURST
MINEHEAD
MUDEFORD
NANTWICH
NEWHAVEN
NINFIELD
NORTHIAM
NORTHOLT
NUNEATON
OLLERTON
ORMSKIRK
OSWESTRY
PAIGNTON
PATCHWAY
PEASLAKE
PENZANCE
PERSHORE
PETERLEE

PETWORTH
PLYMOUTH
PLYMPTON
POLEGATE
POLPERRO
PORTLAND
PURFLEET
RADSTOCK
RAINHILL
RAMSBURY
RAMSGATE
RAYLEIGH
REDBOURN
REDDITCH
RICHMOND
RINGWOOD
ROCHDALE
ROCHFORD
ROTHBURY
ROTHWELL
RUDGWICK
ST ALBANS
ST COLUMB
ST HELENS
SALCOMBE
SALTBURN
SALTFORD
SANDBACH
SANDIWAY
SANDWICH
SEASCALE
SEDBERGH
SELBORNE
SHANKLIN
SHARDLOW
SHEFFORD
SHELFORD
SHERBURN
SHIPSTON
SHOREHAM
SIDMOUTH
SKEGNESS
SLEAFORD
SOLIHULL
SOUTHALL
SOUTHEND
SOUTHERY
SOUTHSEA
SPALDING
STAFFORD
STAMFORD
STANDISH
STANFORD
STANMORE
STANSTED
STAVELEY
STEYNING
STOCKTON

STRATTON
STUDLAND
SURBITON
SWAFFHAM
SWANWICK
TAMWORTH
TANWORTH
THETFORD
THORNLEY
THORNTON
TIDWORTH
TINTAGEL
TIVERTON
TORCROSS
UCKFIELD
UXBRIDGE
WAKERING
WALLASEY
WENDOVER
WESTBURY
WETHERAL
WETHERBY
WEYMOUTH
WHITWELL
WICKFORD
WILLITON
WILMSLOW
WOLLATON
WOMBWELL
WORFIELD
WORTHING
YARMOUTH

9
ADDINGTON
ADLINGTON
ALDBOURNE
ALDEBURGH
ALDERSHOT
ALFRISTON
ALRESFORD
AMBLESIDE
ASHBOURNE
ASHBURTON
ASHINGTON
AXMINSTER
AYLESBURY
AYLESFORD
AYLESTONE
BATTERSEA
BEBINGTON
BECKENHAM
BEMBRIDGE
BLACKBURN
BLACKPOOL
BLANDFORD
BLETCHLEY
BRAINTREE

BRANKSOME	HARLESTON	ROCHESTER	WHITWORTH	DESBOROUGH
BRANSGORE	HARPENDEN	ROSS-ON-WYE	WINCANTON	DORCHESTER
BRENTFORD	HARROGATE	ROTHERHAM	WINTERTON	DOVERCOURT
BRENTWOOD	HASLEMERE	ST AUSTELL	WOKINGHAM	DUCKMANTON
BRIGHOUSE	HAVERHILL	SAINT BEES	WOODSTOCK	DUKINFIELD
CAMBERLEY	HAWKHURST	SAINT IVES	WORCESTER	DURRINGTON
CAMBRIDGE	HODDESDON	SAINT JUST	WYMONDHAM	EASINGWOLD
CAMELFORD	HOLMFIRTH	ST KEVERNE	YELVERTON	EASTBOURNE
CARBIS BAY	ILCHESTER	ST MARTIN'S		ECCLESHALL
CARNFORTH	ILMINSTER	ST STEPHEN	10	EVERCREECH
CATTERICK	ILSINGTON	ST STEPHEN	ACCRINGTON	FAILSWORTH
CAYTHORPE	IVYBRIDGE	SALISBURY	ADDLESTONE	FELIXSTOWE
CHARFIELD	KETTERING	SANDHURST	ALBRIGHTON	FOLKESTONE
CHARLWOOD	KIDSGROVE	SANDIACRE	ALPHINGTON	FRECKLETON
CHARMOUTH	KING'S LYNN	SAVERNAKE	ALTRINCHAM	FRESHWATER
CHATTERIS	KINGSWOOD	SELLINDGE	ALVECHURCH	GILLINGHAM
CHIPSTEAD	KNEBWORTH	SEVENOAKS	ALVERSTOKE	GLOUCESTER
CHISELDON	KNUTSFORD	SHEERNESS	ATHERSTONE	GUNNISLAKE
CLITHEROE	LANCASTER	SHEFFIELD	BARNSTAPLE	HADLEY WOOD
COLESHILL	LANGSTONE	SHERBORNE	BARROWFORD	HALESWORTH
CONGLETON	LEICESTER	SHERFIELD	BEAMINSTER	HANDSWORTH
CORBRIDGE	LICHFIELD	SMETHWICK	BEDDINGTON	HARTLEPOOL
CRANBROOK	LINDFIELD	SOUTHPORT	BEDHAMPTON	HASLINGDEN
CRANFIELD	LINGFIELD	SOUTHWELL	BEDLINGTON	HATHERSAGE
CRANLEIGH	LIVERPOOL	SOUTHWOLD	BELLINGHAM	HAZEL GROVE
CREWKERNE	LONG EATON	STAINLAND	BICKENHILL	HEATHFIELD
CRICKLADE	LONGRIDGE	STANDLAKE	BILLERICAY	HIGHBRIDGE
CUCKFIELD	LOWESTOFT	STEVENAGE	BILLINGHAM	HILLINGDON
DARLASTON	LYME REGIS	STOCKPORT	BILLINGHAY	HOLSWORTHY
DARTMOUTH	LYMINGTON	STOGUMBER	BILSTHORPE	HOLYBOURNE
DONCASTER	LYNDHURST	STOURPORT	BIRKENHEAD	HORNCASTLE
DONINGTON	MAIDSTONE	STRATFORD	BIRMINGHAM	HORNCHURCH
DRIFFIELD	MANSFIELD	STRETFORD	BOLLINGTON	HUNGERFORD
DROITWICH	MARKFIELD	TADCASTER	BRIDGNORTH	HUNSTANTON
DULVERTON	MIDDLETON	TANKERTON	BRIDGWATER	HUNTINGDON
DUNCHURCH	MISSENDEN	TARPORLEY	BRIERFIELD	ILFRACOMBE
DUNSTABLE	MOBBERLEY	TAVISTOCK	BROMSGROVE	KENILWORTH
EAST COWES	MORECAMBE	TENTERDEN	BROWNHILLS	KIDLINGTON
EASTLEIGH	MOUSEHOLE	THORPE BAY	BROXBOURNE	LAUNCESTON
EFFINGHAM	NETTLEBED	THROCKLEY	BUCKINGHAM	LEAMINGTON
ELLESMERE	NEW BARNET	TIMPERLEY	BURGH HEATH	LEIGH-ON-SEA
ESSINGTON	NEWBIGGIN	TODMORDEN	CALLINGTON	LEOMINSTER
FARINGDON	NEWCASTLE	TONBRIDGE	CANTERBURY	LETCHWORTH
FARNCOMBE	NEWDIGATE	TOWCESTER	CARSHALTON	LITTLEPORT
FARNWORTH	NEWMARKET	TYNEMOUTH	CASTLE CARY	LIVERSEDGE
FAVERSHAM	NEW ROMNEY	ULLSWATER	CHELMSFORD	MAIDENHEAD
FERNHURST	NORTHWICH	ULVERSTON	CHELTENHAM	MALMESBURY
FLEETWOOD	OLD WOKING	UPMINSTER	CHICHESTER	MANCHESTER
FOREST ROW	ORPINGTON	UPPINGHAM	CHIPPENHAM	MESSINGHAM
FOUR MARKS	PAINSWICK	UTTOXETER	COGGESHALL	MEVAGISSEY
GATESHEAD	PENSHURST	WADDESDEN	COLCHESTER	MILDENHALL
GODALMING	PETTS WOOD	WAINFLEET	COLTISHALL	NAILSWORTH
GOSBERTON	PICKERING	WAKEFIELD	CROWTHORNE	NORTHFIELD
GOUDHURST	PLYMSTOCK	WARKWORTH	CULLOMPTON	NORTHLEACH
GRAVESEND	PORTSLADE	WESTCLIFF	CURRY RIVEL	NOTTINGHAM
GUILDFORD	PRESTBURY	WESTERHAM	DARLEY DALE	OKEHAMPTON
HALBERTON	PRESTWICH	WEST KIRBY	DARLINGTON	OLD SODBURY
HALESOWEN	RADCLIFFE	WEST MOORS	DERSINGHAM	OLD WINDSOR
		WEYBRIDGE		

PANGBOURNE
PATRINGTON
PEACEHAVEN
PORTISHEAD
PORTSMOUTH
POTTERS BAR
PRINCETOWN
PUDDLETOWN
PULBOROUGH
RAMSBOTTOM
ROCKINGHAM
RUDDINGTON
RUSTINGTON
SAINT AGNES
SAINT ANNES
ST LAWRENCE
ST LEONARDS
SAINT MARY'S
SAINT NEOTS
SAMLESBURY
SAXMUNDHAM
SCUNTHORPE
SEDGEFIELD
SEFTON PARK
SHEVINGTON
SHREWSBURY
SOUTH BRENT
SOUTH MIMMS
STAPLEFORD
STOWMARKET
SUNDERLAND
SWAYTHLING
SYMOND'S YAT
TEDDINGTON
TEIGNMOUTH
TEWKESBURY
TITCHFIELD
TOLLESBURY
TORRINGTON
TOTLAND BAY
TRESILLIAN
TROWBRIDGE
TWICKENHAM
WADEBRIDGE
WALLINGTON
WARMINSTER
WARMSWORTH
WARRINGTON
WASHINGTON
WATERBEACH
WEDNESBURY
WELLINGTON
WEST GORTON
WESTWARD HO
WHITCHURCH
WHITEHAVEN
WHITLEY BAY
WHITSTABLE

WHITTLESEY
WILLENHALL
WILLINGTON
WINCHCOMBE
WINCHELSEA
WINCHESTER
WINDERMERE
WITHERNSEA
WITHINGTON
WOLSTANTON
WOODBRIDGE
WOOLACOMBE
WORKINGTON
WORPLESDON

11

ALDERMASTON
ALMONDSBURY
BARLBOROUGH
BARTON-ON-SEA
BASINGSTOKE
BERKHAMSTED
BEXLEYHEATH
BIGGLESWADE
BIRCHINGTON
BOGNOR REGIS
BOREHAM WOOD
BOURNEMOUTH
BOVEY TRACEY
BRIDLINGTON
BROADSTAIRS
BURGESS HILL
CARISBROOKE
CHILCOMPTON
CHISLEHURST
CHORLEYWOOD
CHURCH STOKE
CIRENCESTER
CLEETHORPES
COCKERMOUTH
COLNEY HEATH
COMBE MARTIN
CROWBOROUGH
DUNTON GREEN
EARLS BARTON
EAST DEREHAM
EAST HORSLEY
EAST PECKHAM
EAST RETFORD
ECCLESFIELD
FARNBOROUGH
FRAMLINGHAM
GLASTONBURY
GRASSINGTON
GREAT DUNMOW
GREAT OFFLEY
GUISBOROUGH
HALTWHISTLE

HIGH WYCOMBE
INGATESTONE
KESSINGLAND
KINGSBRIDGE
KINGSWORTHY
LEATHERHEAD
LONG LAWFORD
LONG MELFORD
LOSTWITHIEL
LUTTERWORTH
MABLETHORPE
MARKET RASEN
MARLBOROUGH
MATLOCK BATH
MICHELDEVER
MILNETHORPE
MOUNTSORREL
MUCH WENLOCK
MYTHOLMROYD
NEW BRIGHTON
NEWTON ABBOT
NORTHAMPTON
NORTH TAWTON
OLD TRAFFORD
OULTON BROAD
PETERSFIELD
PEVENSEY BAY
POCKLINGTON
PORTCHESTER
RAWTENSTALL
ROTTINGDEAN
ROWLEY REGIS
SAINT ALBANS
SAINT COLUMB
SAINT HELENS
ST MARGARET'S
SANDERSTEAD
SCARBOROUGH
SEDLESCOMBE
SHAFTESBURY
SOUTHAMPTON
SOUTH MOLTON
STAPLEHURST
STOCKBRIDGE
STORRINGTON
STOURBRIDGE
SUNNINGDALE
SUTTON-ON-SEA
SWADLINCOTE
SWALECLIFFE
THEYDON BOIS
WALLINGFORD
WEDNESFIELD
WEST BYFLEET
WEST DRAYTON
WEST MALLING
WEST WICKHAM
WEST WYCOMBE

WHITTINGTON
WOLVEY HEATH
WOODHALL SPA
WOOLHAMPTON

12

ALDERLEY EDGE
ASTLEY BRIDGE
ASTON CLINTON
ATTENBOROUGH
ATTLEBOROUGH
BAMBER BRIDGE
BEACONSFIELD
BEXHILL-ON-SEA
BISHOP SUTTON
BLETCHINGLEY
BOROUGH GREEN
BRIERLEY HILL
BROCKENHURST
BURNHAM-ON-SEA
CAISTER-ON-SEA
CANVEY ISLAND
CHESTERFIELD
CHIPPERFIELD
CHRISTCHURCH
CLACTON-ON-SEA
CLIFTONVILLE
EAGLESCLIFFE
FRINTON-ON-SEA
GAINSBOROUGH
GREAT MALVERN
HOCKLEY HEATH
HUDDERSFIELD
KING'S STANLEY
KINGSWINFORD
LOUGHBOROUGH
MACCLESFIELD
MILFORD HAVEN
MILFORD-ON-SEA
MILTON KEYNES
NEEDINGWORTH
NORTH FERRIBY
NORTH SHIELDS
NORTH WALSHAM
OVERTON-ON-DEE
PETERBOROUGH
ROWLANDS GILL
SAINT AUSTELL
SAINT KEVERNE
SAINT MARTIN'S
SAINT STEPHEN
SCOTCH CORNER
SHOEBURYNESS
SKELMERSDALE
SOUTHBOROUGH
SOUTHMILFORD
SOUTHMINSTER
SOUTH SHIELDS

STEEPLE ASTON
STOKENCHURCH
STOKE-ON-TRENT
SUTTON BRIDGE
SWALLOWFIELD
TENBURY WELLS
THORNTON DALE
WALTHAM CROSS
WELLESBOURNE
WEST BROMWICH
WEST HOUGHTON
WHITTLESFORD
WIVELISCOMBE

13

ABBOT'S BROMLEY
ABINGER HAMMER
ALLENDALE TOWN
BARNARD CASTLE
BIDFORD-ON-AVON
BILLINGSHURST
BOROUGHBRIDGE
BRIGHTLINGSEA
BUCKFASTLEIGH
BUCKHURST HILL
BURY ST EDMUNDS
CHANDLER'S FORD
DOWNHAM MARKET
EAST GRINSTEAD
EAST WITTERING
ELLESMERE PORT
FORDINGBRIDGE
GERRARDS CROSS
GREAT SHELFORD
GREAT WAKERING
GREAT YARMOUTH
HAYLING ISLAND
HAYWARDS HEATH
HENLEY-IN-ARDEN
HIGHAM FERRERS
HILDENBOROUGH
HOUGHTON REGIS
KIRKBY STEPHEN
KNARESBOROUGH
LEAMINGTON SPA
LITTLEBOROUGH
LITTLE CLACTON
LITTLEHAMPTON
MARKET DRAYTON
MELTON MOWBRAY
MINSTER LOVELL
NEEDHAM MARKET
NEWARK-ON-TRENT
NEWTON FERRERS
NORTHALLERTON
RICKMANSWORTH
ROBERTSBRIDGE
SAFFRON WALDEN

SAINT LAWRENCE
SAINT LEONARDS
SHEPTON MALLET
SHOREHAM-ON-SEA
SITTINGBOURNE
SOUTH BENFLEET
SOUTHEND-ON-SEA
STOW-ON-THE-WOLD
SUTTON-ON-TRENT
THORNTON HEATH
UPTON-ON-SEVERN
VIRGINIA WATER
WATERLOOVILLE
WESTGATE-ON-SEA
WICKHAM MARKET
WOLVERHAMPTON
WOODFORD GREEN

14

ANGMERING-ON-SEA
ASHBY-DE-LA-ZOUCH
BILLINGBOROUGH
BLANDFORD FORUM
BRADFORD-ON-AVON
CASTLE BROMWICH
CHIPPING NORTON
CHURCH STRETTON
CLAYTON-LE-WOODS
DEEPING ST JAMES
GORING-ON-THAMES
GREAT DRIFFIELD
GREAT MISSENDEN
HAMPTON-IN-ARDEN
HEMEL HEMPSTEAD
HENLEY-ON-THAMES
KIRKBY LONSDALE
KIRKBY MOORSIDE
LEE-ON-THE-SOLENT
MARKET WEIGHTON
MIDDLETON-ON-SEA
MORETON-IN-MARSH
MUNDESLEY-ON-SEA
NEWBRIDGE-ON-WYE
NEWPORT PAGNELL
ROWLANDS CASTLE
SAWBRIDGEWORTH
SIBLE HEDINGHAM
SOUTH NORMANTON
STANFORD-LE-HOPE
STOCKTON-ON-TEES
STONY STRATFORD
TUNBRIDGE WELLS
WALTON-ON-THAMES
WATH-UPON-DEARNE
WELLINGBOROUGH
WESTCLIFF-ON-SEA
WEST HARTLEPOOL
WOOTTON BASSETT

15

ASHTON-UNDER-LYNE
BARROW-IN-FURNESS
BURNHAM-ON-CROUCH
BURTON-UPON-TRENT
CHALFONT ST GILES
CHALFONT ST PETER
CHAPEL-EN-LE-FRITH
CHARNOCK RICHARD
CHESTER-LE-STREET
CHIPPING CAMPDEN
CHURSTON FERRERS
DALTON-IN-FURNESS
GREAT TORRINGTON
ENGLEFIELD GREEN
GRANGE-OVER-SANDS
IRTHLINGBOROUGH
KIRKBY-IN-FURNESS
LEIGHTON BUZZARD
LITTLE GADDESDEN
NEWNHAM-ON-SEVERN
NORTH SOMERCOTES
ST LEONARDS ON SEA
SHIPSTON-ON-STOUR
SUTTON COLDFIELD
WELLS-NEXT-THE-SEA
WEST CHILLINGTON
WESTON-SUPER-MARE
WIMBORNE MINSTER
WISBOROUGH GREEN
WOTTON-UNDER-EDGE

Cities, Towns and some villages of Scotland

3
AYR
UIG

4
COVE
DUNS
ELAN
FORD
LUIB
OBAN
STOW
TAIN
WICK

5
ALYTH
ANNAN
BANFF
BEITH
BRORA
CRAIL
CUPAR
DALRY
ELGIN
ELLON
GARVE
KEITH
KELSO
LAIRG
LARGS
LEVEN
NAIRN
PERTH
TROON

6
ABOYNE
ALFORD
ALNESS
ANCRUM
BEAULY
BIGGAR
BUCKIE
COMRIE
CONTIN
CORRIE
CRIEFF
CULLEN
DARVEL
DOLLAR
DRYMEN
DUNBAR
DUNDEE
DUNOON

EDZELL
FINTRY
FORFAR
FORRES
GIRVAN
GRETNA
HAWICK
HUNTLY
IRVINE
KILLIN
KIPPEN
LANARK
LAUDER
MOFFAT
RHYNIE
ROSLIN
ROSYTH
ROTHES
STEPPS
THURSO
TONGUE
WISHAW

7
AIRDRIE
AMULREE
AULTBEA
BALLOCH
BRAEMAR
BRECHIN
BRODICK
CARLUKE
CUMNOCK
DOUGLAS
DUNKELD
DUNNING
FALKIRK
GLASGOW
GLENCOE
GOLSPIE
GOUROCK
GULLANE
KILMORY
KILSYTH
KINROSS
LAMLASH
LERWICK
LOCH AWE
MACDUFF
MALLAIG
MELROSE
PAISLEY
PEEBLES
POLMONT
PORTREE

PORTSOY
RENFREW
SELKIRK
TARBERT
TYNDRUM

8
ABERDEEN
ABERDOUR
ABERLADY
ABERLOUR
ABINGTON
ALLANTON
ARBROATH
ARMADALE
ARROCHAR
AVIEMORE
BALLATER
BANCHORY
BANKFOOT
BARRHEAD
BARRHILL
BATHGATE
BEARSDEN
CARNWATH
CRAWFORD
DALKEITH
DINGWALL
DUFFTOWN
DUMFRIES
DUNBLANE
EARLSTON
EYEMOUTH
FISHNISH
FORTROSE
GAIRLOCH
GIFFNOCK
GLENFARG
GREENOCK
HAMILTON
INNELLAN
JEDBURGH
KILLEARN
KIRKWALL
LANGHOLM
LOCHGAIR
MONTROSE
MUIRHEAD
NEWBURGH
ROSEBANK
ROTHESAY
SANQUHAR
SOUTHEND
STIRLING
ULLAPOOL

WHITBURN
WHITHORN

9
ABERFELDY
ARDROSSAN
ARINAGOUR
BALMACARA
BELLSHILL
BLACKFORD
BLACKWOOD
BONNYRIGG
BROADFORD
BROUGHTON
CALLANDER
CARTER BAR
CHIRNSIDE
CLYDEBANK
CRUDEN BAY
DUMBARTON
EASTRIGGS
EDINBURGH
FOCHABERS
GLENCAPLE
INVERARAY
INVERNESS
INVERURIE
KILMACOLM
KINGUSSIE
KIRKCALDY
LOCHINVER
LOCKERBIE
LOGIERAIT
MILNGAVIE
MONIFEITH
NETHERLEY
NEWBRIDGE
PETERHEAD
PITLOCHRY
PRESTWICK
ST ANDREWS
SALTCOATS
STEWARTON
STORNOWAY
STRANRAER
STROMNESS
SYMINGTON
THORNHILL
TOBERMORY
TOMINTOUL
WEMYSS BAY

10
ANSTRUTHER
ARDISHAIG

BALLANTRAE
BISHOPSTON
CARNOUSTIE
COATBRIDGE
COLDSTREAM
DALBEATTIE
DODDINGTON
GALASHIELS
GLENROTHES
HADDINGTON
INVERSANDA
INVERSNAID
KILCREGGAN
KILMARNOCK
KILMICHAEL
KILWINNING
KINCARDINE
KIRKNEWTON
KIRRIEMUIR
LINLITHGOW
MILNATHORT
MOTHERWELL
NEWTONMORE
OLD MELDRUM
PITTENWEEM
RUTHERGLEN
ST BOSWELLS
SKELMORLIE
STEVENSTON
STONEHAVEN
STRATHAVEN
TWEEDMOUTH
UDDINGSTON
WESTERKIRK
WHITING BAY

11
BLAIR ATHOLL
BLAIRGOWRIE
BONAR BRIDGE
CAMPBELTOWN
CONNEL FERRY
COUPAR ANGUS
CUMBERNAULD
CUMMERTREES
DUNFERMLINE
ECCLEFECHAN
FORT WILLIAM
FRASERBURGH
HELENSBURGH
LOSSIEMOUTH
MUSSLEBURGH
PETERCULTER
PORTPATRICK
QUEENSFERRY

STRATHBLANE
WHITEBRIDGE

12
AUCHTERARDER
BALLACHULISH
BRIDGE OF EARN
BRIDGE OF WEIR
CROSSMICHAEL
EAST KILBRIDE
FORT AUGUSTUS
GARELOCHHEAD
INNERLEITHEN
LAURENCEKIRK
LOCHGILPHEAD
NEWPORT-ON-TAY
NORTH BERWICK
SAINT ANDREWS
STRATHPEFFER
TILLICOULTRY

13
BRIDGE OF ALLAN
BROUGHTY FERRY
CASTLE DOUGLAS
INVERKEITHING
KILLIECRANKIE
KIRKCUDBRIGHT
KIRKINTILLOCH
NEWTON STEWART
SAINT BOSWELLS

14
GRANTOWN-ON-SPEY

Cities, Towns and some villages of Wales

3
USK

4
BALA
FOEL
MOLD
RHYL
ROSS
SARN

5
BARRY
BORTH
BWLCH
CARNO
CHIRK
CONWY
NEATH
NEFYN
RADYR
TENBY
TYWYN

6
AMLWCH
ARTHOG
BANGOR
BEDWAS
BRECON
BUILTH
CORWEN
MOSTYN
NEVERN
ROGIET
RUTHIN
TREVOR
VALLEY

7
BARGOED
CARDIFF
CWMBRAN
CWM-Y-GLO
DEGANWY
DENBIGH
HARLECH
MAESTEG
MUMBLES
NEWPORT
NEWTOWN
NORTHOP
PEMBREY
PENARTH
RHYMNEY

ST ASAPH
SWANSEA
TINTERN
WREXHAM

8
ABERAVON
ABERCARN
ABERDARE
ABERGELE
BARMOUTH
BETHESDA
BRIDGEND
BRYNMAWR
CAERLEON
CARDIGAN
CHEPSTOW
DOLYWERN
EBBW VALE
FERNDALE
HAWARDEN
KIDWELLY
LAMPETER
LLANBEDR
LLANELLI
LLANRWST
LLANWNDA
MONMOUTH
NARBERTH
PEMBROKE
RHAYADER
RHUDDLAN
ST CLEARS
ST DAVIDS
SCURLAGE
TALGARTH
TALYBONT
TALYLLYN
TAMWORTH
TREDEGAR
TREGARON
TREMADOC
TREORCHY
VELINDRE

9
ABERCYNON
ABERDARON
ABERDOVEY
ABERGWILI
AMMANFORD
BEAUMARIS
CEMAES BAY
COLWYN BAY
COWBRIDGE

CRICCIETH
DOLGELLAU
FISHGUARD
KINMEL BAY
LLANBERIS
LLANDEILO
LLANDUDNO
LLANGEFNI
LLANGELER
LLANHARAN
MANORBIER
PONTANTWN
PONTERWYD
PONTFADOG
PONTYPOOL
PORTHCAWL
PRESTATYN
ST MELLONS
SKENFRITH
SOUTHGATE
TON PENTRE
TONYPANDY
TRECASTLE
WELSHPOOL

10
ABERPENNAR
BONT NEWYDD
CAERNARVON
CAERPHILLY
CARMARTHEN
CASWELL BAY
FFESTINIOG
GLYNCORRWG
LLANDDULAS
LLANDOVERY
LLANDYSSUL
LLANFAIR PG
LLANFYLLIN
LLANGOLLEN
LLANIDLOES
NEWBOROUGH
PONTYPRIDD
PORTHMADOG
PORT TALBOT
PRESTEIGNE
SAINT ASAPH
ST DOGMAELS
THREE COCKS
YSTALYFERA

11
ABERGAVENNY
ABERTILLERY
ABERYSTWYTH

BARRY ISLAND
BUILTH WELLS
CONNAH'S QUAY
CRICKHOWELL
LANGLAND BAY
LLANLLECHID
MACHYNLLETH
MENAI BRIDGE
MOUNTAIN ASH
NANTGAREDIG
PENMAENMAWR
SAINT CLEARS
SAINT DAVIDS
TRAWSFYNYDD

12
LLANBRYNMAIR
SAINT MELLONS
SAUNDERSFOOT
SEVEN SISTERS
TREARDDUR BAY
YSTRAD MYNACH

13
BISHOP'S CASTLE
HAVERFORDWEST
MERTHYR TYDFIL
PENRHIWCEIBER
SAINT DOGMAELS
YSTRADGYNLAIS

14
LLANFAIRFECHAN

Cities, Towns and some villages of Northern Ireland

3
MOY

5
ARMOY
CLOGH
GLYNN
KEADY
LARNE
NEWRY
OMAGH
TOOME

6
ANTRIM
ARMAGH
AUGHER
BANGOR
BELCOO
BERAGH
CLAUDY
COMBER
KILREA
LURGAN

7
BELFAST
BELLEEK
CALEDON
CARRICK
CLOGHER
CRUMLIN
DERVOCK
DROMORE
DUNDRUM
DUNMORE
FINTONA
GARVAGH
GILFORD
GLENARM
KILKEEL
LISBURN
POMEROY

8
AHOGHILL
ARDGLASS
DUNGIVEN
HILLTOWN
HOLYWOOD
KILLYLEA
LIMAVADY
MILEBUSH
PORTRUSH

STRABANE
SWATRAGH
TRILLICK

9
BALLYMENA
BALLYMORE
BANBRIDGE
BUSHMILLS
CARNLOUGH
COLERAINE
COOKSTOWN
CRAIGAVON
DUNDONALD
DUNGANNON
LISNASKEA
MONEYMORE
NEWCASTLE
PORTADOWN
RASHARKIN
ROSTREVOR
TOBERMORE
WHITEHEAD

10
AUGHNACLOY
BALLYCLARE
BALLYKELLY
BALLYMONEY
BALLYRONEY
CASTLEDERG
CUSHENDALL
DONAGHADEE
KILLYLEAGH
MARKETHILL
PORTAFERRY
SAINTFIELD
STRANGFORD
TANDERAGEE

11
BALLYCASTLE
BALLYGAWLEY
BALLYNAMEEN
BROUGHSHANE
CARRICKMORE
CROSSMAGLEN
DOWNPATRICK
DRAPERSTOWN
ENNISKILLEN
LONDONDERRY
MAGHERAFELT
NEWTOWNARDS
PORTGLENONE

PORTSTEWART
RANDALSTOWN
RATHFRILAND
RATHFRYLAND
WARRENPOINT

12
BALLYNAHINCH
CASTLEDAWSON
CASTLEWELLAN
HILLSBOROUGH
SIXMILECROSS
STEWARTSTOWN

13
BROOKEBOROUGH
CARRICKFERGUS
DERRYGONNELLY

14
LOUGHBRICKLAND
NEWTOWNSTEWART

Towns of Eire

4
ATHY
BIRR
BRAY
COBH
CORK
GORT
NAAS
TRIM
TUAM

MALLOW
MENAGH
NENAGH
ROOSKY
SHRULE
SWORDS
TALLOW
TRALEE
TULLOW

5
ADARE
ARDEE
BALLA
BOYLE
BRUFF
CAHER
CAVAN
CLARA
CROOM
EASKY
ENNIS
FERNS
GOREY
KEADY
KELLS
LUCAN
MOATE
NAVAN
NEWRY
SLIGO
TULLA

7
ATHENRY
ATHLONE
AUGHRIM
BALLINA
BLARNEY
CARRICK
CLIFDEN
CLONMEL
DONEGAL
DRANGAN
DROMARD
DRUMSNA
DUNDALK
DUNMORE
FETHARD
FOXFORD
GRANARD
KANTURK
KENMARE
KILCOCK
KILDARE
KILLALA
KILRUSH
KINSALE
LEIXLIP
LIFFORD
LISMORE
MULLAGH
NEWPORT
NEW ROSS
PORTLAW
ROSCREA
TAGHMON
TARBERT
THURLES
TRAMORE
WEXFORD
WICKLOW
YOUGHAL

6
ARKLOW
ARVAGH
ATHBOY
BANDON
BANGOR
BANTRY
CALLAN
CARLOW
CARNEW
CASHEL
CLOYNE
COLLON
DINGLE
DUBLIN
DURROW
ELPHIN
FERMOY
GALWAY
GOWRAN
KILKEE

8
ARDNAREE
ASKEATON
BANAGHER

BUNCLODY
CLOGHEEN
COOLANEY
DAINGEAN
DROGHEDA
DRUMLISH
DUNLAVIN
GLENAMOY
KILKELLY
KILKENNY
KILLALOE
LIMERICK
LISTOWEL
LONGFORD
LOUGHREA
MAYNOOTH
MIDLETON
MONAGHAN
ORANMORE
PORTUMNA
RATHDRUM
SKERRIES
TINAHELY
WESTPORT

9
ABBEYLEIX
BALLYHACK
BALLYMOTE
BELLAVARY
BELMULLET
BELTURBET
BUTTEVANT
CAPPOQUIN
CASTLEBAR
CASTLEREA
CLONEGALL
CLONROCHE
COLLOONEY
DONERAILE
DUNCANNON
DUNGARVAN
DUNMANWAY
EDENDERRY
FRESHFORD
INISTIOGE
KILBEGGAN
KILCULLEN
KILLARNEY
KILNALECK
KILTAMAGH
MILESTONE
MOUTHRATH
MULLINGAR
NEWMARKET
OLDCASTLE
PORTACLOY
RATHKEALE

RATHLOIRC
ROSCOMMON
TEMPLEBOY
TIPPERARY
TULLAMORE
WATERFORD

10
BALBRIGGAN
BALLINDINE
BALLINROBE
BALLYCANEW
BALLYMAHON
BLACKWATER
BRIDGETOWN
CLONAKILTY
FRENCHPARK
GREYSTONES
KILFINNANE
KILLORGLIN
KILMALLOCK
KINGSCOURT
MILLSTREET
MUINE BHEAG
PORT LAOISE
RATHANGLAN
RATHDOWNEY
SKIBBEREEN
STRADBALLY
TEMPLEMORE
THOMASTOWN
TOBERCURRY
URLINGFORD

11
BALLINAKILL
BALLINASLOE
BALLINGARRY
BALLYBUNION
BALLYCASTLE
BALLYHAUNIS
BALLYVAGHAN
BALTINGLASS
BELLANANAGH
BLESSINGTON
BORRISOKANE
CAHERSIVEEN
CASTLECOMER
CHARLESTOWN
CLARECASTLE
CLAREMORRIS
CROSSMOLINA
DUNMORE EAST
ENNISCORTHY
ENNISTIMMON
GORESBRIDGE
KNOCKNALINA
LETTERBRICK

PASSAGE EAST
STROKESTOWN

12
BALLINCOLLIG
BALLYRAGGETT
CASTLEBRIDGE
CASTLEISLAND
CROCKETSTOWN
DUN LAOGHAIRE
MITCHELSTOWN
MONASTEREVIN
MOUNTMELLICK

13
BAILIEBOROUGH
BALLYLONGFORD
CARRICK-ON-SUIR
CASTLEPOLLARD
KNOCKCROGHERY
NEWCASTLE WEST
NEWTOWN FORBES
PORTARLINGTON

14
BALLYJAMESDUFF
BORRIS-IN-OSSORY
CARRICKMACROSS
EDGEWORTHSTOWN
LEIGHLINBRIDGE

15
BALLAGHADERREEN
GRAIGUENAMANAGH
MILLTOWN MALBRAY

17
NEWMARKET-ON-FERGUS

Towns of the Channel Islands and the Isle of Man

4
PEEL

6
RAMSEY

7
DOUGLAS

8
ST HELIER

10
CASTLETOWN

11
SAINT HELIER
ST PETER PORT

14
SAINT PETER PORT

Towns of the World (see also Capitals; Ports)

Towns of Europe (excluding the British Isles and the USSR)

Key to abbreviations

A = Austria; *AL* = Albania; *B* = Belgium; *BU* = Bulgaria; *C* = Cyprus; *CZ* = Czechoslovakia; *D* = Denmark; *EG* = German Democratic Republic; *F* = France; *FD* = Finland; *G* = Germany (Federal Republic); *GR* = Greece; *H* = Hungary; *I* = Italy; *M* = Malta; *N* = Netherlands; *NY* = Norway; *P* = Portugal; *PD* = Poland; *R* = Romania; *S* = Switzerland; *SN* = Sweden; *SP* = Spain; *T* = Turkey; *Y* = Yugoslavia

4
BARI *(I)*
BONN *(G)*
BRNO *(CZ)*
CLUJ *(R)*
COMO *(I)*
GERA *(EG)*
GRAZ *(A)*
KIEL *(G)*
LINZ *(A)*
LODZ *(PD)*
NICE *(F)*
OSLO *(NY)*
PISA *(I)*
ROME *(I)*
VIGO *(SP)*

5
ARRAS *(F)*
BASEL *(S)*
BERNE *(S)*
BREDA *(N)*
BREST *(F)*
CADIZ *(SP)*
DELFT *(N)*
DIJON *(F)*
EMMEN *(N)*
ESSEN *(G)*
GENOA *(I)*
GHENT *(B)*
GIJON *(SP)*
HAGEN *(G)*
LIEGE *(B)*
LILLE *(B)*
LYONS *(F)*
MAINZ *(G)*
MALMO *(SN)*

MILAN *(I)*
NANCY *(F)*
PADUA *(I)*
PARIS *(F)*
PARMA *(I)*
ROUEN *(F)*
SOFIA *(BU)*
SPLIT *(Y)*
TOURS *(F)*
TURIN *(I)*
YPRES *(B)*

6
AACHEN *(G)*
AARHUS *(D)*
AMIENS *(F)*
ANCONA *(I)*
ANGERS *(F)*
ARNHEM *(N)*
ATHENS *(GR)*
BERGEN *(NY)*
BERLIN *(EG/G)*
BILBAO *(SP)*
BOCHUM *(G)*
BREMEN *(G)*
BRUGES *(B)*
BURGOS *(SP)*
CALAIS *(F)*
CRACOW *(PD)*
ERFURT *(EG)*
FOGGIA *(I)*
GDANSK *(PD)*
GENEVA *(S)*
KRAKOW *(PD)*
LE MANS *(F)*
LEYDEN *(N)*
LISBON *(P)*

LUBECK *(G)*
LUBLIN *(PD)*
LUGANO *(S)*
MALAGA *(SP)*
MUNICH *(G)*
NANTES *(F)*
NAPLES *(I)*
NARVIK *(NY)*
ODENSE *(D)*
OPORTO *(P)*
OSTEND *(B)*
OVIEDO *(SP)*
POZNAN *(PD)*
PRAGUE *(CZ)*
RAGUSA *(I)*
REGGIO *(I)*
RENNES *(F)*
RHEIMS *(F)*
RIJEKA *(Y)*
ST MALO *(F)*
SKOPJE *(Y)*
TIRANA *(AL)*
TOULON *(F)*
TROYES *(F)*
VENICE *(I)*
VIENNA *(A)*
WARSAW *(PD)*
WEIMAR *(EG)*
ZAGREB *(Y)*
ZURICH *(S)*

7
AALBORG *(D)*
AJACCIO *(F)*
ALCAZAR *(SP)*
ALMERIA *(SP)*
ANTWERP *(B)*

AVIGNON *(F)*
BAYONNE *(F)*
BELFORT *(F)*
BERGAMO *(I)*
BOLOGNA *(I)*
BOLZANO *(I)*
BRESCIA *(I)*
CAMBRAI *(F)*
CATANIA *(I)*
COIMBRA *(P)*
COLOGNE *(G)*
CORDOBA *(SP)*
CORUNNA *(SP)*
DRESDEN *(EG)*
FERRARA *(I)*
GLIWICE *(PD)*
GRANADA *(SP)*
HAARLEM *(N)*
HAMBURG *(G)*
HANOVER *(G)*
KOBLENZ *(G)*
LEGHORN *(I)*
LE HAVRE *(F)*
LEIPZIG *(EG)*
LIMOGES *(F)*
LUCERNE *(S)*
MESSINA *(I)*
MULHEIM *(G)*
NICOSIA *(C)*
ORLEANS *(F)*
PALERMO *(I)*
POTSDAM *(EG)*
RANDERS *(D)*
RAPALLO *(I)*
ROSTOCK *(EG)*
ROUBAIX *(F)*
SALERNO *(I)*
SEVILLE *(SP)*
TARANTO *(I)*
TILBURG *(N)*
TRIESTE *(I)*
UTRECHT *(N)*
ZWICKAU *(EG)*

8

BAYREUTH *(G)*
BEAUVAIS *(F)*
BELGRADE *(Y)*
BESANCON *(F)*
BIARRITZ *(F)*
BORDEAUX *(F)*
BRINDISI *(I)*
BRUSSELS *(B)*
BUDAPEST *(H)*
CAGLIARI *(I)*
DORTMUND *(G)*
DUISBURG *(G)*
ENSCHEDE *(N)*

FLORENCE *(I)*
FREIBURG *(G)*
GLADBACH *(G)*
GOTEBORG *(SN)*
GRENOBLE *(F)*
HELSINKI *(FD)*
ISTANBUL *(T)*
KATOWICE *(PD)*
LA SPEZIA *(I)*
LAUSANNE *(S)*
MANNHEIM *(G)*
MONTREUX *(S)*
NIJMEGEN *(N)*
PAMPLONA *(SP)*
SALONICA *(GR)*
SALONIKA *(GR)*
SALZBURG *(A)*
SANTIAGO *(SP)*
SARAJEVO *(Y)*
SCHIEDAM *(N)*
SORRENTO *(I)*
SYRACUSE *(I)*
SZCZECIN *(PD)*
THE HAGUE *(N)*
TOULOUSE *(F)*
VALENCIA *(SP)*
VALLETTA *(M)*

9

ABBEVILLE *(F)*
AMSTERDAM *(N)*
APELDOORN *(N)*
BARCELONA *(SP)*
BUCHAREST *(R)*
BYDGOSZCZ *(PD)*
CHERBOURG *(F)*
DARMSTADT *(G)*
DORDRECHT *(N)*
DUBROVNIK *(Y)*
EINDHOVEN *(N)*
FRANKFURT *(G;EG)*
GRONINGEN *(N)*
HILVERSUM *(N)*
KARLSRUHE *(G)*
LJUBLJANA *(Y)*
MAGDEBURG *(EG)*
NUREMBERG *(G)*
OLDENBURG *(G)*
OSNABRUCK *(G)*
REMSCHEID *(G)*
ROTTERDAM *(N)*
ST ETIENNE *(F)*
SAINT MALO *(F)*
SALAMANCA *(SP)*
SANTANDER *(SP)*
SARAGOSSA *(SP)*
STAVANGER *(NY)*
STOCKHOLM *(SN)*

STUTTGART *(G)*
SUNDSVALL *(SN)*
TARRAGONA *(SP)*
TIMISOARA *(R)*
TRONDHEIM *(NY)*
WIESBADEN *(G)*
WUPPERTAL *(G)*

10

AMERSFOORT *(N)*
BADEN-BADEN *(G)*
BRATISLAVA *(CZ)*
CIUDAD REAL *(SP)*
COPENHAGEN *(D)*
DUSSELDORF *(G)*
HEIDELBERG *(G)*
LA ROCHELLE *(F)*
LEEUWARDEN *(N)*
MAASTRICHT *(N)*
MARSEILLES *(F)*
STRASBOURG *(F)*
VALLADOLID *(SP)*

11

CZESTOCHOWA *(PD)*
SAARBRUCKEN *(G)*

12

LUDWIGSHAFEN *(G)*
SAINT-ETIENNE *(F)*
SAN SEBASTIAN *(SP)*

13

FREDERIKSHAVN *(D)*
KARL-MARX-STADT *(EG)*

14

RECKLINGHAUSEN *(G)*

15

CLERMONT-FERRAND *(F)*
FRANKFURT AM MAIN *(G)*
MORAVSKA OSTRAVA *(CZ)*

Towns of the USSR

4
BAKU
KIEV
OMSK
PERM
RIGA
TULA

5
GORKY
KAZAN
KIROV
MINSK
PENZA
TOMSK

6
EREVAN
FRUNZE
GROZNY
MOSCOW
ROSTOV
TIFLIS
TYUMEN
URAL'SK

7
ALMA ATA
BARNAUL
IRKUTSK
KALININ
KHARKOV
LUGANSK
SARATOV
TALLINN
TBILISI
ULAN-UDE
VILNIUS
VORKUTA
YEREVAN

8
DUSHANBE
KEMEROVO
KISHINEV
MURMANSK
ORENBURG
SMOLENSK
TASHKENT
VORONEZH

9
AKMOLINSK
ASHKHABAD
ASTRAKHAN

KRASNODAR
KUIBYSHEV
LENINGRAD
NIKOLAYEV
SAMARKAND
USSURIYSK
VOLGOGRAD
YAROSLAVL

10
KHABAROVSK
SVERDLOVSK

11
ARKHANGELSK
CHELYABINSK
KALININGRAD
KRASNOYARSK
NOVOSIBIRSK
VLADIVOSTOK

12
MAGNITOGORSK
NIZHNIY-TAGIL

13
PETROPAVLOVSK
SEMIPALANTINSK

14
DNEPROPETROVSK

Towns of Asia outside the USSR

4
ADEN
AGRA
AMOY
CEBU
HOMS
KOBE
LINI
SIAN

5
ADANA
AHVAZ
AJMER
AKITA
AMMAN
BASRA
BURSA
DACCA
DAVAO
DELHI
HAIFA
HANOI
IZMIR
JIDDA
JUKAO
KABUL
KIRIN
KOCHI
KYOTO
MECCA
MOSUL
OMUTA
OSAKA
OTARU
PATNA
POONA
PUSAN
QOMUL
RASHT
SEOUL
SHASI
SIMLA
SURAT
TAEGU
TOKYO

6
ABADAN
ALEPPO
ANKARA
ANKING
ANSHAN
ANTUNG
BARODA

BEIRUT
BOMBAY
CANTON
CHEFOO
FUSHUN
HANKOW
HARBIN
HOWRAH
HUFHUF
ILOILO
IMPHAL
INDORE
JAIPUR
KANPUR
KERMAN
KUWAIT
LAHORE
MADRAS
MANAMA
MANILA
MUKDEN
MULTAN
MYSORE
NAGOYA
NAGPUR
NINGPO
PEKING
QUETTA
RAJKOT
RIYADH
*SAIGON
SASEBO
SENDAI
SHIRAZ
SWATOW
TABRIZ
TAEJON
T'AI-NAN
TAIPEH
TEHRAN
TOYAMA
TSINAN
WUCHOW

7
BACOLOD
BAGHDAD
BANDUNG
BANGKOK
BENARES
BIKANER
CARVERY
CHENGTU
COLOMBO
CUTTACK

ESFAHAN
FOOCHOW
FUKUOKA
GWALIOR
HAMADAN
HENYANG
HUHEHOT
ISFAHAN
JODHPUR
KAIFENG
KARACHI
KASHGAR
KUCHING
KUNMING
KWEILIN
LANCHOW
LATAKIA
LIUCHOW
LUCKNOW
MASHHAD
NANKING
NANNING
NIIGATA
PAOTING
RANGOON
SAPPORO
SINUIJU
SOOCHOW
TAIYUAN
TEHERAN
TEL AVIV
TOURANE
URUMCHI
USKUDAR
WENCHOW
YINGKOW
ZAHEDAN

8
AMRITSAR
BAREILLY
CALCUTTA
CHANGSHA
CHINCHOW
CHONGJIN
DAMASCUS
DJAKARTA
HAIPHONG
HAKODATE
HANGCHOW
JABALPUR
KANDAHAR
KIAMUSZE
KWEIYANG
LIAOYANG

LYALLPUR
MANDALAY
NAGASAKI
NANCHANG
PESHAWAR
SEMARANG
SHANGHAI
SHOLAPUR
SRINAGAR
SURABAJA
T'AI-CHUNG
TANGSHAN
TIENTSIN
TSINGTAO
VARANASI
VICTORIA
WAKAYAMA
WANHSIEN
YENCHENG
YOKOHAMA

9
AHMADABAD
ALLAHABAD
BANGALORE
BHAGALPUR
CHENGCHOW
CHIANG MAI
CHINKIANG
CHUNGKING
ESKISEHIR
HIROSHIMA
HYDERABAD
JALALABAD
JERUSALEM
KAO-HSIUNG
KOZHIKODE
MANGALORE
MORADABAD
NYITKYINA
PALEMBANG
PHNOM PENH
PONTIANAK
PYONGYANG
SINGAPORE
TSITSIHAR
ULAN BATOR

10
CHANCHIANG
CHENGKIANG
GEORGE TOWN
JAMSHEDPUR
JOGJAKARTA
KERMANSHAH
MUTANKIANG
*PORT ARTHUR
RAWALPINDI

SAHARANPUR
TRIVANDRUM

11
CHANGKIAKOW
KUALA LUMPUR
SHIMONOSEKI

12
LUANG PRABANG

13
†HO CHI MINH CITY

14
VISHAKHAPATNAM

*former name
†new name

Towns of Africa

3
FEZ

4
JUBA
KANO
ORAN
SUEZ

5
ACCRA
ASWAN
ASYUT
*BEIRA
CAIRO
DAKAR
ENUGU
KABWE
LAGOS
LINDI
LUXOR
NDOLA
OUTJO
RABAT
TUNIS
ZOMBA
ZONGO

6
AGADIR
ASMARA
BAMAKO
BANJUL
BISSAU
BUKAVU
DOUALA
DURBAN
HUAMBO
IBADAN
KISUMU
LUSAKA
†MAPUTO
NIAMEY
†SOFALA
SOUSSE
TABORA
TOBRUK
UMTALI

7
ABIDJAN
ALGIERS
BERBERA
CALABAR
CHIPATA

COTONOU
KAMPALA
MOMBASA
NAIROBI
SEEHEIM
TANGIER
TRIPOLI
YAOUNDE

8
BALOVALE
BENGHAZI
BENGUELA
BLANTYRE
BULAWAYO
CAPE TOWN
DJIBOUTI
FREETOWN
HARGEISA
KHARTOUM
LILONGWE
MAFEKING
N'DJAMENA
OMDURMAN
PORT SAID
PRETORIA
ZANZIBAR

9
BUJUMBURA
KIMBERLEY
LADYSMITH
LAS PALMAS
MAIDUGURI
MARRAKESH
MOCAMEDES
SALISBURY
SANTA CRUZ
WADI HAIFA

10
ADDIS ABABA
ALEXANDRIA
CASABLANCA
EAST LONDON
LIBREVILLE
LUBUMBASHI
MOZAMBIQUE
NACHINGWEA

11
DAR ES SALAAM
OUAGADOUGOU

12
BLOEMFONTEIN
JOHANNESBURG
PORT HARCOURT

13
BOBO-DIOLASSO
PORT ELIZABETH

14
*LOURENCO MARQUES

Towns of North and Central America

4
GARY
LEON
NOME
RENO

5
BOISE
FLINT
MIAMI
OGDEN
OMAHA
TAMPA
TULSA

6
ALBANY
AUSTIN
BELIZE
BOSTON
DALLAS
DENVER
DULUTH
EL PASO
GANDER
HAVANA
MERIDA
MOBILE
NASSAU
OAXACA
OTTAWA
PANAMA
PEORIA
PUEBLA
QUEBEC
ST JOHN
ST PAUL
TOLEDO

7
AKLAVIK
ATLANTA
BUFFALO
CALGARY
CHICAGO
DETROIT
HALIFAX
HOUSTON
LINCOLN
MANAGUA
MEMPHIS
NEW YORK
NORFOLK
OAKLAND
PHOENIX

ST JOHN'S
ST LOUIS
SAN JOSE
SAN JUAN
SAN LUIS
SEATTLE
SPOKANE
TORONTO
TORREON
TRENTON
WICHITA

8
AMARILLO
CAMAGUEY
CHEYENNE
COLUMBUS
EDMONTON
GOOSE BAY
HAMILTON
HARTFORD
KINGSTON
MONTREAL
NEW HAVEN
NORTH BAY
PORTLAND
RICHMOND
SAN DIEGO
SAVANNAH
SCRANTON
SYRACUSE
VERACRUZ
VICTORIA
WINNIPEG

9
ANCHORAGE
BALTIMORE
CHARLOTTE
CLEVELAND
DES MOINES
FAIRBANKS
FALL RIVER
FORT CHIMO
FORT WAYNE
FORT WORTH
GUATEMALA
HOLLYWOOD
KNOXVILLE
MILWAUKEE
MONTERREY
NASHVILLE
SAINT JOHN
SAINT PAUL
VANCOUVER

10
BATON ROUGE
BIRMINGHAM
CINCINNATI
COPPERMINE
JERSEY CITY
KANSAS CITY
LITTLE ROCK
LOS ANGELES
LOUISVILLE
MEXICO CITY
MONTGOMERY
NEW ORLEANS
PITTSBURGH
PORT ARTHUR
PROVIDENCE
SACRAMENTO
SAINT JOHN'S
SAINT LOUIS
SAN ANTONIO
SHREVEPORT
WASHINGTON
WHITEHORSE
WILMINGTON

11
BEAVERLODGE
BROWNSVILLE
CHATTANOOGA
DAWSON CREEK
FORT SIMPSON
GRAND RAPIDS
GUADALAJARA
MINNEAPOLIS
SAN SALVADOR
TEGUCIGALPA
YELLOWKNIFE

12
INDIANAPOLIS
JACKSONVILLE
OKLAHOMA CITY
PHILADELPHIA
PORT-AU-PRINCE
PRINCE GEORGE
PRINCE RUPERT
SALT LAKE CITY
SAN FRANCISCO
SANTO DOMINGO

13
CORPUS CHRISTI
GUATEMALA CITY

14
SANTIAGO DE CUBA

*former name
†new name

Towns of South America

4
CALI
LIMA

5
BELEM
CUSCO
CUZCO
LA PAZ
NATAL
ORURO
QUITO
SUCRE

6
BOGOTA
CALLAO
CUIABA
CUMANA
MANAUS
PARANA
POTOSI
RECIFE
TEMUCA

7
ARACAJU
CARACAS
CAYENNE
CORDOBA
GOIANIA
ITABUNA
LA PLATA
MENDOZA
NITEROI
SANTA FE
TUCUMAN
VITORIA

8
AREQUIPA
ASUNCION
BOA VISTA
BRASILIA
CHICLAYO
CURITIBA
MEDELLIN
PARNAIBA
SALVADOR
SANTIAGO
SAO PAULO
VALDIVIA

9
CARTAGENA

FORTALEZA
MANIZALES
MARACAIBO
RIO BRANCO
RIO GRANDE
SANTA CRUZ

10
AVELLANEDA
CONCEPCION
FRAY BENTOS
GEORGETOWN
MONTEVIDEO
VALPARAISO

11
BAHIA BLANCA
BUCAMARANGA
BUENOS AIRES
PORTO ALEGRE
PORT OF SPAIN
PUNTA ARENAS

12
BARQUISIMETO
BARRANQUILLA
RIO DE JANEIRO

13
BELO HORIZONTE
FLORIANOPOLIS

Towns of Australasia

3
CUE
HAY

5
DERBY
DUBBO
NHILL
PERTH

6
DARWIN
HOBART
KERANG
MACKAY
PARKES
SYDNEY

7
BENDIGO
DUNEDIN
GEELONG
IPSWICH
LEONORE
MILDURA
RENMARK
WHYALLA
WYNDHAM

8
ADELAIDE
AUCKLAND
BALLARAT
BRISBANE
CANBERRA
CLERMONT
COOKTOWN
HAMILTON
NORSEMAN
SWAN HILL
TOCUMWAL

9
CARNARVON
CLONCURRY
ESPERANCE
FREMANTLE
GERALDTON
MELBOURNE
NEWCASTLE
PORT PIRIE

10
BROKEN HILL
COOLGARDIE

DENILIQUIN
KALGOORLIE
LAUNCESTON
NARRANDERA
PROSERPINE
TOWNSVILLE
WAGGA WAGGA
WELLINGTON

11
MOUNT MAGNET
PORT HEDLAND
ROCKHAMPTON

12
ALICE SPRINGS
CHRISTCHURCH
MOUNT GAMBIER
TENNANT CREEK

Treaties

3
ABO

4
CAEN
LAUF
LODI
RIGA
ROME

5
ALTON
ARRAS
ATHIS
BADEN
BASEL
BLOIS
BREDA
BREST
DELFT
HAGUE
JASSY
LYONS
MEAUX
MELFI
NOYON
OLIVA
OUCHY
PARIS
PERTH
REDON
REVAL
SUTRI
THORN
TRENT
WORMS

6
AMIENS
ANAGNI
ARDRES
BAGDAD
BERLIN
BJORKO
BRUGES
CALAIS
COGNAC
DURHAM
GISORS
KALISZ
KARDIS
LABIAN
LONDON
LORRIS
LUBECK

MADRID
MANILA
MERSEN
MOSCOW
NYSTAD
OLERON
OLMUTZ
PASSAU
PEKING
PRAGUE
ST OMER
SALBAI
SENLIS
TILSIT
TOLEDO
TROYES
TYRNAU
VENICE
VERDUN
VIENNA
VOSSEM
WARSAW
XANTEN
ZURICH

7
ALTMARK
BADAJOZ
BAGHDAD
BAGNOLO
BERWICK
BOLOGNA
BRIGHAM
BUCZACZ
CAMBRAI
CORBEIL
DUNKIRK
FERRARA
GASTEIN
GUILLON
HAGENAU
KASCHAU
LAMBETH
LATERAN
MECHLIN
NANKING
NETTUNO
RASTATT
RYSWICK
ST CLAIR
SEVILLE
SISTOVA
STETTIN
TANGIER
TESCHEN

UTRECHT
VERVINS
WEDMORE
WINDSOR
ZURAWNA

8
ARANJUEZ
AUGSBURG
BARWALDE
BELGRADE
BOULOGNE
BRETIGNY
BRUSSELS
CHERASCO
ESCORIAL
GANDAMAK
GUERANDE
KHAEROED
MURZSTEG
NIJMEGEN
PRETORIA
PYRENEES
ROSKILDE
ROXBURGH
STOLBOVA
TARASCON
TIENTSIN
UCCIALLI
VALENCAY
WAITANGI

9
ABERDARON
ALGECIRAS
AMSTERDAM
AQUISGRAN
BARCELONA
BROMSEBRO
BUCHAREST
COMPIEGNE
DORDRECHT
EDINBURGH
EISENBURG
LUNEVILLE
NEWCASTLE
PICQUIGNY
PRESSBURG
ST GERMAIN
SAINT OMER
SALISBURY
SARAGOSSA
SCHONBRUN
STOCKHOLM
VANCELLES
VINCENNES

10
ADRIANOPLE
DUSSELDORF
GERSTUNGEN
MONTEBELLO
NICOLSBURG
SAINT CLAIR
SAN STEFANO
SHREWSBURY
VERSAILLES
WASHINGTON
WESTPHALIA

11
ALTRANSTADT
CAMPO FORMIO
FURSTENBERG
HUBERTSBURG
NORTHAMPTON
PASSAROWITZ
REICHENBACH
SHIMONOSEKI
TORDESILHAS
VEREENIGING
VILLAFRANCA
WALLINGFORD
WESTMINSTER
ZSITVA-TOROK

12
ANTANANARIVO
BREST-LITOVSK
BRETTON WOODS
GROSSWARDEIN
HAMPTON COURT
HERRENHAUSEN
SAINT GERMAIN
ST PETERSBURG
SAN ILDEFONSO
WUSTERHAUSEN

13
AIX-LA-CHAPELLE
CLAYTON-BULWER
FONTAINEBLEAU

14
CHARLOTTENBURG
CONSTANTINOPLE
FREDERICKSBORG
FREDERICKSHAMM
ST CLAIR-SUR-EPTE

15
CATEAU-CAMBRESIS
KUCHUK KAINARDJI
SAINT PETERSBURG

United States of America

2
DC

4
IOWA
OHIO
UTAH

5
IDAHO
MAINE
TEXAS

6
ALASKA
HAWAII
KANSAS
NEVADA
OREGON

7
ALABAMA
ARIZONA
FLORIDA
GEORGIA
INDIANA
MONTANA
NEW YORK
VERMONT
WYOMING

8
ARKANSAS
COLORADO
DELAWARE
ILLINOIS
KENTUCKY
MARYLAND
MICHIGAN
MISSOURI
NEBRASKA
OKLAHOMA
VIRGINIA

9
LOUISIANA
MINNESOTA
NEW JERSEY
NEW MEXICO
TENNESSEE
WISCONSIN

10
CALIFORNIA
WASHINGTON

11
CONNECTICUT
MISSISSIPPI
NORTH DAKOTA
RHODE ISLAND
SOUTH DAKOTA

12
NEW HAMPSHIRE
PENNSYLVANIA
WEST VIRGINIA

13
MASSACHUSETTS
NORTH CAROLINA
SOUTH CAROLINA

18
DISTRICT OF COLUMBIA

British Universities

4
BATH
CITY
HULL
KENT
OPEN
YORK

5
ASTON
ESSEX
KEELE
LEEDS
WALES

6
BRUNEL
DUNDEE
DURHAM
EXETER
LONDON
OXFORD
QUEEN'S
SURREY
SUSSEX
ULSTER

7
BELFAST
BRISTOL
GLASGOW
READING
SALFORD
THE CITY
THE OPEN
WARWICK

8
ABERDEEN
BRADFORD
STIRLING

9
CAMBRIDGE
EDINBURGH
LANCASTER
LEICESTER
LIVERPOOL
NEWCASTLE
ST ANDREWS
SHEFFIELD

10
BIRMINGHAM

BUCKINGHAM
EAST ANGLIA
HERIOT-WATT
MANCHESTER
NOTTINGHAM

11
SOUTHAMPTON
STRATHCLYDE

12
LOUGHBOROUGH
SAINT ANDREWS

16
KENT AT CANTERBURY

17
ASTON IN BIRMINGHAM
ROYAL COLLEGE OF ART

18
CRANFIELD INSTITUTE

Volcanoes

4
ETNA
LAKI
TAAL

5

ASAMA
ASKJA
HEKLA
PELEE
TEIDE
THERA

6
ELBRUS
EREBUS
KATMAI
MARAPI
MERAPI
SEMERU

7
CHILLAN
ILIAMNA
KILAUEA
ORIZABA
RUAPEHU
VULCANO

8
ANTISANA
CAMEROON
COTOPAXI
DEMAVEND
FUJIYAMA
HUALALAI
KRAKATAU
KRAKATOA
MAUNA KEA
MAUNA LOA
TARAWERA
VESUVIUS

9
ACONCAGUA
HALEAKALA
KARISIMBI
MONT PELEE
NGAURUHOE
PARICUTIN
PUY DE DOME
SOUFRIERE
STROMBOLI
TONGARIRO

10
CHIMBORAZO
HALEMAUMAU
LASSEN PEAK
MOUNT BAKER
NYAMLAGIRA
NYIRAGONGO
SANTA MARIA
VILLARRICA

11
IXTACIHUATL
KILIMANJARO
LA SOUFRIERE
MOUNT SHASTA
NYAMURAGIRA
PICO DE TEYDE

12
CITLALTEPETL
FALCON ISLAND
IXTACCIHUATL
IZTACCIHUATL
KLUCHEVSKAYA
LLULLAILLACO
POPOCATEPETL

13
KLYUCHEVSKAYA
MOUNT WRANGELL

14
TRISTAN DA CUNHA

Weapons

2
AX
DA

3
ARM
AXE
BAT
BOW
DAG
DAH
GAD
GAT
GUN
RAM

4
ARMS
BILL
BOLT
BOMB
CANE
CELT
CLUB
COLT
COSH
DART
DIRK
EPEE
FOIL
GAFF
GOAD
KIRI
KRIS
MACE
PIAT
PIKE
STEN
TANK
TUCK
WHIP

5
A-BOMB
ARROW
BILBO
BLADE
BOLAS
BOWIE
BRAND
ESTOC
FUSEE
FUSIL
FUZEE
H-BOMB

KNIFE
KNOUT
KUKRI
LANCE
LASSO
LATHI
LUGER
MAXIM
ORGUE
PANGA
POKER
RIFLE
SABER
SABRE
SHAFT
SHARP
SKEAN
SKENE
SLING
SPEAR
STAFF
STAVE
STICK
SWORD
WADDY

6
AIRGUN
ALPEEN
ANLACE
BODKIN
BOFORS
CANNON
COHORN
CREASE
CREESE
CUDGEL
DAGGER
ESPADA
GINGAL
GLAIVE
HAGBUT
HANGER
HANJAR
JINGAL
LARIAT
LASSOO
MAUSER
MESAIL
MINNIE
MORTAR
MUSKET
NAPALM
PARANG
PETARD

PISTOL
POLE-AX
POMPOM
POMPON
POPGUN
QUARRY
RAPIER
SALADE
SALLET
SICKLE
SPARKE
SPARTH
STYLET
SWIVEL
TOLEDO
TULWAR
WEBLEY

7
ANELACE
ASSAGAI
ASSEGAI
ATAGHAN
BALISTA
BAYONET
BAZOOKA
BLOWGUN
BREN GUN
BULLDOG
CALIVER
CARBINE
COEHORN
CURTANA
CURTAXE
CUTLASS
DRAGOON
DUDGEON
ELF-BOLT
ELF-SHOT
FIREARM
FIREPOT
GATLING
GINGALL
HACKBUT
HALBERD
HALBERT
HAND-GUN
HAND-JAR
HARPOON
HATCHET
JAVELIN
KURBASH
LONGBOW
LONG TOM
MACHETE
MATCHET
MISSILE
MORGLAY

OIL-BOMB
PEDRERO
POLE-AXE
POMPOON
PONIARD
QUARREL
RABINET
SANDBAG
SHOTGUN
SIDE-ARM
SJAMBOK
SPARTHE
SPURTLE
STEN GUN
SYMITAR
TEAR-GAS
TORPEDO
TRIDENT
TWIBILL
WAR-CLUB
WARHEAD
WHINGER
WIND-GUN
YATAGAN

8

ARBALIST
ARQUEBUS
ATOM BOMB
BALLISTA
BASELARD
BASILISK
BATTLE-AX
BIRDBOLT
BLOWPIPE
BLUDGEON
BRICKBAT
CARABINE
CASE-SHOT
CATAPULT
CLAYMORE
CROSSBOW
CULVERIN
CURTAL-AX
DAMASKIN
DYNAMITE
EEL-SPEAR
ELF-ARROW
FALCHION
FALCONET
FIELD-GUN
FIREBALL
FIRELOCK
FIRESHIP
GAVELOCK
HALF-PIKE
HOWITZER
LANCEGAY

LANGRAGE
LEWIS GUN
MANGONEL
MAXIM GUN
NAVAL GUN
OERLIKON
ORDNANCE
PADERERO
PARAVANE
PARTISAN
PATERERO
PEDERERO
PETRONEL
PISTOLET
PYROXYLE
REPEATER
REVOLVER
SCIMITAR
SCORPION
SEMITAUR
SHRAPNEL
SIEGE-GUN
SKEAN-DHU
SKENE-DHU
SMALL-ARM
SPADROON
SPONTOON
STILETTO
STONE-BOW
SYMITARE
TOMAHAWK
TOMMY-GUN
WHINYARD
YATAGHAN
ZOMBORUK

9

ARBLASTER
ARQUEBUSE
ARROW-HEAD
ARTILLERY
AUTOMATIC
BASTINADO
BATTLE-AXE
BIG BERTHA
BLACKJACK
BOAR-SPEAR
BOFORS GUN
BOMBSHELL
BOOMERANG
BROWN BESS
BROWNBILL
CARRONADE
CARTRIDGE
CHAINSHOT
CHASSEPOT
DEMI-LANCE
DERRINGER

ESCOPETTE
FISH-SPEAR
FLINTLOCK
GELIGNITE
GRAPE-SHOT
GUNCOTTON
HANDSTAFF
HARQUEBUS
LANGRIDGE
LIGHT TANK
MATCHLOCK
MILLS BOMB
MINUTE-GUN
MUNITIONS
MUSKETOON
NEEDLE-GUN
POISON GAS
SHILLELAH
SLINGSHOT
SLUNG-SHOT
SMALL ARMS
SPRING GUN
STARSHELL
STINK-BOMB
SWIVEL-GUN
SWORD-CANE
TRUNCHEON
TURRET-GUN
WELSH-HOOK
WHIZZBANG
XYLOIDINE
ZAMBOORUK
ZUMBOORUK

10

AMMUNITION
ARBALESTER
ARBALISTER
ARCUBALIST
ATOMIC BOMB
BOWIE KNIFE
BROADSWORD
BURREL-SHOT
CANNONBALL
CANNON-SHOT
DEMI-CANNON
FIELDPIECE
GATLING GUN
HARQUEBUSE
HARQUEBUSS
KNOBKERRIE
LEE-ENFIELD
MACHINE-GUN
MINIE-RIFLE
MISERICORD
MUSQUETOON
MUSTARD GAS
PAIXHAN-GUN

PEASHOOTER
SHILLELAGH
SIX-SHOOTER
SMALLSWORD
SMOOTHBORE
SWORDSTICK
ZUMBOÒRUCK

11

ANTI-TANK GUN
ARMOURED CAR
BLUNDERBUSS
BOW-AND-ARROW
DEPTH-CHARGE
GARAND RIFLE
HAND-GRENADE
HORSE PISTOL
JACOB'S STAFF
LOCHABER-AXE
MAGAZINE-GUN
MINETHROWER
MISERICORDE
MORNING-STAR
MOUNTAIN GUN
STERNCHASER

12

BATTERING-RAM
BOARDING-PIKE
BOMBING PLANE
BREECHLOADER
DEMI-CULVERIN
FLAMETHROWER
FOWLING-PIECE
MITRAILLEUSE
MUZZLE-LOADER
QUARTERSTAFF
RIFLE-GRENADE
SPURTLE BLADE
STOKES MORTAR
SWORD-BAYONET
TRACER-BULLET
TRENCH-MORTAR

13

AERIAL TORPEDO
GUIDED MISSILE
HIGH EXPLOSIVE
KNUCKLEDUSTER
LIFE-PRESERVER
MAGAZINE-RIFLE
POISONED ARROW
SCALPING-KNIFE
SUBMACHINE-GUN
TWO-EDGED SWORD

14

INCENDIARY BOMB
REPEATING RIFLE

15

ANTI-AIRCRAFT GUN

Welsh Sovereigns and Princes

4
IAGO
RHUN
RHYS

5
CYNAN
HYWEL
IDWAL
MADOG
OWAIN

6
CADVAN
DAFYDD
MERVYN
RHODRI

7
ANARAWD
BLEDDYN

8
GRUFFYDD
IORWERTH
LLEWELYN
LLYWELYN
MAREDUDD
MEREDITH
TRAHAERN

9
CADWALADR
CADWALLON

12
OWAIN GWYNEDD

English Princes of Wales since 1301

5
HENRY

6
ARTHUR
EDWARD
GEORGE

7
CHARLES
RICHARD

9
FREDERICK

10
HENRY TUDOR

11
ARTHUR TUDOR
HENRY STUART

12
ALBERT EDWARD

13
CHARLES STUART

14
FREDERICK LEWIS
GEORGE AUGUSTUS

18
JAMES FRANCIS EDWARD

22
GEORGE WILLIAM FREDERICK